Hail, Columbia

★

Hail, Columbia

Robert Gray, John Kendrick
and the
Pacific Fur Trade

★

JOHN SCOFIELD

OREGON HISTORICAL SOCIETY
PRESS

COVER ILLUSTRATION by Dennis Cunningham.

Designed and produced by the Oregon Historical Society Press.

The paper used in this publication meets the minimum requirements of American National Standard for Information Sciences—Permanence of Paper for Printed Library Materials, ANSI Z39.48-1984.

Number nineteen in the North Pacific Studies Series.

Production of this volume was supported by funds made available by The Thomas Vaughan Fund for Publications in Oregon Country History, and the editorial work was assisted financially by the Bureau of Educational and Cultural Affairs of the United States Information Agency under the authority of the Fulbright-Hays Act of 1961, as amended.

Library of Congress Cataloging-in-Publication Data

Scofield, John, 1914–
  Hail, Columbia: Robert Gray, John Kendrick and the Pacific Fur Trade / John Scofield.
    p. cm. — (North Pacific studies series: no. 18)
  Includes bibliographical references and index.
  ISBN 0-87595-234-8
  1. Northwest Coast of North America—Description and travel. 2. Northwest, Pacific—Description and travel. 3. Fur trade—Northwest Coast of North America—History. 4. Fur trade—Northwest, Pacific—History. 5. Gray, Robert, 1755–1806. 6. Kendrick, John, ca. 1740–1794. 7. Voyages to the Pacific Coast.
    I. Title. II. Series
    F851.S36 1993
    910.4´5—dc20   91-22354 CIP

Printed in the United States of America.

FOR AUDREY

AS AN EXPRESSION OF MY LOVE AND ADMIRATION.

AND FOR

JOHN KENDRICK LOCKWOOD

ANNA KENDRICK LOCKWOOD

ELIZA KENDRICK LOCKWOOD

EMILY KENDRICK LOCKWOOD

KENDRICK SCOFIELD

★

Contents

★

Illustrations and Maps

★

Preface

★

Before the great overland expansion of the United States had even started, another westward movement occurred that took a growing tide of New Englanders in one breathtaking leap south almost to Antarctica, then around Cape Horn into the Pacific Ocean and north to the coasts of what are now Oregon, Washington, and British Columbia. In its time— from 1787 to about 1817—this seaborne expansion proved to be of far greater moment to the young, trade-starved United States than did its overland counterpart. By bartering for sea-otter furs with the Indians of the Northwest Coast and then exchanging them for tea and textiles in Canton, the captains of these pioneering vessels—led by Boston's *Columbia Rediviva* and *Lady Washington*—established a world-girdling trade that brought a heady scent of prosperity to depression-wracked New England, provided a badly needed source of pride for the freshly independent colonies, and changed the Pacific from a Spanish lake to a happy hunting ground for Yankee mariners and their merchant backers.

I grew up, in a sense, with the voyages of *Columbia* and *Lady Washington*. John Kendrick, one of the two captains, was an ancestor of mine. As a child, I heard from my paternal grandmother all the fine, fancy stories that the family had treasured for generations: Captain Kendrick had been the first American to sail around the world. He had also discovered the Columbia River. Kendrick had smuggled himself into China—again, the first American to do so—by disguising himself with a pigtail, which he eventually brought home to Massachusetts. (There was some indignation in the family at the idea that a great aunt of Victorian days had worn out this precious relic by making a hairpiece of it.)

Kendrick died as dramatically as he had lived. His friend, the British explorer Captain George Vancouver, lying at anchor in Honolulu Harbor next to Kendrick's frigate *Columbia*, fired a salute on the old mariner's birthday. Accidentally, the gun had been left loaded. The ball killed Kendrick as he sat at his cabin table.

Each of these tales, of course, was the purest fantasy. It was Kendrick's fellow captain Robert Gray, I learned as a teenager, who sailed over the bar of the Columbia River and, in command of the *Columbia*, completed the voyage that first carried the Stars and Stripes around the world. Kendrick never returned to Boston, a fact that effectively repudiated that wonderful yarn of his having brought home a Chinese pigtail to his wife and children. No one knows what his birthday was. And while Kendrick knew Vancouver, and although he was killed aboard his ship by an accidental cannon shot, Vancouver had nothing to do with it. One historian has even suggested, with considerable justification, that Kendrick deliberately stole *Lady Washington*, one of the two vessels entrusted to him by Boston merchants who sent him and Robert Gray into the Pacific, and used the ship for his own ends for the rest of his life.

Eventually I came to realize the pivotal nature of *Columbia*'s and *Washington*'s voyages in the larger story of this nation's first great mercantile adventure. Despite the incompetence, or worse, of both commanders, Boston's pioneering essay into the China and Northwest fur trades exerted an influence on American history far beyond its immediate ends. In the wakes of *Columbia* and *Washington*, the hazards of Cape Horn ceased to terrify Yankee sea captains. The Stars and Stripes was shortly showing up all over the Pacific. Unheard-of wealth flowed into the coffers of Boston's merchants, playing a major role in lifting New England out of the post-Revolutionary depression of the late 1780s.

More and more foreign seamen in exotic costumes appeared on Boston's cobbled streets—who can forget Queequeg, the tattooed, harpoon-carrying cannibal of *Moby Dick*? Bostonians who had never been farther away from home than Newburyport suddenly found themselves making one voyage after another to China or Fiji or the Spice Islands. A whole new mood swept coastal New England. From being a provincial center whose ships rarely ventured out of the Atlantic, Boston became one of the world's commercial hubs. Though neither Gray nor Kendrick delivered to Boston the riches their backers expected, the ships that followed them into the Pacific did. Captains were shortly returning to Massachusetts with as much as a 400-percent profit for their merchant backers and tidy fortunes for themselves.

The whalers, too, lost no time following Kendrick and Gray's lead and making their way into the Pacific. Though the ship was British-owned, the *Emilia* sailed in 1788 under Captain James Shields, with Archaelus Hammond as first mate. Both were Nantucket whalemen. Rounding Cape Horn only a few months behind *Columbia* and *Washington*, Hammond successfully struck a whale off the coast of Peru—the first sperm whale killed in the Pacific. By 1792 there were at least nine whaleships operating in that vast ocean. Though only three were American-owned, all but one were commanded by Massachusetts captains and crewed largely by Massachusetts whalemen. Before long, as they had with the fur trade, United States ships and their crews were dominating the Pacific whaling grounds from the coasts of Chile and Peru to Japan and the Bering Sea.

Of even greater importance to the infant republic than any of this, in the longer view, was Robert Gray's determination one spring morning in 1792 to enter the mouth of a great stream he saw pouring into the Pacific. He named it "Columbia's River," for his ship. Had some British captain been the one to sail across that forbidding, surf-lashed bar (Vancouver had seen it only a few days earlier but had passed it up), the old Oregon Country—now the states of Washington, Oregon, and Idaho—would almost surely today be a part of Canada.

Though the news of Gray's discovery would be slow to enter the American consciousness—the mythical "Oregon River" would continue for a decade to be the chief goal of overland explorers—the existence of the Columbia pointed inevitably to Thomas Jefferson's dispatch of Lewis and Clark to search out a land route to the Pacific. Their success in reaching the Columbia River in its turn paved the way for United States ownership of the Oregon Country. "One can hardly conceive of the

Lewis and Clark expedition without the preliminary work of these early Cape Horners," wrote maritime historian Carl C. Cutler in *Greyhounds of the Sea*, his great survey of the clipper-ship era, "yet the major credit for extending the territory of the United States beyond the Rockies is usually given to the overland explorers."

At first, it seemed to me that there simply were not enough facts to correct that lapse in our history books by telling the stories of *Columbia* and *Lady Washington* and the pioneer American fur traders who followed them around the Horn. Many of the logs and journals had disappeared, and most of those that survived were mere fragments. Only a handful of letters and other documents seemed to have been preserved. Retirement, however, brought me the opportunity to spend as much time as I wished in tracking down contemporary references and new manuscript sources. Gradually a consecutive picture emerged. *Columbia*'s and *Washington*'s pioneering explorations in the Pacific can now be told with a degree of detail I would not have thought possible a few years ago. So too can the personalities of the two captains confidently be drawn in almost equal detail.

Not surprisingly, both emerge in an unaccustomed light. Robert Gray's great success, the discovery of the Columbia River and the impetus that discovery gave to United States claims on the Northwest Coast, has obscured the cold ruthlessness and cruelty of the man. John Kendrick, on the other hand, sidesteps the charge of outright dishonesty only by falling headlong into what young John Quincy Adams characterized at the time as "unpardonable stupidity."

I want to express my appreciation to Louis L. Tucker, Director, and John D. Cushing, Librarian of the Massachusetts Historical Society; the late Marion V. Brewington of the Peabody Museum of Salem; Prudence K. Backman, Essex Institute, Salem; George T. Miles, Curator of Western Americana at the Beinecke Rare Book and Manuscript Library of Yale University; Margaret Titcomb, Librarian, the Bernice P. Bishop Museum, Honolulu; Chapin D. Foster and Alta F. West of the Washington State Historical Society; Professor Iris H.W. Engstrand, University of San Diego; Fred Schamel of the National Archives; Laurence G. Hill, Free Public Library, New Bedford, Massachusetts; Richard K. Doud and Margaret C.S. Christman of the National Portrait Gallery, Smithsonian Institution; and Thomas Vaughan, former Executive Director, Priscilla Knuth, Margaret

N. Haines, and Susan Seyl of the Oregon Historical Society for their willingness to share information with me, to search out items I needed, and for
their courtesy in making available to me typescripts, photocopies, micro-
films, photographs, and permission to quote from manuscript material in
their care. Thanks are due also to Bruce Taylor Hamilton, Director of the
Oregon Historical Society Press, and to my able editor, Kim L. Carlson, of
the Society's North Pacific Studies Center, who tactfully smoothed rough
spots in the manuscript and saved me from many a stylistic and factual
slip. Research in published material, particularly in the rare original editions of eighteenth-cenury British shipmasters' accounts of their voyages,
was largely accomplished in the unparalleled collections of the Library of
Congress. Julian Bach read the manuscript and offered valuable editorial
suggestions. Herbert Beals and John Frazier Henry also reviewed the manuscript and submitted helpful comments.

Lastly, I owe a more than routine acknowledgement to two historians I never met. The late Frederic W. Howay of New Westminster, British
Columbia, spent much of his life seeing to the publication of, and com-
menting wisely on, the original chronicles of Northwest Coast maritime
exploration. His monumental *Voyages of the Columbia to the Northwest Coast*,
published by the Massachusetts Historical Society Press in 1941 and reprinted by the Oregon Historical Society Press in 1990, consists of meticulously transcribed texts of most of the surviving journals and many of the
documents and letters relevant to *Columbia*'s two circumnavigations. My
study would have been a far more formidable undertaking had these
source materials not been so readily available. The bibliography reveals
the extent of my debt to Judge Howay in other respects. The second is
Professor Warren L. Cook, whose splendid *Flood Tide of Empire—Spain and
the Pacific Northwest, 1543-1819* makes accessible for the first time so much
that was previously available only in untranslated documents in the Spanish Colonial archives of Madrid, Seville, and Mexico City.

★

Editorial
Principles

★

It will become obvious that I wanted to let the people who experienced these great voyages tell their own stories in their own ways, without meddlesome "improvements" in either their grammer or their spelling. Except for the addition or deletion of a few commas where this would make meanings clearer, and the insertion of periods and initial capitals when sentences tended to run together, the quotations herein are given whenever possible as they appear in the original journals, documents, and letters. The small loss in readability this occasions is compensated for by the sound of authenticity and the sense of closeness one gains to these adventuresome eighteenth-century mariners. With Indian names, I have used familiar forms—Maquinna and Wickananish—rather than the more correct but awkward equivalents Ma-kwee-na and Wee-ka-na-nish. In the case of Chinese place names, I have used forms that were familiar to our eighteenth-century mariners—Canton, for instance, instead of the currently correct Guangzhou, Whampoa instead of Huang-pu, and Lintin rather than Neilingding.

Finally, a caution. In the prologue particularly, I have tried to flesh out the principal characters in this long and complex saga by filling in between the lines of historical fact—chiefly by imagining what might have passed through the mind of the homeward-bound Robert Gray. Though based insofar as possible on fact or reasonable supposition, this and a few other easily reconizable passages are, of course, only informed guesses, and must be read as such. The rest is history.

★

PROLOGUE

Home
Is the Sailor

★

The weary ship barely moved through greasy summer swells, almost as if she were reluctant to finish this last leg of a lonely and desperately long journey around the world. Captain Robert Gray, two years three-hundred-twelve days away from Boston—no, three-hundred-*thirteen* days; they had lost one day as the ship circled the globe west about—craned aft over the taffrail to look for the hundredth time at the snake-like tentacles of seaweed that trailed from the ship's fouled rudder. Below the waterline, he knew, would be more weed, as well as barnacles the size of hens' eggs, clutching invisibly at the ship as she struggled these last painful leagues back to Boston. More than six months had slipped by since *Columbia*'s hull had been graved at Canton. The hateful weed was still there, Gray could see. So too, he could sense in the ship's sluggish progress, were the barnacles.

The captain leaned back now against the taffrail and tipped his one good eye aloft, past his new nation's starred and striped flag, or at least what was left of it, hanging dispirited and frayed from the tip of the spanker gaff. High above the flag, golden coins of sunlight glistened

1

through tattered holes in a weather-chafed topsail. Columbia's worn and strained canvas barely filled in the stagnant air. The ship ghosted silently across the flat sea, unaccompanied by the cheerful chorus of squeaks and groaning noises that would have marked her passage had the rigging been taut and the sails filled and drawing. Just as well, thought Gray. Every sail we own is rotten. Any more of a breeze and there'll be rips in all of them before we sight Castle William.

Gray ran a hand through his hair as if to fend off the sense of foreboding that clawed at his mind. Damn it, this was a moment when he should feel elation. In another few hours he would be back in Boston, the first man ever to have carried the American flag around the world. That should make a hero of anyone. And the flag had crackled in the gales, too, on that awful passage around Cape Horn. No American captain had gone through there before, either. And in the dead of winter, Gray added to himself with bitter satisfaction, thanks to John Kendrick's infernal caution. Caution? No, Gray almost said aloud as his knuckles whitened on the rail. It was cowardice, and he had told his fellow captain so to his face.

New England ship captains and New England shipowners had long been terrified of that stormy gateway to the Pacific Ocean. But until someone could find a Northwest Passage over the top of America or dig a canal across Mexico—that was one of John Kendrick's crazy dreams—a voyage southward down the Atlantic almost to Antarctica and then around Cape Horn would continue to offer American ships the shortest route between one ocean and the other. Now that he had challenged those bitter seas and won, Gray sensed other captains would be quick to follow his daring lead around Cape Horn and into the Pacific. Like Kendrick, he too had been terrified during that months-long night of blinding gales and menacing ice, but he had forced his ship through them. That should count for something with old Barrell, Columbia's principal owner, who waited impatiently for him now in his comfortable Boston counting house.

Next morning at dawn, with a thimbleful of air helping Columbia along, first mate Joseph Ingraham called out a landfall, a low smudge of gray on the southwestern horizon. Gray had made a sun sight the day before, so he knew within a few leagues where he was. This had to be Race Point, at the tip of Cape Cod's curled finger. Boston lay dead ahead. One more day on the old tub!

Every man on deck went silent and felt a little weak-kneed as the word raced from one crewman to another, then aloft to a sailor on the lower main yard and below to the cook and his sweaty helper. The reality of this homecoming that had been so long and powerful a dream —every crewman had been sustained by it from the very day he left Boston—suddenly overcame them, as if they could not quite cope with it. A hush fell over *Columbia*'s usually garrulous seamen. Only Attoo, the young Sandwich Islands "prince" who had attached himself to Captain Gray in Hawaii, seemed unmoved. Unmindful of the news that had struck his shipmates dumb, he went on with his boyish chatter, a strange mixture of Polynesian and proper Boston English.

This rich new dialect had become the prized patois of *Columbia*'s seamen, a sort of inside joke, as the young islander learned from his crew mates to use English words and they in turn imitated his many-voweled Hawaiian phrases. This outrageous mixture had become spiced too with a smattering of Chinese and snippets of half a dozen Indian languages picked up as the Bostonians traded for sea-otter furs along the shores of "new Albion," the name Sir Francis Drake had given to the coasts of northern California and Oregon, broadened now to include the whole coast of western North America. During the long passage home from China, Gray had remained aloof from this good-natured linguistic pastime. It irked him now to realize that he could no longer understand a conversation between two of his own crewmen!

Watching the handsome young Polynesian with his tawny unblemished skin—so unlike the pale Bostonians who awaited him ashore— Gray managed an inward smile. His had been the first American ship to drop anchor off Hawaii's golden isles—another honor the uneasy captain was bringing home to Boston. At Gray's instigation, Attoo had brought aboard *Columbia* one of the splendid feather cloaks of his people, patiently assembled from the red and gold feathers of island birds. Each of the hundreds of tiny creatures needed to fashion such a garment, the islanders had told him, provided only one thumbnail-size bit of color for this great knee-length cape. To go with it, Attoo also carried aboard a fantastic carved headdress, it too covered with brilliant feathers. Gray had it in mind to parade up King Street—he would find that in his long absence, Boston's main artery had been renamed State Street to confirm the nation's independence from European royalty—at the head of his crew, with Attoo at his side in all that heart-stopping finery. Then every living soul in Boston would know with no mistake that Captain Robert Gray had brought *Columbia* safely home from around the world.

Gray thumbed softly back through the whole improbable adventure, though his always practical mind would have given an eighteenth-century twist to that romantic term. A business *venture*, he would have defined it, entailing significant risks—and risks enough there had been, starting with fellow captain John Kendrick's prickly tantrums as Kendrick's flagship *Columbia* and his own little sloop *Lady Washington* crossed the Atlantic from Boston to Africa's Cape Verde Islands and then labored back again across the same ocean to Patagonia.

It had seemed so simple back there in Boston. Captain Kendrick and he, as second in command, would take their two ships around Cape Horn and make their way to the Northwest Coast, where sea-otter furs could be traded from the Indians for whatever oddments one had—beads or bits of iron—and then sold to the Chinese in Canton for a fortune in shining Spanish dollars. The money thus so easily acquired would buy tea to be brought home around the world to the thirsty townspeople of Boston, who would grant an even greater fortune for the privilege of filling their silver tea caddies with fragrant Oolong and Hyson.

But the risks had come tumbling down upon them, beginning in earnest with Cape Horn. No wonder mariners quailed at the thought of that stormy passage. Both of the ships had barely squeaked through. There had been shortages of water, and the ravages of scurvy as the two vessels, now separated, made their way north. On the coast of New Albion, hostile Indians had taken their toll. Rival British traders, arriving ahead of the Americans, had swept the coast almost clean of furs and shattered the dream of easy riches waiting to be gathered up for a pittance. But gather them up they did—*he* did, Gray corrected himself, painfully, patiently, one at a time, while Kendrick dreamed and dawdled the time away.

With his customary unpredictability, Kendrick had suddenly decided to send Gray on to China with *Columbia* to dispose of the furs thus far gathered, while he remained behind with the smaller ship to scrape up a second cargo. Once in Canton, the entrepreneurial Yankees had proven no match for canny Chinese merchants. Gray knew that his homebound cargo would put no smiles on the shipowners' faces. But he was nearly home. That was the main thing.

An incongruous bleat shattered Gray's reverie. Nancy! The captain smiled openly, and the barnyard sound broke the constraint that had hushed the crew. Nancy the goat had joined the ship at the Cape Verde Islands more than two years earlier, when *Columbia* was only a few weeks out of Boston. Her flock mates had long ago been butchered and salted down or had died seasick and half-starved on that endless passage around Cape Horn and up the Pacific. Only Nancy had survived and prospered. Now she browsed gratefully in her tiny pen by the foremast on any scraps the crew could spare from their own spartan meals. In return, Nancy had become pet and ship's mascot. Her uncomplaining presence lightened the burden of long passages, and her milk gave officers and seamen alike their one luxury, a drop of white to soften the bite of the ship's strong tea. She'll have a long stay ashore, Gray promised with unaccustomed warmth, and all the fresh grass she can eat.

The cloud settled over Gray's mind again. His thoughts moved past that triumphant procession with Attoo—if indeed Joseph Barrell would countenance such a show at all. Along with Attoo and his finery, Gray had brought home gifts for Barrell and the other owners of *Columbia*—Indian basketry, bows and arrows, a spear, and other gimcrackery from the Northwest Coast. But that too would postpone for only a short time the awkward matter of explaining why he and not Captain John Kendrick, who had been given command of the adventure from the start, had brought *Columbia* home.

Would any sensible person believe Gray's story—that Captain Kendrick had ordered him to take command of the larger ship before she had left the Northwest Coast, to proceed to China where the furs were to be sold, and then to bring her back to Boston with a cargo of tea? It was true, but who would believe that the leader of the expedition had preferred to stay behind as captain of the little sloop *Lady Washington* to continue trading for furs among the Indians while his underling came home in the tiny squadron's flagship to tell his story as he saw fit and to take as much of the credit as he could manage.

And the cargo, the tea that was to make Barrell and his partners rich overnight? After the Chinese merchants had finished with *Columbia*'s new captain and the ship had been put to rights for the voyage home, there were precious few Spanish dollars left from the sale of furs to pay for those chests of tea. It had been a skimpy enough cargo, and now many of the few chests they had managed to buy were damaged by the saltwater that leaked constantly through the ship's dried out and gaping seams.

Gray had moments of respite from the black fears that gripped him. At the sight of Columbia hurrying the last few leagues homeward before a fresh breeze, with her frayed sails somehow holding together, joyous salutes rocketed from the garrison of craggy Castle William at the entrance to Boston's busy harbor. Huzzahs burst from the throats of Bostonians, too, at the city's Long Wharf when Columbia's anchor chains finally tumbled overboard. It was Monday, 9 August 1790.

The next morning, Tuesday, Gray marched triumphantly up the Massachusetts capital's cobbled State Street from Long Wharf to the State House itself, trailed by his crew, with the befeathered Attoo resplendent at his side. There could have been no one in the whole of Boston that thrilling summer day who did not know that Robert Gray had come home with Columbia. And Nancy the goat, true to Gray's unspoken promise, got her lush pasturage for a few precious weeks ashore.

Predictably, though, when the balance sheet had been tallied, no huzzahs sounded for Gray himself. Even less approbation accrued for the absent Kendrick, presumably still gathering up sea-otter skins somewhere on the other side of the world. Yet Gray—and Nancy the goat— were at sea again after a scant two months ashore. Reluctantly, Joseph Barrell and Columbia's other owners confirmed Gray as commander of a second expedition, though they sent an agent along to keep an eye on his bookkeeping. Whatever Gray's shortcomings, the owners were forced to accept one unassailable fact: no one else was available with Gray's experience of the route, his knowledge of the wild coast of New Albion and the ways of the Chinese with whom perforce their profits eventually lay. So on 25 July 1793, nearly three years after he had sailed away from Boston a second time, Captain Robert Gray watched the city's island-dotted harbor reaches rise once again from the sea as he completed his and Columbia's second voyage around the world.

This time there was a better cargo, though still not so great as to make up for the financial losses of the first voyage, nor to allay entirely some nervousness on Gray's part at once again coming to accounts with Columbia's profit-hungry investors. But there was one shining difference between this voyage and the last. Though he would have been only dimly aware of its meaning, Gray had brought home to Boston this time a prize more valuable than any cargo of tea—far more valuable, in fact, than all the tea that would ever cross old Boston's weathered wharves.

The story of those two voyages, which were destined so profoundly to change the history of the United States, is a long and fascinating one. The men who shaped its chapters were as eminent as Benjamin Franklin and Thomas Jefferson, as varied as the luxury-loving Boston merchants with their small silver-hilted swords and powdered periwigs, and those hard-eyed and fiercely ambitious sea captains who established United States dominion over the eastern Pacific under the very noses of their British and Spanish counterparts. Great Indian chiefs clad in rich furs and eagle down walked that stage, along with aristocratic Spanish dons, shrewd Chinese merchants, British traders—some as unprincipled as pirates—and handsome Sandwich Islanders, who would one day be friends, and the next, deadly enemies of the seafarers who came their way.

Writing about the ship's first voyage, historian Samuel Eliot Morison summed up, "*Columbia* had solved the riddle of the China trade." Joseph Barrell's bold adventure, though he little intended it, had unalterably launched New England on a collision course with European dominion over the Pacific—a course in which the energetic Yankees inevitably emerged the victors. The outcome of that struggle forever changed the economic fortunes of the brash young nation that was just then taking form along the seaboard of the western Atlantic.

In what would become the highlight of *Columbia*'s second voyage, Captain Gray on 11 May 1792 took his ship across a perilous bar to enter the Columbia River. This encounter was the great gift Gray brought back to Boston—to the United States, really—that second time around. But the infant nation remained scarcely aware of the importance of Robert Gray's entrance into the "Great River of the West" until Lewis and Clark reached it overland in 1805. From that day on, the Columbia River would beckon unceasingly until the borders of the United States reached from New England's rock-rimmed harbors to the restless surf of the Pacific Northwest. "Empire," said Morison of *Columbia*'s second circumnavigation, "followed in the wake."

★

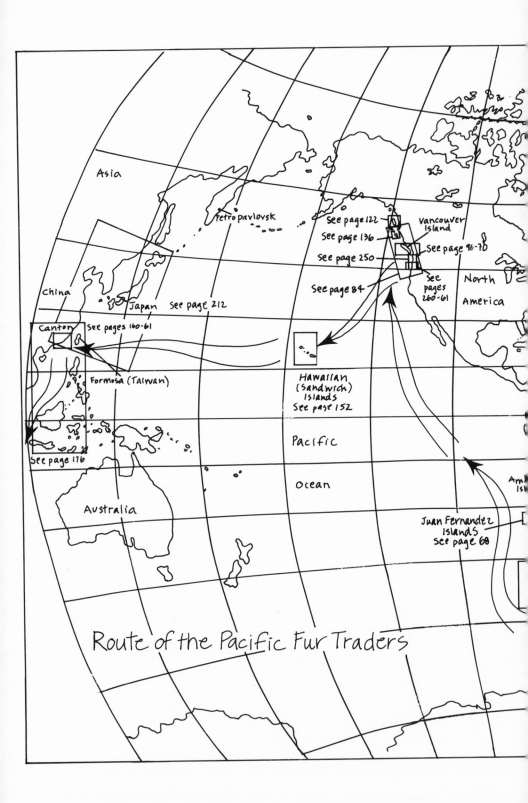

Asia

Petro pavlovsk

See page 122
See page 136
See page 250

See page 84

Vancouver
Island

See page 96-70

See
pages
260-61

North

America

China

Japan   See page 212

Canton   See pages 160-61

Formosa (Taiwan)

See page 176

Australia

Hawaiian
(Sandwich)
Islands
See page 152

Pacific

Ocean

Am
Isl

Juan Fernandez
Islands
See page 68

Route of the Pacific Fur Traders

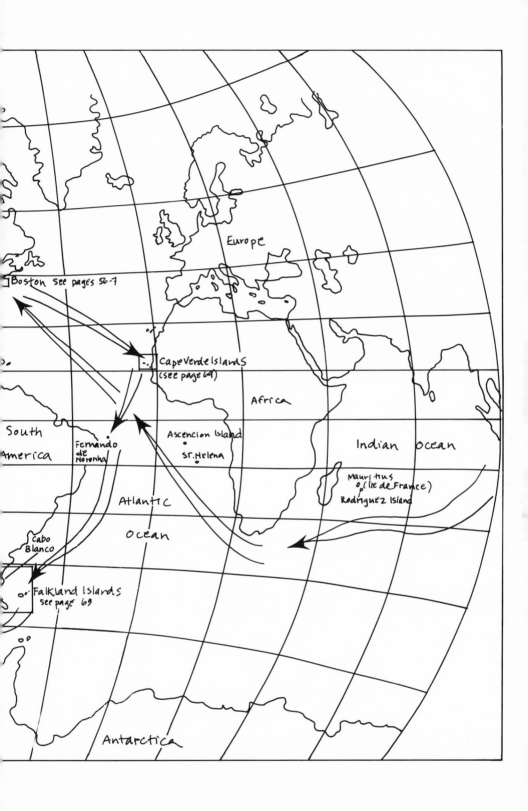

Boston See pages 56-7

Cape Verde Islands
(see page 69)

Europe

Africa

South
America

Fernando
de
Noronha

Ascencion Island
St. Helena

Indian Ocean

Mauritius
o (Ile de France)
Rodriguez Island

Atlantic

Ocean

Cabo
Blanco

Falkland Islands
See page 69

Antarctica

CHAPTER ONE

Resolution and Discovery Sow the Seeds of a China Trade

★

The anchor chains had barely stopped rattling before the two ships were surrounded by a fleet of huge painted and carved canoes, each hewn from a great cedar log. The Indians who stood at their bows wore splendid ankle-length robes of sea-otter fur and held other furs aloft as an invitation to trade.

Captain Cook's men, exploring and mapping the Pacific Ocean for King George III, had been two years at sea. The sailors' clothing, unlike the glistening robes of the Indians, hung in torn and greasy tatters. Shivering in the chill of late March, ordinary seamen and gentlemen officers alike looked enviously at the warm "cutsarks" worn by the Nootka chiefs. Each garment was fashioned of sea-otter skins—five to six feet in length—two sewn together vertically, with a third attached horizontally across the bottom.

The ships' surgeon, William Ellis, recorded with surprise that the natives were eager to part "with their black beavers Skins . . . for any little trifles." The Indians eagerly handed over their furs—often leaving themselves unabashedly naked—for blue and green beads, old swords, English

11

ha'pennies, even rough scraps of pewter, copper, or brass. The sailors stripped buttons from their ragged uniforms and brass handles from the ships' furniture, and knocked to pieces every spare pot and pan they could lay hands on in their haste to put something between themselves and Nootka Sound's Arctic winds. Never mind that some of the furs were worn and jumped with lice. They were warm.

The shivering Britons could thank only themselves for their predicament. Before *Resolution* and *Discovery* had dropped anchor in this ice-rimmed harbor on the western coast of British Columbia's Vancouver Island, the two ships and their crews had tarried long and pleasantly through the balmy Hawaiian winter of 1777-78. Pursuing sexual favors from the women of these beguiling islands, the explorer's men had traded away most of their warm clothing. Alas, instead of proceeding to China, as they had expected, the next station for these ill-clad argonauts proved to be the ice-locked coast of Northwest America.

The plight of Captain Cook's half-clothed seamen would survive only as a minor footnote in the history of the great explorer's third voyage around the world, were it not for the way trifles have of triggering distant and sometimes momentous events. Had James Cook been more successful in discouraging his men's off-duty amours that winter in Hawaii, neither they nor their shivering officers would have had to trade so eagerly for the Indians' furs in that chill March of 1778. And had Cook's people not then carried their raffish capes and bedcovers of sable and sea otter on to Kamchatka and the fur markets of China, the chronicle and even the boundaries of the United States might be startlingly different. The long history of Oregon, Washington, and Idaho as thirty-third, thirty-fourth, and forty-third stars on the American flag started in a very real sense with that curious and slightly comic encounter at Nootka Sound more than two centuries ago.

As *Resolution* and *Discovery* made their way northward to Alaska, the mariners, snug now in their startling garb, continued to add to their stores of furs, particularly the rich, shiny sea-otter skins. The Englishmen were not alone in this. The Britons were astonished to find small Russian settlements in this unexplored and icy wilderness devoted to the same end. The furs the Muscovites gathered from the Indians and Aleuts were sent to Kamchatka, across the Bering Sea in Asiatic Russia, from where they would be shipped overland to Peking. One of *Discovery*'s officers learned that the skins of sea otters, which the Russians also called sea beavers—*morskoi bobr*—"sold in general for twenty Rubles apiece," the equivalent of four British pounds. That was nearly four months' pay for an ordinary seaman!

Resolution and *Discovery* crossed the Bering Sea to Petropavlovsk, the Russian's main gathering point for furs. The expedition's seamen were still unaware of the value of their outlandish costumes and bedclothing, and might have remained in ignorance had not a Russian merchant been invited one day to dine aboard ship. "The Merchant having gained intelligence of our having Sea Beaver Skins on board desired leave to trade with our people," wrote David Samwell, *Resolution*'s surgeon, "and in a short time a brisk traffic was carried on between Decks. They were sold at first much under value as our people were unacquainted with their worth, but perceiving the Merchant exceedingly eager after them they raised the Price of them & good Skins sold for 20 to 30 rubles & a few at 35 rubles or 7 pounds Sterling. Some of our people as well as the Officers had great numbers of them. The most that any one person made by Skins here was 60 pounds."

An even greater surprise awaited the two ships when they finally reached Canton in December, "the Chinese being very Eager to purchase [sea otters] and gave us from 50 to 70 dollars a skin . . . for what we bought with only a hatchet or a Saw." The silver coins the Chinese handed out were the handsome Spanish "pillar dollars," so called for the Pillars of Hercules that flanked the shield of Castille and Leon on the reverse. An international currency of the day, they were also known as "head dollars" for the likeness of Spain's Carlos III on the other side.

The market improved steadily. "A brisk trade arose," recorded Captain James King, who had assumed command of the expedition after Captain Cook had been murdered by natives in the Hawaiian Islands in February 1779 and then his successor, Captain James Clerke, had died of tuberculosis only six months later. "One of our seamen sold his stocks, alone, for eight hundred dollars; and a few prime skins, which were clean, and had been well preserved, were sold for one hundred twenty each."

The trade the officers and men had been carrying on so successfully with the Chinese, King noted wryly, "produced a very whimsical change in the dress of all of our crew. On our arrival . . . nothing could exceed the ragged appearance both of our younger officers and seamen . . . almost the whole of our original stock of European clothes had long ago been worn out, or patched up with skins. These were now again mixed and eked out with the gaudiest silks and cottons of China."

One can imagine the feelings aboard ship, especially among the seamen and junior officers, when they realized the money they might have piled up had they but known the skins' value back there on the Northwest Coast. "The rage with which our seamen were possessed to return," wrote Captain King, "and, by another cargo of skins, to make their fortunes, at one time, was not far short of mutiny." Two men did manage to desert, in fact, after stealing one of *Resolution*'s boats—a six-oared cutter—and headed back across the Pacific. They were never heard from again. But King stood firm. Orders were orders. The expedition was at an end. The ships would return directly to London.

King had a practical eye for all this, and penned in his journal a plan for a Northwest fur trade. Suggesting an expedition, like his own, consisting of two ships—"single ships ought never to be sent out on discoveries"—he recommended that each

> should have five tons of unwrought iron, a forge, and an expert smith, with a journeyman and apprentice, who might be ready to forge such tools as it should appear the Indians are most desirous of. For though six of the finest skins purchased by us were got for a dozen large glass beads, yet it is well known that the fancy of these people for ornament is exceedingly capricious; and that iron is the only sure commodity for their market. To this might be added a few gross of large-pointed case knives, some bales of coarse woolen cloth (linen they would not accept from us), and a barrel or two of copper and glass trinkets. It cannot be doubted, from our experience in the present voyage, that two hundred and fifty skins, worth one hundred dollars each, may be procured without any loss of time.

As for *Resolution*'s and *Discovery*'s transactions in China, King wrote in one of those marathon sentences that characterize so many eighteenth-century ship's journals:

> The whole amount of the value, in specie and goods, that was got for the furs, in both ships, I am confident, did not fall short of two thousand pounds sterling; and it was generally supposed that at least two-thirds of the quantity we had originally got from the Americans were spoiled and worn out, or had been given away, and otherwise disposed of, in Kamtschatka when, in addition to these facts, it is remembered, that the furs were, at first, collected without our having any idea of their real value; that the greatest part had been worn by the Indians

from whom we purchased them; that they were afterwards preserved with little care, and frequently used as bed-clothes and other purposes during our cruize to the North; and that, probably, we had never got the full value for them in China; the advantages that might be derived from a voyage to that part of the American coast, undertaken with commercial views, appear to me of a degree of importance sufficient to call for the attention of the Public.

Despite King's recommendation, the British Admiralty intended not to let the public in on this particular secret—or, for that matter, any of the expedition's other discoveries—until much later. The existence of furs that could be bought for tuppence worth of beads and then sold for half a year's pay apiece would be a difficult secret to keep, but the British intended to try. While the ships were still well at sea, making their way to Canton, off the Lema Islands, the captains of the vessels, complying with an Admiralty order given them before their departure from London three years earlier, "desired every Gentleman to deliver up to them their Journals, charts, drawings and remarks of all kinds relative to the Voyage; and a diligent search was likewise made among the sailors." The intent of this, Captain King explained in his own journal, which was among those obediently handed over to the authorities, "was to prevent any person publishing an account of our discoveries, but such as their Lordships should appoint, and when they thought proper."

The best-laid plans of their lordships, however, had not taken into consideration the contrary ideas of second lieutenant John Rickman of *Discovery*. Rickman obediently handed over his journal of the voyage, "a good straightforward log, as logs go, with no particular merit or demerit." Rickman had kept two journals, however, or perhaps the act of writing the one he surrendered had so fixed the details of the voyage in his mind that he could reconstruct it once he was back on shore. Adding fanciful incidents—one told of a love affair between a beautiful New Zealand maiden and one of the expedition's sailors—and turning every gale into a "dreadful tempest," Rickman handed his anonymous manuscript over to the London printer Newbury, who issued it in 1781, only a year after the expedition had returned to England. Its success was immediate. Fanciful or not, it caught the imagination of the British public, and scooped the Admiralty's handsome three-volume account of the voyage by three years. Another edition of Rickman's work appeared in London the same year, and a Dublin printer also published a pirated version.

The other actor in this particular drama was a young Connecticut-born Colonial named John Ledyard, who had also served with Cook during the whole of his third voyage. Turning up in London in 1776, he had somehow contrived to become a corporal of marines aboard *Resolution*. An imaginative and ambitious twenty-five-year-old when Cook's ships left England, Ledyard managed a front-row seat for a good deal of the excitement of the voyage. The climax came in the unfortunate encounter with Hawaiian islanders in which Captain Cook was killed. As the final straw in a series of thefts while *Resolution* and *Discovery* lay at Kealakekua Bay on the western shore of the island of Hawaii, one of the ships' boats was stolen.

Captain Clerke, Cook's second in command, was already ill with the tuberculosis that soon would carry him off. Cook, angry and determined to teach the islanders a lesson, went ashore himself, intending to kidnap the local chief and hold him hostage until the boat was returned. Putting a cordon of armed boats across the harbor to prevent help from coming to the Hawaiians from neighboring villages, Cook was rowed ashore with a bodyguard of six marines commanded by Lieutenant Molesworth Phillips, Ledyard's best friend on the voyage. Among the marines was corporal Ledyard.

After seizing the chief, Cook and his guard made their way back to the shore, where the cutter bobbed in the surf. An angry crowd of warriors boiled around them. Cook ordered Phillips back to the boat. Firing broke out, and in the melee Cook was fatally stabbed and fell face down in the water. Though wounded, Phillips managed to swim to the cutter. Ledyard and one of the marines followed, and were rescued by Phillips as they floundered in the sea.

This tragic incident left command of the expedition in the hands of the ailing Clerke, who gamely tried to carry out the Admiralty's instructions for the remainder of the voyage. He died at sea only a few months later and was buried in Petropavlovsk, in Kamchatka. Captain King took command of the two ships for the remainder of the voyage.

Ledyard is not listed among those who surrendered their journals when the ships neared Canton, but he almost certainly kept one. His shipmate James Burney wrote that "Ledyard had the most romantic enthusiasm for adventure of any man of his time," and commented on the American's flamboyant literary style. Somehow, Ledyard must have smuggled his notebooks through to the end of the voyage.

Still wearing his corporal's red coat, Ledyard remained in England for two years. We know little of what kept him busy during this period except that he certainly snapped up a copy of his shipmate John Rickman's bootleg account of Cook's final voyage the moment it appeared. The Revolution was then in full cry, but the young American managed somehow to escape duty that would have put him in combat against his native land. Homesickness, however, must finally have struck. He had not seen his family for seven years.

In December of 1782 he turned up, still in his Royal Navy uniform and a sergeant now, aboard a British man-of-war in Huntington Bay, Long Island. Ostensibly to visit his mother, who kept a tavern and boarding house sixty miles away in Southold, Long Island, Ledyard secured a seven-day leave from his ship. Probably walking the whole way, he found her establishment crowded with British officers. Ledyard quietly made himself known to his mother but quickly arranged a passage across Long Island sound to Connecticut. He was a deserter now, the Revolution was still to go on for many months, and he had to find a safe haven. It proved to be the home of his uncle and former guardian in Hartford.

"I am now at Mr. Seymour's, and as happy as a bee. I have a little cash, two coats, three waistcoats, six pair of stockings, and a half a dozen ruffled shirts. . . . I eat and drink when I am asked, and visit when I am invited; in short, I generally do as I am bid." It sounded like a quiet and leisurely existence, the perfect antidote for those eventful years at sea. In fact, the next four months were probably the busiest of John Ledyard's life, holed up as he was at his uncle's comfortable home and amid the pleasant bookishness of his law office. Hartford printer Nathaniel Patten had promised him twenty guineas for a book that would compete with Rickman's account of Cook's discoveries and had advanced him enough to pay for those waistcoats and shirts and a bit more to keep him afloat. In those sixteen weeks Ledyard completed his *Journal of Captain Cook's Last Voyage to the Pacific Ocean.* Biographer Helen Augur wrote that when the American Revolution officially ended on 19 April 1783, and Ledyard was no longer wanted as a deserter, "he wound up work on the book in a great hurry, almost as if he were no longer interested in it. But he knew precisely what he wanted to do, and there was not a moment to be lost in getting out his book and launching his project." Using either his own journal or his memories of the voyage, plus John Rickman's unsigned account to fill out his own sketchy notes on the expedition's return to

England, he dedicated the volume to Connecticut Governor Jonathan Trumbull, a family friend. It was mostly warmed-over Rickman—the last thirty-nine pages word for word—including the fanciful romance in New Zealand and the dreadful tempests, plus a few details of his own invention. Almost as if he needed to get rid of it, Ledyard handed his manuscript over to Patten and got what was still due him of his twenty guineas. In fact, it has been theorized that Ledyard was so eager to see the end of it that he gave the manuscript unfinished to the printer, who picked up from Rickman those thirty-nine last pages.

Whatever the details, Ledyard could now get on with his great dream. He was determined to be the first American to lead an expedition back to the Northwest Coast and its wealth of furs.

CHAPTER TWO

John Ledyard's Stubborn Quest

★

To a modern mind, Ledyard's proposal seems a bold one, but practical enough. Remember, though, that this was two hundred years ago. The Mississippi Valley belonged then to Spain, or perhaps to France, if it belonged to anyone other than the Indians. The Rocky Mountains had barely entered the American consciousness. The western coast of America? Spain again, and perhaps Britain. Colonies on the moon were not a more distant possibility than trying to struggle through or around those wild barriers to establish trade on so remote a shore.

It will help our perspective at this point if we digress for a moment. What was life like in John Ledyard's America, that embryonic United States that had so recently been spawned by the Revolutionary War? Who lived there?

By 1790, when the nation's first census was undertaken, the citizenry of the thirteen original colonies numbered a bare four million. Nearly all were clustered in a narrow 1,600-mile corridor along the Atlantic seaboard, from Canada's still-uncertain border to Spain's bristling outposts in northern Florida. At the settlers' backs rose the green, still essentially unbreached Alleghenies. Beyond that lay only empty wilderness.

In Ledyard's America, one citizen in twenty lived in a city. New York, sprawling over lower Manhattan Island, boasted thirty-three thousand souls—roughly the population of today's Manhattan, Kansas. Only Philadelphia was larger, with forty-two thousand. The other Americans, nineteen out of twenty, were small farmers or those who dealt with small farmers. They scratched a living from small forest clearings or huddled for convenience and comfort in villages and towns sheltering from a few score to a thousand or two.

Roads? Better to call them bridle paths through the still unbroken forest. The only highways over which a stagecoach or a wagon might pass —unpaved, dusty, agonizingly rough—joined city to city. Most travelers, if they could afford it, went by ship.

In that post-Revolutionary era, good news of any kind was hard to come by. Inflation brought extravagant living to those with money to manipulate, and bitter poverty to those who lacked it. The newly created and inexperienced Congress was having little luck convincing the governments of thirteen fractious onetime colonies into dropping their old jealousies and working in tandem. In a dark mood spreading from Massachusetts, where Daniel Shay agitated for agrarian reform, bankrupt farmers throughout the Northeast talked of something very close to open rebellion.

And there was the problem of foreign trade. At war's end the urban residents of the eastern seaboard had turned their attention to the pursuits of peaceful commerce—but where? Independence be damned, the British had no intention of letting the upstart Americans invade their commercial domains in Europe and Africa. Nor had they any wish to buy American fish and timber. There was little to be done in the West Indies, either, where our old allies the Spanish and French were now acting more like competitors. The classic three-cornered Atlantic trade—Yankee goods to Spain and Africa, slaves from Africa to the West Indies, and sugar, rum, and molasses back to New England—had been permanently shattered.

There was also the matter of ships. Ledyard would find them difficult to come by. Most American merchant vessels of any size had been converted to privateers during the long conflict; many others had been lost, and the remainder were rarely in shape to undertake a major voyage. There had been little new shipbuilding, so the few vessels that might be available were already booked up for whatever trade might be found. But Ledyard's dream was not to be denied. Could the financing be secured, every other problem, he was sure, would vanish.

John Ledyard's plan was grandiose but simple. He intended to guide the first American ship to sail around Cape Horn and thence northward to Nootka Sound. After a season gathering furs on the Northwest Coast, he would head westward across the Pacific to Canton, with a stop at Hawaii for food and fresh water. With the money gained from the sale of the furs, he would then pick up a cargo of China goods and run southward around Africa and up the Atlantic to Boston—and fame. He would even propose the purchase of land from the Indians for the establishment of a permanent trading post. This was exactly what happened—eventually. All in all, though, the idea John Ledyard would try to sell to his countrymen was about as audacious for its time as was President Kennedy's promise nearly two centuries later that we would send men to the moon.

Interestingly, though it hardly comes as a surprise, Ledyard had had much less to say in his book about the eagerness of the Chinese for Northwest Coast furs than would the official account of Cook's last voyage. That was still a year away. The American contented himself with a few sentences. The Northwest Coast had, he wrote, "a species of weazel called the glutton; the skin of this animal was sold at Kamchatka, a Russian factory on the Asiatic coast, for sixty rubles, which is near 12 guineas, and had it been sold in China it would have been worth 30 guineas." His only other comment on the value of the furs so abundantly available on the Northwest Coast was that skins acquired there that had "not cost the purchaser sixpence sterling sold in China for 100 dollars." That was enough to give away in his book. He could tell prospective backers the rest of the story himself.

As soon as the book was completed, and with his dream burning in his mind, Ledyard left his uncle's comfortable retreat for the banks and merchant houses of New York and Philadelphia. Counting his fortune of the moment, exactly three guineas, he decided to walk.

Such an escapade would have daunted most men even in those self-reliant days. But Ledyard was already a great walker, and would continue so throughout his life. Once, years later, he slogged in the dead of winter for 1,200 miles around the Gulf of Bothnia to get from Stockholm to St. Petersburg, averaging twenty miles a day through the snow. He even seriously entertained the idea of walking around the world, thus to become "the first circumambulator of the globe." So Hartford to New York was a modest enough goal.

There he goes, clutching a canvas bag stuffed with his razor and his spare waistcoats, jacket, stockings, and ruffled shirts. He foots his way down the pleasant Connecticut River Valley, glowing now in the electric green of spring. Then he turns westward along the shore past those quiet villages still called New Haven, Bridgeport, and Stamford. Figure the trip at 150 miles, give or take a few—perhaps a week of walking—to reach New York.

The city received him coldly. Its financiers lay all but drowning in the dismal let-down that followed the Revolution. Their glorious cause, which had sustained them through seven uncertain years of brimming excitement and high hopes, now appeared to have fallen into leaden ruins at their feet. Independence seemed such a hollow prize, soured by rampant inflation, destructive internal bickering, and a crushing loss of overseas markets. Was this what happens, they seemed to ask plaintively, to a nation that has just *won* a war?

Ledyard explained his great dream to these gloomy merchant bankers. They listened courteously enough to the intense young visitor's proposal. An expedition to where? By way of Cape Horn? These good, cautious men exchanged glances and then firmly shook their heads.

"Not meeting with encouragement adequate to his sanguine expectations," Ledyard's first biographer, Jared Sparks, summed up primly, "he hastened onward to Philadelphia." Another four or five days and another hundred dusty miles were fatal to Ledyard's only shoes. After breakfast at the Crooked Billet, a favorite inn of Penn's busy city—Benjamin Franklin had lodged there decades before—Ledyard again surveyed his fortune. Counting his cash, he "turned it over and looked at it; shook it in my hand, recounted it, and found two French crowns, half a crown, one-fourth of a dollar, and just twelve coppers." He also looked at his shoes. If he bought new ones, "my two crowns and I shall part. We did part; I put my new pumps on, washed, shaved," and went out. This was in a letter to his cousin, which concluded with the frantic postscript: "For God's sake, send me some money."

In Philadelphia the situation at first appeared even gloomier than it had in New York. Unemployed American sailors loafed about the docks, while foreign sailors cheerfully unloaded the foreign ships that crowded the wharves. American ships? There were almost none. A few weeks later, though, Ledyard was able to write to his cousin in a more hopeful vein. He had met Robert Morris, the "financier of the American Revolution." Morris was now looking to his own finances as a partner in Willing and Morris, the largest importing house in the new nation.

"The Honourable Robert Morris," Ledyard wrote ecstatically, "is disposed to give me a ship to go to the North Pacific Ocean.... What a noble hold he instantly took of the enterprise!" Gloating that he would "take the lead of the greatest commercial enterprise that has ever been embarked on in this country," Ledyard added that he expected to set off shortly for New England—Morris had advanced him enough money that there would be no need this time to walk—to find seamen and a ship. "Morris," he added, "is wrapped up in the idea of Yankee sailors."

In Boston, Ledyard actually found a ship available at one of the city's rotting wharves, but as luck would have it, someone else snapped her up for a different voyage. Ledyard tried in New London, where he contracted for the Continental frigate *Trumbull*, only to have that one too slip out of his fingers. A ship was discovered in New York, but she proved to be so old as to be unfit for the voyage. By this time Robert Morris's enthusiasm had begun to wane. Instead of tackling the Northwest Coast, he decided he would send a vessel around Africa to Canton. Explaining the change of mind, Ledyard said only that Morris "had shrunk behind a trifling obstruction." Probably it was fear of the dreaded passage around Cape Horn, and the problem of finding an American captain willing to attempt it.

Discouraged and defeated, Ledyard once again counted his finances —Robert Morris had paid him enough while the two negotiated to stay afloat a little longer—and concluded he could do no more in the United States. Armed with letters of introduction from Morris, he sailed for Cadiz, Spain, and a month later moved on to the great French port of Lorient. The success of Cook's voyage had alarmed the French and Spanish, and both were planning "scientific" expeditions of their own to look for lands undiscovered by Europeans—and for other overlooked markets like China's for North American furs. After being in Lorient only a few days, Ledyard had secured what sounded like a firm agreement for a voyage to Nootka Sound.

That too slipped away. He had arrived too late in the season, the merchant backers decided; he should wait over in Lorient until the following summer. Reluctantly, Ledyard agreed. Then Louis XVI sent his own ships under La Pérouse into the Pacific, effectively killing any possibility of French cooperation in Ledyard's venture. "My envious fate has again unhorsed me," Ledyard wrote to his cousin in America, "—the devil's in it, said I, if *this* negotiation falls through—and yet it did fall through, as easily as a needle would pass the eye of a camel."

Amid bewildering doubts about his whole project, and again painfully aware of his poverty, John Ledyard hastened off to Paris for one last try. He arrived in the French capital with the usual three guineas in his pocket —plus his letters of introduction from Robert Morris. As an American, he could hardly have picked a more propitious time. Benjamin Franklin, eight years his country's minister to France, was staying on long enough to ease the transition for his successor, Thomas Jefferson. John Paul Jones was also in Paris.

This "most ambitious and intriguing officer in the American Navy," as President-to-be John Adams described Jones after a meeting with him in 1779, was another eccentric in the mold of Ledyard. "Eccentricities and Irregularities are to be expected from him—they are in his Character," noted Adams, "they are inside his Eyes. His voice is soft and still and small, his eye has Keen[n]ess and Wildness and softness in it." The doughty little commodore lived in rented quarters in Montmartre whence he spent his days acting under a commission from the Congress of the United States authorizing him to collect prize money for vessels he had taken during the Revolution, particularly in his famous capture of the *Serapis.* In the evenings he pursued successful affairs with some of the most beautiful women of the city. There was something about him, it seemed, that brought out their instinct to protect. Abigail Adams, though she remained unmoved by this facet of Jones's charm, observed nonetheless of this battle-tried warrior that she "should sooner think of wrapping him up in wool, and putting him in my pocket, than sending him to compete with cannon-balls."

Here was a foursome to reckon with—the brilliant Jefferson, wise Franklin, the flamboyant Jones, and the ever-penniless Ledyard. We know a great deal about the first three. But Ledyard? One wonders just what sort of man he was, what he looked like. A single dubious portrait exists, a drawing executed years after Ledyard's death. The long, aquiline nose, the full lips, the wide untroubled eyes could have belonged to anyone; they betray no hint of the forces that drove this tormented, restless man again and again to dare the odds so clearly set against him. He had been to Dartmouth, and one of his classmates there had recalled tactfully: "He . . . had an independence & singularity in his manners, his dress, & appearance that commanded the particular notice & attention of his fellow students." Fortunately, however, no aspect of Ledyard's eccentricity, either in dress or action, became a social liability. Paris proved that.

Ledyard met all the great men who had been drawn to the French capital by the political currents of the American Revolution. Franklin, suffering from gout and "the Stone"—a bladder ailment that since 1782 had left him few pain-free moments—defied his illnesses to hear first-hand of the death of his old friend James Cook, whom he had known and admired in London, from one who had shared Cook's last great voyage. Franklin would have received Ledyard at his house in rural Passy, half a mile from Paris, on which he had erected one of his new lightning rods. Perhaps the two strolled in Franklin's favorite retreat, "a large garden to walk in," Ledyard talking excitedly of the voyage and of his plans to return to Nootka Sound, the aging Franklin in his familiar plain brown coat listening carefully and peering with curiosity through the bifocals he had invented. He promised his intense young guest letters of introduction to Jefferson and John Paul Jones. It was to be Ledyard's only meeting with Franklin.

When he met Jefferson, Ledyard quickly became an intimate of the Virginian's town house, the Hôtel de Langeac, at what is now the traffic-choked intersection of the Champs-Elysées and the rue de Berri. In the 1780s the house, now long gone, stood beside the Grille de Chaillot, a great iron gateway blocking the Champs, where peasants bringing their rabbits, ducks, and chickens into the city stopped to argue loudly about how much toll they should pay.

The poverty-stricken Ledyard gratefully joined the American visitors, sometimes as many as twenty of them at a time, who regularly shared the hospitality of Jefferson's table. Good conversation would have been Ledyard's passport to regular attendance in that changing, always fascinating company; the articulate Jefferson would hardly have encouraged him had he not contributed at least his share of it. Jefferson, ever one to let conversation flow undisturbed, set a style in his Paris home that he was later to bring to the White House: a small table placed between each pair of guests to hold the current course, so that the servants could leave the dining room until the time came for the next serving. Meanwhile, guests helped themselves and the talk went on unimpeded.

Jefferson, who a few years earlier had proposed an exploring expedition beyond the Mississippi, was fascinated by Ledyard's adventurous tales and by his ideas about trade with the American Northwest, and filed it all away in his mind. Writing enthusiastically to the Marquis de Lafayette, he spoke of Ledyard as having "a spirit of enterprise, an education better than the common, and a talent for interesting and useful observation.... To all this he adds just as much singularity of character, and of that particular kind too, as was necessary to make him undertake the journey he proposes." So Lafayette in his turn became Ledyard's friend and, like Jefferson, his sometime financial benefactor.

One of the richest men in France, the Marquis held court in a house on the rue de Lille for which he had paid the equivalent of nearly a million dollars, and had spent half again as much on its furnishings. Like Jefferson's Hôtel de Langeac, Lafayette's salon buzzed with good talk of America, most of it in French, of course, from the tongues of the young noblemen who had served with Lafayette in the cause of the United States. The Marquis himself spoke English with equal facility, and his home, again like Jefferson's, attracted every American of note who turned up in the French capital. The John Adamses knew Lafayette's hospitality, as did Franklin when his health allowed it. So did John Jay, who with Franklin and Adams had negotiated the treaty of peace with Great Britain at the end of the Revolutionary War.

On the strength of Jefferson's fulsome introduction, Ledyard would surely have been invited to some of the Lafayettes' regular Monday night dinners, at which the Marquis delighted in showing off two of his prized possessions. One was a great picture frame, half of which held a copy of the Declaration of Independence. The empty half was reserved, Lafayette liked to tell his American visitors, for the Declaration of Rights that would one day be enacted for the citizens of his beloved France. The second was "an American savage clad in his native costume" who, as Ledyard would come to do with Jefferson, addressed the Marquis as "Father."

The third of the Americans who would succumb to John Ledyard's spell was the cocky English-born John Paul Jones, whom he probably met at Thomas Jefferson's hospitable table. The two men shared an uncommon spirit; no wonder they became such good friends. Jones seized on Ledyard's project with sweeping enthusiasm. The commodore, Ledyard wrote to his cousin Isaac, has gone so far as to desire me to procure my cargo, send to London for goods, etc. and advanced me necessary cash . . . we do not risk all on a single voyage, but shall establish a factory upon the coast under my direction and under American colours. The first six months after our arrival we collect our furs, purchase the sovereignty of some little spot—most probably an island, and build a stockade sufficient to keep in safety myself, a surgeon, my assistants in business and twenty soldiers.

One of the ships, at the expiration of the six months, proceeds to China; when she returns she stays six months longer and then both ships leave me and my factory, proceed to China and thence by way of the Cape of Good Hope to New York . . .

What a dream! And how profoundly it would have changed the history of the North American West if, instead of waiting until the Spanish had a fortified outpost at Nootka Sound and the British were moving up and down the coast, someone had helped John Ledyard establish his trading station there under the Stars and Stripes.

Jones spent much of the summer and fall of 1785 in Lorient and Nantes looking after his own affairs while Ledyard remained impatiently in Paris. Unbeknownst to Ledyard, though, Jones was having cautious second thoughts. He had written to Robert Morris asking his opinion of the project. Morris sent back an enthusiastic affirmative. But it became clear that no financial aid would be forthcoming from the French. Jones would have to dig deeply into his own pocket to finance an expedition. The French had finally paid Jones about $35,000 in prize money to be split among his men, but his share would not go far on such a grandiose project.

The sensitive Jones was also feeling diplomatic pressures. He had written to Spain to assess the feeling there toward an American foothold in what the Spaniards considered part of their domain. The answer was so obvious he should never have asked. "Spain is too jealous," the commodore shortly wrote to a friend in America, "to permit any commercial speculation in the neighborhood of California."

Poor John Ledyard was back exactly where he had been two and-a-half years before, when he had left the sanctuary of his uncle's house in Hartford. And so was the march toward American ownership of that distant shore called New Albion.

★

CHAPTER THREE

Empress of China
Finds a Market for
Home-Grown Ginseng

★

While John Ledyard's grand hopes had been crumbling, other Americans had begun to move. If the idea of putting a fortune into a trading expedition to the Northwest Coast and then risking it in a voyage around Cape Horn continued to terrify American shipowners and their captains, there was still China. Canton could be reached east about—southward across the Atlantic, around the Cape of Good Hope, and then up through the Indian Ocean. That way, winds and currents would help a ship around, instead of battering her on the nose as they do on the Cape Horn route. And America, unlike Europe, had one home-grown commodity the Chinese would eagerly take in exchange for the tea Americans so desperately wanted.

Ginseng, in the minds of the Chinese, was known as the "dose for immortality." Good quality roots were worth as much as $400 an ounce—their weight in gold, even by today's inflated standards. In fact, ginseng root has no curative powers whatever, but its shape—roughly that of a human body—had since medieval times suggested almost magical properties. It continues to find a ready market throughout East Asia.

American ginseng, which still grows wild in the forests of the eastern seaboard, was of lesser quality than the ginseng of Manchuria, but it nonetheless commanded a substantial price in China. Before the American Revolution, the British had taken all the ginseng the colonies could export for reshipment by the East India Company to Canton. Acquiring it was a trade not unlike the fur bartering of the Northwest Coast. Indians were offered trinkets and whiskey—much to the discomfiture of Puritan divine Jonathan Edwards, who saw in the activity only an excuse for the aborigines to escape their "public worship and their husbandry"— and the forests of New England, New York, and western Pennsylvania were ransacked for the magical "mandrake root." Even worse, complained Edwards, the Indians were accustomed to bringing their ginseng to market in Albany, where they were put "much in the way of temptation and drunkenness."

Not surprisingly, the first cargo loaded for China aboard an American ship consisted of ginseng. But it *is* surprising that this trailblazing voyage pioneered the American-China trade without ever going to China. The little forty-ton sloop *Harriet*—not much larger than a good-sized yacht— left Hingham, Massachusetts, in December 1783. Like nearly every later ship would do on this African run, the *Harriet* put in at the Cape Verde Islands for wood, water, and livestock, and again at Cape Town. In Table Bay, near Africa's southern tip, Captain Hallet anchored beside a fleet of homeward-bound East Indiamen. He must have mentioned his cargo to the British captains. The thought of a Yankee challenge to the East India Company's monopoly of the ginseng trade prompted them to propose an unusual exchange. Captain Hallet planned to take tea back to Hingham? Then they would offer the New Englander double the weight of his cargo of ginseng in Hyson tea. The canny Captain Hallet saved himself that eight thousand-mile round trip between Africa's tip and Canton. Glory could wait. Captain Hallet was more interested in showing a profit for himself and his owners. On 29 July 1784, only seven months after leaving Hingham, *Harriet* was back in New England again, and the Boston *Independent Chronicle* could advertise "fresh teas taken out of an Indiaman and brought by Captain Hallet from the Cape of Good Hope." The voyage cleared $30,727, a 30-percent profit for *Harriet*'s owners.

Credit for the first American voyage to China would finally go to John Ledyard's almost-partner in the Northwest fur scheme, the Philadelphian Robert Morris. Morris's financial interests were not confined to the

City of Brotherly Love. Working through the New York firm of Daniel Parker and Company, Morris and his partners had a ship designed and built in Massachusetts expressly for the China trade. They named her, appropriately enough, *Empress of China*. The merchants loaded their new 368¼-ton vessel with wine and brandy and 473 piculs, about thirty tons, of ginseng. The wines and brandy, and the money on board, would be traded en route for other commodities the Chinese favored: cotton, lead, and roughly half a ton of pepper. On 22 February 1784, George Washington's fifty-second birthday, *Empress* moved out of the East River to make this country's first direct mercantile contact with China.

The sea letter *Empress* carried, signed by President Washington, re-flected the high hopes and the unknown character of the voyage. Taking no chances, it was addressed to the "Most Serene, Serene, most puissant, puissant, high illustrious, noble, honorable, venerable, wise and prudent Emperors, Kings, Republicks, Princes, Dukes, Earls, Barons, Lords, Burgo-masters, Councillors, as also Judges, Officers, Justiciaries, & Regents of all the good Cities and places, whether ecclesiastical or secular who shall see these patents or hear them read."

Captain John Green, who had commanded privateers during the Revolution, made an uneventful passage, stopping first at the Cape Verde Islands, off the west coast of Africa, where he took on the usual water, meat, and fresh vegetables. The sailors, in the manner of seamen every-where, acquired three monkeys to amuse themselves on the long voyage ahead. One evening, after they had set sail for the Cape of God Hope, one of the pets, a "little green monkey with a black face," fell overboard. Next morning "Pug" was found quite unharmed, holding fast to a fishing line that had been left trailing behind the ship all night. It was a good omen.

In the Sunda Strait, which would lead *Empress* into the most dangerous leg of the voyage, the pirate-infested South China Sea, the Americans met two French ships also bound for Canton. The Frenchmen greeted *Empress* warmly and insisted that all three stay together for mutual protection. Captain Green was delighted to do so.

At Portugal's little China-coast colony of Macao, which Captain Green consistently spelled "McCaw" in his log of the voyage, *Empress* had to apply to the Chinese customs house for permission to proceed up the Pearl River to Canton. While the ship lay at anchor, "Mr S Shaw our Suppercargo accompaneyed by Mr Swift Purser had the honour of hoisting the first Continentol Flagg Ever Seen or maid Euse of in those Seas."

In Canton itself, representatives of all the nations whose ships were tied up there—French, British, Dutch, and Danish—welcomed the first American vessel to reach China. Most surprising, perhaps, was the reaction of the Britons, who had so recently been at war with their rebellious colonies. "It was impossible to avoid speaking of the late war," wrote Major Samuel Shaw, who had been sent as *Empress's* supercargo to handle the business affairs of the voyage. The Englishmen he met "allowed it to have been a great mistake on the part of their nation,—were happy it was over,—glad to see us in this part of the world,—hoped all prejudice would be laid aside,—and added, that, let England and America be united, they might bid defiance to all the world." It was a heady welcome.

The only thing that came even close to marring *Empress's* voyage occurred at Whampoa anchorage below Canton, when the Hoppo, Canton's chief customs officer, came aboard to measure the vessel. This would determine the duty to be collected for the Imperial Treasury. British supercargoes had learned that this was a problem that could be eased by bringing to Canton a small assortment of "sing-sings"—European watches, clocks, music boxes, and the like, along with "smellum water"—European perfume. The Hoppo was now accustomed to set aside anything of this sort he fancied. Eventually he would ask the price. The supercargo, who understood such matters perfectly, would quote about 5 percent of the actual cost, for the Hoppo would never accept such things as gifts.

When *Empress* was measured, the Chinese official asked if the crew had brought any sing-sings. Major Shaw had to admit nervously that he was from a new country coming to China for the first time and had not known about the custom. The Hoppo's displeasure moderated somewhat, though he impressed on Shaw the need to bring such luxuries should the American ship come again. But Shaw's diplomatic manner carried the day. Though there had been no sing-sings, the Hoppo that afternoon sent *Empress* his customary gifts-in-return: two bulls, eight bags of flour, and seven jars of Chinese wine.

Empress remained four months in Canton, easily disposing of the cargo and taking on 2,460 piculs—each of 133⅓ pounds—of black tea, 562 piculs of green tea, 24 piculs of coarse cotton cloth called nankeen, 962 piculs of chinaware, 490 pieces of silk, and 21 piculs of cassia, an inferior grade of cinnamon. To make the voyage even more successful, Thomas

Randall, Empress's other supercargo, remained in Canton when the ship sailed for New York and chartered another vessel, the Pallas, that would follow Shaw and Green home with a second cargo, $50,000 worth of tea. On 11 May 1785, Empress of China dropped anchor in New York City's East River, where she "saluted the city with thirteen guns, and finished our voyage." Pallas proceeded to Baltimore, where Thomas Randall supervised the unloading not only of the tea but of a quantity of Chinese porcelain carried home as ballast. Much of it—302 pieces, including some painted with the insignia of the Order of the Cincinnati—was eventually bought by George Washington for use at Mount Vernon.

The charmed life Empress led on that pioneering visit to China failed the ship in later years. Sold on her return home in 1785 and sold again following a second voyage to Canton in 1786-87, also under Captain Green, the ship was rechristened Edgar and put into service between New York and European ports. After having been stranded in 1789 off Waterford, on the south coast of Ireland, the ship was given still another identity, Clara, to avoid the stigma of being an unlucky vessel. But ill fortune continued. Clara blundered onto a shoal off Dublin Harbor on 22 February 1791—ironically, George Washington's fifty-ninth birthday— seven years to the day since the ship had begun her great voyage from New York Harbor to Canton. All hands were saved, but Clara, ex-Edgar, ex-Empress of China, had made her last voyage.

Not long after Empress had delivered its cargo of China goods to New York, Captain Ebenezer West brought Elias Hasket Derby's Grand Turk back to Salem. Her return, wrote Samuel Eliot Morison, "brought fabulous profits to her owner, whetted the appetite of every Massachusetts merchant, and (what was equally important) fixed their good wives' ambition on a chest of Hyson, a China silk gown, and a set of Canton china."

During this same period there had even been faint signs of interest in a Northwest fur trade. The English captain James Hanna in 1785 took his little merchantman Harmon from Canton to America where, either in anticipation of gathering up a cargo of furs, or in celebration of having already done so, he renamed his vessel Sea Otter. He stayed only about five weeks on the Northwest Coast, but that was long enough for him to gather 560 sea-otter skins, which he took back across the Pacific and sold in China for $20,600. When the Boston men finally overcame their fear of Cape Horn and made it to the Northwest Coast, it was becoming clear that they would find English ships had been on the coast ahead of them.

There may even have been a New York ship there on the coast, though the evidence is far from clear. All we have are tantalizing hints. East India Company archives record the *Elenora*, Captain Simon Metcalfe, as having arrived in Canton from Bengal and the Dutch Indies on 12 August 1788. "She left America last season," says the entry. That she might have come by way of the *west* coast of America rests on a single sentence in a log of Captain John Boit, who as we shall see plays a considerable role later in these pages. In Hawaii, seven years after the event, Boit was told of Metcalfe's arrival in China "in the *Elenora* from the NW coast," and noted that she thereafter sailed "for the coast *again*" in company with the little Nor'westman *Fair American*, commanded by Metcalfe's eighteen-year-old son Thomas. On so dubious a record, that first American contact with the Pacific Northwest seems doubtful. We shall probably never know for sure if Simon Metcalfe pioneered the United States maritime fur trade.

Certainly it was not John Ledyard. Disillusioned and chronically penniless, he would spend what little remained of his short life in futile attempts to revive his great dream, or to substitute another for it. His mentor Jefferson, on whom he leaned increasingly for both advice and financial support (Ledyard once addressed him in a grateful letter as "My friend, my brother, my Father") remained enthusiastic about the idea of an expedition to Nootka Sound. In one of those sudden, almost miraculous moments of inspiration, Jefferson proposed a bold new approach to Ledyard's undertaking that would have the most extraordinary consequences for the United States, though it would have little for the unfortunate Ledyard. "I suggested to him," Jefferson recalled some years later, "the enterprise of exploring the Western part of our continent, by passing through St. Petersburg to Kamschatka, and procuring a passage thence in some of the Russian vessels to Nootka Sound, whence he might make his way across the continent to the United States . . ."

Here was the first, almost timid appearance of one of those startling, nation-shaping concepts—Jefferson's dream of an expedition that would in one bold swoop unlock the entire North American West. All of this would come to pass, but only after Boston mariners had shown the way by following John Ledyard's original plan of going around Cape Horn to the Northwest Coast. Then Jefferson in 1804 could dispatch Lewis and Clark with a known objective—the Columbia River, which he would still be confusing with the mythical "Oregon River"—on their epochal march across America. Poor John Ledyard, though, who might conceivably have succeeded in carrying out Jefferson's extraordinary notion of walking alone from one side to the other of the North American continent, was to be denied any role in bringing that bold dream to reality.

In another reminiscence—his 1813 biographical tribute to Meriwether Lewis—Jefferson explained his idea for Ledyard's journey as even more clearly a prelude to his creation of the Lewis and Clark expedition. From Nootka, he wrote, he wanted Ledyard to "fall down to the latitude of the Missouri, and penetrate to, and through," to the seaboard states of the Union. This is almost exactly what Lewis and Clark would end up doing. Never mind that Ledyard would have gone from west to east, while Lewis and Clark eventually did it the other way around. West to east would have changed American history just as surely as east to west, and might have done it a good many years sooner.

"I undertook," recorded Jefferson of his efforts to put the plan into action, "to have the permission of the Empress of Russia." Unhappily for the whole project, he continued, "the Empress refused at once, considering the whole enterprise as chimerical." So Ledyard turned back with fierce determination to his original idea of a voyage to Nootka Sound via Cape Horn. Going to London, he actually found a vessel that was readying for a trip to Nootka. With borrowed funds he went aboard in September 1786, only to have the vessel and himself brought back to the Thames by government revenue cutters with attachment papers from the ship's creditors.

Stubbornly determined to do *something*, John Ledyard just as quickly returned to Jefferson's idea of an overland approach to Nootka Sound by way of Siberia and Kamchatka, whether the Russian empress would give her permission or no. He made his way through Norway, Sweden, and Lapland—that incredible 1,200-mile midwinter walk—to St. Petersburg. By a fluke he was permitted to go on and reached Yakutsk, more than halfway across the great sprawl of Russia, before the empress ordered him arrested and escorted to the Polish border. Back in London, "disappointed, ragged, and penniless, but with a whole heart," this American Marco Polo abandoned his dream of returning to the American west that he had glimpsed as a marine with Captain Cook, and turned his eyes to Africa. Enlisting late in 1788 in a search for the sources of the Niger, he visited Jefferson in Paris. He would return from Africa, he promised his friend, and then undertake a westward crossing of North America starting from Kentucky. He then went on to Egypt.

Ledyard died in as curious a manner as he had lived. In Cairo, awaiting the start of his caravan for the interior, this "slave of accident and son of care," as he once called himself, seems to have lost the resilience that earlier had carried him through so many desperate frustrations. Apparently tried beyond human endurance by the Egyptian camel men he had hired, he "suffered himself to be transported with anger . . . because they delayed setting out on their voyage for want (as they said) of a fair wind. He was seized with a pain in the stomach occasioned by Bile and undertook to cure himself." Ledyard, the account goes, "took a dose so strong as . . . to break a blood vessel. In three days he was suffocated and died."

Defeated and alone, the thirty-seven-year-old adventurer gave up his quest forever. Could he only have known it, though, he and Thomas Jefferson had together sowed the seeds for the United States' acquisition of its splendid Northwest Coast—one of the brightest chapters of the American saga yet to come.

Tentacles of trade extended in many directions from the countinghouse of Boston merchant Joseph Barrell. He bought and sold lands on the Allegheny frontier, sent ships to Madeira for wine and to the West Indies for sugar, dispatched a well-heeled agent to Europe to ferret out "promising speculations," and as early as 1784 consigned a quantity of ginseng root—the one commodity North America offered that the Chinese valued enough to exchange for their tea—aboard the Asia-bound *Empress of China*. It comes as no surprise that such a man would seize on an idea originating with the third voyage of Britain's Captain James Cook: a globe-girdling trade that would exchange trinkets and bits of iron for the furs of Northwest Coast Indians. Sale of the pelts to China's mandarins would pay for cargoes of Souchong and Bohea to be brought home to the teapots of New England by way of the Cape of Good Hope. There was one catch. If American merchants wanted those furs, their ships would have to reach the Pacific Ocean by way of Cape Horn's fury. No American vessel had ever braved that terrifying passage. In 1787, Joseph Barrell took up the challenge— and forever changed United States history.

(*Pastel by John Singleton Copley, Worcester Art Museum, Worcester, Massachusetts*)

CHAPTER FOUR

Boston
Takes Up
the Challenge

★

Bostonians finally listened to what John Ledyard had been trying to tell them. Joseph Barrell, one of the city's wealthiest merchants, had surely been one of those approached by Ledyard when he had come to the Massachusetts capital to sell his idea of a Northwest Coast voyage. In fact, Barrell and some of his merchant friends had earlier attempted to organize just such a voyage as Ledyard proposed. They had even "procur'd many of the necessary articles of traffick; and got it in some forwardness: when those other gentlemen, deeming it too speculative a voyage, it dropt." Shades of poor John Ledyard!

Barrell had also dipped a tentative toe in China-trade waters in 1784, when he had entrusted twenty-three casks of ginseng and five cases of claret to Captain John Green on *Empress of China*'s pioneering voyage to Canton. There was also a cask of beads. Barrell, in the ignorance of the times, must have thought the Chinese would be as eager for trinkets as Cook had found to be true of the Indians of the Northwest Coast. The beads, predictably, sold for a mere fourteen Spanish dollars and the wine for only $125, but Captain Green realized a handsome $4,055 for the ginseng—enough to let him take back to Barrell several cases of silks, quantities of ready-made satin breeches and waistcoats, and several hundred Malacca canes. Chinese goods immediately became the rage in Boston, and Barrell's profits on his little adventure would have whetted his appetite for a more direct hand in the Canton trade.

At this point it would be well to understand exactly what a merchant was in the Boston of 1787. Samuel Johnson's classic definition, "one who trafficks to remote countries," gives us a start. Historian Samuel Eliot Morison goes further:

> He was no mere shopkeeper, or commission dealer. He bought and sold, at home and abroad, on his own account, and handled "private adventures" on the side. He owned or chartered the vessels that carried his goods . . . The provincial merchants owned not only merchant ships, but fishing craft, whalers, and coasters, sent their vessels to . . . England, the Mediterranean, the West Indies, and the Spanish main for all sorts of commodities; sold their return ladings at wholesale, and at retail from their own shops; speculated in wild lands, did a private banking business, and underwrote insurance policies.

These merchants lived well, Morison continues,

> with a spacious brick mansion in Boston and a country seat at Milton Hill, Cambridge, or as far afield as Harvard and Hopkinton, where great house parties were given. . . . They carried swords, and drew them if not granted proper deference by inferiors. Their wives and daughters wore the latest British fashions, and were painted by Smibert, Blackburn, and Copley. Their sons went to sea on a parental ship, or, if they cared not for business, to Harvard College.

Such were Joseph Barrell and his merchant contemporaries, though their lives may have glittered a little less than this in post-Revolutionary Boston's lean and unsettled times.

Now, after poverty-stricken John Ledyard himself had in total frustration given up his plan for a voyage to the Northwest Coast and was attempting to walk across Russia to get there, the bewigged, well-fed Joseph Barrell had come again to the idea of sending a ship around Cape Horn and on to western America. "There is a rich harvest to be reaped there" he wrote, as if it had been his idea in the first place, "by those who shall first go in."

Barrell shared his renewed interest in the Northwest Coast with his good friend and neighbor Dr. Thomas Bulfinch, and with Thomas's son

Charles, who had graduated from Harvard in 1781 and now at twenty-three had just returned from eighteen months of architectural study in Europe. Young Bulfinch had started out, at his father's request, to become a merchant himself, and spent some time learning the ropes in Joseph Barrell's countinghouse. But to his finely honed mind the details of business were boring, while architecture more and more captured his interest. Charles Bulfinch would become famous not as a merchant, but as the Architect of the United States Capitol, a post in which he succeeded Benjamin Latrobe and saw to the completion of that great building in 1830. He would also one day design a mansion in the Boston suburb of Charlestown for his old friend Joseph Barrell. It would have "an oval parlor projecting on the garden side in the manner . . . adopted the same year for the President's house in Washington."

But now, years before any of this would happen, Joseph Barrell and the Bulfinchs, father and son, sat around a crackling fire in the Bulfinch mansion on Boston's cobbled North Square, only a block from the noise and bustle of the wharves, and planned a daring and, they hoped, profitable venture. One can sense the excitement they felt, the kind of enthusiasm that set Bostonians of those days apart from other Americans. The people of the Massachusetts capital, opined Timothy Dwight, a New Haven contemporary, were "distinguished by a lively imagination. Their enterprises are sudden, bold, and sometimes rash. A general spirit of adventure prevails here."

It was young Charles Bulfinch, in fact, and not Joseph Barrell himself, who was initially responsible for this bold and sudden resurgence of interest in the establishment of a Northwest fur trade. Bulfinch's architectural studies in Europe, financed by an unexpected £200 windfall from the estate of an uncle in Britain, had allowed him to putter at will through England, France, and Italy, absorbing the glories of their splendid buildings along the way. This is beside the point for our interests. What matters is that he carried letters of introduction to the Marquis de Lafayette and Thomas Jefferson. This was in 1785 and '86, the very years that the restless John Ledyard was in Paris inflaming Jefferson's and Lafayette's imaginations with his schemes for a fur-trading expedition to Nootka Sound. Bulfinch joined that shimmering company of Americans around Jefferson's hospitable table at the Hôtel de Langeac, where he absorbed Lafayette's and Jefferson's enthusiasm for Ledyard's stirring dream.

The idea of a business career may have bored the young architect-to-be, but as Bulfinch listened to Ledyard's proposition he thought it sounded more like an adventure than dull commerce. After a month-long voyage back to Boston in the dead of winter—ample time for him to reorder Ledyard's then-abandoned plan and adapt it to his own thoughts —Charles Bulfinch had already sounded out his father and his merchant friend Barrell on the idea of a *Boston-owned* expedition to Nootka Sound, China, and back home around the world to Boston. And why not? Ledyard had given up and was now going about it by way of Russia and Siberia. And there was no patent on the idea anyway.

Almost certainly Barrell and his two friends had with them that night the three beautiful leather-bound volumes of Cook's third voyage issued in London only three years before. Probably young Bulfinch had lugged them home himself. In the last volume was that memorable passage in which Cook's successor, Captain James King, had outlined his own proposals for a Northwest fur trade. Here were all the instructions one would need.

As the three men continued to meet round the Bulfinchs' cheery fire on other evenings, the circle grew to include four others: Boston merchant Samuel Brown; Crowell Hatch, a sea captain of Cambridge; John Derby of Salem, a wealthy shipowner and son of famed merchant Elias Hasket Derby; and twenty-eight-year-old John Marsden Pintard of New York City, who had inherited some money from his grandfather and felt a hankering to establish himself in the China trade. Out of those conversations in the early months of 1787 came a determination to do precisely what John Ledyard had proposed four years earlier. This time the proposal would stick.

Barrell by now was no less enthusiastic about the venture than Ledyard himself had been. "It must appear obvious how very favorable such a trade would be," he wrote at the time, "... for in case of success, a very valuable property would be brought into the country from a trifling advance, and in a short time establish a trade superior to any the country enjoys at present, and the idea may with propriety be extended to an establishment [on the Northwest Coast] at least equal to what Hudson's Bay is to Great Britain."

Barrell and his partners were aware, too, of how great a leap into the unknown such an expedition would be. Captain Cook had recorded at least the dim outlines of the Pacific Coast of North America from northern California to Nootka Sound. Beyond, all the way to Sitka, Alaska, the

Patriot-silversmith Paul Revere engraved this fanciful bird's-eye view of Boston, with
its exaggerated church spires and menacing array of British warships, in 1774 for the *Royal
American Magazine*. Thirteen years later, when Joseph Barrell's two captains, John Kendrick
and Robert Gray, embarked on their great adventure, the harbor sheltered American
merchant ships flying the Stars and Stripes, but little else had changed in the appearance
of the Massachusetts capital. Long Wharf (A, at center), with its row of warehouses and
ships' chandleries, still carried State Street a third of a mile out into Boston Harbor.
The expedition's two ships, *Columbia Rediviva* and *Lady Washington*, were fitted out at
Hancock's Wharf (B, at right). At far left (D) lies Griffin's Wharf,
where the Boston Tea Party took place.
(*Massachusetts Historical Society*)

map remained blank. If there proved to be insufficient furs at Nootka, Barrell wrote in his proposal for the voyage, the ships were "then to proceed along the coast to the northward, examining the same in the most attentive manner for bays, rivers, or harbors suitable for trade between Notooka [sic] and Prince William's sound ... as between these two places the coast was not explored by Captain Cook or any former navigator."

Here was a proposition to appeal to that spirit of adventure Timothy Dwight had observed, and even more to the mercantile interest that, said a French visitor of Bostonians in 1788, "occupies all their thoughts, turns all their heads, and absorbs all their speculation." Six partners among the seven present quickly pledged a total of $49,000—fourteen shares at $3,500 a share. This was an enormous amount in that time of postwar depression and failing trade. Barrell, as originator of the scheme, agreed to take four shares, with two each to the other partners. Dr. Bulfinch was not, by name at least, among the venture's investors, but he must have put up the money for his son's share. Perhaps he was still not sure that architecture would be a suitable profession for his son and clung to the hope that young Charles would make his mark in the mercantile world.

The first problem would be ships. Barrell and his associates remembered well what Captain King had cautioned: "Single ships ought never to be sent out on discoveries," which was but a paraphrase of Sir Thomas More's dictum of more than two centuries earlier: "A wise merchaunt never adventures all his goodes in one ship." With both determination and cash—assets Ledyard's fickle backers never seemed to have had at the same time—Barrell quickly found them.

It would not have been easy in those difficult times. In the palmy days before the Revolution, as many as 125 new vessels had been launched in Massachusetts in an average year. By 1787 that had dropped to fifteen or twenty. Foreign vessels, but few flying the new American flag, crowded Boston harbor. Barrell was lucky to find ships at all, and good ones especially so. Three years earlier, forty-five ships had come down the way in Massachusetts, twelve of them ordered by the French East India Company. But the workmanship had been so shoddy that the Europeans refused to order more. So there was quality to worry about too. These ships would have to survive the battering of a westward passage around Cape Horn—"the most dangerous, most difficult, and attended with more hardships, than that of the same distance in any other part of the world"—and then go on to whatever unknown trials they would find in the Pacific.

Barrell and his partners settled on a ship named *Columbia Rediviva*—and thereon hangs a controversy. Most historians believe *Columbia* was a new vessel that the Bostonians found abuilding in Plymouth, Massachusetts. Others suggest that she was built in 1773 up the coast a way at Scituate, in the same yard that gave birth to *Beaver*, of Boston Tea Party fame, a year earlier. There are also those who see that Latin word in her name—*rediviva*—which translates as "reborn," or "restored to life," as evidence that she was an even older ship undergoing complete rebuilding in 1787 when Barrell and his friends discovered her. Whatever the ship's origin, veteran of the seas or untried newcomer, we know this much with certainty: She was only a few inches over eighty-three feet long on deck—hardly the leviathan one might wish for a voyage round the world and a doubling of Cape Horn. *Columbia*'s beam measured about twenty-four feet, and the ship was rated at a burden of 212-and-8/95th tons. This, even then, was an old-fashioned way of expressing a ship's capacity in *tuns*, huge wine casks that weighed, with their contents, roughly a long ton.

Columbia would be the expedition's flagship. As *Columbia*'s tender, Joseph Barrell and company selected the *Lady Washington*, a sloop of ninety tons, about sixty feet long. Vessels named for Martha Washington were popular in the turbulent years of the Revolution. In Massachusetts alone there were two. *Columbia*'s consort may have been one of them, a sloop fitted out at Boston as a privateer in 1776. The possibility that this was Barrell's *Lady Washington* is strengthened by the fact that one of the partners in the current venture, Samuel Brown, had been at one time half owner of the 1776 vessel. Barrell himself had also been involved in the fitting out of at least half a dozen armed Massachusetts ships given letters of marque permitting them to prey on enemy shipping. *Lady Washington* had done well for the United States, beating off four armed British vessels in one encounter and, in another, capturing the British ship *Weathrill*, carrying a cargo of rum, sugar, and cotton, and bringing ship and cargo home as a prize of war to Boston. So, if we have the right *Lady Washington*, the ship was already a veteran by 1787.

Being fresh off the builder's—or the rebuilder's—ways that spring, *Columbia* would have been a handsome sight, the hull freshly painted with a broad band of bright yellow, with blue, dark green or black above and below. Carved and gilded "gingerbread" adorned the transom, setting off the whole proud name, Columbia Rediviva—"Columbia Reborn"—and the hailing port, Boston. There would have been more gilding and carved "quickwork" about the bows, leading the eye out to the great upthrust bowsprit. Three masts, the highest towering nearly one hundred feet above the water, carried a panoply of square sails. Aft, above her stern, a huge thirteen-starred flag would have billowed. Americans liked their flags large in those glory days of the republic.

Oddly, had Columbia been stripped of all that bright decoration and fresh color, no trim greyhound of the sea would have emerged. The ship was exactly what Barrell thought was needed, a bluff cargo carrier, slab sided and broad of beam. New England shipbuilders, unlike the men who turned out the swift Baltimore clippers of Chesapeake Bay, clung to the old notion that "ships require a spreading body at the water's edge . . . to support them from being plung'd too deep in the sea." Columbia would plow her way through the water instead of parting it cleanly.

Though not a new vessel, Washington had her own appeal. She did look a trifle like a Baltimore clipper: A single soaring mast, raked handsomely aft. A huge mainsail nearly as long at the foot as the entire deck of the vessel. A bowsprit that added another forty-five feet or so to the total length of the sloop. The twenty-foot overhang of that great gaff-rigged mainsail aft and the incredible bowsprit forward doubled the visual length of the little craft, making it seem in fact a greyhound beside the St. Bernard build of Columbia. But that ship, too, stripped of mast and those amazing overhangs at bow and stern, would have been revealed as beamy and capacious despite a rakish appearance.

Both vessels were heavily armed; the need for that kind of protection had been shown time after time on Cook's voyages. The owners would have put aboard Columbia as many as a dozen carriage guns, probably three and six pounders, to be fired through ports in the rails. Swivels—light, easily handled guns of smaller caliber—would have been mounted along the bulwarks. Instead of single balls, these would have fired grape shot, clusters of small round projectiles, or if necessity arose, langrage, which consisted of any murderous bits and scraps of metal the gunner could put his hands on. Washington would have had nearly as many weapons, possibly the same ones she had carried as a privateer. In all of this, the two vessels seemed ideally suited to their purpose—to accommodate a larger than usual crew and more than the usual stores of food, water, and

"That nothing might be wanting to commemorate the voyage," Joseph Barrell and his partners had an engraver—probably Paul Revere—cut the die for a medal to be struck in copper, pewter, and silver. It carried the names of the two ships, the expedition's commander, and the six merchants who financed it. Several hundred of these tokens, today among the rarest of American commemorative pieces, were sent with the ships to serve as "a lasting memento in those countries which might be visited or discovered. . . ." Only a few were struck in silver. This example was given by Barrell to John Kendrick, who left it behind in Massachusetts when he sailed aboard *Columbia*, never to return. Years later his widow passed it on to Hall J. Kelley, an early champion of Oregon statehood, who was endeavoring to press the claims of Gray's and Kendrick's heirs to lands on the Northwest Coast.

(*Oregon Historical Society*, OrHi *2880/259*A)

trading goods on a voyage through dangerous and unknown waters that might stretch out over three or four years. Both were solid, practical ships for the jobs they had to do, and they would prove it again and again.

Barrell and his partners must have scoured every book they could get their hands on that had anything to say about the experiences of Cook's expedition to the Northwest Coast. But the information was meager. The trading done by the British had been without advance planning, using whatever trinkets and supplies they could spare from the ships' regular stores. In the end, Barrell and his partners piled aboard *Columbia* and *Washington* an assortment of trade goods that resembled the inventory of a New England general store: 18 rat traps, 15 dozen necklaces, 19 egg slicers, 600 sail needles, 449 looking glasses, 78 snuff bottles, 22¾ dozen Jew's harps, 14 dozen pairs of "elegant earrings," 92 pounds of beads, plus an assortment of "skillits, potts and kettles, Brass tobacco Boxes, pint Basons, hatchetts" and whatnot, to a total of several thousand items. Also put aboard, as Captain King had recommended, was a large quantity of unworked iron that the ships' smiths could transform into the crude chisels the Indians were known to favor.

All was not dull business, however. Barrell and his friends had a sense of drama, and they knew this venture of theirs would find its way into the history books. "That nothing might be wanting to commemorate the voyage," wrote Barrell's clerk, John Hoskins, who would become *Columbia*'s supercargo on the second voyage, "and to place a lasting memento in those countries which might be visited or discovered, during its continuance: the Owners caused several hundred medals to be struck." On one side of the silver-dollar size tokens Barrell had his engraver— probably his friend and neighbor Paul Revere—fashion portraits of the two ships, pennants bravely streaming as they scudded along before a fair breeze. "COLUMBIA and WASHINGTON," the inscription reads, "Commanded by J. KENDRICK" and on the back, "FITTED at BOSTON. N. AMERICA for the PACIFIC OCEAN, 1787" and the names of the six partners (Derby's, oddly enough, misspelled "Darby"). Most of the medals were of copper or pewter. About a dozen were struck in silver. One of these was sent to General Washington, who "paid the Owners a very flattering comment on the occasion; at the same time express'd his best wishes for their success." Thomas Jefferson and the Marquis de Lafayette also received medals.

In all, some fifty men, including ships' officers, would form this pioneering contingent of Boston's sturdy Nor'westmen—more than the usual complement but still not too many to crew two ocean-going vessels. New England sailors were accustomed to serving under thrifty owners who would never send two men on a job if they could get by with one. But thrift would not be the determining factor when it came to selecting the captains who would command the ships. Once the expedition was launched, there would be no way for the owners to communicate, nor could the captains fall back on the owners for decisions of any kind. The only link might be an occasional letter sent back thanks to some chance encounter with a homeward-bound vessel, and that would arrive only after many months at sea. Once the ships were out of Boston harbor, Barrell and company knew too well, everything would be in the hands of *Columbia*'s and *Washington*'s captains.

Joseph Barrell, Samuel Brown, and Crowell Hatch, shipowners and Bostonians all, would have had a wide range of captains from which to choose a commander for their expedition. Young Bulfinch, the other Bostonian, lacked any experience in the maritime world of New England and would surely have left it up to his partners to make this particular decision. Pintard, familiar with the New York shipping scene, might have had his say, as would John Derby of Salem. Unfortunately, no document survives to give the slightest hint of why they selected big, gregarious John Kendrick of Wareham, Massachusetts—a man of broad experience but who was then nearing fifty—to be captain of *Columbia* and commander of the whole enterprise. Experience may have been the answer, for Kendrick had had many commands in a long life at sea, and had done well with them.

Kendrick's English grandfather, Edward Kenwrick, settled on Cape Cod about 1700. The rest of John's family, good Pilgrim and Puritan stock, had already been there for two or three generations. Edward Kenwrick's wife, Elizabeth, was a granddaughter of Constance Hopkins, who had come to Plymouth as a teenager with her father aboard the *Mayflower*. Called a "trader" in some of the old records, Edward probably was a storekeeper and certainly was a land speculator. Dying a prosperous man, he left half a dozen slaves to his children. He seems never to have had any connection with the sea.

John Kendrick's father, Solomon, however, turned early to the life of a mariner. At the age of thirty he was master of a whaling sloop operating off the mouth of the St. Lawrence River. Not much is known of his life

other than an item in the Boston *News-Letter* of 24 May 1736, which reported that Kendrick's vessel had

> struck and wounded two Whales, which then lay upon the Water
> seemingly in a dying Posture: but one of them suddenly rush'd with
> great Violence over the midst of one of their [whale] boats and sunk
> both the Men and the Boat into the Sea; one Man was thereby kill'd
> outright, and two others much wounded: Tis a wonder they were not
> all destroy'd, for the Whale continued striking and raging in a most
> furious manner in the midst of them (now in the water) for some
> Time, but the other boat came and took them all up (except the man
> that was kill'd, who sunk immediately) and carried them safe to the
> Sloop.

Could this, added to the story of the *Essex* and her fate, have been the
germ of Melville's *Moby Dick*?

Solomon Kendrick's third son, John, was born in Harwich, midway
out on Cape Cod, about 1740. From the few examples of his writing that
survive, he seems to have acquired even less than the usual common-
school education. Certainly he, like his father, went to sea early. At
twenty, John signed on as a seaman aboard Captain Judah Bangs's schooner for a voyage to the St. Lawrence whaling grounds. The voyage was
successful, a local historian wrote, "notwithstanding four of the crew
were Indians." Shortly thereafter, John saw service fighting the French on
the northern frontier in his uncle Captain Jabez Snow's militia company.
From that period in uniform, which spanned eight months in 1762, the
records are sparse until the Revolutionary War. About all that can be said
is that John Kendrick rose to the command of merchant vessels sailing
between Boston and the Colonies' southern ports. At some time in this
same period he also moved from Harwich to Martha's Vineyard, where
in 1767 he married Huldah Pease, a great-great-granddaughter of John
Pease, among the earliest of the island's settlers.

Of course, there was the Boston Tea Party, if a family tradition can be
believed. Half the families of maritime Massachusetts fondly share that
tradition, though, and there were no more than 100 to 150 "Mohawk
braves" risking the King's wrath on that rainy night of 16 December 1773.
To the credit of the belief that John Kendrick might have been among
them, the men who boarded *Beaver*, *Dartmouth*, and *Eleanor* in Boston Harbor were picked for being "not much known in town and not easily
recognized." Though he sailed out of Boston, Kendrick's Martha's Vine-

yard residence would have answered that qualification. And there is one other hint that he may in fact have been among the angry men who tossed those chests of stamp-act tea overboard. Pride in the exploit might well have been at work when he elected two years later to sail in command of a coastwise brigantine brazenly named *Undutied Tea*.

But even if he was only one among the many who watched history being made that night from the safety of stumpy Griffin's Wharf, no question can be raised of John Kendrick's devotion to the patriotic cause. In May of 1777, he turns up as captain of the Massachusetts privateer *Fanny*, a vessel carrying eighteen guns and a crew of one hundred. The fact that his name appears not only as captain but as one of the vessel's bonders suggests that Kendrick had by then acquired a respectable status financially; so does his new address, Wareham, where he and Huldah had built a lavish home, finished internally in accordance with the "foreign order of archetectural designs."

Fanny's activities that summer occasioned some heated diplomatic correspondence when she, with the brigantine *General Mercer*, captured two British ships and carried them into the French port of Nantes. The Americans claimed the two vessels were actually Dutch, bringing cargoes of sugar from St. Eustatia, which led the French to confiscate them both. Eventually the Royal Government approved payment of four hundred thousand French livres prize money to the owners and officers of the privateers. Kendrick's share may have been the money that went for his new house.

In November 1779 Kendrick appears to have been captured by the British ships *Brutus* and *Little Brutus*, and he may have languished for a time in England's infamous Dartmoor Prison. In any event, he was exchanged and made his way back to Boston. The next year he was sailing as commander of the privateer *Count d'Estaing*, a brigantine of sixteen guns and one hundred men. He again appears as the principal bonder. Late in 1780 he had command of the slightly smaller Massachusetts brigantine *Marianne*. Kendrick's activities between 1780 and 1787, when he became *Columbia*'s captain, remain for the most part buried in the Massachusetts archives. We know of only two voyages during that period. After the end of the Revolution he returned at least briefly to whaling, captaining the brig *Fortune* out of Boston on a cruise to the Atlantic grounds, from which he returned in October of 1784. Two years later he was in Charleston, South Carolina, presumably back in the coasting trade between New

England and southern ports. Whatever his commands, they must have brought credit to him, or Joseph Barrell and his partners would never have trusted him with the responsibility for their Northwest venture.

Kendrick must have been much in evidence around Joseph Barrell's countinghouse at the very end of this period, for he and eighteen-year-old John Hoskins, then one of Barrell's clerks, formed a deep and lasting friendship. The two would not meet again until Columbia reached Nootka Sound on her second voyage around the world, when Hoskins was the ship's supercargo and Kendrick, as captain of the Lady Washington, was a rival trader.

Barrell's confidence in Kendrick's experience and judgment was warmly expressed in the order given him before the voyage began.

> Sir: [Barrell wrote] The ship Columbia and sloop Washington being completely equipped for a voyage to the Pacific Ocean and China, we place such confidence in you as to give you the entire command of this enterprise. It would be impossible upon a voyage on this nature to give with propriety very binding instructions, and such is our reliance on your honor, integrity and good conduct, that it would be needless at any time. You will be on the spot, and as circumstances turn up you must improve them.

Barrell enjoined Kendrick to treat the Indians fairly, so that "the most inviolable harmony and friendship may be cultivated between you and the natives, and that no advantages may be taken of them in trading, but that you endeavor by honest conduct to impress upon their minds a friendship for Americans."

The instructions also warned against touching "at any part of the Spanish dominions on the western continent of America, unless driven there by some unavoidable accident." In that case, Barrell instructed Kendrick, stay no longer than necessary and "be careful to give no offense to any of the subjects of his Catholic Majesty."

"The sea letters from Congress and this State," Barrell concluded, "you will also show on every proper occasion; and although we expect you will treat all nations with respect and civility, yet we depend you will suffer insult and injury from none without showing that spirit which will ever become A FREE AND INDEPENDENT AMERICAN."

John Pintard on 18 August 1787, had requested that the Congress of the Confederation, then struggling ineffectually to govern the newly independent and headstrong states, issue sea letters for both Columbia and

Washington. The harried legislators got around to authorizing the documents "in the usual form" on 24 September, less than a week before the ships were to sail, and they were rushed to Boston by stage coach. The language so carefully worked out three years earlier for *Empress of China's* pioneering voyage had now become "the usual form." *Columbia's* letter, still addressed to the "Most Serene, Serene, most puissant, puissant" of earth's rulers, has long since disappeared, but it would have read:

> We the United States of America in Congress Assembled make known that John Kendrick Captain of the Ship call'd the Columbia is a Citizen of the United States of America and that the Ship which he commands belongs to Citizens of the said United States and as we wish to see the said John Kendrick prosper in his lawful affairs, our prayer is to all the before mentioned, and to each of them separately, where the said John Kendrick shall arrive with his Vessel & Cargo, that they may please to receive him with goodness and to treat him in a becoming manner, permitting him upon the usual tolls & expences in passing & repassing, to pass, navigate and frequent the ports, passes and territories to the end to transact his business where and in what manner he shall judge proper: whereof we shall be willingly indebted.

The handsome document, with its pale green ribbon and the Great Seal of the United States glowing in its upper left corner, was signed by His Excellency General Arthur St. Clair of Pennsylvania, who was then sitting as president of the Congress. This was the document Joseph Barrell would so ceremoniously hand over to John Kendrick along with a similar sea letter from the state of Massachusetts and with his own instructions for the voyage.

The old mariner, for all his past commands and experience of the sea, would have been most impressed of all, one guesses, by that federal passport, with its smell of authority and its suggestion of carte blanche to the presence of emperors, kings, princes, dukes, earls, barons, lords, and burgomasters—though Kendrick would find precious few of any of those where he was going.

If the facts of John Kendrick's early life are sketchy, those for the thirty-two-year-old bachelor Robert Gray, named by Barrell and his partners to be captain of the *Lady Washington*, are almost nonexistent. He, too, came of "good New England stock," a distant relative of Governor Edward Winslow of the Plymouth Colony. He was born to William and Elizabeth Gray of Tiverton, Rhode Island, on 10 May 1755. Gray's widow,

No identified contemporary portrait exists of Robert Gray or John Kendrick. This conjectured likeness of Gray was probably drawn years after his death. The artist appears to have been unaware that *Columbia's* captain had lost an eye, a fact noted by both Indian and Spanish observers on the Northwest Coast.
(*Oregon Historical Society*, OrHi 586/458)

many years after his death, said that he had been an officer in the Continental Navy during the Revolution, but no record so far unearthed gives any detail of that service. Gray had commanded the ship *Pacific*, engaged in the South Carolina trade and jointly owned by two of the partners in the *Columbia* venture, Crowell Hatch and Samuel Brown. But that is all we know of Robert Gray until the day *Lady Washington* raised her sails in Boston harbor for the voyage to the Northwest Coast.

They would make a strange pair, the easy-going but mercurial Kendrick, now forty-seven years old, and the businesslike, methodical Robert Gray, fifteen years Kendrick's junior. A large, outgoing man who had come up to his captaincy through the ranks—"through the hawse hole," a New England sailor would have said—Kendrick would prove on this voyage to be a man of unbounded courage at one moment and frustrating vacillation the next. Uninterested in the petty routines of making a dollar at a time, his visionary streak would lead him into one beguiling side issue after another, none of which in the end would come to much.

No identifiable contemporary portrait of Robert Gray or any of his progeny survives, and the visual record is equally blank where John Kendrick is concerned. However, a naive but probably accurate likeness of Kendrick's son Alfred, who was only nine when *Columbia* sailed from Boston, suggests the features his father may have had. Painted when Alfred was in his sixties, it shows a large, big-boned man, as John Kendrick is reputed to have been. Bushy eyebrows jut above dark, frank eyes. A broad forehead balances the strong, stubborn chin. Between them, the long, straight nose dwarfs an abrupt, narrow upper lip. The mouth dominates this face. Alfred's expression was tense and slightly downturned as he sat uncomfortably for some itinerant painter, and there seems to be a hint of a streak of suppressed anger beneath the untroubled facade that might erupt momentarily, as it did so often with his father, into an outburst of uncontrolled temper.

Both John Kendrick and Robert Gray were consummate seamen who could handle their vessels skillfully under the most trying circumstances, though Kendrick's cautious dawdling would keep him out of trouble as often as Robert Gray's foolhardy navigation would get him into it. Both shared a tendency to outbursts of temper, though Gray's seems rarely to have flared as abruptly as did Kendrick's. But there the resemblances end. The evidence is meager, but one imagines Gray in every other way as just the opposite of Kendrick. He was no dreamer, but an eminently practical man. Throughout the voyage he would keep his mind firmly on the "paltry two-penny objects" of commerce that had led the Bostonians to launch the expedition in the first place. Where the flamboyant Kendrick often appears larger than life, Gray seems never to have inspired remarks on his personality or expressions of friendship from his fellows in any of the journals kept aboard his ships. Even the fact that Gray appears to have had the use of only one eye escaped comment except for a passing note in the journal of a Spanish visitor to the Northwest Coast in 1792.

Though it had not yet dawned on them, Joseph Barrell and his partners could hardly have picked two men less suited to share the command of an expedition into the virtually unknown Pacific.

CHAPTER FIVE

Columbia and Lady Washington Raise Sail for New Albion

★

1787. SEPTEMBER. Early in the fitting of the Columbia for a Voyage round the world, I was employed as third Officer. Great expedition was used to forward our departure . . . the Ship was hauled off from the wharf and anchored in the Harbour. Here numberless articles of her provisions, stores, etca. were received . . . The Pilot came onboard and we were removed down to the Castle roads where we anchored with the small bower and mored with the Streem anchor.

Friday the [28th] the Sloop Washington Captain Robt. Gray who is to be our consort, anchored in the Roads.

Thus young Robert Haswell, not quite nineteen, begins his journal, the only surviving account of *Columbia Rediviva*'s and *Lady Washington*'s pioneering voyage to the Northwest Coast.

Since Haswell will be our chief guide during most of this historic voyage, it is not amiss to ask who he was. Not much is known of Haswell's early years. When the Revolution broke out, his father, a lieutenant in the British Navy, was interned by the rebellious Americans; about 1778 the whole family was packed off to Halifax, Nova Scotia. Eventually they

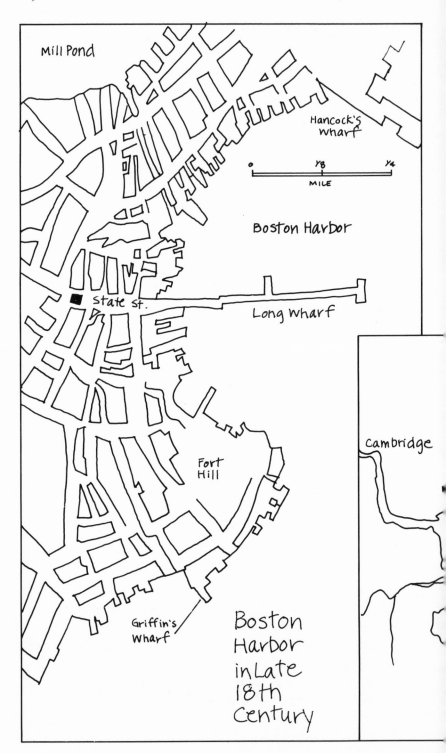

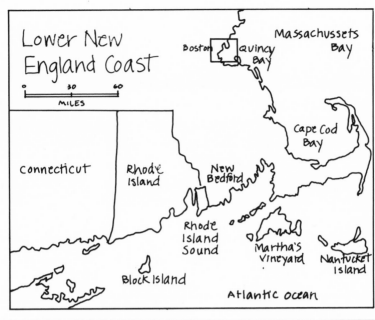

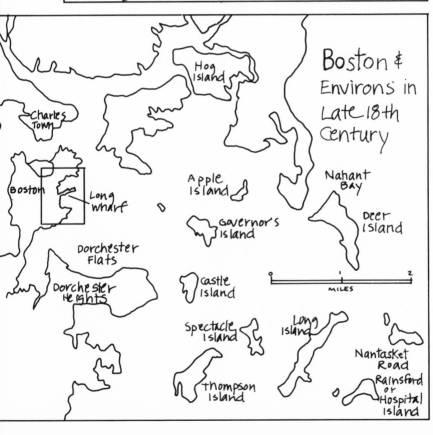

made their way back to England, settling in Yorkshire. Exactly when Robert Haswell returned to his native Massachusetts and how he acquired the experience that qualified him for a third-mate's ticket on *Columbia* is unknown. His journals show him to have been an intelligent though often opinionated observer who matured into an able and dependable mariner. In the two surviving portraits of Haswell, his seaman's hairstyle—long in the back and with the sides combed down over the ears—frames a full, tanned face with humorous, direct eyes and a mouth that appears ready to crackle into a smile.

Barrell and company's two ships had been readied for sea as they lay alongside Hancock's Wharf, a long, improbable finger of earth and pilings crowded on its north side with warehouses, sail lofts, the counting houses of Boston's merchant shipowners, and shops of a dozen kinds. Only neighboring Long Wharf, which carried the city's King Street 1,743 feet out into the water, was larger, its shops and warehouses more varied. The greatest vessels in the world could safely tie up here without fear of grounding even at low tide.

Over this busy hub of maritime trade created by the two outflung wharves hung the rich odors of rum and drying fish, Norway tar and sea wrack, dye pits and baking bread. Here *Columbia* and *Washington* had been loaded with the multitude of goods demanded by so long a voyage to a shore so distant. Bolts of cloth, sides of leather, hogsheads of vinegar and boxes of dried fish, cases of nails and cords of firewood—name it and, if it existed in eighteenth-century Boston, some would likely have been placed aboard one vessel or the other.

Now boatloads of stout oarsmen towed *Columbia* and *Washington* away from the wharves and brought them to anchor in the crowded inner harbor. After last-minute supplies—fresh meats, vegetables, and the like—had been ferried out to them, they were again towed out through the winding channel between Dorchester Neck and Little Governor's Island to the roadstead of Castle Island. In the infant Boston of 1787, "the Castle" and its wrecked British fortifications lay comfortably out to sea. (Today landfills and urban growth have turned them into a part of the mainland.)

Saturday morning Haswell had himself, his barely started journal, and his baggage ferried out to the waiting *Columbia*. He probably also carried aboard a copy of that day's *Massachusetts Centinel*, which included the only official notice Bostonians would be given of *Columbia*'s departure. In fact,

A boyish countenance belies the maturity of Robert Haswell, who on *Columbia's* second voyage rose to become first mate and captain of Gray's trading sloop *Adventure.* Haswell's later career was as eventful, but tragically short. After service in the United States Navy, where he took part in the capture of the French corvette *Berceau,* the thirty-three-year-old mariner signed on as captain of the *Louisa* for what would have been his third voyage to the Northwest Coast. Clearing Boston in 1801, the ship was never heard from again.
(*Pastel by James Sharples, Massachusetts Historical Society*)

an advertisement for "a dark-red cow of a middling size" that had strayed from Boston Common received considerably more space that day than the start of this historic adventure. Under shipping news, among listings of vessels bound for such familiar Atlantic destinations as Virginia, Surinam, the West Indies, and Nova Scotia, was the single line "Cleared since our last, Ship Columbia, Kendrick, for New Albion." Lady Washington and Robert Gray received no notice at all.

Haswell was to be joined that afternoon by Columbia's second mate, Joseph Ingraham. Already a veteran seaman at twenty-five, Ingraham once described his early life as "a series of storms, dangers, and troubles." Probably the storms and dangers were experienced during service in the Continental Navy and, one historian suggests, a voyage on one of the first American ships in the Asian trade. If true, the latter would have been reason enough for his selection as one of Columbia's officers. Though he would have had no experience on the Northwest Coast—no American vessel had yet been there—he might have known some of the tricks of doing business with the Chinese.

Ingraham, like Haswell, would keep a journal of the voyage, probably in greater detail than Haswell, and for the entire circumnavigation. Ingraham's account of another round-the-world voyage as captain of the brigantine Hope, carried out in the years 1790 to 1792, is peppered with references to this earlier journal. An entry of October 1791, for instance, tells us that in his account of Columbia's voyage, "I took great pains to learn every particular respecting the [Hawaiian] Islands and their inhabitants, the description of which occupies many pages in that work." Of the Falkland Islands, he says in another entry, "I was able on my last voyage to give a short description, relating to Brett's Harbor in particular, where the Columbia lay a fortnight." Referring to the British fur trader William Douglas, captain of the Iphigenia Nubiana, he speaks of him as "my friend of whom I made frequent mention in the journal of my last voyage."

It is one of the tragedies of American maritime history that the journal Ingraham kept aboard Columbia as she became successively one of the first two American ships to round Cape Horn and to explore the coasts of what would become Oregon, Washington, and British Columbia, the first American vessel to call at Hawaii, and the first to carry the American flag around the world, has disappeared—thrown out as valueless trash, perhaps, by some nineteenth-century descendant.

Had it survived—and one can dream that it may yet lie forgotten in

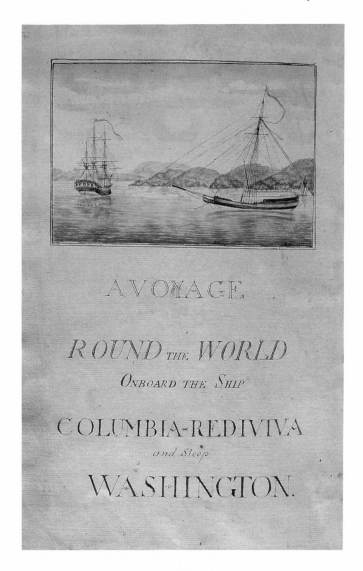

Not yet nineteen, Robert Haswell left Boston in 1787 with two precious possessions—a
third mate's berth aboard *Columbia* and a blank volume that would become one of the
treasures of American maritime history. As the voyage unfolded—dissension aboard
ship, a near disastrous rounding of Cape Horn, a fateful encounter with the Indians, and
unexpected competition for furs on the Northwest Coast—Haswell crammed his journal
with details of his country's first exploration into the Pacific. On the title page he
portrayed *Columbia* (left) and *Lady Washington*—the latter, except for a crude rendering
on Joseph Barrell's medals, the only likeness in existence of the famous little vessel.
(*Massachusetts Historical Society*)

some unswept New England attic—we would have a far better understanding of this pivotal piece of American history, and a fuller portrait of the two puzzling and strangely different men who were its principal actors. Where Haswell in his boyish assurance nearly always passes bitter and critical judgment on John Kendrick's behavior—and occasionally on Robert Gray's—Ingraham's account would surely have balanced that assessment by reflecting his warm friendship with Kendrick and the respect he felt for him. But the blank spots in the wake of Columbia's and Washington's first voyage are unlikely ever to be filled, or the contradictions resolved. Haswell is all we have.

Sunday morning was sailing day, Haswell tells us. The decks of both vessels grew crowded with family members and well-wishers. About noon Captain Kendrick came aboard Columbia, trailed by his "clerk," Lieutenant Richard S. Howe. Actually, Howe appears to have been the vessel's supercargo, the owner's business agent aboard. It would be his job to oversee the obtaining of a cargo of furs on the Northwest Coast and its sale in China and the purchase of "China goods" for the return voyage to Boston.

Behind Kendrick and Howe, John B. Treat clambered onto Columbia's deck. He was the "furrier," who would care for the skins Kendrick expected to acquire from the Indians. With him came the ship's surgeon, Dr. Roberts, and John Nutting, variously called the expedition's "Astronimer" and schoolmaster. The first probably meant navigator; what the latter implied is uncertain. Possibly the owners of the ships felt an obligation to provide some sort of schooling for the very youngest among the crew. Cabin boys in those days were often only eight or nine.

Curiously, for more than a month Haswell makes no mention in his journal of the man both he and Ingraham would be serving under. Simeon Woodruff, an American who had spent time in the British Navy, had been picked as Columbia's first mate for his very special qualifications. Ingraham might have been to the Orient on an earlier voyage, but whether to China or the East Indies no one can be sure. But Woodruff, we know, had sailed with Captain James Cook on the explorer's great third voyage around the world. Woodruff alone among Columbia's men knew the Northwest Coast and the Indians who would trade their furs for Boston trinkets. He knew Hawaii—the Sandwich Islands, as they were then called. And he would have known at least some of the tricks of dealing with Chinese merchants and officials in Macao and Canton.

Clearly, Joseph Barrell and his partners had seen in Simeon Woodruff an opportunity to tap the very experiences that had led them to launch this expedition in the first place.

All told, *Columbia*'s complement totalled about forty men. Among them, as fifth mate, was John Kendrick, Junior, the commander's eldest son, who was about seventeen, and, as an ordinary seaman, his brother Solomon, a year or so younger. *Washington* seems to have carried a crew of ten. Among the fifty or more aboard the two vessels, in addition to ordinary seamen—"the people," as they were called in those days—were men with trades that would be vital on ships that might have to be self-sufficient for two or three years before they saw home again: carpenter, sailmaker, gunner, blacksmith, caulker, and cooper—the last to build and maintain the water casks whose contents would sustain the crew during long passages offshore.

There was also a tailor—John Kendrick's tailor, to be precise. Captains were great dandies in those days, and would have felt their authority crumble had they not been able to lord it over ill-clad seamen while immaculate themselves in crisp ruffles, a scarlet waistcoat with a touch of gold piping, and a properly fitted jacket. The men would need new clothing too after a few months at sea. For them, the tailor would issue out ready-made watch coats, pea jackets, and stout duffle trousers from the ship's slop chest—at cost plus a substantial advance, of course, to be totted up against their meager pay. The seamen, self-sufficient with thread and needle as with so much else, would be expected to keep their own clothing in repair.

Captains, mates, and crew members alike had drawn advance wages so they could set in the small stores—needle and thread, tobacco, a few sheets of paper and a pencil, a change of clothing bought ashore where the prices were lower than from the slop chest, perhaps a stock of sugar or chocolate—things they would not have another chance to buy until the vessels were halfway around the world. Most, being young men without families, had drawn only a month's pay, occasionally two. They would rather have the money pile up—it would be slow enough at only one pound ten a month for an ordinary seaman—until they reached home again.

Only two, Kendrick and Woodruff, took heavy advances. Captain Kendrick drew forty-five pounds—a little over a year's pay at his salary of three pounds twelve shillings a month. Much of that amount probably was posted to Wareham, Massachusetts, where Kendrick's wife waited in the couple's "costly gambrel roof house" with six-year-old Huldah and her brothers, Benjamin, Alfred, and Joseph. The eldest was only eleven.

Woodruff was likely the oldest man on either ship. Haswell would refer to him in his journal as "the Aged Gentleman." So he, too, probably had a family in need of the twenty-seven pounds—nine month's pay—that he received before the ships left Boston.

Columbia and Washington, complete now with their crews plus a gaggle of friends and relatives and a delegation of Boston's prosperous merchants, were towed in a dead calm out to Nantasket Road, where only a shoal or two lay between them and the open sea. That evening, Haswell records warmly, "was spent in murth and glee . . . Jovial songs and animating sentiments passed the last evening we spent on that side of the Continent . . . Wishes for our prosperity resounded from every tongue." By sunrise next morning, 1 October 1787, the guests had all been rowed the several miles back to Boston and the two ships slipped out into the Atlantic.

Little occurred that was worth recording during the first few weeks at sea, though it took Haswell less time than that to register his first criticism of the captain. In a sharp squall, Kendrick ordered Columbia reduced to a single foresail. The weather soon moderated, Haswell noted acidly, "but alltho' there was not more wind than would forse Us four knots we still continued, under that sail nineteen hours."

On 18 October the crew was treated to a display of northern lights. On the thirty-first they saw three "Amphibious Animils" they could not identify. It was probably just as well that sometimes boisterous but essentially uneventful weather marked this first leg of the voyage. It would have been a time of adjustment and testing for all hands; for Kendrick to see what kind of men Woodruff and his second and third mates were, and for them to size him up as well. Chances are all three mates had been picked by Barrell and the other owners. Surely Woodruff was.

And then there was Lieutenant Howe. Supercargoes and their captains were notorious for getting under each other's skins. Ingraham would learn that with his own supercargo, Ebenezer Dorr, when he commanded the brigantine Hope on its voyage to the Northwest Coast. The crew would have been less of a problem; too much of a gulf existed between an ordinary seaman and even a second or third mate for likely trouble there. No, it was the captain and his ship's officers who would have to tread softly those first few weeks while they worked out their relationships so they could settle down to the demands of life in a world that was only eighty-three feet long by about a quarter of that wide.

CHAPTER SIX

Braving the Terrors of Cape Horn

★

Far from easing relationships on this particular voyage, *Columbia*'s leisurely passage eastward across the Atlantic seemed to magnify existing tensions. "Much discord . . . subsisted in our Ship ever since our departure from Boston," Haswell observed, though he piously claimed to have no idea why. He continued to snipe at Kendrick. The ship raised craggy Maio— the Isle of May in Portugal's Cape Verde Islands—on 9 November, forty days out of Boston. *Washington* soon dropped anchor within half a mile of *Columbia*. "We had found . . . that both our vessels sail exceeding well," Haswell observed. But had they carried more sail, he added acidly, "we might have made a verry quick passage."

"Two Ships four Briggs and a schuner" shared Maio's uncomfortable, reef-flanked anchorage with the Americans. Some at least were probably slavers, for the Cape Verdes lay directly opposite Dakar's Ile de Gorée, where slave pens still crumble in the hard African sunlight. The Cape Verdes were a regular stop for "blackbirders" plying between Senegal and the Americas. Samuel Shaw, who had come to the Cape Verdes only three years earlier as supercargo of *Empress of China*, found four slavers lying here—one, he noted unhappily, with a deck load of naked captives. Other ships would have been cramming their holds with salt from the islands' evaporation pans, or with asses and mules for the West Indies. Kendrick too was here for livestock; somehow room was found on the already crowded decks of one ship or another for two bulls and a cow, three hogs, three sheep, and 140 goats.

One among the latter would achieve a kind of immortality. Adopted as a pet by Captain Gray, Nancy the goat provided milk for ship's tea all the way back to Boston. When *Columbia* set out a second time under Gray, Nancy was again an honored member of the crew. She survived much of this second voyage, including another passage around Cape Horn and on into the Pacific, making her the first *American* goat to sail around the world. Unfortunately for Nancy's record, a nameless nanny some twenty years earlier had beaten her out for both first goat and most circumnavigations by circling the globe aboard British Captain Samuel Wallis's *Dolphin* and then being transferred to Captain James Cook's *Endeavour* for a second trip around the world.

Kendrick, to young Haswell's disgust, continued his dilatory progress at Maio. More than a week slipped by in getting the livestock aboard the two vessels. On 16 November, *Columbia* and *Washington* moved to neighboring São Tiago, where the ships' water casks would be filled for the long haul to Cape Horn. "Had the stock been procured [here] at St. Jago's while other work was doing," Haswell grumbled, "all this time would have been saved."

Of course, for all his self-righteousness, Haswell was correct. Time *was* wasting, and the ships risked losing the best of the Antarctic summer before they could dare the perilous passage around Cape Horn, which no American vessel had attempted before.

Two more days passed before Kendrick took Gray ashore with him to call on the governor of São Tiago. They were given permission to use the little Island of Quails in the harbor of Praia, São Tiago's capital. Next day Kendrick had all hands turn to building a tent out of two of the ship's sails and getting the livestock ashore. Probably a majority of the animals —Nancy notably not among them—would be butchered and salted down. Except for the possibility of wild game in the remote Falkland Islands or Patagonia, there would be no further opportunities for resupplying the ships until they were far into the Pacific Ocean.

This precipitated an even greater delay. Casks had to be brought

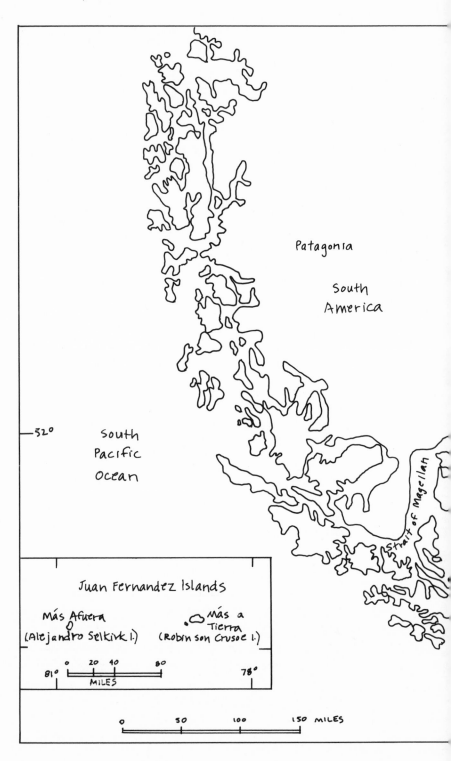

Patagonia

South
America

—52°

South
Pacific
Ocean

Strait of Magellan

Juan Fernandez Islands

Más Afuera
(Alejandro Selkirk I.)

Más a Tierra
(Robinson Crusoe I.)

0   20   40   80
81°   78°
MILES

0   50   100   150 MILES

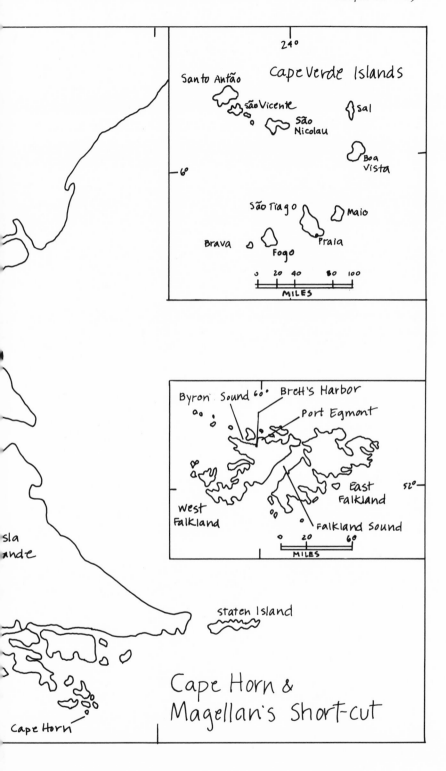

24°

Cape Verde Islands

Santo Antão

São Vicente

Sal

São
Nicolau

6°

Boa
Vista

São Tiago

Maio

Brava

Praia

Fogo

0   20   40   80   100

MILES

Byron Sound 60°   Brett's Harbor

Port Egmont

East
Falkland

52°

West
Falkland

Falkland Sound

0   20   60

MILES

isla
ande

staten Island

Cape Horn &
Magellan's Short-cut

Cape Horn

from both ships to receive the salted meats. The water casks, which Kendrick himself had insisted be put in the lowest tier of *Columbia*'s hold, had now to be moved so they could be filled. The captain decided to completely reorganize the cargo. This was no easy task. Great ironbound hogsheads of rum, barrels of flour and of tar, hogsheads of hard ships' bread, cases of tin pots and beads, bright cloth and Jews' harps, buttons and iron to make "chizzles"—trade goods for the Indians of Northwest America—all had to be hauled out on deck and put back again. To make matters worse, Kendrick "supposed that no person could do the work so well as himself," so "every other person was allmost always idle."

"Heavy indeed the work seemed to hang" as Kendrick labored on in the hold. November became December when suddenly the "discord" that had smoldered since Boston burst into open flame. Kendrick ordered Simeon Woodruff no longer to consider himself *Columbia*'s first mate, and conferred the situation on Ingraham. Haswell in turn became second mate. Piling insult upon injury, the captain demanded that Woodruff either earn his passage by "catoring," working in the ship's galley—a suggestion the elderly man contemptuously rejected—or leave the vessel. Woodruff cleared out his stateroom and shifted his baggage to *Washington* for the night.

One can only guess at the cause of all this dissension, though Woodruff's boastful claims may provide a clue. He had commanded ships out of London, he told the impressionable Haswell—and probably told Kendrick the same thing. He was a skilled navigator as well. The latter may have been true, but for the other claim—well, maybe. As far as the record goes, he was an American-born seaman who had shipped as gunner's mate on Captain James Cook's *Discovery*. And then there was Woodruff's age. Kendrick may have resented Joseph Barrell's saddling him with an elderly know-it-all instead of a younger man of his own choice. From later events, it seems likely that third-mate Haswell sided openly with his friend Woodruff, and in the process did himself no good in Kendrick's eyes.

Howe, *Columbia*'s supercargo, was sent aboard *Washington* with papers for Woodruff to sign. They may have pertained to the money Woodruff would have owed after drawing a large advance and then serving only a couple of months. The papers "were not wrote in a manour that suted him," so he refused to sign. The excitable Kendrick ordered Woodruff back to *Columbia*, but denied him use of his bedding, "inconsequence of

Which he was exposed to the inclemency of the Weather the whole night on deack." In the morning Woodruff reluctantly signed and was allowed to go ashore, where the captain of a passing Spanish vessel offered him a passage to Madeira. From there he eventually made his way back to America; he is known to have been living in Litchfield, Connecticut, as late as 1820.

For the details of this fracas, of course, we have only the testimony of one bitterly prejudiced witness. Haswell's account appears to have been written some weeks after the quarrel, when his distaste for Kendrick had had ample time to mature—even, in fact, after Haswell's own role in the proceedings had come to outright violence. Whatever the details of this and subsequent clashes of personality, however, it seems almost impossible to excuse Kendrick's laggard progress toward Cape Horn. The dates tell their own story.

In this, for a change, we also have the testimony of two witnesses. Where Haswell had to confide his misgivings to his journal—he would have been in black trouble had Kendrick read some of those scathing judgments—Gray, as a fellow captain, albeit a junior one, could take his case directly to Kendrick, though still to no avail. "From the time of leaving Boston," Gray complained in a letter to Joseph Barrell, "we had good weather and excellent winds to St. Jago, where we lay forty-one days, which was thirty-six more than I thought was necessary . . . All this I have mentioned over and often to the Commodore at St. Jago, but all to no purpose, he being very absolute and would not hear to reason."

Roberts, the ships' surgeon (his first name appears nowhere in the records), was to become the next casualty of the volatile captain's temper. Alleging ill health, the doctor asked for his discharge. Kendrick refused unless he would pay his passage to the Cape Verdes. The doctor would not—or could not—and the matter appeared to have been dropped.

A few days later, Roberts requested permission to visit the island capital. A message next day from the Portuguese governor asked that two of the ships' officers confer with him at his palace. Kendrick and Ingraham went ashore to be told that the doctor, entering a complaint of inhumane treatment, had claimed the governor's protection. Insisting that Roberts was a deserter, Kendrick demanded that he be turned over to him. The governor refused.

The whole thing might have blown over had Kendrick not caught sight of the doctor as he and Ingraham made their way back from the governor's palace. Drawing his sword, Kendrick tried to force Roberts down to the ship's boat. When a group of Portuguese soldiers came to Roberts' aid, Kendrick prudently sheathed his weapon and "Came quiately onboard."

Fearful that the governor would detain anyone he could collar from *Columbia* or *Washington* until Dr. Roberts' baggage had been sent to him, Kendrick thenceforth allowed no one ashore. This meant an end to the filling of water casks, though there was "grate defishancy of that article." It took a week more to round up the surviving cattle and goats from their little island pasture and get them aboard. Roberts, in the meantime, had taken refuge on a passing ship of the Danish East India Company, from which he sent a message that he would return to *Columbia* provided he not be flogged. This was a common punishment of the time, aboard merchant vessels as well as naval. If this were denied, might he have a shift of linen sent him? Kendrick refused both requests, and then had to cut a cable and leave behind one of *Columbia*'s anchors in his haste to get clear of São Tiago.

Interestingly, Kendrick seems never to have bothered himself to offer Joseph Barrell and the other owners his own explanation of first-mate Simeon Woodruff's dismissal or Dr. Roberts's departure from the ship—merely a terse acknowledgement some nineteen months later that "the Doctr and Mr. Woodruffe" were no longer aboard "which probably you have been informed of previous to this." In not troubling to put forward his side of the story in the face of the version that Woodruff himself certainly presented to Barrell when he made his way back to America, one almost feels that Kendrick even then knew in his bones that he would never return to Boston, so any concern about the owners' reactions was beside the point.

Aboard *Columbia* now were three new faces, recruits signed on in the Cape Verdes. Their names—George Monk, Hanse Lawton, and John Hammond—suggest that they were American or English seamen who, for one reason or another, had dropped off in the Cape Verdes to seek a berth under a different master. (Kendrick's wasn't the only ship in the world that suffered crew losses because of personality clashes.) On *Washington*, Gray had a new servant, a young Cape Verdean known by a single reference in Haswell's journal as Marcus Lopius—Lopez, perhaps? Of the four men, only one would live to reach Boston.

Columbia and *Washington* stood out of the harbor of Praia in company with a group of "Foreign Indeia Ships." Like *Empress of China*, the Indiamen would follow along the African coast to the Cape of Good Hope and thence northward again through the Indian Ocean to the Orient. The American vessels pointed their bowsprits almost due south—back across the Atlantic from the bulge of Africa to the bulge of Brazil. Beyond lay Cape Horn.

Amid all this wrangling and dissension, there could have been desperately little holiday spirit aboard either vessel as *Columbia* and *Washington* furrowed their way across the Atlantic again. Not that there was ever more than a token observance of Christmas aboard any eighteenth-century merchantman. An extra ration of grog, maybe, or a dab of plum duff to go with melancholy thoughts of husbandless wives and fatherless children left behind to celebrate as best they could. New Year's Eve might have been, for a fleeting moment, a little more cheerful. Nautical custom directed that at midnight the oldest man aboard—on *Columbia*, with the loss of first-mate Woodruff, this would probably have been the fiftyish captain himself—should strike the midnight bells, to be followed immediately by eight more hammered out by the youngest of the ship's company. A ration of straight rum for all hands would have made it official, with a ragged volley of windblown shouts to welcome the first day of 1788 before the seamen went back to their watch or drifted below to the hammocks.

In a little more than two weeks out of the Cape Verdes, the ships sighted the towering central peak of Fernando de Noronha, which lies about two hundred miles off the Brazilian coast. Tropical showers now helped top up the water casks, only partially filled at São Tiago. Ten days into January, it was noticed that *Columbia*'s mizzenmast was split. Shears were erected and, with favorable weather for a repair at sea, the ship's carpenter had the mast out, fixed, and quickly back in place. Even so, by the time the sails were set and the ship underway again, another five days had been lost.

That same day, another misfortune befell the ship, apparently unconnected with any previous difficulty. John Nutting, the astronomer-schoolmaster, was lost at sea. Kendrick, in a belated letter to *Columbia*'s owners, said only that he was "unfortunately drowned." The ship's furrier, John B. Treat, wrote in another letter of "our Astronomer, who being *insane* threw himself overboard and was lost." Haswell, usually at no loss for words when it came to ships' troubles, seems to have overlooked the incident altogether. We do not have to wait long to find out why.

Very shortly after this melancholy event—exactly when is not clear —Captain Gray and *Washington*'s first mate, R. David Coolidge, came aboard *Columbia* for a meal with Kendrick and his ship's officers. In the course of the afternoon Kendrick several times ordered crewmen out of the hold and up to the afterdeck. When they failed to move smartly enough to suit Haswell, he added his orders to those of the captain, still with no effect. This was not a new problem, if we are to believe Haswell. While *Columbia* had lain becalmed with her mizzenmast out, Haswell wrote, crewmen had been "encouraged to dissobey the Command of there Offisers and continually intoxicated with Licure delivered them by Capt. K. orders."

Whatever his other imperfections, this charge against Kendrick becomes too much to swallow. Yankee sailors, like their British counterparts, looked on their ration of grog as practically a God-given right, so ships of those days routinely carried "ardent spirits." Nor was there lack of reason to do so. Neither fresh water nor beer could be kept indefinitely in casks, so a ration of alcohol made it possible for sailors to choke down the foul-smelling and slimy water that became their only salvation after a few months at sea—a few weeks even, if the ships were in the tropics.

No inventory of *Columbia*'s cargo survives from this first voyage, but the liquor she carried would not have differed greatly from that aboard when she sailed from Boston the second time around: 311 gallons of New England rum at two shillings and a penny a gallon, and 225 gallons of West Indies rum at three shillings five pence. At first glance this sounds like enough to float the ship. Parcelled out to a forty-man crew during a nearly three-year voyage, as *Columbia*'s would be, it works out to less than a pint a man per week. Kendrick himself may have hit the bottle on occasion. Most captains did, when they had a chance. But no captain would allow, much less encourage, his own crew to do likewise.

Taking matters into his own hands—this by his own account— Haswell leaped down the hatchway, collared a rebellious sailor named John Lipscomb, and tried to drag him up on deck. Lipscomb's language grew so abusive that Haswell lost his temper and struck the man a blow "that instantly covoured him with bludd." The hubbub drew the attention of the other officers. First-mate Ingraham, says Haswell, used the opportunity to make matters look as unfavorable for him as possible.

Seemingly with greater anger than the situation deserved, Kendrick ordered Haswell off the quarterdeck, striking him several times until Haswell pinned the commander's arms. "With horrid oaths," Kendrick threatened to blow Haswell's brains out with a pistol, and charged "his people"—Ingraham and supercargo Howe, presumably—to knock him down with a handspike if he ever ventured on the quarterdeck again. He was also refused the use of his stateroom, which was immediately occupied by Howe.

Reading between the lines, one sees in this contretemps an echo of the Woodruff affair. Haswell's having sided with Woodruff in that earlier quarrel certainly did him no good in Kendrick's view. And perhaps Kendrick was somehow aware of the unflattering portrait this brash nineteen-year-old was painting of him in his journal. (How desperately one yearns for just one quick look through Joseph Ingraham's long-vanished journal!)

In any event, Haswell wrote Kendrick a note asking to be discharged. The captain sent back a message that Haswell should be allowed to transfer to the first ship they encountered.

The northeast trade winds hurried the two vessels southward along the coast of Brazil, though Haswell continued to complain that *Columbia* could have done even better had Kendrick ordered more sail carried. With his usual caution, Kendrick had stayed well offshore the whole way —a sensible course, one would think, when *Columbia*'s and *Washington*'s only interest in the Patagonian shore was to put it behind them. But it earned another scathing comment from young Haswell, who complained that the captain's "naturel timidity" deprived him of the knowledge he might have gained by sailing closer to the land. Interestingly, Gray's habit of doing just that would later inspire some of Haswell's most bitter criticism.

Argentina's Cabo Blanco loomed a few leagues to the west. Already they were halfway down the Patagonian shore. From there, "fresh gales and boisterous weather" drove them to the Falklands, a jumble of two hundred or more isles and islets lying about four hundred miles northeast of Cape Horn. Due west of them now lay the Magellan Strait, through which the great Portuguese navigator whose name it bears had fought his way in 1520. It had taken a month for his three little ships to struggle through to the Pacific against forty-foot tides and freakish currents. They became the first European vessels ever to put their keels into that ocean.

Shunning Magellan's shortcut, *Columbia* and *Washington* would take the long but prudent way around Cape Horn, as most vessels had done for the two and a half centuries since Magellan and would continue to do for another century. Icebergs, screaming gales, and seas so mountainous they could sweep an entire watch off the deck made it just as dangerous to continue southward in the open sea to round the dread cape. But at least there was room to maneuver a clumsy square-rigger. Better to take your chances in the open sea, any deep-water sailor would tell you, than to risk smashing yourself to bits on a rock. Of course, Magellan could not have known there was another way to get from the Atlantic to the Pacific when he made his historic transit.

Navigating through the Falklands using a beautiful copper-engraved map in a 1773 volume of voyages by John Hawkesworth, Kendrick overshot the entrance to Port Egmont and had to sail into Brett's Harbor through a channel that was foul with kelp, which floated up from the bottom in seventy- and eighty-foot strands and lay in a choking mass on the surface. After making their way through the mess, the two vessels anchored opposite "an excellent streem of water." Kendrick, Gray, and one of the mates celebrated their arrival by going ashore and shooting a large number of geese.

Next morning Kendrick sent for Haswell. The captain's anger had cooled. He sat the young man down in his cabin and acknowledged the rashness of his previous behavior. Haswell angled for more of an apology, but "this hint the Gentleman either coold or woold not take." Haswell asked to be transferred to the sloop. Kendrick agreed. Privately, Haswell still clung to the hope that a ship would appear on which he could get completely clear of Kendrick and his unpredictable ways.

After a hasty examination of Brett's Harbor, Kendrick announced his intention of staying in the Falkland Islands over the winter. This provoked unanimous opposition among the ships' officers. Haswell informed Kendrick, he tells us, "that was I in his case the Commander of the Ship, after spending so much time in the Cape de Verds and making such long passages I would go round the Cape or loos the Vessels in the attempt." Whether the cheeky teenager really said this to a captain nearly thirty years his senior or merely put in his journal what he wished he had said is anyone's guess.

We can be sure that Gray, a fellow captain, did speak forthrightly. There was not a stick of wood to be procured anywhere in the treeless

Falklands. A winter there, he pointed out, would expose them to greater hardships than could possibly attend a passage around the Horn. And now Gray expressed for the first time what had clearly been on his mind for much of this interminable voyage. If Kendrick was adamant about wintering in this godforsaken harbor, he would round the cape himself "in the Sloop and had not the least doubt of succeeding provided Capt. Kendrick would allow him."

There seems little question that Kendrick was terrified by the prospect of a winter rounding of that fearsome barrier. Alan Villiers, in *The Way of a Ship*, commented that "the dread of Cape Horn had an effect on the nerves of far too many masters. As soon as they got near 50 South in the Atlantic they feared the worst, and shortened their ships down to wait for it. Of course, they got it, then."

Kendrick probably would have stayed over until spring had it not been for the solid front put up by his officers. He was not "*positively* determined" to wait it out, he finally admitted. It gradually became clear that the voyage would proceed, if not on schedule, at least according to plan. But even then, no great urgency seems to have been felt about getting ready. A tent would have been improvised ashore from one of the ships' sails, and the water casks floated in to the beach where they could be refilled with fresh water. Nancy the goat, along with whatever remained of the meat animals penned on deck, would have been sent ashore to browse. All hands would have turned to the jobs of checking ships' gear and securing everything for the battle with Cape Horn that lay ahead.

For his part, Haswell continued to hope for the sight of a passing vessel on which he could secure passage back to Boston. The islands were then a port of call for Atlantic whalers and sealers as well as for an occasional British vessel bound into the Pacific, but with the season so far advanced, few were likely now to come this way.

Haswell nonetheless contrived to have what he thought might be one more chance to find a homeward-bound vessel. A few days before they were to start toward Cape Horn, he, supercargo Howe, and Mr. Treat, the furrier, went ashore and walked the four miles from Brett's Harbor to the abandoned British settlement at Port Egmont. This was where Kendrick had intended to shelter, had he not overshot its entrance. It was a better anchorage than Brett's, and a more likely place to encounter a passing ship.

The three men explored ruins where English garden flowers still grew spontaneously, and shot some wildfowl. "Making a fier we broiled them with some rashers of pork which with bread and Cheas a bottle of rum etca ... we made an excessive hearty meal to which we added a good salit." As the voyage progressed, the crews of both vessels would come to regret not having laid in a store of Haswell's salad materials— wild celery, chickweed, garden sorrel, and "several other sorts of excel- lent greens which would prove strong antiscerbutics ... on long voy- ages." As *Columbia* and *Washington* made their months-long way up from Cape Horn to the Northwest Coast, crewmen of both vessels suffered sorely from scurvy, which might have been avoided had they gathered enough of Haswell's "good salit."

As the three men walked back toward the ships, Haswell discovered that the bayonet on which he had roasted the fowl had been left behind. He went back for it, secretly deciding to spend the night in the faint hope that a ship might yet show up off Port Egmont. Howe and Treat returned to Brett's Harbor.

Finding a rocky cavern, Haswell filled it with the six-foot-high tussock grass that clothes much of the Falklands and slept comfortably. The next day he surveyed the whole of Port Egmont without sighting a sail, and returned to Brett's Harbor in midafternoon. A shore party in one of *Columbia*'s boats spied him and ran up their flag. To his surprise, *Columbia* discharged three guns. Kendrick, it turned out, had become concerned over Haswell's absence and had himself gone to Port Egmont to search for him, leaving behind orders that if Haswell showed up, he should be notified by the firing of two or three guns. Here was the kindly side of Kendrick's complex nature. It would reappear often in the future and lead some of Kendrick's friends to record fulsome praise of the captain in their journals.

On 28 February 1788, with water casks full and the ships ready for sea, Kendrick ordered Haswell to transfer to *Washington*. Now reduced in rank—he was still second mate but aboard a much smaller vessel— Haswell had his duffle, including the precious journal, moved to the sloop.

As one of his final pieces of business while the ships still lay in Brett's Harbor, Kendrick penned a series of instructions for Robert Gray. These and one shorter directive to Gray appear to be the only existing docu- ments entirely in Kendrick's hand. All of his other communications were apparently written by one ship's clerk or another and merely signed by him.

> ... my orders [Kendrick wrote] is that you Sail with the Columbia and do all in your power to keep company with her But should you get Seperated from her By Bad weather or any other axerdent What Ever you air to proseed on your voige Round Cape horn into the Pacific ocan and then Stand to the Northward ... you will find a harbour By the Name of Nootka Sound on the West Side of North America.
>
> I would have you purchase as much furs as possibal of the Natives and in perticuler the Sea otters But not Refuse any Should you git five hundered Sea otters Skins and other furs in perpotion the First season I would have you proseed from thence to Macao in China.
>
> After you have Sold what Ever you have got on the Coast of America in China lay out your money in Such goods as you think Be Most Sailabel in America and take the proper Season to Return to Boston in America By way of the Cape of good hoop.

With a flood tide and a northeast wind, the two vessels stood out of Brett's Harbor. By dark they were clear of land. Haswell expressed his misgivings in his journal: "At this advanced season of the Year we were launching forward in a sloop scarcely 90 tuns to make a passage at the same season of the Year when Lord Anson in one of the finest ships in the British Navy mett with allmost insermountable diffi[c]ulties. The account of his Voyage was truely discouraging."

The 250 miles or so to Staten Island, which lies off the upcurved tip of South America, produced no heavy gales, though "the sea generaly ran very cross and to a mountaineous highth." Then the dreaded passage began to live up to its reputation. Both the currents and the heaviest winds came out of the west—exactly where the little flotilla wanted to go. Hourly the air grew colder. *Washington* was almost continually under water. Haswell began to wonder about his wisdom in requesting transfer to the sloop. "Far more comfortable indeed must there situation be who are onboard the Ship whose sides are so high that a man is nevour wett on her deacks." On 17 March, Haswell noted morosely, "Our prospect of wethering the Cape is very unfavourable. We have seen several Large Islands of ice and the Weather excessive coald."

The angry westerlies were now hurling themselves at the two struggling ships day after day, night after awful night. Driven before these icy blasts, gale crowded upon gale. Each new storm seemed to force the great crouching waves to terrifying new heights. These waves did not simply sweep over *Washington*'s low, open decks. Instead, every few moments it seemed as if some huge hand were pressing downward on the little sloop until everything but the mast disappeared beneath a huge roiling meadow of green water. Each time, after a long, heart-stopping moment, the ship would bob to the surface, shake herself free of the water's clutch like some huge, wet dog, and struggle ahead again.

After each of these immersions the noise of the storm, which had been momentarily stilled in the rush and sluice of water, would drive itself again like a rusty nail into the consciousness of Gray and his exhausted men—the lunatic roar and clatter of wind through rigging that, though tightened down with all the strength the crew could summon, still shuddered and slammed in the gale's clutch as if it intended to tear the little vessel apart. Orders became impossible to give or to receive; the screaming wind tore away the words before they could leave Gray's or Haswell's lips. The men on deck—at least half the crew had to be there if the ship was to be kept under any control at all—could only screw their eyes shut, hold their breath, and cling grimly to whatever handhold they could grab when one of those monstrous waves engulfed their little cork of a vessel.

Chafe became a continual worry, the fear that a critical stay, sawing back and forth to the wind's angry tattoo, might part and bring the stumpy lower mast smashing down onto the deck or, worse, tumble it into the maelstrom alongside. There, still held fast to the ship by other lines, this mammoth balk of floating timber would slew back and forth insanely like some huge tethered bull, threatening before they could cut it away to smash head-on into the fragile hull planking. Adrift in these freezing seas with no mast and a gaping hole below the waterline? Gray tried not to think about that.

Miraculously, the rigging held. The icebergs, those "Large Islands of ice" that Robert Haswell so anxiously recorded in his journal, somehow kept their distance through the endless nights when they could not have been seen until it was too late. The mast creaked and snapped against the stresses of *Washington*'s wild rolling, sometimes sounding like a pistol shot above the scream of the wind. But it stayed resolutely in place, swinging reassuringly in great arcs against the sky, and flaunting its rags of reefed-down sails that were all Robert Gray dared carry. The battered ship survived, and so did all the battered crew. Gray could occasionally glimpse distant *Columbia* through the gale-driven spume, barely winning her own fight against Cape Horn's horrors.

As March dragged into its final week, with *Columbia* and *Washington* still managing to keep each other in sight, shifting winds allowed them to make some headway, though aboard both ships the crewmen remained as uncomfortable as before, clothing and bedding drenched with icy salt water and no chance of drying anything. *Columbia*'s high sides, which Haswell remembered so longingly after his transfer to *Washington*, availed the larger vessel little. Her crew suffered as badly as the sloop's.

Slowly, slowly, the fury seemed to abate. "The Weather was very chaingable," Haswell recorded of a typical Cape Horn day as March came to an end, "from Clear and pleasant to snow hail Rain and sleet and from that to clear in the space of half an hour—we have the frost intensely hard at sertain times and sudonly again a thaw." Taking advantage of every favorable slant of wind, the two vessels managed most days to gain a little more westing than they lost. By 1 April, *Columbia* and *Washington* had clawed their way past the dread cape, though not beyond the reach of its turbulent seas. They would not be clear of that danger until they had struggled westward and then north another five hundred miles.

On that stormy April Fool's Day, in the darkness before dawn, the wind suddenly veered from northwest to southward. *Columbia* wore ship, a complex and dangerous maneuver in heavy seas. It meant running off before the wind, where the ship would roll unmercifully in the trough of the sea, and a wave might easily slam across her deck and sweep away a whole watch. It took planning and above all, plenty of room, to get the wind back in the sails where it belonged. *Washington*, having only fore-and-aft sails (the ship would not have been carrying a topsail or topmast in those raging seas) could handle a sudden wind shift with much less fuss. But to keep *Columbia* in view she followed as the larger vessel made a wide swing to starboard.

Washington lost sight of *Columbia*. A violent gale followed, "a perfect hericain accompanyed with rain, hail, snow and Sleet with an intence frost. The sea imediately [rose] to an immoderate highth and frequently thretened us with instant distruction for had the smalest of these Huge overgrone seas struck us it would infallibly have put a period to our existance."

Fortunately, the sloop showed her true worth, scudding safely off before the wind. One of the quarterboards was stove in, but the stout little vessel suffered no other damage. However, the storm had driven *Columbia* and *Washington* far apart. There was only the barest chance that they would meet again before reaching the Northwest Coast.

Gray was delighted.

★

CHAPTER SEVEN

A Fatal Brush
with the
Tillamook Indians

★

Free at last of Kendrick's leisurely ways, Gray drove Lady Washington as hard as he dared, but Cape Horn had not yet tired of toying with the little vessel. The day after the sloop parted with Columbia, a sudden nighttime squall carried away the jibstay. "It was now we first meterialy felt how greatly our hardships had debili[t]ated all the Crue," wrote Haswell, "for there was not one sailor onboard who was able to go aloft and take down the Old Jibb Stay or fitt a new one." The job fell to David Coolidge and Haswell, the first and second mates. Only by luck and last-ditch determination did the exhausted pair manage to climb the shrouds in the darkness and clear away the wreckage.

For two more weeks Washington encountered constant gales, one of them more violent than anything they had suffered before. But Gray threw caution aside in his haste to get to the Northwest Coast. He insisted that the sloop carry "an incredable press of Sail and pushed on with the most urgent diligence." On 13 April a gust split their one good mainsail. But their trial was over. As they put faith in their only replacement, an old and badly worn sail that would never have stood up to the lash of a

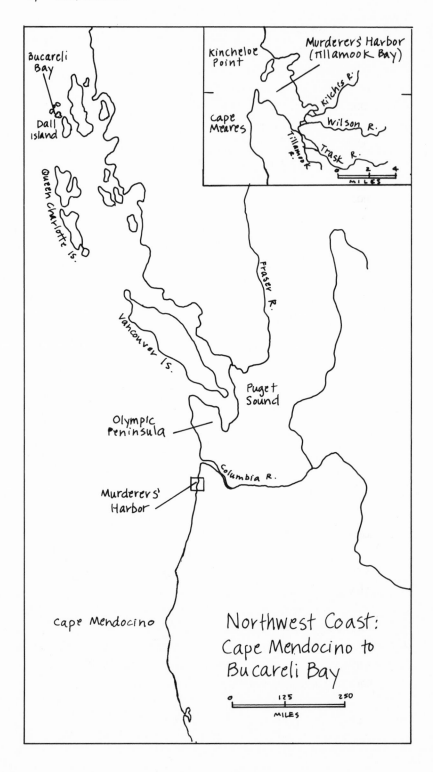

Northwest Coast:
Cape Mendocino to
Bucareli Bay

gale, the storms abated and "temperate weather welcomed us into the Pacifick Ocean." The sloop was now opposite the western end of the Strait of Magellan and out of the clutches of Cape Horn. "We viewed the remainder of our passage to the Coast of America with indifference," Haswell noted happily, "the worst part . . . being over."

Now porpoises and flying fish escorted *Lady Washington* northward toward Más Afuera, westernmost of the Juan Fernández Islands, some five hundred miles off the coast of Chile. Today Más Afuera carries a second name, Alejandro Selkirk, for the Scottish mariner left ashore in these islands in 1704. Its sister, Más a Tierra, is known also as Robinson Crusoe Island, for the fictional character based on Selkirk's life. In the orders given Gray before the two ships started for Cape Horn, Kendrick had written: "Should you want wood or water after you have arived in the pacific ocean I advise Stoping at Masafuero . . . But take great Care not to put your Self in the power of the Spaniards If possibal to avoide it." Gray was not eager to jeopardize his voyage by placing himself in a situation in which the Spanish might confiscate his vessel. He was even less eager, one supposes, to put *Washington* back under Kendrick's erratic command.

Columbia was not at Más Afuera on 22 April, when Gray sighted the island, but there was always the chance the larger ship might show up before they had collected firewood and filled their water casks. Gray had the ship's longboat hoisted out and sent his first mate to reconnoiter a safe landing place. Mr. Coolidge's report that swells and heavy surf rendered landing dangerous was enough for the captain, who "conclooded on departing without making aney further tryal."

Kendrick had given *Washington* an alternative if circumstances forbade a stop at Más Afuera: to sail on to Más a Tierra. Haswell, whose journal reflects his reading of every account of every voyage he could get his hands on—after all, knowledge of these was the intelligent mariner's substitute for a college education—rhapsodized about this island he had never seen. It offered, he told his journal, "allmost all the tropical and European fruts and grane," as well as "Cattle hoggs Horses and Goats in incredible numbers, and indeed everything else in great abundance." He was hoping for a stop not only for water and wood, of which they were already short, but fresh vegetables.

Perhaps scurvy had even then shown itself aboard the ship. Curiously, Captain Cook's successful measures for keeping scurvy under control during long voyages—a fanatic attention to cleanliness; fresh greens at every possible opportunity; a mix of dehydrated meat broth and dried greens called "portable soup"; sauerkraut, a quart a week while at sea whether the men wanted to eat it or not; and as little salt food as could be managed—were well enough known but had made scant impression on the Americans. Haswell mentions scurvy often in his journal and knew what would prevent it. Other captains forced greens and evil-tasting spruce beer on their crews when they could get them—both valid preventives for scurvy—and once a week washed the fo'c'sle down with vinegar and gunpowder, but neither Kendrick nor Gray seemed particularly interested in taking any serious measures against the problem.

In their defense, the two captains were probably innocent of any direct experience with this most loathsome peril of the eighteenth-century circumnavigator. The disease often killed half or more of a ship's complement on voyages as lengthy as this one. But Kendrick and Gray would have read of its ravages in the accounts of earlier Pacific voyages. Note this chilling description of scurvy's symptoms left us by Richard Walter, chaplain of Lord Anson's flagship *Centurion*. That ship together with three others had left England in 1740 with nearly a thousand men aboard. When they reached Juan Fernández after rounding Cape Horn, only 351 remained alive. The handful of able-bodied seamen among the survivors were barely able to bring the ship to anchor. Scurvy's effects, reported the horrified clergyman, included "large discoloured spots dispersed over the whole surface of the body, swelled legs, putrid gums . . . fevers, pleurisies, the jaundice, and violent rheumatick pains . . . At other times the whole body, but more especially the legs, were subject to ulcers of the worst kind, attended with rotten bones, and such a luxuriancy of funguous flesh, as yielded to no remedy." Small wonder that death itself was sometimes looked upon as one of the lesser of scurvy's afflictions.

Haswell, with the optimism of youth, put aside these gloomy preoccupations—his journal shows that he remembered much of what he had read about Lord Anson's disastrous passage around Cape Horn—in favor of more cheerful musings. From other readings—perhaps those journals of Captain Cook's third voyage—he was longing, it seems, to put in at the Sandwich Islands on the way to Northwest America. He permitted himself a flight of fancy as *Washington* made her way the few leagues east to Crusoe's Island. A generous mind could show its benevolence to the maritime world in general and to a numerous race of human beings, he wrote, by carrying a few cattle, goats, and horses to the Hawaiian Islands. In Hawaii's fertile clime, he fancied, the animals would multiply "and in a fue Years Its verdent launs [would] be strown with hurds and flocks that might give the most ample suplies to fueture adventurers in this very remote Clime, and much increase the felisity of these now happy people." What a different view from the gifts Pacific traders actually brought those "happy" islanders: firearms, whiskey, new diseases—all the discontents of civilization!

When *Washington* reached Crusoe's Island, Gray was in no mood to tarry. Lord Anson, he might well have known, had put in there in 1741 and carried away stocks of fresh goat meat and fish, as well as quantities of celery, sorrel, watercress, parsley, turnips, radishes, and "cabbage" from the island's palm trees. But Gray took one look at what he thought appeared to be land in that direction and kept his sails filled. He was determined not to wait around and have Kendrick catch up with him.

There was one more chance, at least for wood, water, and perhaps fodder for Nancy the goat and whatever was left of the ship's meat animals: Chile's elusive San Ambrosio Island, another five hundred miles to the north. Sometimes voyagers found it. At other times, it seemed to disappear into the Pacific haze.

Three days after passing up Crusoe's Island, *Washington*'s captain decreed a reduced allowance of water: two quarts per man a day. Four days later, Gray found San Ambrosio easily enough, but it took another forty-eight hours before they were close enough to send the longboat ashore. Separately, both the small boat and the sloop sailed nearly around the island without finding signs of fresh water. When they landed, the crewmen were unable to scale the cliffs that towered above the shore and had to content themselves with catching a quantity of fish and killing "a vast number of ceals and sea lyons which were incredibly numerous." *Washington*'s crewmen extracted the oil of the seals and dried their skins. Only four years later another Boston vessel, the *Jefferson*, would stop here for seven weeks, during which the crew would salt down thirteen thousand sealskins for their China-bound cargo!

Gray hurried on, making his way past the Galapagos Islands without sighting any of them. In late May rain finally fell. Crewmen caught enough to fill several hogsheads as it ran off the sails, "to which we were indebted for preservation on [the] remaining part of our passage."

Haswell was by now criticizing Gray almost as severely as he had Kendrick. The captain should have put in at St. Felix, San Ambrosio's neighbor, which lay only a few hours' sail out of the way. And now, in Haswell's view, he was staying too far to the east. *Washington* had, Haswell calculated, spent twenty-one days with only a light northward breeze while she bucked a strong southerly current, thus gaining only twenty miles in three weeks of sailing. In this sort of thing, Haswell was right as usual. Had Gray taken *Washington* farther west he would quickly have picked up the northeast trade winds and materially improved his daily runs.

Gray would have known this as well as did his second mate, even had Captain Kendrick not also spelled it out in his orders: "You must Not Come nigher to the Continent of america than Seventy or Eighty Leagues till you get thrue the Trade Wind into the varibel [variables] on the Coast of California on account of the indraft of Wind that Blowes in on the Coast." But Gray, in his eagerness to stay as far as possible from Kendrick, stubbornly insisted on "pursevearing in with the Land," and the days thus lost saw his frightened crewmen threatened ever more seriously by the ravages of scurvy.

June, and then July, slipped away. Fortunately, regular rains meant that water was no longer a problem. Crewmen would have held up unused sails to catch the precious drops and direct them into casks on deck. And sea turtles were added to the menu, "which, by the by," commented Haswell, "were not very delicate eating." By now, finally, the northeast trade winds and then favorable gales kept *Washington's* sails filled. Birds played about the sloop, and fish were seen jumping. On August first—after more than five months at sea since *Washington* had left Brett's Harbor to make that terrifying passage around Cape Horn, and nearly a year since they had left Boston—Robert Haswell recorded a greenish hue to the water, and "the Clouds had strong apearances of our nigh approach to the American Continent." On the second, "to our inexpressable joy we saw the Coast of New Albion."

Gray made his landfall on California's redwood coast midway between Cape Mendocino and the present Oregon border. Though several of the crew were now seriously afflicted with scurvy, the captain chose not to land but made his way cautiously up the seemingly deserted shore. Two days passed before the Bostonians saw their first West Coast Indians: "a canoe with ten natives of the Countrey paddling towards us. On there nigh approach they made very expressive seigns of friendship." These were the peaceable Yurok, a small tribe classified by many anthropologists as members of the great Algonquian nation who had been somehow displaced from their relatives two thousand miles away in the northeast. The Yurok were noted chiefly for their use of tusk-shaped dentalia shells as a surprisingly sophisticated form of money and for their big, blunt-ended redwood canoes, "hued," noted Haswell, "from a tree of vast bulk . . . the boat, tho' of the most clumsy shape in the world, yet so well was it finished that it looked very pasable." The Bostonians' faint praise of the Yuroks' awkward boats was justified. Designed for maneuverability on the small streams of the redwood coast, Yurok canoes were notably unseaworthy. Only overwhelming curiosity about their strange visitors had drawn this canoe full of Indians from the sheltered Klamath River out into the Pacific, where they were in imminent danger of being capsized by even a moderate wave.

As Gray continued to feel his way north, he kept *Washington* as close to shore as he dared, at times so close that the crew could see men running along the beaches, gesturing, shouting, and waving spears "with an air of defeyance." Haswell again remembered what he had read. From Cook's account of his third voyage the young Bostonian knew that the strange white costumes of these people were in fact tanned elk hides, in three and four thicknesses, which they used as arrow-proof armor. These were not the friendly Yurok, but warlike Alsea tribesmen. Their reluctance to approach within range of *Lady Washington's* guns perhaps stemmed from some unhappy encounter with earlier Spanish explorers of that unknown shore.

Farther north, men of still another tribe approached in great seagoing log canoes with images carved at bow and stern—the first sight the Americans had of the work of the Northwest Coast's skilled woodcarvers. These were the Tillamook, who "boiled and roasted crabbes which our people purchaced for buttons etca." At night, as *Washington* coasted northward, fires were often visible, and during the day "Culloms of smoak" lofted above villages hidden behind the screen of great trees. Whenever a likely harbor appeared, Gray sent the ship's longboat to see if there was sufficient protection and depth for the sloop. Repeatedly he chose to continue northward. At one such stop, while the ship's boat was inshore, men approached in two small canoes, bringing several sea-otter skins and, says Haswell mysteriously, "one of the best peces"—meaning something less than a complete pelt—"I ever saw."

Where Haswell could previously have seen sea-otter furs is a puzzle. And this is not the only time his record of the voyage hints at prior experience in the Pacific. Earlier he had noted of the Juan Fernández Islands that "the fir Ceal is in greater abundance [here] than at any place I ever saw." Conceivably he could have been speaking of fur-seal colonies the expedition had encountered in the vicinity of Cape Horn. But no such explanation comes to mind for another entry. As Lady Washington made her way up the southern coast of Oregon—the first American vessel ever to do so—Haswell wrote that "the natives on this part of the Coast live on hunting, for they most of them live in land. This is not the case to the Northward for the face of the Countery [there] is widly different." How could he have known? Again, Haswell earlier had implied a familiarity with the approaches to Cape Horn when he criticized Kendrick for missing the entrance to Port Egmont in the Falklands. "Captain Kendrick being totaly Ignorant of the place" (as Haswell, one might assume, was not), "the ship was kept too far to the Southward and we entered Bretts harbr." This anchorage, added Haswell, seemingly with the authority of personal experience, "tho' good is far inferior to Port Egmont."

That the nineteen-year-old Haswell was already an experienced seaman and a veteran of some voyaging goes without saying. He would otherwise never have been entrusted with a third-mate's berth, let alone be promoted to second mate on so important an expedition. And his whereabouts during almost the whole of his teenage years, after he had moved with his Loyalist family to England, remain unknown. But a voyage into the Pacific during those years hardly seems credible, least of all one to the Northwest Coast itself. When, and aboard what ship? Haswell's maritime experiences during the years prior to his selection by Joseph Barrell as his flagship's third officer remain among the most intriguing little mysteries of the whole Columbia and Lady Washington saga.

Whatever his familiarity with sea-otter pelts—real or gained through his insatiable reading of other people's voyages—Haswell would have been as excited that day as anyone else. How the Americans must have fondled and stroked those lustrous pelts, the first anyone aboard—except possibly Haswell—had ever seen. Nearly six feet long and two feet or more wide, they were a glossy jet black that shaded to the silver of the underfur in the lightest breath of air. One of the Boston traders who would come to the Northwest Coast in the wake of Washington and Columbia rhapsodized that except for a beautiful woman and a lovely infant, a prime sea otter skin was the most beautiful natural object in the world. And if this were not enough, fine skins like the ones they were now holding were literally worth their weight in gold to the mandarins of distant China. This was what Gray and his men had come from Boston to find and what they intended to carry a shipload of to Canton!

It was 14 August, two weeks since they had first glimpsed the smoky outline of California on the horizon, before the cautious Gray found a harbor he felt was safe. *Washington* went in and anchored half a mile from shore. The crew spent the afternoon trying to entice some Indians in a small canoe—they were still in Tillamook territory—to approach the ship. Finally, late in the afternoon, the Indians came alongside and were given small presents. Others followed, bringing berries and crabs that had already been boiled. "These they liberaly handed onboard as preasants seemingly without any Idea of payment. [They] were the most accepta-ble things that they could have brought to most of our seamen who were in a very advanced state of scurvy and was a means of restoration of health to 3 or four of our Companey who would have found one months longer duration at sea fatal to them so advanced were they in this malig-nant distemper."

By the next afternoon, a seemingly friendly trade had been estab-lished. Knives, axes, and adzes were exchanged for more sea-otter skins. The Americans quickly learned that small pieces of sheet copper, of which they had brought little, would have been more welcomed by the Indians. Gray felt uncertain about this anchorage—with reason, as it turned out. The only source of fresh water they could find lay so far from the shore that a party venturing there would be beyond the protection of the ship's guns. Several boat loads of wood were gathered, but one load of water was all Gray was willing to risk. The natives, Haswell wrote, "behaved with great propriety" while the armed water and wood crews were ashore, but their fear of the strangers was obvious. They never ventured near the Americans except with daggers uplifted, ready to strike.

The next day, *Washington* weighed anchor and raised her sails in a light easterly breeze. Suddenly the wind died and a flood tide swept the sloop gently onto a rocky shoal. *Washington* was unharmed, but a sea breeze now arose and prevented the ship's departure until the next day's tide. With time on their hands, Haswell and first-mate Coolidge decided to take the longboat ashore to gather forage for Nancy the goat and the few meat animals that remained on board. The five crewmen most seriously stricken with scurvy made up the rest of the party. Though they might have been dimly aware of Captain Cook's successes in controlling scurvy, seamen of those days still clung steadfastly to their traditional belief that the mere scent of land and the feel of it under their feet would alleviate the ailment's baleful effects.

Haswell admitted ruefully that the group went ashore poorly armed: two muskets and three or four cutlasses, while he and Coolidge each carried a sword and pistol. At the Tillamook village, a flimsy encampment of houses and storage sheds made of woven mats, they were offered food but found it "so intolerable filthey" they accepted only fruit. The Indians put on a dance for the visitors, "long and hedious acompaneyed with frightfull howlings." As soon as they could leave without insulting their hosts, Haswell and Coolidge wandered past their longboat to a sand flat where they thought they might find some clams.

While they were digging, Marcus Lopius, the young Cape Verdean who had shipped as Captain Gray's servant, carelessly stuck his cutlass in the sand as he piled grass into the boat. One of the Tillamooks snatched the weapon and ran. Lopius foolishly chased after the thief, and both disappeared in the direction of the village.

Coolidge and Haswell made their way back to the village, where the first mate offered the Indians "several articles . . . of great value" if they would return the boy. The Indians indicated the Americans should find him themselves.

Suddenly, beyond a clump of trees, Coolidge and Haswell saw a group of men, with Lopius in the middle holding the thief and calling loudly for help. When the Indians saw the two Americans, "they instantly drenched there knives and spears with savage feury in the boddy of the unfortunate youth. He quited his hold but rose again and stagered towards us but having a flight of arrows thrown into his back . . . he fell within fifteen yards of me and instantly expiered while they mangled his lifeless cor[p]se."

Haswell and Coolidge were now between two groups of Indians, both heavily armed and aroused. Dodging arrows and spears, they succeeded in reaching the boat, which had kept pace with them as they returned to the village. Now they had to wade out to the boat, with the Indians following them into the water. Both Coolidge and Haswell were wounded, as was one other man "who fainting with loss of blud lay lifeless several hours and continued to bleed a torant till the barb of the arrow was extracted."

The Indians continued their pursuit, trying to cut off the small boat, until it reached *Washington*. "As we got onboard we discharged two or three swivel shot at them and in a few Moments not one Canoe was to be seen all having fledd. Duering the whole of the night it was dismal to hear the hoops and houlings of the natives. They had fiers on the beach near the spot where the ladd was killed and we could see great numbers of them passing too and froo before the blaze."

Haswell was all for sending a few rounds of grapeshot in the direction of the celebrating Indians. "I must confess I should not have lett them enjoy there festervile so peasabley had I been Cap. Gray," he wrote, "but his humanity was commendable." Haswell's eagerness to avenge the death of his shipmate had a macabre sequel. Whereas Gray, displaying a humanity he would rarely grant the Indians in later encounters, spared Marcus's murderers, the white man's diseases, brought first by the Spaniards and then by the British and Americans, did not. Epidemics swept through the Tillamook villages, and by the end of the nineteenth century the tribe, once two thousand strong, had virtually ceased to exist.

Haswell guessed that Murderers' Harbor, as they would call it thereafter, was in fact the mouth of the "River of the West," which was vaguely known to exist. Actually, "Columbia's River," as Gray would later name the great waterway, lay about fifty miles to the north. *Washington's* crew would pass the Columbia River this time without knowing it was there. The harbor they now lay in was probably Tillamook Bay.

Next morning at dawn Gray made another attempt to get out of the ill-fated anchorage. They had nearly cleared it when the wind died as they tried to cross the outer bar. As the tide ebbed, the surf rose, slamming the little vessel repeatedly onto the hard sand bottom so violently that crewmen struggled to avoid being thrown overboard. Green water broke over the deck and smashed out the windows of the great cabin, all but filling it. At slack tide, Gray sent out the longboat with an anchor and warped *Washington* back into deeper water. Fortunately, the sloop showed her real qualities in this mishap, as she had on the Cape Horn passage. Only the rudder fittings suffered minor and repairable damage. But now the flooding tide had trapped them for another night in Murderers' Harbor.

Morning dawned calm and foggy. A little after noon three war canoes, each crowded with as many as thirty Indians, materialized out of the murk. The Americans could see that they sat with bows ready and spears in their hands. Gray tried to warn them off but they continued to approach. The gunner fired three swivels and the Indians fled. Now, with a fair tide, *Washington's* anchor was quickly brought up and the sloop finally made her way out of this unhappy place.

CHAPTER EIGHT

Unexpected Competitors:
The "Kintshautsh Men"

★

As he made his way northward toward the rendezvous with *Columbia* at Nootka Sound, Gray stayed prudently at sea, trading with the Indians only from their canoes. Few sea-otter skins rewarded him, and the prices were high. The sloop passed the coast of Washington, where the Bostonians could glimpse the distant snowy peaks of the Olympic Mountains. At Barkley Sound, on British Columbia's Vancouver Island, one chief was allowed aboard *Washington* out of a party of three canoes. He startled the newcomers by mentioning several English names. This was the first clear indication that Gray might have competition for the furs he had been sent so far to find.

Here, finally, Gray had reached the territory of the stunning Nootkan Indians, those great whale and sea-otter hunters, those splendid warriors, those skilled builders and carvers whose shapely ocean-going canoes with their high, upcurved bows, some say, inspired New England shipwrights to create in the same image the swift and graceful clipper ship. Vancouver Island's Barkley Sound, where *Lady Washington* now lay at anchor, was the southern gateway to the empire of the Nootkans, who would play so

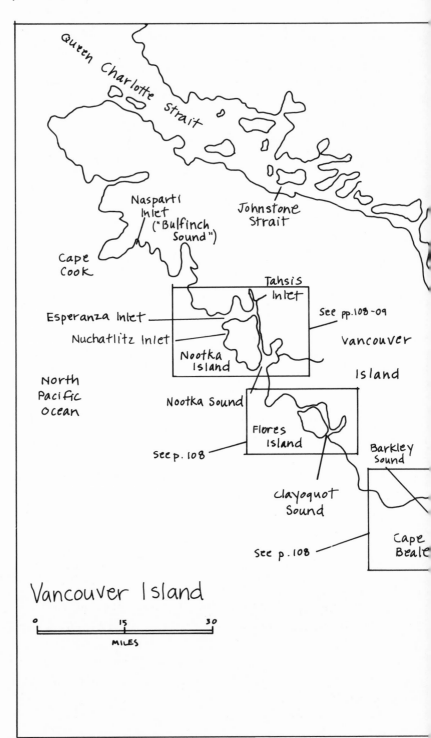

Queen Charlotte Strait

Nasparti Inlet ("Bulfinch Sound")

Johnstone Strait

Cape Cook

Tahsis Inlet

Esperanza Inlet

Nuchatlitz Inlet

See pp. 108-09

Vancouver

Nootka Island

Island

North Pacific Ocean

Nootka Sound

Flores Island

Barkley Sound

See p. 108

Clayoquot Sound

Cape Beale

See p. 108

Vancouver Island

0   15   30

MILES

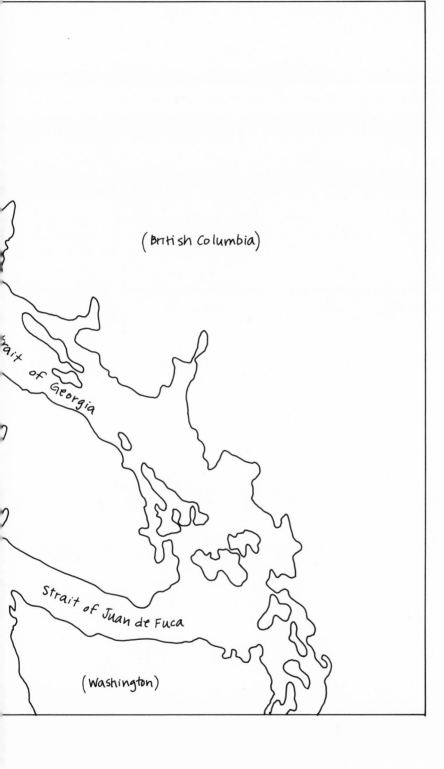

(British Columbia)

Strait of Georgia

Strait of Juan de Fuca

(Washington)

towering a role in the history of the North Pacific maritime fur trade.

Viewing the Nootkans' island home for the first time, Gray found himself facing a land of rugged and powerful impact. Gaunt sawtoothed peaks soared nearly a mile into the sky behind steep, densely wooded shores slashed by narrow fjords where the Pacific's waters surged deep and bitingly cold even in midsummer. The whole island was, in fact, a drowned mountain range with only those great jagged pinnacles thrusting above the sea.

Gray nearly lost his vessel a little farther along that frightening coast. He would have been dangerously unfamiliar then with the hazards of Vancouver Island's racing tides, which sometimes varied as much as thirteen feet between high and low water. When this happened in a harbor with a narrow mouth, the water boiled in and out at a speed as great as six or seven knots, far more than a sailing ship could hope to cope with.

As *Washington* approached Clayoquot Sound a flooding tide swept her toward surf-lashed rocks. Only by frantically manning the sweeps—oversize oars with which the sloop could be maneuvered—was the crew able to pull clear of the danger. While *Washington* was in "this pittiable situation," canoeloads of Indians were waving sea-otter skins and beckoning the Americans ashore. Overcoming his caution, Gray hoisted out the longboat and, helped by the Indians, the sloop was towed to a sheltered anchorage.

Now the threat of competition became obvious. The natives of Clayoquot had been visited by British traders often enough that they knew how badly the foreigners wanted furs, and had raised the ante accordingly. Coming the next morning with an abundance of skins, they demanded the one thing the Americans were least able to afford: guns. Gray would probably not have hesitated to give muskets in trade for skins, had he had them, despite the risk this would have created for himself as well as for the next trader who came along. But *Washington* had barely enough arms for her own defense. And after the unhappy incident at Murderers' Harbor, that was the one item Gray would hardly countenance going short of. The Indians scorned everything else—the rat traps, the mirrors, the egg slicers, the beads, all of the trade goods that Joseph Barrell and his partners had so hopefully put aboard the two vessels. Much of it would go back untouched to Boston.

"Were we possessed of Copper or Muskets, or even chizles made in the proper form," Haswell noted ruefully, "fifty or sixty excellant skins of sea otters might be purchaced in a few hours and very probabley five times that number." But of muskets they had none to spare, and copper little. Iron, as well as a blacksmith to forge it into crude chisels—inch-wide bits of soft iron hammered to a cutting edge that the Indians could provide with a handle and use like an adze—were aboard *Columbia*.

The Bostonians found other evidence of the presence of rival traders. Wickananish, the head chief of Clayoquot—"a tall, raw-boned fellow" who would play a major and continuing role in the whole fur-trading saga—visited *Washington* "compleetely Dressed in a genteel suit of Cloths which he said Capt. Mears had given him." They heard too the names of British fur traders other than John Meares: Captain Barkley, Captain Hanna, Captain Duncan, Captain Douglas. To the first Americans on the Northwest Coast, it began to look as if Nootka Sound might already be a little crowded.

The sound now lay less than fifty miles away, but gales and contrary winds drove *Washington* first southward and then as much as fifty miles beyond her target. Cloudy weather gave the Americans few opportunities to check their position. Two weeks dragged by before Gray picked up the entrance to the sound at sunset on 16 September 1788. Making his way in the next morning by the sketch map of Nootka Sound in Cook's account of his third voyage, Gray headed for Ship Cove, today's Resolution Cove on Bligh Island, where Cook's vessels had anchored in 1778.

Robert Gray had by this time conceived a plan that might remedy his lack of proper trade goods. All would be well if *Columbia* showed up, though even then he would not have the plentiful copper and the muskets that would guarantee a maximum harvest of furs in the face of the British competition.

But *Columbia* might not show up. The ship had faced the same battering Cape Horn storms as had *Washington*. There was little likelihood *Columbia* would be at Nootka ahead of him—Gray was all too familiar with Kendrick's leisurely pace—and always the possibility that the worst had happened and *Columbia* would not get there at all. Determined to make a success of this expedition despite the cloud of ill luck that seemed to hang over it, he decided to collect as many skins as he could before winter ended the season, and then to sail for China. Even a partial cargo would easily bring enough cash to load *Washington* with the right trade goods—copper and muskets, particularly—for a return to the sea-otter grounds in the spring. Gray was sure he could then reach China a second time with the best cargo of furs ever taken from the Northwest Coast.

For a moment the captain's dream tumbled when a ship's boat under sail appeared in the distance. *Columbia* had beat them to Nootka Sound after all! Instead, it turned out to be the longboat of the ship *Felice Adventurer*. The captain, John Meares, was one of the British fur traders with whose names Chief Wickananish had so startled the Americans back at Clayoquot Sound. Meares himself was in the boat, with Captain William Douglas of the *Iphigenia Nubiana* and Douglas's first mate, Robert Funter. Both ships were lying in Friendly Cove, near the western entrance to the sound. Seemingly welcoming the Americans, Meares ordered his boatmen to assist *Washington's* in towing the sloop to the cove. In the meantime the three Englishmen joined Gray and his officers at breakfast. By noon *Washington* was riding at anchor beside *Felice* and *Iphigenia*, and Nancy the goat was probably browsing contentedly ashore.

Gray had become acutely aware over the past few weeks that there would be competition for the Northwest's furs, but he could hardly have prepared himself for this. The British vessels were both larger than *Washington*—*Felice* 230 tons and *Iphigenia* 200, compared to his 90. *Felice* alone carried fifty crew members. *Washington's* crew, after the loss of Marcus Lopius, totaled only ten.

Many of Meares's people were Chinese, and there were Portuguese nationals as well as Malays, Hindus, Filipinos, and Hawaiians aboard both ships. Only gradually did the Americans piece together the story. The two vessels had been fitted out by a group of British merchants in India, in company with a trader in Canton named Daniel Beale, who posed as the Prussian consul, and one Senhor João Carvalho. Secretly a partner of the governor of Portuguese Macao, Carvalho had been given one share in the venture in return for his "services," which consisted primarily of his entrée to the governor's ear. Meares had spent the winter of 1786-87 on the Northwest Coast, during which he almost lost his own life and did lose the lives of twenty-three of his scurvy- and rum-ridden crew. But he knew the fur trade and had convinced this strangely assorted group of investors to send him back in a brash attempt to corner the market.

This was clearly not a venture that would play out according to the rules. Macao, a Portuguese colony on the Chinese coast below Canton, had always dealt in shady business. There, where money would buy almost anything, John Meares had outfitted his two ships. The crews,

Imagination runs riot in this engraving of John Meares's "fort" at Nootka Sound and
the launching of his sloop *North-West America*. The British trader, after establishing himself
on the Northwest Coast ahead of the Americans, had run afoul of Spain's territorial
claims. The Spanish commandant confiscated three of Meares's ships, including the
newly launched sloop, and took possession of his improvised trading post. Meares
angrily returned to London and had an artist create this fanciful, cliff-girt settlement at
Friendly Cove, where only a makeshift shelter guarded by a few cannon had in fact
existed. The affair nearly led to war between Spain and Great Britain. In the end,
Meares was awarded compensation of more than $200,000.
(*Oregon Historical Society*, OrHi 086267)

except for the Chinese, were what one might expect to pick up in Bengal and the stews of Macao. The Chinese were boat builders. Meares's plan was to build a substantial and well-armed fort at Nootka, to take control of the native labor if he could get away with it, and to build a series of small trading vessels that could operate up and down the coast gathering furs that his two ships could then take back to China.

One other thing Macao offered—for money—was the protection of the Portuguese flag. Though he legitimately carried British ship's papers and flew the British flag, Meares acquired, through Carvalho and the governor of Macao, sets of Portuguese papers for both vessels, and even brought along on each a Portuguese supercargo. Should the necessity arise, the Portuguese flag would be hoisted, the supercargoes would become "captains" as specified in the Portuguese papers, and Meares and Douglas could pass themselves off as underlings.

By claiming their ships to be Portuguese, Meares and Douglas would avoid embarrassing situations with the British East India and South Sea companies, which had a monopoly on British trade in the Pacific, as well as make themselves eligible for the lower duties charged on Portuguese vessels at Macao. Their British papers would gain the respect of the Russians and Spaniards, both of whom were eagerly extending their areas of influence in the northern Pacific.

The Portuguese papers read like permits for piracy. Should the vessel carrying them meet with Russian, Spanish, or British ships, they were enjoined to meet force with force. "Should you, in such conflict, have the superiority, you will seize the vessel that attacks you and bring both her and her cargo, with her officers and crew, to China where they may legally be condemned as prizes and the crews punished for piracy."

Meares, in the *Felice*, had reached Nootka Sound nearly four months earlier than *Washington*. Giving Maquinna, the Nootkan chief, two pistols in exchange for a suitable location at Friendly Cove, Meares quickly brought cannon ashore and, says Haswell, "built a tolerable strong garison or place of Defence." Meares would later claim that he had erected a proper fort at Friendly Cove. In fact, except for the ship's guns he dragged ashore, his "fort" appears to have been nothing more than an abandoned Indian hut of rough posts covered with boards. Meares's Chinese shipwrights now began work on what would be the first sailing vessel built in the Pacific Northwest, and Meares himself took advantage of the haven the "fort" provided to begin seizing the Indians' furs and paying for them only with the trinkets he could most easily spare. By the time Douglas arrived in *Iphigenia*, after trading his way along the coast north of Nootka, the Indians had tired of Meares's behavior and moved to their winter village some fifteen miles inland.

This was the situation Gray and his crew walked into. The trading vessel, to be christened *North-West America*, was nearly ready for launching. The Chinese, able shipbuilders that they were, had laid the keel in June, only about three months before.

The Britons discounted the effect Gray's arrival might have on their operations. "The master of the Washington was very much surprised," Meares wrote in the account of his own voyage, "at seeing a vessel on the stocks, as well as on finding anyone here before him ... He appeared, however, to be very sanguine in the superior advantages which his countrymen from New England might reap from this track of trade; and was big with many mighty projects, in which we understood he was protected by the American Congress." Scorning the Americans' presence, regardless of their supposed sponsorship, as of no immediate concern, Meares recorded smugly that he "treated Mr. Grey and his ship's company with politeness and attention." The English captain might have been less condescending could he have known how quickly he and his fellow "King George men"—*kintshautsh*, the Indians called them—would lose their preeminence on the Northwest Coast to these upstart Boston men.

The handsome and worldly Meares, late an officer in His Majesty's Navy, well-garbed and well-spoken here in the North American wilderness, would have awed at least the younger among the Americans. But Gray was of harder stuff. With prickly Yankee pride he put his back up at the casual effrontery of the aristocratic captain and his cool assurance that he had come here first and therefore had a right to whatever could be squeezed from the aborigines of Nootka Sound. We'll see about *that*, thought Robert Gray.

The American captain returned the outward courtesy of his British counterparts by inviting them to celebrate with him aboard *Washington* that first night in Nootka Sound, and he learned that Meares expected to return to Macao in only two or three days. Douglas would stay behind to finish rigging *North-West America*. Then he also would leave to spend the winter in balmy Hawaii before returning to the Northwest Coast.

The Britons lost no opportunity to warn the Americans of the dangers of this wild coastline and the "Monsterous Savage disposition" of its inhabitants. It would be a madness, Meares insisted, for so weakly armed a vessel to remain among them through the winter. And why bother? Since he and Douglas had been on the coast, Meares swore upon his sacred word and honor, they had not collected fifty skins. "So intent was this Gentleman in deceiving us [Haswell wrote] that he hesatated not to forfit his word and Honour to what we were convinced was a notorious falsity."

Though Meares made much of the dangerous disposition of the Indians, the Americans at this juncture were unaware of any tension between the Meares group and the natives. Haswell simply noted that the Indians had "quitted there village and remooved far up the sound." But the fact that there were no Indians in evidence raised its own problems. Desperate now for fresh fish and vegetables, Gray took the longboat to the other side of the sound in search of their villages. They saw not one Indian. In the meantime, *Washington* was pulled over to a convenient beach and careened so the bottom could be scraped and tarred. Meares, ever the gracious host to the little group of Americans, allowed his blacksmith to repair the damage the sloop's rudder had suffered on the bar at Murderers' Harbor.

That afternoon, 19 September by Haswell's count, *North-West America* was launched, and curiosity overcame the Indians. Crowds of them arrived to watch unbelieving as the beamy little schooner, still without masts and rigging, slid down a railway of greased logs. In their exuberance, the builders had failed to put an anchor and cable aboard that could be thrown over the side to stop the ship's motion and *North-West America* was almost carried out of the cove. Nootka Sound's strangely mixed foreign community—British, American, Chinese, Hindu, Malay, Filipino, Hawaiian—spent the rest of the day in "festivity and mirth." The Indians apparently drifted quietly back to their distant villages. Meares, in his account of *Felice*'s voyage, would record the launching as on the twentieth. He had come from China. The Americans, for whom it was the nineteenth, had come the other way around, from Boston.

As his sailing date drew near, Meares put aboard *Felice* a deckload of mast and spar timbers cut from the majestic Douglas firs that surrounded Friendly Cove. These would find a ready market among the shipbuilders of Canton and Macao. "Indeed, the woods of this part of America," Meares wrote enthusiastically, "are capable of supplying with these valuable materials all the navies of Europe." This was perhaps the first recognition of the role timber would one day play in the economy of the entire Pacific Northwest.

Still exuding friendship for the Americans, Meares offered to take letters to China, from where they could be sent on to Boston. Gray gave Meares a packet of twenty-two. By way of thanks, he ordered his longboat to help Douglas's boats tow *Felice* out of the harbor. When Douglas returned, he brought back the bundle of letters with a note from Meares "apolagiseing for returning them saying he was not certain what part of India he should go therefore could not insure a safe Delivery of them." Meares, Haswell recorded angrily, "was fearfull that through the letters to our connections, some information would be communicated relative to the trade on the Coast that would be of disadvantage to . . . his company."

Meares's shabby trick effectively put the Americans out of touch with their employers in Boston. So rare were ships on that still-unexplored coast that nearly a year would pass before another opportunity arose for letters to be dispatched from Nootka Sound. Haswell was particularly contemptuous of Meares's ungentlemanly behavior, especially given *Columbia*'s generosity. Meares, before his departure, had put all the foodstuffs he could spare aboard Douglas's *Iphigenia*, so his own ship, *Felice*, started for China severely short of rations. "But for the provisions we supplied [Meares] with," the offended Haswell wrote, "they would have had maney a scanty meel."

By some strange quirk of luck, the text of Robert Gray's letter to Joseph Barrell, though refused by Meares and returned two centuries ago to its disappointed sender at Nootka Sound, has survived. The draft written by Gray himself for copying by the ship's clerk eventually made its way to Boston aboard *Columbia* with the rest of the captain's papers. In terms of grammar and spelling, it reveals Robert Gray as a man with at least a common school education, something Kendrick missed out on by going so early to sea.

Expressing his concerns over Kendrick's failure to reach Nootka and *Washington*'s shortages of supplies—"I Have only Nine Months Provisions & I Ought to Have fifteen Months, So That I Shall be in a Poor Condition to Winter By my Self"—Gray nonetheless assured Barrell that he was "Determined to Stay on the Coast One More Season, But I Expect to Meet With Poor Success for their is Plenty of Vessels Besides My Self & But few fur Skins to Be Had." This last was Gray's understandable overreaction to finding even one other vessel on the coast ahead of him. As it turned out, with Meares's *Felice* on her way back to China, only four other ships, including the still-unfinished *North-West America*, would be competing with him along that whole six-hundred-mile stretch of coast.

Gray's draft letter, compared with the instructions Kendrick presented to Gray in the Falkland Islands, casts an interesting light on the differing personalities of Joseph Barrell's two captains. Kendrick's big, self-confident penmanship, with its exuberant, inch-high *d*'s and *s*'s, matches the comfortable way in which he gives orders and the relaxed fashion in which he writes to Barrell as an equal. Gray, almost the opposite, writes in a small, tightly controlled hand, and his changes in the wording betray the unease and ambiguity he feels in his relationship with his employer. Starting out by hoping that his letter to Barrell "Will find you in Good Health," he hastily backs away from such familiarity, and feels constrained to adopt a more humble tone. He changes "You" to read "Your Honour." In closing, Gray signs himself "Your Excellencys Most Humble Servant." On reflection, he must have felt uncomfortable now with too much humility. He inks a line through the word "Servant," and in its place writes "Friend."

Gray put aside his letters and his bitter disappointment at not being able to send them home, "which was worse than anything else," he later wrote, and turned to the problem of getting *Washington* ready for sea. It was late September, but he might still pick up enough furs elsewhere along the coast to pay for a cargo of trade goods in China. He was convinced that, Meares gang or no, he could still turn this ill-starred expedition into a profitable voyage. If Kendrick made it to Nootka Sound while he was away, well and good. If not, even better.

CHAPTER NINE

"I Have Seen Them
Eat Human Flesh
Myself"

★

What Robert Gray had not known during that agonizing struggle up the
west coast of the Americas from Cape Horn to Nootka Sound—every
mile of it the territory of His Catholic Majesty Carlos III of Spain—was
that the Spanish commandant at San Francisco had been given orders to
capture both *Columbia* and *Washington*.

> Should there arrive at the port of San Francisco, [the directive read,] a
> ship named Columbia, which they say belongs to General Washington
> of the American states, and which under the command of John
> Kendrick sailed from Boston in September 1787 with the design of
> making discoveries and inspecting the establishments which the
> Russians have on the northern coasts . . . you will take measures to
> secure this vessel and all the people on board with discretion, tact,
> cleverness, and caution, doing the same with a small craft which she
> has with her as a tender . . .

The voyage must have been common knowledge among the European diplomats stationed in the United States. The French and Dutch
consuls in Boston had both provided letters recommending Kendrick and

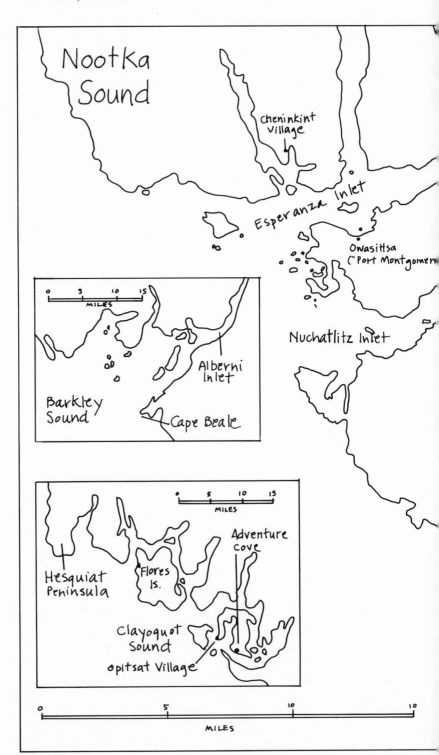

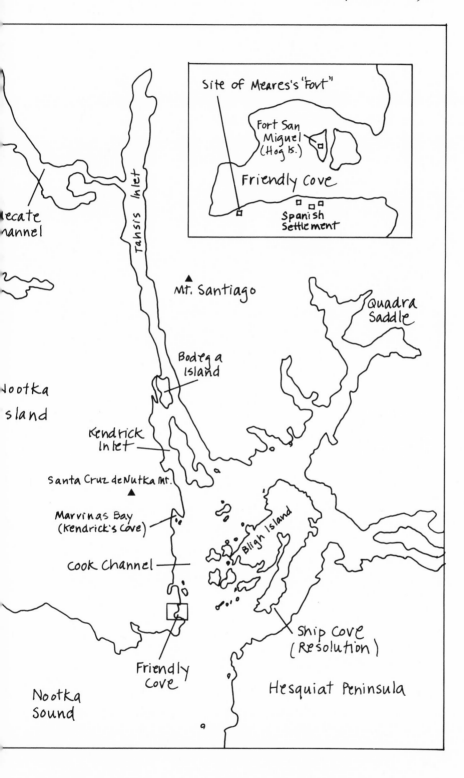

Site of Meares's "Fort"

Fort San Miguel (Hog Is.)

Friendly Cove

Spanish Settlement

Hecate Channel

Tansis Inlet

Mt. Santiago

Quadra Saddle

Bodega Island

Nootka Island

Kendrick Inlet

Santa Cruz de Nutka Mt.

Marvinas Bay (Kendrick's Cove)

Cook Channel

Bligh Island

Ship Cove (Resolution)

Friendly Cove

Hesquiat Peninsula

Nootka Sound

Gray to any ships of those nations they might encounter. Probably the Spanish ambassador to the United States, who may also have been asked to give Kendrick and Gray letters addressed to his countrymen in the Pacific, had allowed his imagination free rein when he learned the details of the voyage. President Washington, of course, had no connection with the venture, nor had Joseph Barrell any intention of challenging Spain's Pacific dominions or Imperial Russia's fur-trading activities in Alaska. But the ambassador's report, with its implication that *Columbia* and *Washington* were on a mission of empire for the new United States government, alarmed the Spanish colonial authorities.

Kendrick, like Gray, was happily unaware of all this when he set out for Cape Horn. He had enough worries as *Columbia* battled the same storms *Washington* had fought. But either Kendrick was not as determined as Gray to get on quickly to Nootka Sound, or *Columbia* had suffered damage that could not be repaired at sea. Kendrick himself says only that "my ship, the Columbia, was considerably disabled, and I was in great want of wood and water." One would guess that the captain's deliberate nature was once again showing itself. Whatever the answer, once *Columbia* had doubled Cape Horn, Kendrick headed for the Juan Fernández Islands.

The ship touched briefly at Más Afuera, but found, as Gray had, that wood and water were going to be difficult to secure. He went on to Robinson Crusoe Island, where he anchored in Cumberland Bay on 24 May 1788. "We were immediately visited by a Spanish boat with two officers in it; and on their return, my first officer, Mr. Ingraham, was sent on shore to request permission to anchor and continue there for a few days, which the governor, Don Blas Gonzáles, major in the cavalry of his Catholic Majesty, very humanely granted."

Apparently the warrant for *Columbia*'s detention had not reached those remote islands. The commandant informed his superiors, the viceroy of Peru and the military authorities in Chile, that he had granted Kendrick permission to remain at Juan Fernández for six days. When a storm delayed the Americans' departure, he courteously allowed them another four days.

It was not until 1792, four years after *Columbia* had left Juan Fernández on her way to Nootka Sound, that Kendrick's son Solomon, then one of the officers of the American fur-trader *Jefferson*, called at Valparíso, Chile, and learned the aftermath of this incident. For having failed to seize the

American ship, his father's friend Don Blas González had been arrested and dismissed from his post. A Spanish ship of war had even been sent from Callao, in Peru, to try to overtake *Columbia*. Posts in Mexico and Chile had also been alerted to capture the American ship if they could.

Solomon met his father a year later, in 1793, on the Northwest Coast, where he gave Captain Kendrick a letter from the unhappy Blas González. Kendrick was touched by the situation of this Spaniard who had suffered so grievously for having offered him a few days of hospitality. He wrote a long and thoughtful letter to Thomas Jefferson, then George Washington's secretary of state, "which I request you to lay before the President, hoping that in his humanity the oppressed will find a protector." Jefferson, in turn, instructed William Carmichael, acting chargé d'affaires in Madrid, to put the matter before Spanish authorities. "A redress of this hardship on the Governor would be received here with pleasure," wrote Jefferson, "as a mark of attention towards us, and of justice to an individual for whose sufferings we cannot but feel." Whatever the result, Kendrick's effort showed once again the kindly side of this puzzling and unpredictable man.

No log or journal survives to chronicle *Columbia*'s passage from Juan Fernández to Nootka Sound, but it could have differed little from that of *Lady Washington*—light winds, adverse currents, the inevitable onset of scurvy. On 23 September 1788, *Washington*'s crew members at Nootka were hurrying their preparations for sea, cutting wood, filling water casks, and overhauling the sloop's rigging. "Some of our Gentlemen were onshore and saw a sail in the offin which by our glasses we soon knew to be the Columbia," Haswell recorded. "I concluded at first sight her people were in an advanced state of the scurvy for tho' [the weather was] very moderate and pleasant her topsails were reefed and her topg[allan]t Masts down on deack." Gray met them in the sloop's longboat.

Columbia had been at sea for two and a half months since Juan Fernández, and scurvy had taken a deadly toll. John Hammond, one of the seamen who had joined *Columbia*'s crew at the Cape Verdes, died only four days before the ship reached Nootka Sound. Another, Hance Lawton, was so far gone that he died there only four days after *Columbia* arrived. With Marcus Lopius's death at Murderers' Harbor, only George Monk was left now of the four who had signed on at the Cape Verdes eight months before.

The ambitious Gray was clearly disappointed that *Columbia* had reached Nootka before he could put into action his plan for a quick voyage to China, and he said so in a letter written a few months later to Joseph Barrell. The ship had arrived from Juan Fernández on 21 September, he added, and "all [were] well on board, except a small touch of the Scurvy." *Columbia* had actually reached Nootka, according to Haswell, on the twenty-third. Curiously, Gray totally ignores the deaths from scurvy of Hammond and Lawton. "I being then nearly ready for Sea," he went on, "which I intended to went to Macao, in China in case the ship had not arriv'd here; there to get some articles of Trade which I had not on board, that suits best on this Coast; which in case had I done it I should have made the best voyage that ever was made on this Coast, but Capt. Kendrick's arriving depriv'd me of my intentions . . ."

Though immediately pressed by Gray and Haswell to push ahead with such trading as could still be done before winter closed in, Kendrick focused more on the problem created by the presence of Douglas and Robert Funter, Douglas's one-time first mate, who was now captain of *North-West America.* "We can do nothing," *Columbia*'s captain insisted, "till these Englishmen have left the place." Lending them his caulkers, carpenters, and blacksmiths, Kendrick did his best to speed their departure. Haswell, of course, grumbled that the Britons "menopolized all the skins nor could we get intercourse with one of the Natives even for the purchace of fish or deer."

Outwardly, no tensions appeared to exist between the British and American traders. The first day of October marked the anniversary of *Columbia*'s and *Washington*'s departure from Boston. The American ships each fired a thirteen-gun salute, which was returned with seven by Captain Funter from Meares's fort ashore and six from Captain Douglas aboard *Iphigenia.* "All the oficers of each vessell were invited to dine onboard Columbia and the remainder of the Day was spent in mirth and festivity."

Though Kendrick shared his stores with Captain Douglas in an effort to get him in his way, the rival vessels still did not have enough food aboard to take them to Hawaii. *North-West America,* under Captain Funter, made a last sally up the coast to secure oil and fish from the Indians. Joseph Ingraham, *Columbia*'s first officer, supercargo Howe, and the furrier, Mr. Treat, went along. They brought back a discouraging account of Funter's methods of dealing with the Indians. "There mode of trading with the natives was. On there arrival at a village to plunder them of all the fish and oil they could find and give them perhaps a small pese of copper ... far less valuable than the provision they had taken by forse, and leav the poor harmless wretches unprovided for a long and rigerous winter."

On 26 October, a Sunday, Kendrick and Gray were finally able to extend Captain Douglas one last courtesy: all of their boats joined forces to tow *Iphigenia* and *North-West America* out of Friendly Cove and see them off in rain and a light breeze for the Sandwich Islands. The Indians no sooner saw the British vessels disappear than they flocked to the Americans, bringing fish oil and venison and even a few sea-otter skins.

It was perhaps then that the Americans had their first glimpse of Maquinna, Nootka Sound's paramount chief. Though he sometimes dressed in trade blankets or garish brass-buttoned jackets acquired from the ships that visited Nootka, he seems for the most part to have preferred the traditional and splendid garb of his people. Maquinna, wrote a Boston seaman of an 1803 encounter,

> was a man of dignified aspect, about six feet in height ... of a dark copper hue, though his face, legs, and arms were ... so covered with red paint that their natural color could scarcely be perceived. His eyebrows were painted black, in two broad stripes like a new moon, and his long black hair, which shone with oil, was fastened in a bunch on the top of his head and strewed or powdered all over with white down, which gave him a most curious and extraordinary appearance. He was dressed in a large mantle or cloak of the black sea otter skin ... fastened around his middle by a broad belt of the cloth of the country, wrought, or painted with figures of several colours.

All of this, said the young Bostonian, gave the chief "an air of savage magnificence."

Stripped of paint and eagle down, Maquinna was still a handsome man, direct of gaze and assured of bearing, with more than a hint of cruelty in the high cheekbones and the slightly hooded eyes. Probably in his thirties at the time, he was the son and grandson of chiefs and even then was grooming his own son to one day inherit both his authority and his name. The Nootkan chief, marveled one admiring visitor, "was endowed with remarkable ability and quickness of intelligence, and knew very well his rights as a sovereign." In this impressive leader, he summed up, were "united the qualities of a legislator, judge and father of his people."

A man of "subtle intellect and considerable diplomatic skill," Maquinna used his
position as paramount chief of Vancouver Island to play off the ambitions of Nootka
Sound's stream of visitors—Americans, Britons, and Spaniards—one against the other.
Clinging proudly to tribal garb, he associated as comfortably with English ship captains
and courtly Spanish dons as he did with his own people. Only toward the end of his
career, sorely tried by the excesses of the fur traders, did he revert to bloody reprisal.
In this woodcut portrait, Maquinna wears a basketry hat woven of split cedar and
spruce bark and pale surf grass; its symbols attest to his prowess at whale hunting,
a highly developed skill of the Nootkans.
(From A Spanish Voyage to Vancouver and the North-West Coast of America, *Cardero*)

Worth their weight in gold to the mandarins of China, glistening furs of the sea otter (*Anhydra lutris*) fueled the first United States commercial venture in the Pacific. Driven to the edge of extinction by greed and fashion, the species was barely hanging on when international protection was decreed in 1911. Happily, the animals responded, and now survive over much of their original habitat, from California's Big Sur to Soviet Kamchatka.
(*Engraving from Cassell*, Popular Natural History, *Library*, The Academy of Natural Sciences of Philadelphia*)

This is not to suggest that Maquinna, much less his vassals, exhibited all the veneers of Western civilization. As the Americans grew to know Maquinna and his tribe at Nootka Sound, they became convinced that they were living among cannibals. "These people . . . eat the flesh of their vanqu[i]shed enemies," claimed Haswell, "and frequently of their slaves, who they kill in Cool blud. They make but little seremoney in owning the fact and I have seen them eat human flesh Myself." Captain Cook had come to the same conclusion in 1778, as did later visitors, including John Meares. Kendrick would tell of having been offered a human hand and a piece of flesh from a four-year-old boy. All three of the journals kept aboard Columbia on her second voyage to the Northwest Coast express the same opinion. This would probably have been ritual cannibalism, resorted to only "on some very particular Occasion," noted a Columbia crewman, rather than for food, with which the Nootkans were lavishly provided by nature without having to eat one another.

Despite the horror the Americans expressed at such behavior, which quickly led the Indians to deny what they had at first readily admitted, the thought that Maquinna and his fellows were cannibals seems to have created no particular uneasiness among the ships' companies. Maquinna brought presents of salmon and deer, and gave every indication that the Bostonians would be welcome guests in his domain.

This tolerant attitude on Maquinna's part occasions some surprise in the light of the chief's experiences at the hands of previous visitors to his shores. The first of these, not counting the Spaniard Juan Pérez, who in 1774 brought his frigate Santiago only to the mouth of Nootka Sound, and the judiciously behaved Captain Cook in 1778, was the Englishman James Hanna, the first fur trader to reach the Northwest Coast. Hanna on this pioneering voyage arrived from China in 1785 in the merchantman Harmon, and appears to have been warmly welcomed to the sound by Maquinna. In response, Hanna invited the chief aboard his ship and offered him what Maquinna took to be a place of honor, a chair placed on the vessel's deck. At this, a practical joker among the Harmon's crew—with the connivance of the captain, one presumes—piled a quantity of gunpowder under the chief's improvised throne and dribbled a trail of it outward to where it could be ignited. Having no idea of what was going on, Maquinna allowed the fuse to be lit and was blown out of his seat in a terrifying blast of flame and acrid smoke. The injury Maquinna thus suffered, both to his backside, which was unprotected by the fur robe that was his only garment, and to his pride, appears to have been the immediate cause of the first known attack by Northwest Coast Indians upon a European vessel. Unfortunately for its success, Maquinna chose a daylight assault as his means of revenge. This tactical error, coupled with the Indians' almost complete ignorance at that time of the efficiency of ship's cannons, led to major losses on their side, with none on that of the *Harmon*'s crew.

Hanna, to his credit, seems to have realized the foolishness of his behavior, and did his best to minister to the injured Indians. As a result, he was able to reestablish amicable relations with Maquinna and his people, which enabled him to carry to Canton a cargo of sea-otter skins that sold for more than $20,000, and to come back for more furs the following year. More to the point, Hanna's apologetic gesture to the wounded Indians—including Maquinna, who for years afterward was given to exhibiting the burn scars on his buttocks—smoothed over a touchy situation that might otherwise have made the Nootkans implacable enemies of every American and European fur trader who followed in Hanna's trail.

Not long after his explosive encounter aboard *Harmon*, Maquinna trustingly assayed another experience with gunpowder, again at the expense of his image among his own people. The British trader James Strange in 1786 decided to cure the Nootkans of their fledgling interest in personal ownership of firearms. Having rammed the barrel of a flintlock musket as full of black powder as he could, Strange offered Maquinna the honor of shooting it off. The chief, he wrote, "very composedly took aim & fired." Luckily, the overloaded weapon failed to blow up in Maquinna's face, but its kick was so great that "had not some of his attendants been standing near him, he could not have failed measuring his length of the ground." Maquinna, "when he recovered [from] his fright ... complained bitterly of the pain which the shock occasioned." The chief's companions, as Strange intended, declined their turns with the musket and each declared his intention of never again having anything to do with firearms.

Thanks in part to these humiliating experiences, Maquinna developed what some have seen only as a mercurial ambivalence toward the traders, imperialists, and explorers who flocked to his domain. Others have found far more to admire in this remarkable native American: the development of a canny pragmatism toward the Europeans and Americans and a willingness to use the ambitions of these competing visitors to further his own control over the entire Nootka region. Historian Warren L. Cook, for instance, sees him as a man "of subtle intellect and considerable diplomatic skill, [who] quickly learned to pit one nation against another."

Maquinna knew all of the players on Vancouver Island's vast, spruce-clad stage, from the Spaniard Juan Pérez and the Englishman James Cook to the American John Salter and the crewmen of his ill-fated *Boston*, all but two of whom were murdered in 1803 by an embittered Maquinna (and their severed heads lined up for identification by the survivors on the vessel's gore-stained deck). But between his unhappy experiences with Hanna and Strange and the resort to murder in 1803, the chief played a welcoming and protective role in the affairs of nearly everyone who came to the Northwest Coast. Kendrick and Gray were no exception. Despite John Meares's dire warnings about the "Monsterous Savage disposition" of the Nootkan Indians, the Americans relaxed gratefully into the warmth of Maquinna's hospitality.

Reassured now that there was little to fear from Nootka's inhabitants, and that he had at least a few months to anticipate without competition from Meares and his roughneck crew, Kendrick decided that both *Columbia* and *Lady Washington* would winter at Nootka Sound. The vessels had arrived too late in the season to lay up a proper cargo of skins for China—thanks, of course, to Kendrick's having taken at least a month longer than necessary in getting to Cape Horn. But there was no cure for that now. They would stay here and then make a season of it beginning in March.

Washington's and *Columbia*'s crews, like the Nootkans, would find themselves in a sense prisoners of the great forest that lay at their backs, pressing them close against Vancouver Island's surf-scoured shore. Here was true forest primeval—nothing like the gentle woods the Bostonians were accustomed to back home. Even the Nootkans knew better than to challenge those tangled slopes very deeply—just far enough in to chop down a great cedar and drag it out to where they could shape from it another of their sleek canoes. The Americans were unlikely to penetrate even this far.

"After one finally breaks through the luxurious growth along the margin," wrote ethnologist Philip Drucker in his classic study of the Nootkan tribes and their soggy homeland,

> he finds himself in a dark gloomy moss-covered world. Huge trunks
> rise straight and branchless, the crowns forming a high canopy almost
> impervious to sunlight.... One must climb over one windfall, duck
> under the next ... and go around a third.... And everywhere the
> scum of moss conceals the footing: in one place it slips underfoot ... at
> the next it covers ... a rotten shell of tree trunk into which one sinks
> to the knees.... And everywhere water drips from the rocks, seeps
> through the moss, drips from branches overhead.

If the forest itself was forbidding, the narrow fjords that slice this
dramatic land made up for that. One could travel for miles inland in a
small boat, helped along, if the time was right, by the push of a flooding
tide. And fortunately for both Indians and Bostonians, the narrow waterways so easily reached offered an ample larder for all. In the fall the
channels would be choked with runs of dog salmon, steelhead, and trout.
Herring spawned there in their billions in late winter. "Codfish," or so the
Bostonians called them, were always at hand for the taking, and so were
the abundant shellfish. Once the New Englanders found their way about,
the island offered an easy and familiar life: the whir of flights of wildfowl
—Vancouver Island lay astride the busy Pacific flyway, the rustle of
browsing deer, even the occasional scream of a panther somewhere in
that green tangle. And if the traders could not snare it or shoot it themselves, the Indians would bring it to them in return for a few buttons or a
couple of beads.

With no urgency to trade until spring, Kendrick turned his mind to a
pet project, one that he had probably thought much about before. He
would rerig *Washington*, turning her from a sloop, with one vulnerable
mast and that great unwieldy mainsail, to a brigantine, with two masts
and smaller, more easily handled sails. Haswell took his usual position,
chiding Kendrick for not "consider[in]g he had not the cordage duck nor
blocks suffisiant for the purpose." That much may have been true. But
actually, it was not a poor idea. John Boit, who took an almost identical
vessel around the world only a few years later, wrote of *Union*, the first
sloop to make a circumnavigation, that "she proved to be an excellent
sea boat & was a very safe vessel. Still I think it too great a risque for to
trust to one mast on such a long voyage ..."

In the light of subsequent events, this could have been Kendrick's
first step toward relieving himself of the burdens of too much boat and
too many details. A superb seaman when it came to the command of

small vessels, he must at times have looked longingly at Washington with her simple rig and crew less than a third that of his own vessel. And he was clearly at a loss when it came to the administrative problems of two ships, two crews—and two captains.

Kendrick had a few spars cut, but he must quickly have realized the hopelessness of so major a conversion in the wilds of the Northwest Coast. Instead, he decided to build a house ashore, as Meares had done. All hands were occupied with the new project for a few days. Haswell scornfully notes that "again this fell through."

To take the place of his planned house so far as storage was concerned, Kendrick had a longboat brought ashore and turned bottom up as a storehouse. Despite around-the-clock guards, Indians slipped in one night and stole five small cannon Kendrick had acquired from Captain Douglas and fifteen of the ships' water casks. The local Indians blamed tribesmen from the opposite side of the sound. "This story pasafied Captain Kendrick for fearfull of punishing an inosent person he let the matter drop unnotised." But the loss of that many water casks was serious. The cooper was set to work making replacements.

As December slipped into January, Haswell recorded that "Captain Kendrick had been for several weeks up to his elbos in morter building a brick chimne[y] where the mizon mast had stood tho' he had a good brass stove. Its bad consequences we all dredded and endevered to disswade Capt. Kendrick from it, but to no purpose." The captain's intent, which the critical Haswell managed to ignore, appears to have been the building on deck of a forge for the ship's blacksmith, with a chimney close to the mizzenmast. Around it he had a sail rigged so that it could shelter the whole crew in bad weather. Charcoal was burned ashore so the smith could fashion bits of iron into the crude little chisels the Indians would accept in trade for their furs. A few days later the cry went up that the ship was on fire. Cabin curtains had gone up, and coals had dropped into a sail locker, setting some of the canvas ablaze. Fortunately, the fire was discovered soon enough to prevent any major loss.

And so the winter went, if we are to believe Haswell. The two crews seem to have been comfortable enough, for there is never a mention of hardship. This is a little surprising. Throughout the winter, shrieking southwesterly storms would have swept that sodden coast, bringing drenching rains and driving the surf to terrifying heights. The cold would have been mild compared to a Boston January, but the men could not have suffered much more from damp and chill had they spent the whole time at sea.

A few sea-otter skins were purchased, but more remained in the Indians' hands. The price too often was either copper or muskets. Toward the end of January a stout bulwark was added entirely around *Washington*'s decks, with ports for additional cannon. In case of an Indian attack, this would help make up for the lack of boarding nets, which many of the traders employed to prevent the Indians from clambering onto their ships.

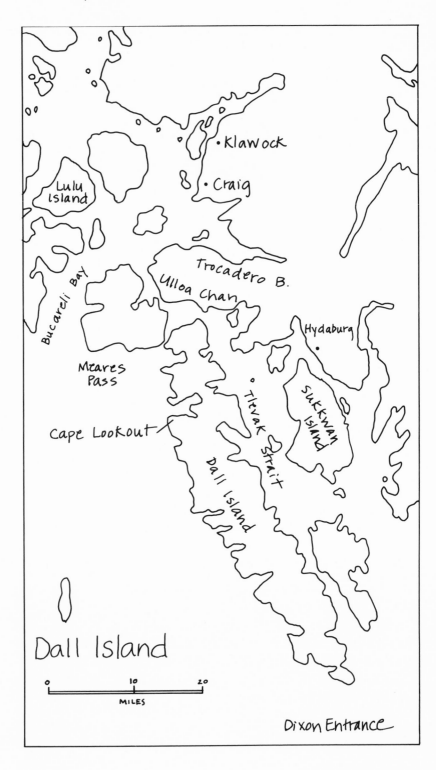

Klawock

Craig

Lulu
Island

Trocadero B.

Ulloa Chan

Bucareli Bay

Hydaburg

Meares
Pass

Sukkwan
Island

Tlevak Strait

Cape Lookout

Dall Island

Dall Island

0   10   20

MILES

Dixon Entrance

CHAPTER TEN

Lady Washington
Was "Dashed ... Against the Rocks
With The Utmost Feury"

★

With the first signs of spring, preparations were made to send *Washington* cruising southward for furs. The sloop would head directly for Clayoquot Sound and work her way farther south along the coast of Vancouver Island until late April. The previous August, Gray had tried to buy the Clayoquot Indians' abundant furs but had lacked the trading truck they demanded. There were still no muskets to spare and little or no copper, but *Columbia*'s blacksmith by late February had forged 450 small adze-like blades of soft iron and turned them over to *Washington*'s crew. The Americans termed these bits of metal "chisels." To the British traders who had introduced them among the Indians of the Northwest Coast as almost a form of currency, they were "toes."

Behind that curious name lay considerable history. Twenty years earlier the English navigator Samuel Wallis had brought home from Tahiti in his *Dolphin* several stone adzes, for which the Tahitian name was *toë*. Captain Cook saw them in London and, knowing the Pacific islanders' overwhelming hunger for metal, had some copies made up in iron. Cook found these an enormous success when he later touched at Tahiti in

Endeavour. When British fur traders made their way to the Pacific Northwest in the wake of Cook's third voyage, the little iron adzes, now popularly known as toes, went along too. Among the British they continued to be called by their Tahitian name.

Gray gave his smith two more casks of iron—large shipwright's adzes, axes, and the like—to be reforged into even more of the little chisels. Ship's supplies—hogsheads of bread, barrels of salt pork and beef, molasses, and corn—were passed back and forth on Kendrick's orders between the sloop and the ship.

Rare was the departure or arrival of a vessel in those days that was not accompanied by some show of ceremony. On the morning of 16 March, *Washington* saluted *Columbia* with five guns and, as befitted her lesser rank, was given three in return. Kendrick and his officers sped the sloop on her way with three cheers, which were returned by Gray and his crew. By sunset a smart easterly breeze had carried *Washington* to within a few miles of Clayoquot.

At anchor in the sound, Gray purchased "a number of Good skins," most of them from the chief of a neighboring village who called himself "Captain Hanna." This was Kleaskinah, who had exchanged names as a token of friendship with the first European trader on the coast, the Englishman James Hanna of the *Harmon* in 1785. The old chief became something of a favorite among later traders for his easy-going manner. "He sold us many skins," Haswell wrote of him, "and seemed a very inteligent old Fellow." John Meares also left a description of Hanna as a man of "about forty [who] carried in his looks all the exterior marks of a man of pleasantry and good humour."

At noon on 10 April, Haswell records, the Americans were startled by "hearing a very suden and Loud shout and seeing allmost every Boddy running from the village to their canoes." Alarm quickly changed to curiosity. "I was soon eased from my suspence by my Friend Hannah who told me that Chief Wickananish [the paramount chief of Clayoquot] had struck a whale and that all the Villagers were going to his assistance." Here was a spectacle that no New England sailor could resist. With John Treat, the expedition's furrier, Haswell clambered into a small sealing canoe and had himself rowed out to where the stricken animal lay.

Exhausted now by the ropes and harpoons of the hunters and prevented from diving by sixteen sealskin floats, the great beast lay quiet, its body rocking gently in the long Pacific swells. One of its huge dark eyes seemed to focus on Haswell's canoe, but the whale appeared too tired to do more than look reproachfully at its tormentors. Wickananish had left the wounded animal to seek another whale that had sounded nearby. Meanwhile, tribesmen in a smaller canoe had retrieved the long harpoon shaft and carried it back to the village, where it now rested against the wall of Wickananish's house. Inside, his principal wife lay quietly beneath a mat of cedar bark, hardly daring to breathe. This was an act of sympathetic magic designed to make the "noble lady," as the Nootkan whalers called their quarry, similarly quiet and manageable.

Having lost the second beast, Wickananish, standing in the bow of his massive cedar-log whaling canoe, returned to the side of the wounded whale. His six muscular paddlers were exhausted. Their face paint of deer tallow and red clay had been smeared by sweat and exertion, and their wide-brimmed basketry hats, their sole bits of clothing, sat askew on their heads. But they and the chief smiled in happy anticipation. There was no chance that this whale could escape them. And Wickananish was pleased that his men had so perfectly observed their ritual preparations for the hunt, which demanded many days of abstinence both from fresh meat and from their wives' inviting beds. Had any of the hunters been lax in these all-important observances, the "noble lady" might well have towed the hunters many miles out to sea instead of obediently coming to rest almost at the doorstep of the village.

Now Wickananish rigged another harpoon with a fresh blade of giant mussel shell lashed to the shaft along with barbs of elkhorn that would remain imbedded and immovable in the whale's flesh even if the fragile shell blade shattered on impact. The chief balanced himself on the canoe's gunwale, holding the harpoon high overhead as his naked oarsmen gently eased the vessel toward the whale. Half a dozen sealskin floats lay on the floor of the canoe atop the coiled line, more than two hundred feet of it, patiently twisted of fiber from the same great cedars that had yielded their trunks to fashion the huge canoe.

As the high bow of the vessel almost touched the wounded animal, Wickananish drove the harpoon downward behind the massive head and then rolled himself swiftly backward into the canoe to escape the impact of thrashing flukes. But the whale, weakened by loss of blood, merely quivered at this new onslaught and made no attempt to dive. The moment had come for the kill.

Wickananish gave the order and, says Haswell, "his mandate was answered by a low but universal acclamation." The young Bostonian, eager to see at close range how these skilled hunters would finish off their quarry, changed into the canoe of Wickananish's younger brother, who had been chosen to end the drama. "We were paddld up to the fish with great speed and gave him a deadly pearce and the enormious creature instantly expiered."

After tying the whale's upper and lower jaws together, the hunters attached lines to the limp carcass so that it could be towed into shallow water fronting the village, where every tribesman waited now for the distribution of meat and blubber to begin. But first there were rituals to attend to. Wickananish's wife approached the shore, welcoming the "noble ladye" to her home by pouring a cup of fresh water on its head and sprinkling the carcass with eagle down.

> They say it is particularly pleasing to their Deaty [Haswell noted] to adorn a Whale with Eagles fethers for they suppose that thunder is caused in conflicts between that Bird and fish. [They believe] that an Egle of enormious size takes the Whale high in the air and when it falls causes the noise [of] thunder. On their Whaling excertions [the Indians] frequently cut their tongues and paint themselves with the blud [so] that the Whale may not be afraid of them and run from them or they [be] afraid of it.

Ever the amateur anthropologist, Haswell kept his pen busy. "They have many other superstisious Id[e]as relative to this fish," he told his precious journal. "On my Return onboard I made particular inquieries relative to their customs in whaling. They told me the first Whale that was killed in a season it was their custom to make a sacrifise of one of their slaves. The corps[e] they lay beside a large pece of the Whales head adorned with eagles feathers." With commendable objectivity (only the horror of cannibalism led him to an outright condemnation of the Indians' way of life), Haswell concluded his observations: "After [the slave's body] has lay'd there a sertain time they put it in a Box as usual." Nor did this gruesome revelation of human sacrifice dampen Haswell's admiration for the skill and bravery of these hunters. He closed his journal that day on an admiring note: "To consider the imperfection of their utentials, musel shell harpoons and lances with Roaps, we must allow them [to be] expurt Whalemen."

Despite the diversions offered by these friendly Indians and the presence of an ample supply of furs in Wickananish's domain, Gray's restless temperament denied him the pleasure of trading in one place for any longer than a few days. The next village, the next anchorage always beckoned with the lure of cheaper, more plentiful furs. Haswell records that, after less than a week at Clayoquot, "Captain Gray determined to keep the remainder of his Chizles for the southern trade and tho' there were an abundance [of furs] offer'd we purchaced none." For several days, says Haswell, "we lay Doing nothing but amuse ourselves by Shooting etca . . . Dewering which Time I took a tolerable accurate survey of the Harbour."

At Chief Wickananish's village, Opitsat, which lay by the entrance to Clayoquot Sound, the Americans were once again reminded of the poverty of their trade goods. "In these houses they have plenty of skins which they told us they would rediely part with for Chizles or Copper but of the former they demand an exorbitant price, ten for a skin, and the latter we are totally destitute of."

At a harbor to the south of Clayoquot, Haswell noted of the Indians that "we were glad to find they spoke a dialect of the Nootka Language," a testimonial to the diligence with which these Bostonians applied themselves to learning the tongues of the people among whom they traded. The New Englanders' reverence for learning shows in nearly every journal of those early days of the maritime fur trade in the form of a carefully recorded vocabulary. Haswell's gives nearly five hundred words and phrases, including numbers, verbs, the names of places and chiefs, and such bits of information as "kleet see oop, a Root like Sassaparilla, tastes like a Carolina Potatoe."

Furs in any quantity continued to elude Gray, so much so that one anchorage was dubbed "Poverty Cove." At another harbor they learned why Wickananish and his people at Clayoquot were so well-stocked with sea-otter pelts. "A great many of the natives were round us but we were disappointed in finding they had no skins. They told us Wickananish had been down there and purchased all they had."

Gray pushed on as far as the Washington coast, where he finally found plentiful skins for which the natives asked only five chisels each. This turn of fortune was short-lived, however. "At daylight several Canoes came off and upwards of 30 sea otter skins were purchaced, but we had the Mortification to see them carey off near 70 Others all of excellent quality for want of Chizels to purchace them and they repeatedly told us they had left great abundance onshore." The Americans' disappointment was compounded next day as they made their way back toward Nootka Sound. A chief paddled out to *Washington* with "maney good skins. Had we ben provided with aney thing that would have purchaced Skins," mourned Haswell, "we should no doubt at this place have got near 200."

As it was, Gray returned to Nootka in late April, his supply of chisels exhausted and with fewer than a hundred sea-otter skins to show for his six-week cruise. He went first to the old anchorage, where he found *Iphigenia* riding at anchor. Captain Douglas, fit and tanned from his winter in Hawaii, had brought the British vessel into Nootka only three days before. Next morning the schooner *North-West America* came over the horizon. Gray must have groaned. There would be the same cutthroat competition this season, and this time there would be no chance of speeding the competing traders on their way. It was only April!

Kendrick had stayed behind to ready *Columbia* for a trading cruise of her own but had never quite gotten around to it, though he had moved the ship from Friendly Cove, where *Iphigenia* now lay, to Marvinas Bay, four miles farther inland. When Gray brought the sloop up to Marvinas Bay, he was shocked to see that *Columbia* was no more ready for sea than she had been when they left Nootka. Less so, in fact. Haswell, with his customary exaggeration, wrote that the ship "was now mearly a Hulk." Kendrick had clearly taken his lead from the fort and house Meares had built at Friendly Cove the year before. His little stronghold, which he had patriotically named Fort Washington and armed with some of the ship's guns, now commanded the bay, and a house stood nearby. In it he had established the blacksmith's forge. Most of the ships provisions and stores were now also on land.

Gray, not one to let anything stand in the way of his own ambitions for the voyage, agreed to another cruise, this time to the north, as quickly as *Washington* could be readied. "The smiths were immediately employed to furnish us with another Cargo of Chizels and all our people in refiting our Vessel for sea repairing the sails and recruting our stock of wood and water."

One would expect to find in Haswell's journal some reflection of the tension that must have existed at times like this between the two captains: Gray coldly determined to take a fortune in skins to China, and Kendrick with his mind on some distant goal of empire. And one wonders about the relationship between Kendrick and Haswell, in the light of the furious encounter during the Atlantic passage that ended in the

younger man's transfer to *Washington*. But there are no clues. At one
moment Haswell paints Kendrick as a vacillating incompetent. Then, in
almost the next breath he and the captain are off together on some
friendly excursion.

One such outing took place while *Washington* lay at Marvinas Bay
fitting out for her northern cruise. Taking probably two or three men to
handle the longboat's oars when the wind failed, Kendrick and Haswell
went off on a shooting excursion in the waterways that thread inland
from Nootka Sound. They made their way northward through Tahsis
Inlet, which lies between high, tree-clothed hills, all of the way to the
deserted winter village of the Nootkan Indians. The two shot ducks and
roasted them for dinner in an improvised shelter where they spent the
night. On the way back they explored an arm of Tahsis Inlet that seemed
to lead the rest of the way around Nootka Island and back into the
Pacific. Indians they talked with confirmed their guess. The whole way,
Haswell noted, the waterway was "generaly about a mile in bredth [and]
navigable for Vessels of the largest burden to its head." Kendrick would
remember, when he came this way again two years later, both this back
route around Nootka Island to the Pacific and the beauty of the land he
and Haswell had seen at the head of Tahsis Inlet.

When Kendrick and Haswell returned from their expedition to
Tahsis, they found Captain Douglas, on *Iphigenia*, still lying comfortably at
Friendly Cove. But to their dismay they found that *North-West America*,
under Captain Funter, had stolen a march on *Washington* by slipping away
on a trading cruise to the northward—exactly where Gray intended to
go. There would be competition for the Indians' furs, all right.

Gray cursed his luck and hurried his preparations. Within forty-eight
hours of Kendrick's return he had put to sea again, hoping to get ahead of
North-West America if she paused in nearby waters to trade. "But as soon as
we were out," mourned Haswell, "the wind hauled to the westward, and
as we were bound to the northward [we] were necessi[t]ated to beat."
All night and into the next day *Washington* slogged wearily into quar-
tering seas. By afternoon the sloop had made little headway northward,
which put her squarely in the way of what Robert Gray least wanted at
that moment—an encounter with a new and totally unexpected actor,
representing still another nation with an oar ready to dip into these
already muddled waters.

"At 4 PM saw a sail inshore of us," Haswell recorded. The ship would

have slowly gained in visibility as she approached Washington: Three masts
—clearly not North-West America. "In a little time she fiered a gun and
hoisted spanish colours. She hauled her wind toward us and at 5 we
spoke."

This looked like trouble—the kind of trouble Barrell had feared
when he warned Kendrick and Gray to stand clear of Spanish possessions.
As far as Spain was concerned, the Pacific was a Spanish ocean. Spain was
worried that the Russians were moving southward from their Bering Sea
outposts, and though the Spanish had little or no interest in fur trading,
they did want to know what other mischief the Americans and British
might be up to. Don Esteban José Martínez, commanding the frigate
Princesa, the vessel under whose guns Lady Washington now lay, and Don
Gonzalez López de Haro, in the packet boat San Carlos, had been sent from
Mexico to make contact with the Russians and to see what else might be
going on along this Spanish shore.

The Americans particularly worried Spain. "We ought not to be
surprised," the viceroy of New Spain had reported to his superiors in
Madrid, "that the English colonies of America, being now an independent republic, should carry out the design of finding a safe port in the
Pacific and of attempting to sustain it by crossing the immense country of
the continent above our possessions of Texas, New Mexico, and California." So the Spanish were already worrying, sixteen years before Lewis
and Clark would actually accomplish it, about an American attempt to
extend their influence from the Atlantic to the Pacific coast of North
America.

Martínez had been given instructions specifically mentioning Columbia and Lady Washington, which had eluded Spanish efforts to capture them
the year before. "In case you are able to encounter this Bostonian frigate
or the small boat which accompanied her," the orders read, "this will give
you the government's authority to take such measures as you may be
able and such as appear proper . . ." Though there was nothing specific
this time about capturing either of the American vessels, the instructions
were worded loosely enough that Martínez could have justified almost
any action he chose to take. And the orders were firm on one thing: The
foreigners, flying the "American colors of the Congress of Boston," must
be made to understand that they were trespassing in Spanish waters.

"Having forced her to bring to," Martínez wrote in his diary of this
first encounter with Washington, "I ordered her boat let down into the

water and her captain to come on board." Instead of following Martínez's direction, Gray sent two of his officers to meet with Martínez aboard *Princesa.* Gray's men, in spite of themselves, would have warmed instantly to this fatherly looking Spaniard. His clean-shaven, rather handsome face, somewhere in middle age and topped with a high, domed forehead, seemed to emphasize the receding hairline that Martínez flaunted by scorning to wear the curled and powdered wig his position entitled him to. It was characteristic, one guesses, of this straightforward, unpretentious man that he expected to be taken exactly as he was.

Martínez asked the two Americans—Haswell's journal fails to record who they were—what their purpose was in being in Spanish waters, and then sent his own pilot, José Tobar y Tamáriz, to *Lady Washington* to check the men's answers against those of their captain. Both Gray and his officers had been well rehearsed against just such a meeting. Neither mentioned sea-otter skins. "They replied that . . . they were sailing along the coast of America in search of material for . . . barrel staves," noted Martínez. The Americans were referring to the loss the previous winter of the fifteen water casks stolen by the Indians of Nootka Sound, which the ship's cooper had been ordered to replace as soon as the materials could be found. The Spaniards also examined *Lady Washington*'s "passport," as they called it, "which was signed by General Washington and countersigned by Captain John Kendrick."

That Gray's sea letter was countersigned by Kendrick one can readily believe. "Absolute" as ever, *Columbia*'s captain would likely have seen to it that anyone Gray encountered should know who was *really* in charge of this expedition. But also endorsed by General Washington? Well, hardly.

Amid the confusion of a vessel named *Washington* and the Spaniards' mistaken belief that she "belongs to General Washington of the American states," a signature misread in haste would have been an easy error for Martínez or his pilot Tamáriz to make. They could not have known that during that sunny September of 1787, when the American Congress in New York was issuing sea letters to *Columbia* and *Washington,* General Washington had finished his stewardship of the Constitutional Congress in Philadelphia, which had finally put the government of the United States on a workable footing—and in the process also paved the way for the nation to elect him as its first president—and had already slipped back into the life of a country squire at Mount Vernon.

That misread signature—in the florid handwriting of the day, getting "G. Washington" out of "A. St. Clair" would not have been unthinkable—was perhaps what led Martínez to take such a temperate view of Gray's and Kendrick's trespass in Spanish waters. Certainly Gray would have taken no pains to correct the idea that George Washington was somehow involved with the expedition. Whatever the reason, the Spaniard chose to overlook the implicit authority his orders gave him to seize *Washington* as a prize. Instead, he interpreted his loosely worded instructions in as friendly a manner as possible. Gray, for his part, wanted only a successful voyage and a hold full of sea-otter skins. He would have made every effort to assure Martínez of his agreement that this was indeed Spanish territory and he only a guest.

The Spanish captain expressed great interest in knowing what ships other than *Columbia* were then lying in Nootka Sound. With no eagerness to help the cause of a rival, Gray told him that the only other vessel there was Douglas's *Iphigenia*, "a packet from Macao, whose captain was a Portuguese, the first mate a Scotchman, and the crew English." She would "make him a good prize," Martínez commented.

The two captains parted on the friendliest basis. Martínez graciously asked if the sloop stood in need of anything he might supply and sent his boat to the *Washington* with "preasants of Brandy wine hams sugar and in short everything he thought would be acceptable." Gray returned the courtesy with two red feather robes, a basketwork hat, three colorful bird skins from Hawaii, and an assortment of harpoons and bows and arrows acquired from the Indians of the Northwest coast. Where the Hawaiian birds and feather cloaks came from has never been explained. Probably Gray got them from Captain Douglas or Captain Funter, both of whom had spent the previous winter in the islands. When *Washington* parted from *Princesa*, Haswell recalled, "we saluted him with 7 Guns and the compliment was returned." Gray must have breathed a heartfelt sigh of relief as the Spanish ship dropped astern and he swung his own bow northward again to resume his quest for furs.

Proceeding on to Nootka, Martínez had another surprise in hand. Having been told that the Russians had plans afoot to take possession of Nootka Sound, the viceroy of New Spain had ordered that a fort be built to firmly establish Spain's claim to this northern coast. To that end Martínez's vessel, *Princesa*, carried fifteen soldiers who would garrison the new post, in addition to the crew of 106. López de Haro's *San Carlos*, which Gray would sight at a distance two days after his encounter with Martínez, was bringing another sixteen soldiers in his ship's complement of eighty-nine. A few of the officers were Spanish, the rest natives of California. The Spaniards' orders were that they would erect not only a fort but buildings to house their forces. Four Franciscan fathers were aboard who would see to the conversion of Nootka's Indians to Christianity, an activity in which the fur traders had been notably disinterested. The Spaniards were also to explore the coast for five or six degrees above and below the sound.

Martínez had been to Nootka once before, in 1774. The Spanish would make much of the fact that four years later, Captain Cook reported buying two silver spoons there that had been stolen from Martínez during this earlier visit. Thus, insisted the Spaniards, their claim to the Northwest Coast clearly antedated any priority the English might advance on the basis of Cook's discoveries.

Meanwhile Gray continued his northward course, sighting López de Haro's vessel but, because "the breeze was so very favourable," choosing to ignore the Spaniard's signal to halt. After the fiasco of the southern cruise, he must have felt desperate in his determination to secure a cargo of sea-otter skins. Hurrying up the coast, he passed up one harbor after another in his eagerness to find a new trading ground and reached the northern tip of Vancouver Island without having bought a skin. Turning toward the mainland, *Washington* finally reached an area where the Indians still placed a high value on iron. "We purchaced of them between twenty and thurty Sea Otter skins for a very trifling number of Chizles," Haswell wrote happily. "There were also," he noted, "a vast number of Sea Otters continualy playing in the water."

Not long after this first purchase, two canoeloads of Indians approached *Washington* and sold a few skins. By gestures they indicated that the Americans should remain at anchor and that they would return with more pelts. When they reappeared three days later, Gray was chagrined to find that they had not gone to inform their tribe of the traders' arrival, as he had supposed, but had instead gone themselves to kill a few more otters. They had ten in their canoe, "several yet warm with life," and spent the following night stretching and drying the skins. Despite the indications that patience would produce more skins where he was, Gray nervously moved on when a favorable wind arose, "meening to explore the Islands more thuroughly on his return."

Making his way as far north as Dall Island in southeastern Alaska, Gray nearly lost *Washington* in one of the foolhardy maneuvers that would threaten the lives of his vessel and crew time after time on both voyages. His courting of disaster had already become a pattern. Three times during the previous cruise first mate David Coolidge and second mate Haswell had joined forces in criticizing their captain's navigation and his rash disregard for the safety of both vessel and crew. Twice Gray had given in, but in one instance, with a hard wind driving the sloop dangerously close to shore, he stubbornly carried on. "Deef to our persuasions, Captain Gray would not heav about but persisted in a southwardly direction," though a change of tack would have carried him safely clear of the land.

In this fourth instance, Gray at nightfall had worked the sloop into a small mountain-girt cove with far too little room for maneuvering. The ship was taken by a sudden gust and slammed onto a ledge. The jib-boom and bowsprit were carried away and the sloop was repeatedly picked up by the surf and dropped onto the rocks with terrifying force. "We ware surrounded with huge craggy clifts nearly as high as our mast head. . . . Every surf that arose lifted us high in the air and as it desended dashed us against the rocks with the utmost fuery . . . every surge left us resting dry on the pinacles of this murcieless Iron bound coast."

By the greatest skill and good luck the ship's longboat was launched without capsizing and managed to carry an anchor and line seaward through the surf. The crewmen ran out the entire length of line, then dropped the anchor. Luckily, it caught. By keeping the line taut, the men remaining aboard *Washington* were able to gain a few feet toward deeper water each time a wave lifted *Washington* off the rocks. It took nearly two hours to kedge off into deeper water, and by the time the sloop was safely free, much of the copper sheathing had been torn from the vessel's bottom and two anchors were lost. The crew lowered the yards and topmast and managed to secure the bowsprit so that it could carry a sail.

"A situation more critical than ours had been for about two hours cannot be immagined," wrote a relieved Haswell, who wondered what might have been his fate had the ship been wrecked on this coast "inhabited by a most horrid race of savage Canables. . . . This disasterous place we called Distress Cove."

Once more the tough little sloop had proved her worth. Gray, however, abandoned all idea of going farther north and turned back toward Nootka Sound where repairs could be made.

★

CHAPTER ELEVEN

Captain Gray
Takes Command of
Columbia

★

Happy to be alive, *Washington's* determined captain continued to trade as his vessel limped southward. A few days after the near-fatal mishap in Distress Cove, Gray reached Parry Passage in the Queen Charlotte Islands, where two years earlier the British fur trader George Dixon had in half an hour bought three hundred sea-otter skins. Gray struck nearly as rich a bonanza. A great parade of canoes, some twenty to thirty of them, approached *Washington,* their occupants "singing a very agreeable air." From them Gray acquired "in a very fue moments" two hundred pelts, then worth some $8,000, for one chisel apiece.

Here, finally, was what he had been looking for. Trade continued into the night, when the Indians "returned to their Village [Haswell wrote] ..." But Gray's restlessness once more asserted itself. He started *Washington* slowly southward again through dense fog. Haswell "was greved to leve them so soon, as it appeared to be the best place for skins that we had seen." He was probably even more grieved when he later learned that Captain Douglas had put in there a few days later in *Iphigenia* and gathered up all the remaining furs.

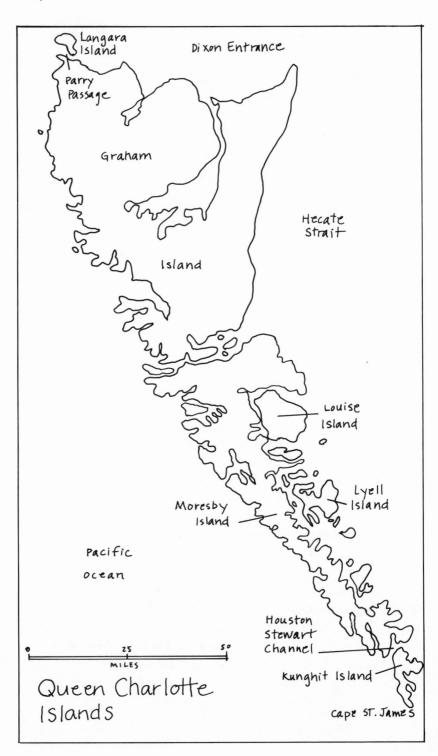

Langara
Island

Dixon Entrance

Parry
Passage

Graham

Island

Hecate
Strait

Louise
Island

Lyell
Island

Moresby
Island

Pacific

ocean

Houston
Stewart
Channel

Kunghit Island

Cape St. James

0   25   50
         MILES

Queen Charlotte
Islands

Nearly a fortnight passed as the crippled *Washington* made her way slowly south along the Queen Charlotte Islands. Near their southern tip, a canoe appeared unexpectedly in an area Gray had judged to be uninhabited. Threading his way between islands, he sighted a village and a cove that offered safe anchorage. Known today as Houston Stewart Channel, the inlet was called Barrell's Sound by the Americans aboard *Washington* in honor of the expedition's principal sponsor. It would become a popular though sometimes dangerous port of call for the fur seekers.

This was the land of the warlike Haida. Numbering nearly ten thousand, they made up one of the largest and most powerful of the Northwest Coast tribes. Theirs were the largest canoes, sometimes as long as seventy feet, unmistakable with the boldly carved and painted symbols of their owners' Raven and Eagle clans. The Haidas' reputation among the fur traders was already one of untrustworthiness and thorny pride. Gray cautiously did his trading from the vessel, so he would have seen only at a distance the Haida village with its big gabled houses of cedar planks drawn up in rows above the shore. They, like the canoes and the soaring totem poles staring seaward beside each doorway, had been fashioned by skilled artisans with the simplest of tools: wooden wedges to split off the planks and adzes of volcanic basalt or hard native jade to shape the huge cedar logs.

"A brisk trade was soon set on foot by Coya, the chief," wrote Haswell, and sea-otter skins began to come aboard in exchange for clothing. "The intercourse with the natives . . . was on the strictest Friendship. They indeed pillaged aney little trifling thing they could find a good opportunity to take unobserved, but as we took no rash means with them it never interrupted our trade." The tendency toward petty thievery among Coyah's people would play a major part in Kendrick's experience when he returned *Washington* to Barrell's Sound a few months later.

Gray and his officers "stript the natives of allmost all the skins they were possessed of" in exchange for every piece of clothing they could spare, much of it probably drawn from *Washington*'s slop chest. There would almost certainly have also been individual bargains made between crew members and Indians in which personally owned garments were exchanged for skins. When the sloop headed south again for the passage back to Nootka Sound, Gray finally had on board the better part of the cargo he had struggled so long and restlessly to acquire.

Now they turned *Washington* southward in earnest. Gray must have felt chagrined at the prospect of having to bring a damaged ship back to Nootka Sound—explanations were always awkward and would be doubly so if Kendrick's mood was ugly—but he would have been elated too at finally having struck it rich among the Indians of the Queen Charlottes. And Haswell's head, at least, buzzed with an exciting new thought. They had, he was sure, discovered the Northwest Passage!

The lure of that mythical seaway that in its most believable version would allow a ship to sail up the St. Lawrence River from the Atlantic, across the Great Lakes, and thence westward by some still-undiscovered strait or great river into the Pacific, had haunted the minds of every explorer since Sir Francis Drake. The story first surfaced in the form of a manuscript allegedly written about 1609, in which a Spaniard named Lorenzo Maldonado told of having sailed in 1588 from the Atlantic across the top of North America to the "Strait of Anian," which in turn led him into the North Pacific. This intrepid discoverer even claimed to have returned by the same extraordinary route.

An elderly Greek pilot, Juan de Fuca, added to the tale by claiming to have discovered another such passage in 1592. (When a wide body of water between Vancouver Island and Washington State's Olympic Peninsula was discovered in 1787 at about the latitude claimed by de Fuca for his discovery, the strait was promptly given the old mariner's name.) Finally a British magazine, the *Monthly Miscellany, or Memoirs for the Curious*, inflamed imaginations in 1708 when it published the story of a voyage in 1640 (news sometimes traveled slowly in those days!) of a Spaniard, Admiral Bartholomew de Fonte, who, it revealed, had also discovered such a passage.

This was enough to convince the world's map makers, who added one version or another of the mythical shortcut to their charts. Mariners, perforce, had no choice but to believe that such a strait existed. And so did governments. Faced with so great a body of evidence—all of it worthless, as it turned out—Parliament in 1744 offered £20,000—an enormous fortune at that time—to the first British captain and crew to sail across the top of North America from one ocean to the other. Captain James Cook's third voyage—the very one that had inspired *Columbia's* and *Lady Washington's* dispatch to the Northwest Coast—had, in fact, been an official search for the Northwest Passage. So far as that goal was concerned, the expedition had come to naught. But then, neither had it disproved the idea.

Oddly, it was Admiral de Fonte's account, by then nearly a century old, that stuck in people's minds. Perhaps it had received the widest circulation. In any event, it was the one that came to Haswell's mind a few days before *Lady Washington*'s terrifying encounter at Distress Cove, when Gray and his crew "discouvered a large inlett trending to the Westward. This . . . is I suppose the entrance to Adml. de Fonts Straits . . ." But Gray had his eye on more practical matters. "We stood out, resolving to examine it some other time," Haswell observed sadly. But *Lady Washington*'s grounding and the attendant damage changed all that. Gray on the homeward leg kept his bow headed firmly toward Nootka Sound.

"Had we not met with the misfortune of running on-shore," Haswell wrote regretfully, "our discoveries would have been very interesting." At least, he was able to say, "we discovered that the straits of Adml. de Font actually exist and I have but little doubt that they penetrate very far into the Continent." Poor Haswell probably went to his grave still thinking that he had actually glimpsed the elusive entrance to that fabled waterway. "It is probable when that shall be penetrated too and explored, large rivers and Lakes may be found that may overlap the western bounds of the Lakes that have their vent in our Eastren coast and perhaps lakes are now discovered that is the sourse of Large navigable Rivers that empty themselves in the North Pacific Ocean." Alas, it would be another half century before the last diehard would forget the tall tales of Maldonado, de Fuca, and de Fonte and give up hope of finding such a convenient passage across the top of North America.

Gray returned to Nootka Sound from his six-week cruise on 17 June 1789. The Spaniard Esteban José Martínez had arrived there in *Princesa* more than a month before, and as soon as the ship had dropped anchor he had hoisted the Spanish colors. The two priests aboard had led the officers and crew in a prayer of thanksgiving for their safe arrival. A fifteen-gun salute and three cheers to the health of Carlos III firmly established a Spanish presence at Nootka Sound, for that day at least. Captain Douglas, aboard *Iphigenia*, interpreted the salvo as a courtesy to his ship and, deciding to hoist his Portuguese colors—a decision he would come to regret—responded with a return salute.

Gray found the Spanish fort, Santa Cruz de Nutka, already taking shape on Hog Island, now rechristened San Miguel, opposite Friendly Cove. In the cove Meares's schooner *North-West America* and an English sloop lay snugly at anchor alongside *Princesa* and *San Carlos*. One of *Princesa*'s gunners fired a round to bring *Washington* to, but Gray confidently continued up the sound toward Marvinas Bay where *Columbia* lay. Partway there, *Washington* was met by Kendrick and Martínez, who obviously had already established a friendly relationship. The fourth vessel, Gray learned, was the newly arrived fur-trading sloop *Princess Royal*, commanded by Thomas Hudson, another of Meares's "gentleman adventurers." Much had happened at Nootka in his absence, Gray could see.

Promptly on his arrival at Nootka Sound, Martínez had demanded an explanation from Kendrick of what he was doing in Spanish waters. Carefully avoiding any mention of sea otters—an omission that could have fooled no one—Kendrick quickly acknowledged that he was in the territory "belonging to the King of Spain," and explained that *Columbia* and *Washington* were on a voyage of discovery. The rest of his letter to Martínez told a pitiful tale of distress and accidental arrival at Nootka:

> .... haveing prior to my arrival sprung the Head of My mizn mast & in a Gale from the N E my Rudder received some considerable Damage, likewise my Stern post became lose. To repair these Defects & recover my men the most of which were sick with the scurvy and two actually Died with the Disease . . . I was infallibly obliged to anchor. Finding the natives Inofensive & a good Harbor to repair my ship which had then been near 12 months from Boston . . . I was induced to remain the Winter . . . & now as you may Observe we are getting our Ship in readiness for Sea with all possible dispatch.

Between his orders to establish a fort at Nootka Sound and the question of what to do about John Meares's British-Portuguese vessels, Martínez had his hands full and seems gratefully to have accepted Kendrick's explanation. He would have been fully aware that Gray and Kendrick were on the Northwest Coast to gather a cargo of sea-otter skins. But that was all right. So long as their interest was commercial and not territorial, he was glad to have them off his mind. "I observe with pleasure," Kendrick shortly wrote to Martínez, "you are satisfied with my Answer . . ." As to *Washington*'s current cruise, Kendrick added diplomatically, "I thought best to employ her on Discovery to the Northward." Again, no reference to furs.

Kendrick was very nearly undone in his protestations when the Indians at Nootka gave Martínez two of the expedition's pewter medals with the ships depicted on one side and "Fitted at Boston, N. America, for the Pacific Ocean" on the other. Coupled with the warnings the Spanish authorities in Mexico had issued about these two vessels "belonging to General Washington," Martínez at first took the medals to be not mere trinkets but an expression by the United States Congress of its intent to claim this distant part of the North American continent. The commandant planned to send the medals to the viceroy in Mexico.

Kendrick seems easily to have calmed the Spaniard's fears, for Martínez shortly thereafter noted in his diary that the Americans left the medals only "as memorials of their expedition wherever they landed." Only a week later Martínez asked to borrow the services of *Columbia*'s blacksmith. Kendrick eagerly agreed without knowing exactly what the commandant had in mind: "the Letter is so unintelligible as to the English that I can make nothing of it."

Though Martínez had talked of seizing Douglas's *Iphigenia* when he and Gray had first met, the courtly don had let nearly a month slip by before taking any action. In the meantime the three captains—one Spaniard, one American, and the Scot Douglas, enjoyed a lively round of socializing. Martínez invited Kendrick and Douglas to dine on the *Princesa*. All were entertained the next day aboard *Columbia*, during which three toasts were drunk to the Spanish monarch. Following each toast, the patriotic Kendrick responded with a federal salute, one round for each of the thirteen United States. That afternoon the group visited a nearby village, where Kendrick told the Indians in their own language that Martínez was their brother who had come to live among them. Saying "*Wacass, wacass*"—friend, friend—the chiefs grasped Martínez's hand in a pledge of amity.

Douglas, in his turn, invited the American and Spanish officers and the two priests to as much of a meal as *Iphigenia*'s nearly exhausted provisions would allow. "Having one Sandwich Island hog left, and a few yams," Douglas recorded in his journal, "I sent the hog on board the Spanish ship and had it dressed after their own fashion; they added two or three other dishes; so that we made it pretty well."

Perhaps Martínez worried that he was not being firm enough with the Portuguese—or were they British?—interlopers he had found in Nootka Sound, whom he had been sent expressly to turn away from Spanish dominions. On 14 May he asked *Iphigenia*'s captain and supercargo to bring the ship's papers to him aboard *Princesa*. Since Douglas had raised the Portuguese flag in response to Martínez's salute on the day *Princesa* arrived at Nootka, he would now have to go through with the whole charade. The Portuguese supercargo Don Francisco José Viana, a native of Lisbon, arrived with his Portuguese papers in his sometime capacity as "captain." Douglas claimed to be the supercargo. This might have gone down had Martínez not had at least some command of Portuguese. He choked on the "authorization" that purported to allow *Iphigenia* to take possession of Spanish vessels and bring them, their crews, and their cargoes to China, where the ships would be condemned as legal prizes and the crews tried as pirates. Over Douglas's objections that this wording was in force only if his vessel were attacked, Martínez held Viana, Douglas, and their crew as prisoners aboard *Princesa* for two weeks.

Douglas suspected, with good reason, that Kendrick had had some hand in this business. The grounds for his dark suspicions are neither difficult to find nor unconvincing. Shortly before Martínez demanded *Iphigenia*'s papers, the Spanish commandant had gone to see Kendrick at Marvinas Bay and took bed and bedding so that he could stay as long as he wished. Douglas saw in this a conference between the two—which it may well have been—in which Martínez sought the American's support for his forthcoming action. There would have been no problem there. When it came to a choice between his native America and the British Crown, Kendrick's patriotism dictated the answer. To make matters worse in Douglas's eyes, the Scottish captain learned that Martínez's approach to Kendrick's blacksmith, which certainly took place with the American captain's approval, had been to have him make a number of leg irons with which Martínez could secure his British and Portuguese prisoners.

In the end, Martínez had second thoughts about the whole affair. Thinking he might have misinterpreted *Iphigenia*'s Portuguese documents, and knowing that if he stayed at Nootka to complete the fort and settlement his orders called for, there would not be enough men available to escort Douglas's ship back to Mexico as a prize, he relented. Making both Viana and Douglas sign an agreement that they would pay the Spanish authorities the value of both *Iphigenia* and her cargo if the viceroy decided they had been legal prizes, he released the men and their ship. The commandant also demanded a letter from Douglas to Captain Funter of the *North-West America* instructing him when he returned to Nootka Sound to sell his vessel to Martínez at a price to be determined by Kendrick and Gray. This further confirmed Douglas's growing suspicion that the Americans were in league with the Spanish commandant.

Martínez ordered Douglas to leave Nootka and not to return. But by some curious chemistry, Douglas, Kendrick, and Martínez were able to put aside their differences and continue their friendship. Douglas pulled down the fort Meares had built at Friendly Cove and took aboard *Iphigenia* the cedar planks that had formed the walls. The roof he gave to Captain Kendrick, who had it cut up for firewood. Martínez sold Douglas the provisions he would need for the return voyage to China, and on his last night in Nootka, the Scottish captain dined with Martínez. Kendrick and *Columbia*'s first mate, Joseph Ingraham, joined them. "They drank my health," wrote Douglas in his journal, "wishing me a good voyage to Macao, and accompanied it with thirteen guns." Though Douglas grumbled that Martínez had robbed him during his captivity of all his trade goods, *Iphigenia* had barely been escorted out of Martínez's sight when Douglas turned the ship northward for one last cruise for furs. Douglas confided to his journal that he had "no idea of running for Macao with only between 60 and 70 sea-otter skins . . . aboard." In a month of trading, *Iphigenia* added more than seven hundred skins to the cargo before turning her bowsprit west toward China.

When Gray arrived at Nootka, about three weeks after Douglas's departure, Martínez had gotten more than a good start on his fort, which now boasted a battery of ten guns. A second fort, with gun emplacements that commanded the ocean approaches to Friendly Cove, was rising on a height south of the cove. Three other buildings had also been erected, a workshop, a bakery, and a building in which Martínez's troops could spend the winter. There was no question now about a Spanish presence on this particular stretch of North American coastline. During this same period, Douglas's one-time first officer, Captain Funter, had reached Nootka on 9 June in the *North-West America*, to be seized promptly by Martínez. The Spaniards immediately rechristened the schooner *Santa Gertrudis la Magna* to honor the patron saint of sailors, and put the crew aboard *Columbia*.

The skins in the hold of the *North-West America* were transferred to *Princess Royal*, the British sloop that had reached Nootka in mid-June. Even Martínez, though, was not immune to the beauty of sea-otter pelts and the money they represented. He decided *North-West America* owed him a debt, of what kind we can only guess, and as payment kept twelve of the finest skins for himself.

At about this time *Princesa*'s carpenters began building still another schooner at Kendrick's anchorage in Marvinas Bay. Perhaps Martínez chose this location only because he wanted the proximity of Kendrick's blacksmith while the ship was under construction, or he might have seen this as a way of establishing Spanish control over this favorite retreat of the two American vessels. The commandant's artisans had come to Noot-ka ill-prepared for shipbuilding. Kendrick sold them iron, nails, sailcloth, caulking materials, three thousand bricks, a number of two-handed saws, and probably the services of his blacksmith to forge the boat's fittings. Kendrick dispensed these commodities from *Columbia*'s stores as casually as if they belonged to him. On the other side of that particular coin, he was also seeing to it that he and his ships remained in the good graces of the commandant and out of Spanish captivity.

Kendrick, by this time, must have made up his mind about the future movements of *Columbia* and *Washington*—and about his own role in the enterprise. Martínez would not have put *North-West America*'s people aboard *Columbia* if he had not been sure of her departure soon for China. Yet exactly what that decision was, and how it was arrived at, we shall probably never know. Haswell's journal, the only detailed account of the voyage we have, ends mysteriously almost in mid-sentence with a description of Martínez's seizure of Douglas's *Iphigenia* and the subsequent release of ship and crew. "Everything being settled thus Captain Douglass sailed for China" were—so far as anyone knows—the last words Haswell penned on *Columbia*'s first world-girdling voyage.

Gray, in a subsequent letter sent to Joseph Barrell from Canton, was not much more revealing. "Captn Kendrick thought best to change vesels," he wrote, "and take all the property on board the Washington and Cruize the Coast himself and for me to take the best of my way to the Sandwich Islands to procure sufficient provisions to carry me to Canton. Our provisions on the Coast not being sufficient for both vessels to Cruize the Season out was the reason for our separation." Yet that really fails to explain why Kendrick gave command of the larger ship to Gray and, by doing so, also seems effectively to have transferred to him leadership of the whole enterprise.

As commander of the expedition, a role Gray seems never to have openly challenged, Kendrick, ever the "absolute" leader, undoubtedly made the decision himself that he would take command of *Washington* and remain for the rest of the season on the Northwest Coast while Gray would take *Columbia* and the skins thus far collected to China. The reasons are not difficult to see. Except for his diplomatic maneuvering with the Spanish commandant, Kendrick had contributed virtually nothing to the voyage thus far, and could not have been too anxious at this point to show up in Boston. If he stayed on the coast a month or two longer, perhaps he could still salvage his end of the enterprise by meeting *Columbia* in Canton or following her home with another equally successful cargo of China goods.

And there was always his palpable distaste for *Columbia*. The ship was too big and too deep for the rocky coves and wild tides of the coast, and too much of a handful at sea. *Washington* had come this far and had shown her worth. She was not too small to make it back across the Pacific and home to Boston. Whatever the reasons—and they have to be the purest conjecture, for no shred of fact about the trade-off survives—Gray would take the ship to China while Kendrick kept the sloop and finished out the season on the coast. It would take months for Gray to sell his skins in China and put aboard another cargo. Perhaps Kendrick could catch up with him there. The two ships might still sail home together.

There would have been much to do. *Washington* desperately needed repairs after her near-destruction on the Alaskan rocks, and *Columbia* had lain neglected far too long. Neither vessel could go a-cruising now, though the season was at its peak. Kendrick resourcefully made an arrangement with Martínez. A few days after the Spanish commandant had seized *North-West America*, Martínez authorized one of his officers, José Narváez, to undertake a cruise on board the schooner with David Coolidge, *Washington*'s first mate, going along as interpreter to the Indians. Martínez had been ordered by the viceroy to explore the coast south of Nootka. The commandant thought that the narrow inland channels he had learned of from the Indians might possibly enable a ship to reach the headwaters of the Mississippi River. *North-West America* sailed southward to the Strait of Juan de Fuca, at the southern end of Vancouver Island. She returned with no splendid geographic discoveries but did bring back seventy-five sea-otter pelts, presumably to be divided between the Spaniards and Americans.

While Kendrick and Gray both worked furiously to get the two vessels ready for sea, Martínez decided that the time was ripe for a formal show of Spain's title to Nootka Sound. With his forts and their auxiliary buildings now completed, he selected 24 June 1789 as the official day to mark Spain's dominion over Vancouver Island. In elaborate ceremony—

amazing, considering Nootka's isolation then from the rest of the civilized world—Martínez and López de Haro took formal possession of the sound in the name of Spain's Catholic monarch.

A great cross was erected. A document of possession was signed by the ranking Spaniards and witnessed by Kendrick and Captain Hudson of the *Princess Royal* and then sealed in a bottle and buried. Cannon boomed in volleys, and shouts of "*Viva el Rey*" were initiated by seamen in the rigging of the Spanish ships and returned, said Martínez in his diary, by Hudson and the Americans. Kendrick must have loved it, and would remember some of the details on his return to Vancouver Island two years later.

At noon, Hudson and the Americans joined their Spanish hosts at a banquet that Martínez immodestly described in his diary as "*esplendida.*" Repeated toasts to the health of his Catholic Majesty Carlos III punctuated the festivities, as did more volleys of gunfire. In those days news would have reached Nootka Sound more slowly, in all probability, than it did any other corner of the great Spanish kingdom. The assembled guests could hardly be blamed for not drinking to the health of Carlos IV instead of to that of his predecessor, who had died the year before.

Whatever the international complications, Martínez and Kendrick, along with whoever else might sail into Nootka Sound unannounced, made a convivial company. Captain Hudson's *Princess Royal* had arrived at Nootka only ten days before the great ceremony. That night Kendrick and Martínez had spent the night aboard the British ship, along with Martínez's semi-captive Captain Funter of *North-West America*. After the little *Princess Royal*—which carried a crew of only fifteen—had been towed to an anchorage, the three captains repaired to *Columbia*, still lying at Marvinas Bay, where they spent several hours.

Martínez got down to business the next morning. Summoning Captain Hudson, he asked why the Englishman had brought his vessel uninvited into a Spanish port. Hudson's answer, that his ship needed repairs, satisfied the Spanish commandant, who offered assistance to speed Hudson's departure. By late June *Princess Royal* was ready for sea and, presumably at Martínez's request, the longboats of *Columbia* and *Washington* towed her out of Nootka Sound.

Kendrick had by this time become so certain of Martínez's friendship that he decided to leave Marvinas Bay in favor of a berth at the Spanish settlement at Friendly Cove. A few days after the ceremony, *Columbia* and

Lady Washington lay snugly moored under the guns of San Miguel's fort.

No sooner had Captain Hudson and one British ship disappeared over the horizon than another one appeared. *Argonaut*, a Meares vessel again, was under the command of James Colnett, a veteran of Captain James Cook's third voyage. He had come from Macao with orders from John Meares and his backers to build at Nootka "a solid establishment, and not one that is to be abandoned at pleasure." The orders directed that it be called Fort Pitt for Great Britain's then prime minister. Colnett, it became apparent, was not one who would speak softly to this Spanish don who thought he owned Nootka Sound. Martínez, in his diary, noted that Colnett told him he had "come as governor of this port, to establish a factory for collecting sea otter skins."

What upset Martínez even more was the Englishman's patently false claim that he was acting on orders of the King of England in taking possession of Nootka Sound and fortifying it as he thought necessary. To that end, like Meares before him, he had brought a contingent of Chinese artisans—twenty-nine of them, including blacksmiths, bricklayers, carpenters, shoemakers, tailors, and a cook. The ship, jammed with supplies both above and below decks, also carried the pre-shaped timbers for a sloop to be ninety-two feet long at the keel. Appropriate to the golden fleece the ship's owners expected her to gather on the Northwest Coast, the sloop was to be called *Jason*. Once the sloop and the trading post at Nootka were in operation, Colnett had orders to establish posts elsewhere along the coast.

Martínez acted this time without hesitation. He had the *Argonaut* towed into the sound where she was secured by two lines, one to *San Carlos* and the other to *Columbia*. The Spanish commandant went so far in making Kendrick an ally in all this that he asked him to load *Columbia's* guns and train them on *Argonaut*. Martínez and Colnett met aboard *Princesa* the next day and a violent argument ensued. According to Martínez, Colnett several times placed his hand on his sword and, assuming Martínez spoke no English, loudly denounced him as "*gardem Espana*"—a God-damned Spaniard. A Spanish visitor to Nootka, however, recorded a version strongly at odds with Martínez's own account. It was the commandant, he wrote, who had "put his hand on his sword" and otherwise needlessly insulted Colnett. It was likely, he said, that "the churlish character of each of these men led up to the argument. Those who had sailed with both complained of one as much as the other and condemned their uncultivated boorishness." Whatever the origin of the fracas, Martínez declared himself unwilling to put up with such abuse in the cabin of his own ship. He announced that Colnett was a prisoner of war, together with all of his officers and crew, and prepared to send them to Mexico, where they would be dealt with by the viceroy of New Spain.

Once again, the strange distinction at Nootka Sound between social intercourse and politics became evident. The day after Martínez had seized *Argonaut*, gunfire shattered the dawn calm of Friendly Cove. It marked no new development in the problems between Spain and the unwelcome British guests. John Kendrick was simply celebrating the Fourth of July, the thirteenth since the signing of the Declaration of Independence. Wrote Martínez in his diary,

> The frigate Columbia fired a salvo of 13 guns in celebration of the number of years that the American English had separated from their kinsmen in Europe. They fired several more in the course of the day, of the same number of guns.
>
> At noon Captain Juan Kendrique invited me and all the officers and chaplains of the two vessels under my command, besides the missionary fathers and our prisoners and the officers of the British packet ... Argonaut. He had a splendid banquet served for us, in the course of which toasts were drunk to the health of our sovereign, Don Carlos III (whom God protect).

There would also have been toasts to the welfare of the infant United States. The festive meal "was followed by a salvo of 13 guns, to which I ordered the packet San Carlos and the fort of San Miguel to respond. I excepted the frigate Princesa because her guns were loaded with ball and grape."

These wholesale expenditures of gunpowder became routine at Nootka Sound as ships and holidays came and went—too much so, wrote one British officer. "There was scarcely a day past without puffings of this kind from some Vessel or other, & we too followed the example, and puffed it away as well as any of them, till at last we were become so scarce of ammunition to defend ourselves from the treacherous Indians, that we were obligd to get supplies of Powder from both the Spaniards & Traders before we left the Coast."

Shortly after Kendrick's holiday celebration, the first observance of Independence Day on the Northwest Coast, Martínez offered Captain Colnett and "the officers who are my prisoners" another elaborate repast. That same afternoon a lookout at San Miguel reported the sighting of *Princess Royal*, which Martínez had allowed to leave Nootka Sound three weeks before. This time the Spanish commandant again acted decisively, seizing the vessel and making prisoners of everyone aboard. Before the end of July, Martínez had loaded Colnett and his crew aboard *Argonaut* and sent them, under Spanish officers, to Mexico for trial. Captain Narváez took command of *Princess Royal*, with Captain Hudson and his men aboard as prisoners, and followed.

Thanks to the ever-courteous Martínez, the departure of the captured vessels offered the first opportunity since Meares had refused to carry letters for the Americans nearly a year before that they were able to report to their owners in Boston. "The sloop has made two Cruizes and is now ready to accompany the Ship to the North[ward]d part of the Coast, which I intend Cruizing the Season," Kendrick informed Joseph Barrell, "and from thence proceed to China, where I shall follow your further Instructions, and inform you perticularly of the Success of the Voyage, which I am sorry is not by any means equal to your expectations when we left Boston—shall leave this port on the morrow." Whether Kendrick was reluctant to tell Barrell of the planned switch of command between himself and Gray, or had simply not yet made up his mind, is anyone's guess. With his letter to Barrell went one from the captain to his wife, Huldah, probably her first since *Columbia* had left Boston nearly two years before.

Gray's letter, both in what he said and what he was unable to say, much more clearly reflects the relationship between the two commanders. He had, he told Barrell, "made two Cruises with considerable success, considering the way I was sent, but not half equal to going the way that I wanted to . . . I have nothing more to inform you except the voyage will not turn out to the Owners expectations, all for the want of a nimble leader . . ."

The postscript was the most revealing. "I have to request you to call upon Capt. Hatch, and to the Gentlemen of the Company and present my best respects to them, together with Mr. Howe's and inform them that as we have orders not to write them, we must refer them to Capt. Kendricks Letter for all information relative to the voyage."

The Americans would not be on the coast to know of it, but events continued to unfold at Nootka. Martínez busied himself adding gun emplacements to his fort and completing his "schooner of about sixty

English feet in length that should not draw more than six or seven feet."
He, too, it seems, had fallen in love with *Washington* and wanted a vessel
like her that could safely slip in and out of the local inlets. About this
time, however, the Spanish ship *Aranzazú* arrived with supplies for the
Nootka garrison as well as with the astounding news that the viceroy of
New Spain was ordering Nootka Sound abandoned at the end of the
season. Before the close of 1789, Nootka would be once again what it had
been before the British traders, the Boston men, and then the Spaniards
had arrived.

Kendrick and Gray had by now shuffled crew members between
their two vessels in preparation for *Columbia*'s departure. Ingraham would
stay with *Columbia* as first officer and Haswell would go back aboard the
ship as second. Some of *Columbia*'s men were transferred to the sloop,
bringing her complement up to twenty, so the ship would have room to
take the crew of *North-West America* back to Macao. Martínez also put
aboard *Columbia* the furs the schooner had collected before her capture.
Gray was asked to keep a fair number to pay the passages of the British
seamen, and to divide the rest among them to make up for the pay they
had lost because of their imprisonment.

Shortly before *Columbia* and *Washington* left Nootka Sound, John Kendrick, Jr., now "second pilot" of the ship, had approached the Spanish
commandant with the request that he be allowed to transfer to the
service of Spain. The young American had become fluent in both Spanish
and the language of the Nootkan Indians, and Martínez had probably
drawn on his talents already as an interpreter. The Spaniard may even
have encouraged Kendrick to apply. Though several British seamen had
made the same request and been turned down, Martínez agreed now
because, as he recorded in his diary, Kendrick had of his own free will
"abjured the heresies of Luther" and become a Roman Catholic. He was
also, the commandant noted, well educated and an expert pilot. Martínez makes no mention in his diary of young Juan Kendrique's linguistic
abilities. José Tobar y Tamáriz, one of *Princesa*'s mates, recalled that the
elder Kendrick embraced his son, crying, and told him that life held no
greater good fortune than to be a man of goodwill, and advised him to
follow that path throughout his life.

Before the American ships left Nootka's sheltered waters, there
would have been a farewell round of entertainment and exchanges of
salutes between the Boston men and the Spaniards as *Columbia* and *Wash-*

ington completed their preparations to leave. *Columbia*'s first mate, Joseph Ingraham, as a parting gift, presented to Martínez a long paper written in English—"A Description of Nootka Sound and an Indian Vocabulary"—which so impressed the commandant that he sent it with an enthusiastic letter to the viceroy in Mexico.

Martínez, unaware of Kendrick's strange plan to trade vessels with Gray, expected that both ships would head directly to China. Instead, *Columbia* and *Washington*, escorted by Martínez in his launch, made their way out of Nootka Sound and then, with a farewell cheer to their Spanish friend, turned south toward Clayoquot Sound, where they briefly resumed trading. It was there that Kendrick and Gray finalized their exchange of vessels. By 30 July 1789, the arrangements had been made. Gray put aboard *Columbia* all the furs he had gathered while trading in *Lady Washington*. The pelts that had trickled in slowly but steadily during the year that Kendrick had remained at Nootka Sound would also have gone into *Columbia*'s hold.

There were seven hundred in all, according to an "Invoice of Sundry Sea Otter Skins and others Ship'd on board the Ship Columbia by Jno. Kendrick Esqr." This brief document was probably in the nature of a receipt tendered Kendrick by the departing Gray or by *Columbia*'s supercargo, Howe. Since Gray had brought in nearly the entire cargo, the count would have been his as well. As we shall learn, however, there seem in fact to have been more than twice as many furs aboard the ship as were officially acknowledged by Gray.

Now the two ships headed out of Clayoquot together, with salutes and the crews' huzzas echoing from the sound's steep wooded hills. It is difficult to guess what might have been in the minds of the two commanders as Robert Gray started *Columbia* on the long passage to Canton, via the Sandwich Islands, and John Kendrick turned his eyes to the little *Lady Washington* that would be his only home for the rest of his life.

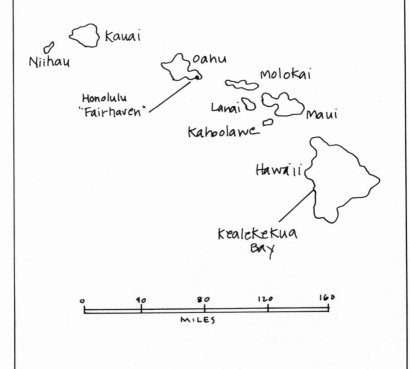

Hawaiian
(Sandwich)
Islands

Kauai

Niihau

Oahu

Molokai

Honolulu
"Fairhaven"

Lanai

Maui

Kahoolawe

Hawaii

Kealekekua
Bay

0   40   80   120   160
MILES

CHAPTER TWELVE

Learning the Tricks
of the China Trade

★

Though no American ship had then touched at Hawaii, Captain Gray and his officers knew where they were going and what to expect when they reached those "happy islands." Among the Portuguese, Hindus, Malays, Chinese, Britons, Bostonians, and assorted others in Nootka Sound's amazingly varied populace during that summer of 1788 there had been three Hawaiians. John Meares had stopped in Hawaii and taken them aboard his ship when he had returned to China from his first voyage to the Northwest Coast in 1787. Two of them, natives of the island of Maui, had been brought back across the Pacific to Vancouver Island when Meares returned in *Felice* and were there when *Washington* and, later, *Columbia* reached Nootka Sound. The other, a young and important chief named Kaiana, had gone to Macao with Meares in 1787 at his own request. Returning in a roundabout way, he sailed from Macao with William Douglas in *Iphigenia*. Douglas reached Nootka by way of Prince William Sound and Cook's River far to the north, much to Kaiana's discomfort. The chill of the near-Arctic, the shivering Hawaiian decided, held no appeal for him.

Kaiana had adopted European ways to the extent of sometimes wearing British clothing, but he never quite understood why these foreigners placed a higher value on silver and gold than they did on iron. All three of the islanders had been with their British friends long enough to acquire a reasonable fluency in English. Two of the Hawaiians had presumably been returned to their home island when Meares sailed back to Macao the second time in September of 1788. Kaiana remained at Nootka until the following month, when Douglas returned him to Kauai aboard *Iphigenia.*

Thus the Americans had had ample opportunity to familiarize themselves with these islands none of them had ever seen, not only from Kaiana and his countrymen but from Captains Douglas and Funter, who had spent a winter in Hawaii. So, after four weeks at sea, Gray knew enough to go straight to Kealakekua Bay, on the western shore of the island of Hawaii. British fur traders had come here often enough in the decade since Captain Cook had discovered the islands to make it something of a clearinghouse for passing ships.

Kaiana had moved from Kauai to Hawaii and was at Kealakekua when *Columbia* arrived. From him, first-mate Joseph Ingraham received a letter left by Ingraham's friend John B. Adamson, an officer aboard William Douglas's *Iphigenia.* Douglas had stopped off at the islands on his way from Nootka Sound to Macao, where he had picked up desperately needed supplies and returned the wandering Kaiana to his people. Adamson told of *Iphigenia's* having been attacked and of her "narrow escape of being destroyed by the natives," and warned Gray and Ingraham of the treachery of the Hawaiians. *Columbia's* supercargo, Richard S. Howe, in turn left a letter with Kaiana repeating the warning, to be handed to Captain Kendrick when *Lady Washington* reached Hawaii later in the year.

Though the Americans were not then aware of Kaiana's own complicity in the changing atmosphere of the islands, he was no longer the friendly mascot of the fur traders he had been at Nootka Sound. The Hawaiians had gained their first taste for firearms here at Kealakekua with the guns taken from the bodies of Captain Cook's slain marines. As traders followed the discoverers, more weapons found their way into the hands of the Hawaiians. Before long the islanders would often sell hogs to a passing ship only if payment were made in guns. No one knows whether or not Gray went along with that demand. On this first voyage he

Dubbed "the Great Stranger" by the awed Chinese of Macao, portly six-foot-four-inch
Kaiana sailed from his native Hawaii to the Asian city with John Meares in 1787, where he
liked to wander its crowded lanes clad in flaming feather cloak and helmet, carrying a
spear. Doubling back across the Pacific to the Northwest Coast aboard William Douglas's
Iphigenia Nubiana, Kaiana was at Nootka Sound when Kendrick and Gray reached there
in 1788. He was returned to Hawaii by Douglas in the autumn of that year, where
he quickly forgot his friendship with the Britons and took part in several attacks
on passing trading vessels.
(Special Collections Division, University of Washington Libraries)

seems never to have expressed any feelings against putting firearms into the hands of the people along the way, only regret that he lacked them when the Indians of the Northwest Coast refused any other payment for their furs. In this he was simply doing what practically every other fur trader—including Kendrick—also did. Once away from Hawaii, he would have had only nominal use for muskets.

However they were paid for, *Columbia's* crew "salted five puncheons of Pork and took on deck One hundred and fifty live hogs." Kendrick had transferred all of the supplies *Columbia* could spare to *Washington* for her own continued trading on the coast, leaving just enough for the ship to reach Hawaii. Gray had arrived short of nearly everything. So he would also have taken aboard in the islands ample stocks of Hawaii's other bounties: fruit and vegetables, along with wood and fresh water.

As long as a guard was kept to see that anchor cables were not cut in the night or squares of copper sheathing pried off the vessel's bottom by these aquatic islanders and that parties collecting wood and water went ashore heavily armed, the time would have passed pleasantly enough. Even Gray seems to have put aside his customary haste. *Columbia* tarried in Hawaii for three weeks, visiting all the main islands. Tropical warmth and ample fresh food for a change would have made it a welcome break after the somewhat spartan life of Nootka Sound. The island women must have swarmed out to the ship by the canoe load—as they often did— and the reserved but practical Gray probably accepted it. The missionary Sheldon Dibble, in his *History of the Sandwich Islands*, records disapprovingly that "many ships from the time of their arrival till the time of their sailing were crowded with naked inhabitants of both sexes, and presented a scene to which it is scarcely possible to allude."

Fortunately for our understanding of eighteenth-century Hawaii, some of the younger mariners of the day found no trouble at all in alluding with great enthusiasm to their stays in the islands. Wrote one British ship's officer, expressing an initial reservation: "Some abominable custom has deprived every woman of her foreteeth. The deuce take the inventor of such a fashion." He was quick to note, though, that despite the missing teeth and hair cropped short, he and his shipmates eagerly welcomed the island girls who swam and paddled out to the ship, which still lay three miles offshore.

"Having several hundred round us in Canoes . . . a slight beckon was a sufficient invitation as they plunged like Sea Nymphs from their Canoes, going under every canoe that obstructed their passage to the ship. No encumbrance of clothes impeded their swimming as they were in a state of nature except a small strip of Cloth applied like [the] Fig leaf worn by our Grandmother Eve. A towel absorbs the saline particles from the skin and leaves them as cool as cucumbers. No bad thing in a tropical country."

Columbia's people, still sharing their cramped quarters with the crew of *North-West America*, reluctantly weighed anchor in mid-September and started for China. It must have been an uncomfortable passage, the decks jammed with extra passengers and odorous with penned hogs. Gray, like Meares, had also acquired a Hawaiian, a new cabin boy to take the place of the murdered Marcus Lopius. Attoo, apparently a member of a chiefly family, brought aboard one of the islands' famed feather cloaks, blazing in red and gold, and a feathered helmet. First-mate Joseph Ingraham also acquired a servant, Kalehua, whom he came to call "Opie." Both of the Hawaiians would see the sights of Canton and Boston before they reached home again from around the world.

Before he sailed, Gray saw to it that some of the *Columbia* medals remained in Hawaii to commemorate the first visit to the islands by an American vessel. Only the next month Lieutenant George Mortimer, aboard the British brig *Mercury*, described them as being "of pewter, and nearly the size of a crown-piece [and] very neatly executed." He added, "The medals seem to have been left at the different places touched at by the Americans . . . to fix them in the remembrance of the natives; in my opinion a very excellent plan, and worthy the imitation of all future navigators who may be sent on voyages of discovery." Supercargo Howe also left behind on Oahu another letter to be handed to Kendrick, reiterating John Adamson's warning of the danger of attack by the islanders.

The passage from Hawaii to the China coast took nine weeks, by a track that took *Columbia* between the islands of Luzon, in the Philippines, and Formosa, the present-day Taiwan. The Americans' first sight of Cathay, long before they had glimpsed China itself, would have been the offshore fishing fleet, sometimes as many as two hundred small boats that worked in pairs with a net trailing between them. Entire families lived on them, spending most of their lives at sea. There would also have been a menacing flotilla of junks—with pirates among them in all likelihood—to worry about. Carriage guns and swivels—and the men behind them—were always kept ready on this passage in case a stranger approached too closely.

At the barren Lema Islands, still a two-day sail from Macao, it was customary for an approaching ship to fire a gun and hoist her national colors as a signal for a Chinese pilot to come aboard. Usually these pilots were old men—fishermen, for the most part—who carried with them testimonials from other captains whose ships they had taken into the river. For the customary price, in *Columbia's* case, $36—agreed upon after much haggling—he would have guided the Americans through the maze of islets and rocks that guard the mouth of Canton Bay to an anchorage in the Typa off Portuguese Macao—the Harbor of the Sea Goddess A-Ma—with its pastel European-style houses facing the sea along the Praya Grande and the spires of its thirteen churches spiking the sky behind them. Here the mandarins, Chinese government officials in their office on the Praya, would issue a "chop" permitting the American vessel to take on a new pilot and proceed up the Pearl River to Canton.

Gray went ashore at Macao and applied for the instructions from Joseph Barrell that he knew would be waiting there for him. Written only a few weeks after *Columbia* and *Washington* had left Boston and intended for whichever captain reached China first, they must have been strangely different from the orders Gray anticipated. Barrell's high optimism of that long-ago October had quickly evaporated. If the voyages had not been "prosperous," and his tone betrays his expectation that they will not have been, he would have his commanders sell the sloop at Canton or Macao. He thought they might "be able to obtain 10 or 12 Thousand Dollars for her." They should then bring home the proceeds aboard *Columbia* in Bohea and Hyson tea. If this failed to work out, perhaps they could arrange for a cargo of freight from Canton to the "East Indias" and there pick up a shipload of cotton and sugar for Boston. Barrell recommended that Kendrick and Gray trade in India through his nephew Nathaniel Barrell, Jr., though he knew not whether the young man did business in Calcutta, or 2,500 sea miles away from there in Bombay, or in some other place altogether.

Before the letter signed off, Barrell completely reversed himself and proposed first that Kendrick sell both ship and sloop, then that he sell the ship only and return in the sloop by way of the Dutch-held Spice Islands. At the Moluccas, Barrell had been told, in parts where the Dutch had no garrisons, "the natives will come off and trade with you and you may get a Load of Spices; if this could be done it would make amends for a bad voyage in the first intention."

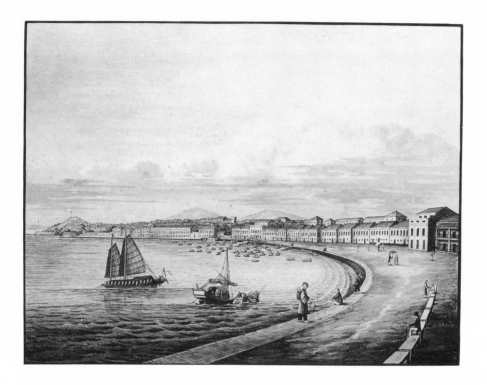

Crouching on China's doorstep but conveniently beyond the reach of Chinese
authorities, Portuguese Macao in the late eighteenth century became a magnet for
smugglers and pirates and an important waystation for ships in the China trade. The
artist Tinqua painted this view of the island city's seaside Playa Grande looking
southwest from the Chinese customs station. Here Robert Gray stopped on both
voyages to pick up mail and apply for clearance before he could take *Columbia* up
the Pearl River to Whampoa anchorage below Canton. In the distance,
Fort Bomparto lies under church-crowned Penha Hill.
(*Peabody Museum, Salem, Massachusetts*)

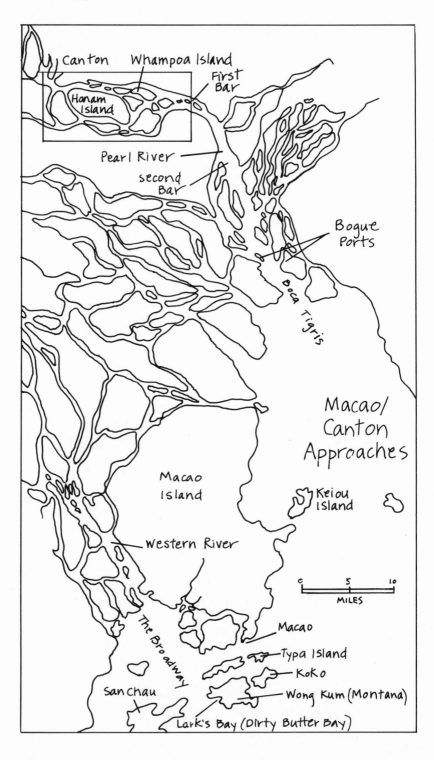

Canton Whampoa Island First Bar Honam Island Pearl River Second Bar Boque Ports Boca Tigris Macao/Canton Approaches Macao Island Keiou Island Western River The Broadway Macao Typa Island KoKo Wong Kum (Montana) San Chau Lark's Bay (Dirty Butter Bay) 0 5 10 MILES

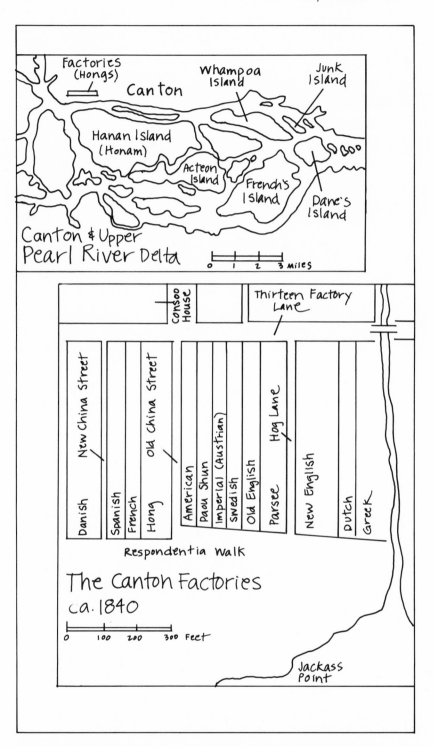

Factories (Hongs)

Canton

Whampoa Island

Junk Island

Hanan Island (Honam)

Acteon Island

French's Island

Dane's Island

Canton & Upper Pearl River Delta

0 1 2 3 miles

Consoo House

Thirteen Factory Lane

New China Street

Old China Street

Hog Lane

Danish

Spanish

French

Hong

American

Paou Shun

Imperial (Austrian)

Swedish

Old English

Parsee

New English

Dutch

Greek

Respondentia Walk

The Canton Factories

ca. 1840

0 100 200 300 Feet

Jackass Point

Barrell wrote that the captains were to "attend to these directions only as hints of what appears to be most beneficial, but in no way binding ... everything is left to your own judgement." The only firm order in the whole three pages was that whichever captain received the letter, assuming he had at least a partial cargo of furs, he was "forbid to go with either Ship or Sloop up to Canton, unless he is certain the price he can obtain will be better than at Macao."

If Gray needed an excuse for a poor return to the owners for the voyage, Barrell's pessimistic letter had just handed it to him. *Columbia*'s captain lost no time in taking advantage of the opening. "My cargo consists of seven hundred Indifferent skins," he wrote to Barrell, capitalizing the word "indifferent" as if to emphasize the poor prospects the Boston merchant had for a profit. Then, either disregarding the one definite instruction given him in Barrell's letter, or convincing himself that he could do better with his skins in Canton than at Macao, Gray headed up the river.

Past Lintin Island, the "Solitary Nail," lay the famed Bogue Forts, where the river narrowed below the city. Here *Columbia* would have backed her topsails and hove to while a pigtailed and silken-robed official examined her before she received permission to continue up the shoal-beset river to Canton. A messenger would also have been dispatched by one of the "fast boats" that plied the river, alerting the firm of Shaw and Randall that *Columbia* had arrived in China.

This was the same Major Samuel Shaw and Thomas Randall who had made their way to China five years before as supercargoes on America's first China-trade ship, *Empress of China*. Now they were both back in Canton, where they had set up a business as brokers to handle the cargoes of the Yankee ships that were already flocking to China. In addition to their mercantile interests, Shaw was the honorary American consul and Randall his vice consul.

Forty miles of the narrow, twisting Pearl River still had to be negotiated above the "Tiger's Gullet," the Bogue Forts that theoretically kept the Chinese port safe from invaders. The protection they offered was more psychological than real, for the guns were mounted on stone carriages that allowed them to fire in only one direction. Gray on board the *Columbia* would have worried more about the problem of making his way up the river, blocked by its First and Second Bars, shoals with only a few feet of water over them even at flood tide, and the inability to tack in the

Columbia's sailors would have gaped in disbelief at their first glimpse of the Whampoa anchorage and its lacy nine-story pagoda. Fifty-eight foreign ships lay there in November of 1789, when Robert Gray arrived in China—fourteen of them American vessels that had reached China ahead of him by way of the Cape of Good Hope. Here, on a quieter day, a dozen ships swing at anchor. Small Chinese craft, "chopboats" and lighters, ferry ships' officers and cargoes upriver to the hongs, or "factories," of Canton, while vigilant police boats lie alongside each of the foreign vessels to discourage smuggling.
(*Painting by Tinqua, Peabody Museum, Salem, Massachusetts*)

river's narrow confines. If the wind died, or came on from the northwest, the Chinese pilot would have had to arrange for a fleet of sampans, as many as two hundred of them, to attach their lines to the ship and tow Columbia to her anchorage at Whampoa.

Let us stand now with Captain Gray on Columbia's deck—up by the bow, as far forward as we can go—while the ship makes her slow way these last few miles toward the city her crew has so long dreamed of, and about which they know so little. The wind did die, the sails hang lifeless. The pilot has summoned a gaggle of sampans—no more than forty or fifty of them, as it turns out—and they have attached their lines to Columbia's towing bitts. The little craft bob ahead of the ship like so many tethered ducks. On each of them a boatman poises at the stern, wielding a long, springy sweep. In a curious repetitive ballet he drives the broad blade to starboard with a forward step, then with a skillful turn of the wrist to reverse the blade's angle he executes a backward step to drive it to port, over and over. The ship, heavy with barnacles and weed, painfully gains a few feet at a time against the sluggish current. The boatmen dance their strange gavotte, and with infinite slowness the muddy banks of the Pearl River slide away aft, and the green bulk of Junk Island rises in the distance.

Captain Gray, tense and expectant, has donned his best for whatever welcome awaits at Whampoa: ruffled shirt, fancy maroon waistcoat beneath a dark calf-length jacket, trousers buckled at the knees above stockinged legs, and a flat, wide-brimmed hat set squarely upon his head. Accustomed to telling others what to do and when to do it, he is ill at ease now as the Chinese pilot shouts his unintelligible directions to the sampan men, and Columbia squeaks her way over the First Bar, the final barrier to Canton's doorsill. Dead ahead lies Whampoa.

Look! What's that? Haswell, with his young eyes, has sighted the tip of the spire that gives the Pagoda Anchorage its name. Slowly, slowly, it rises over the island ahead, one level at a time until all nine gauzy, scalloped stories are visible. A building so lacy and unbelievably tall would have drawn excited gasps of wonder and disbelief from these Bostonian newcomers had another sight not unfolded at the same time—Whampoa anchorage itself. In a ragged file extending from swampy Junk Island well past four-mile-long Whampoa Island, serenely at anchor, lies what must be the world's greatest assemblage of ocean-going sailing ships.

Here is a sight to catch the breath of any Yankee seafarer. Fifty-eight vessels, each crowned by a spiderweb of masts and cocked yards, crowd Whampoa in the dying light of a November afternoon. Fourteen of them are the Americans that have made it here ahead of *Columbia*. All of these others—big *Massachusetts, Sampson, William & Henry*, James Magee's *Astrea*, Thomas Randall's *John Jay*, and nine more—have followed *Empress of China*'s track round the tip of Africa and up the warm Indian Ocean. Only *Columbia* has made her way westward from the Northwest Coast and Hawaii. The Dutch flag hangs limply above five high-sided East Indiamen. Only *Dauphin* and *King of Denmark* represent French and Danish interests here today. The rest of the fifty-eight are British "country" ships, up from Bombay and Madras, from Bengal and the steamy Malabar Coast, or with spices from Batavia in the Dutch Indies. Swirling about them all like ducklings around their mothers are the Chinese: fast boats, sampans, lighters, supply boats, customs boats—one of these last to each foreign ship, stationed there to prevent the foreign devils from smuggling any of their goods ashore.

The Chinese pilot shouts more orders, and the tethered sampans swing *Columbia* into a space near the head of the column where the other American vessels lie at anchor. Now Gray can have his ship back. The tension leaves his face as he gives his own orders and the chain of one of *Columbia*'s bower anchors clatters overboard. The ship swings into the current. Another anchor astern will hold her steady now. The captain gratefully orders his men to drop the sampans' lines, and the little boats gather them in and scuttle away like waterbugs.

Before Gray can think of unloading, *Columbia* will have to be boarded by the chief Chinese customs official at Canton, properly the Hai Kwan Pu, whose sonorous title had been corrupted by unimpressed British traders to the rather denigrating nickname "Hoppo." He would arrive at Whampoa in a barge propelled by ten rowers and flying the great Dragon Flag of China. He was customarily announced, wrote an unappreciative British captain, by a band consisting "of two brass conchs, beat like the English tabor, and three or four pipes . . . the whole forming a harmony resembling a sow-gelder's horn and the cackling of geese." The second-ranking official of the city, below only the viceroy in authority, the Hoppo traveled with "a numerous retinue, who paid him a princely respect, saluting him at his coming upon deck with a bent knee."

Known in Pidgin English as "John Tuck," the Hoppo would have been accompanied by Pinqua, the Chinese merchant selected by Shaw and

Randall to sell Columbia's cargo and procure a new one for the voyage home. The Hoppo's ceremony of "Measurement and Cumshaw," in which his assistants would run a tape from the forward part of the rudder head to the after part of the foremast, and from gunwale to gunwale just aft of the mainmast, would determine the amount to be paid into the Chinese treasury. The figure derived from these two measurements, plus nearly 100 percent for cumshaw—actually a bribe—and 50 percent for John Tuck's "opening barrier fee," 10 percent for the superintendent of the Imperial Treasury, and several lesser assessments—including one for the bookkeeping involved—usually totaled six to seven thousand dollars. Pinqua would sign a bond guaranteeing payment, and the Hoppo would in turn issue a "permit to open hatches."

Officially, this was the only duty levied on a foreign ship entering Canton and, as we have seen, could usually be kept somewhere below the disaster level by generous "sales" to the Hoppo, at a fraction of cost, of perfume and sing-sings—European clocks, music boxes, and similar mechanical wonders. Gray, like Shaw when Empress of China made her appearance in Canton, probably had neither sing-sings nor "smellum water." But he would have been alert enough, if the Hoppo did not himself suggest it, to offer a sea-otter skin or two at a price the Hoppo would find irresistible. Otter skins were in greatest demand among the wealthy of China's cold northern provinces, but even here in the temperate south, Chinese who could afford it liked to add a cape of sea-otter fur to their jackets. Now, with the Hoppo back aboard his barge and his band tootling a dissonant farewell, Gray and supercargo Howe would have hurried off to Canton, a bit anxiously perhaps, leaving Columbia to tug fitfully at her anchors and await the next act in this exotic drama.

No book or description, nothing Meares or Douglas could have told them, would have prepared these no-nonsense Yankees for their first glimpse of an Asian city. Eighteenth-century Canton—the forbidden City of Rams—must have been overwhelming. To eyes that had looked on Boston harbor as the center of the world, the river approach alone would have been a revelation. While their sampan covered those last twelve miles, before the city itself even appeared, there would have been a dizzying concourse of strange native vessels swirling about them. Six-hundred-ton seagoing junks of the Borneo and Java trades and ungainly salt junks peered eerily from the eyes painted at their bows. Gangs of near-naked men endlessly walked paddle wheels or manned great

Opening his door a crack to the *fan kwae*, or "foreign devils," the Chien Lung emperor
permitted alien merchants to operate in China only from this crowded enclave on
Canton's riverbank, screened from the forbidden City of Rams by a high wall. There in
thirteen hongs over which flew the flags of eight nations—England, France, Holland,
Denmark, Sweden, Spain, Austria, and one newcomer, the United States—ships'
captains and their supercargoes matched wits with wily Chinese merchants, paid off
greedy customs officials, and hired compradores, who supplied food and ships'
stores at the highest possible prices.
(*Peabody Museum, Salem, Massachusetts, photo by Mark Sexton*)

sweeps to propel other craft up and down the river. Rowboat-sized sampans, each with a family living aboard and a tiny cooking fire glowing aft, clogged the waterway and moored in clotted masses along the river-banks. Barbers' boats solicited customers with the clatter of scissors, symbols of their owners' profession. Fortune tellers, clothing merchants, even theatrical troupes passed their entire lives afloat in the river's swarming community. These water people were taken ashore only to die, thus sparing their family's floating domicile the ill-luck of a death at home. White and scarlet flags and red sashes tied around the muzzles of their cannon marked the mandarin boats that patrolled the busy river.

Neither *Columbia*'s captain nor her crew would be allowed to wander at will in Canton. China was still forbidden territory to the *fan kwae*, the foreign devils, and all trade with the outside world took place through one enclave outside the city walls on Canton's river bank. Here each nation doing business with the Chinese—England, France, Holland, Denmark, Sweden, Spain, Austria, and now the United States—maintained a "factory," identified by its national flag, where the chests of tea and bales of silk they had bought were stored while awaiting shipment. The river-bank before the factories was usually covered with enormous quantities of merchandise—teas, silks, cotton fabrics—in the process of being un-loaded from the chop boats to the wharves or from them into boats for transfer to the ships waiting at Whampoa for homeward-bound cargoes.

Between the river and the thirteen factories lay a fenced enclosure not more than a quarter of a mile square called the Respondentia Walk, which was reserved for the exclusive use of the foreign merchants and ship captains. They were also permitted access to a few neighboring streets. Thirteen Factory Lane, behind the "hongs," as the factories were called, and Hog Lane and Old and New China Streets, which ran between the hongs, offered "silks, satins, crapes, teas, china, preserves, lackered ware, screens, snuff boxes, chess boards, ivory carvings, and the thousand fanciful things that can be procured only in Canton." Druggists offered deer antler, dried tiger's flesh, and snake gall. The wine shops of Hog Lane catered to foreign sailors with *sam tsu*, a powerful local brew, as well as with *ho tsu*, literally "fire liquor," whose formula has been handed down in the pages of a nineteenth-century missionary quarterly called the *China Repository*. It consisted of alcohol, tobacco juice, sugar, and a touch of arsenic! The effect of this "rare dose," said the *Repository*, was awful.

The Chinese had disliked the foreign devils from their first sight of

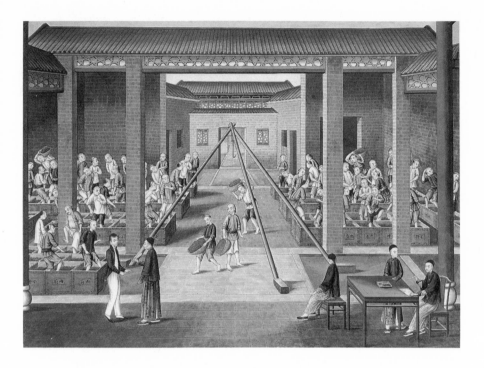

A western trader bargains for the tea that has lured him halfway around the world,
while barefoot laborers tread down the leaves in paper-covered wooden chests. A scale
will be suspended from the tripod at center to weigh the filled boxes. On her first
voyage, *Columbia* could afford only 221 chests of Bohea, a low grade of leaves picked from
plants past their prime; much of that was spoiled by saltwater leakage
before the ship reached Boston.
(Peabody Museum, Salem, Massachusetts, photo by Mark Sexton)

them. "Their clothes and their hair were red," Cantonese officials report-ed contemptuously of Dutch traders in the seventeenth century, "their bodies tall; they had blue eyes sunk deep in their heads. Their feet were one cubit and two-tenths long; and they frightened people by their strange appearance." So, from the start the Chinese had adopted an atti-tude of studied contempt toward Westerners attempting to trade with them. The Ch'ien Lung Emperor, in a haughty message to Britain's George III, implied total ignorance of the imports already reaching his people through Canton when he declared that "our Empire produces all that we ourselves need. But since our tea, rhubarb and silk seem to be necessary to the very existence of the barbarous Western peoples, we will, imitating the clemency of Heaven, who tolerates all sorts of fools on this globe, condescend to allow a limited amount of trading through the port of Canton."

The privilege of commerce with the Sons of Heaven would be hedged about with all kinds of restrictions. Eight regulations conspired to keep the Europeans and Americans unhappily cooped up in Canton's fenced trading compound. One prohibited guns, spears, and—logically enough, it appeared in Chinese minds—women. Another forbade out-ings on the river. Except for three days each month when they were permitted to visit a nearby garden and a local temple—and that "not in droves of over ten at a time"—the foreigners were forced to spend their days confined to the factories, the few streets in and around them, and the crowded recreation square that lay between the factories and the river. "Shopping is the only relief for idleness and *ennui* in Canton," wrote a disillusioned Westerner. Fortunately, he added, "the daily lounge through cool and picturesque streets is as entertaining as a museum."

Most galling of all to the lonely Western traders was the Chinese proscription of all women—extending even to their own wives—in the international compound. The Chinese justified their regulation with dev-astating logic. "If we permit your women to land and live in our coun-try," they said, "you will soon establish your homes amongst us; and by the natural growth of your families and your contented condition, you will in course of time form a permanent colony. But if we forbid your wives, your sisters, and your daughters to reside in, or even visit, the Flowery Land, we may be confident that after you have been successful in trade, you will depart for your native country and make room for another race of dissatisfied bachelors."

And the Chinese meant it. One defiant British official had his wife brought up from Macao guarded by boat loads of armed sailors. Cannon were mounted on the British factory and the sailors were installed there to protect the lady's residence. The Chinese made no effort to stop her progress to Canton, or her installation in the hong. Once she was there, however, they quietly forbade all trade with the foreign devils, whatever their nationality, withdrew their servants, and saw to it that they received no supplies. The lady was shortly shipped back to Macao. Her husband, for having injured British commerce so grievously, was replaced by an official more willing to live by the rules, however odious they might be.

Nor were the foreign devils allowed along the river where the "flower boats" lay moored. These were richly gilded and decorated vessels topped by rows of potted blossoms from which they took their name. From their windows, outlined with carved birds and flowers, painted ladies of pleasure crooned enticingly at dusk. Should a Western sailor have ventured aboard one of these floating brothels, he would likely have been found dead in the Pearl River next morning. Fortunately for ship's morale, the friendly laundry girls—"poor, honest, amphibious animals," observed an early visitor from Baltimore—who plied their soapy trade where the ships moored at Whampoa, were not under the same restriction.

With its insects and its diseases, Whampoa was "about as unhealthy a quagmire as China affords, for the immense banks of alluvial mud, left to dry at low water, give rise to pestilent, fever-breeding exhalations." No wonder it was only the lowly seamen who were left there aboard ship. "The crews, of course, have little holiday, and it is necessary that they should be kept steadily at work to debar them from mischief, but the captains while in port have a jolly time of it." Setting themselves up in Canton, "they visit and dine with each other . . . amuse themselves with the Chinese, and brag of their ships."

The Americans who remained at Whampoa aboard *Columbia* were permitted to summon a sampan and be rowed a few at a time the twelve miles upriver to Jackass Point at Canton. The boats themselves would have seemed the peak of luxury to seamen accustomed at best to the spartan confines of a ship's fo'c'sle—and at worst to a spot somewhere on the windswept deck. "For two dollars," wrote one visiting trader, "you may hire a handsome sampan with good accommodations for eight or ten people.... These boats are fitted up in the inside almost like a parlour, with a table and chairs for the passengers. They have lattices made of pearl, and covered with a neat arched roof of bamboo."

Columbia's tailor, Bartholomew Ballard, drew advance pay of "thirty Spanish Milled Dollars" on 30 January for his sampan trip to the shops of Hog Lane and Old and New China Streets. That was more than three months' pay. One can guess that it bought enough bright silks and stout nankeens for him to start his own tailoring establishment when he returned home to Boston. Seamen Otis Liscome and Abraham Waters went up to Canton on 3 February, taking fifteen dollars each. John Kendrick's son Solomon contented himself with a three-dollar advance. The next day carpenter's mate Joshua Hemingway and seaman John Cocks risked three dollars and fifteen dollars of hard-won pay on the enticements of Canton's shops. So it went during the nearly three months *Columbia* lay at anchor at Whampoa. This was not an unduly long stay. "It seems the Chinese are not very expeditious in transacting their business," observed one frustrated captain, "and there is no remedy for these delays but patience."

Robert Gray had brought *Columbia* up to the Canton anchorage on 17 November 1789. Not until 4 January were the skins—1,215 in all, according to an inventory made that day—sent ashore "in a Chop Boat guarded by 8 Men with Muskets and the Captain." Ninety-six of that total had been part of the cargo of John Meares's *North-West America*, which were turned over to Kendrick, and then to Gray, as security for the costs of carrying the captured schooner's crew to China. Gray kept twenty-four as payment for his charges.

Officially the cargo consisted of only seven hundred skins, attested by the inventory taken by Gray just before *Columbia* left Nootka Sound, and by Gray's letter of 18 December 1789 to Joseph Barrell, which mentioned the same figure. Whatever the number, there was certainly some private commerce going on, and some smuggling, though the only documentary evidence of the latter is the notation on 19 January that James Jones, a seaman who had signed on as a crewman in Canton only six weeks earlier, "carried a Skin under his Jacket to Town for Mr. Ingraham."

Columbia must also have experienced the kind of thing that John Boit would indignantly report on his 1795 fur-trading voyage in the sloop *Union*. "This day," he noted in his journal, "a powder keg was found, which I caus'd to be open'd & found contained three large Sea Otter Skins

The grand chop, certifying compliance with all of Canton's customs duties and
regulations, was issued when a foreign ship was ready to slip down the Pearl River
toward home. *Columbia*'s chop disappeared long ago, but they were all alike: Printed from
a huge hand-carved block and inscribed with an inked brush, they listed the cargo and
the names of both ship and commander. This particular one was issued to Elias Hasket
Derby's *Astrea*, Captain James Magee, which had already reached Canton by way of the
Cape of Good Hope when *Columbia* arrived from the Northwest Coast on her first voyage.
To add to Joseph Barrell's unease, *Astrea* also sped home ahead of her Boston rival,
bringing to neighboring Salem a cargo of teas, silks, and china ware valued at more
than twenty-seven thousand dollars—an enormous fortune in those times.
(*Massachusettts Historical Society*)

& five Large Tails, worth at Canton one hundred & ten Dollars . . . The Furs must have been Embezzl'd out of the Ship's Cargo."

It was becoming clear that Joseph Barrell's brave venture, even where *Columbia* was concerned, would not be a profitable one. Gray wrote to Barrell that the ship was "much out of repair and the expenses will I fear exceed your expectations . . . nor is there any American Ships here but will make bad Voyages." To be sure that his tidings of a poor showing reached Boston ahead of his own return in *Columbia*, Gray dispatched his letter in duplicate. One copy went "pr. favor Capt. Beal," whose ship *Federalist* had come up from Madras and was then loading for her return to the United States. The second, sent the next day "pr. favor Capt. Hodges," would go home on the brig *William & Henry*, which had reached Canton by way of Mauritius. Strangely, in neither letter was there so much as a hint of the ninety-six sea-otter skins entrusted to Gray by Martínez, nor was there a word about Gray's having brought the crew of *North-West America* to Macao, as payment for whose passage he had kept two dozen of the finest skins.

Gray's next letter to Barrell was not much more optimistic. The skins were "yet unsold by reason of the Mandareens putting their Chop upon them, but have great prospects of closieing the business in a few days. Mr. Randall," it continues, "has engaged six hundred chests of Bohea Tea, but cannot tell the amount of our funds untill the Cargo is sold . . ."

(Thomas Randall's account of the transaction, in a 1791 letter to Secretary of the Treasury Alexander Hamilton, was much more revealing. "As Captain Gray had no other funds, [I] advanced the necessary money to refit his ship to take in a cargo for America," wrote Randall, "and upon our estimate of the highest price I might probably obtain for the skins, found the sum would be insufficient, after defraying the expences of the ship, to load her fully with bohea teas. I then determined to fill her up on my own account on freight," he concluded piously, "in order to render the voyage as lucrative as possible for the owners." The profit, in truth, would be largely Thomas Randall's, and the tea he loaded aboard *Columbia* would wind up in the bins and warehouses of Samuel Parkman, one of Joseph Barrell's chief competitors for the pounds and shillings of Boston's housewives.)

> [We] cannot but express our anxiety for Captn. Kendrick, who has not yet arrived, [Gray said in concluding his letter to Joseph Barrell] but are in hopes of seeing him previous to our departure, and of

giveing you pleasing accounts of him on our arrival in America, untill which time we remain with every sentiment of respect to you and the Gentlemen of the Company.

your Devoted and Obedient humble Servants
R.S. Howe for himself and Robert Gray

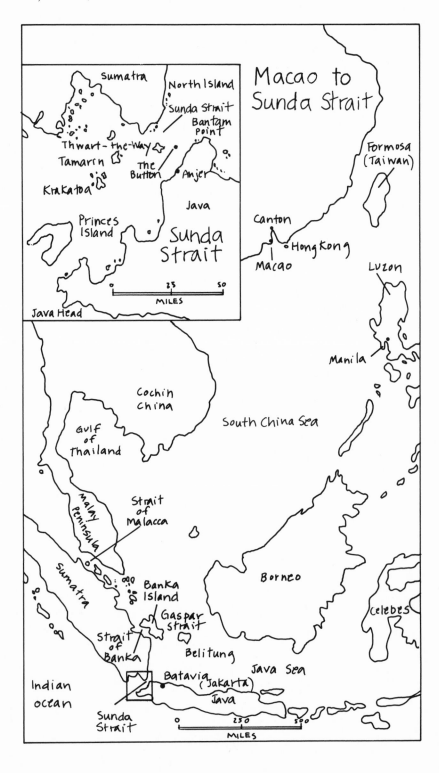

CHAPTER THIRTEEN

"Trifling Cargo" Mars
a Triumphant Homecoming

★

Gray's hope of carrying to Boston "pleasing accounts" of Kendrick's operations after Columbia's departure from the Northwest Coast suggests that the arrangement between the two captains in which they exchanged vessels was just what it appeared to be on the surface: The impatient Gray would take Columbia to China with the skins so far collected, while Kendrick remained behind with Lady Washington to gather another cargo before catching up with Columbia in Canton. Gray's and supercargo Howe's concerns for Kendrick's safety were laid to rest on 27 January, when they learned that Washington had arrived at Macao the day before.

After Columbia's departure from Clayoquot Sound in July, the sloop spent the rest of the 1789 season successfully trading along the coast of Vancouver Island to the north of Nootka Sound and then even farther north in the Queen Charlotte Islands. Believing the latter to consist of one great island, Kendrick patriotically named it for the first president. From this fur-traders' paradise, the American captain returned to Nootka for a reunion with commandant Martínez before starting for China and his rendezvous with Columbia.

Despite his close friendship with Kendrick, Martínez had at no time been fooled by the American's insistence that *Columbia* and *Washington* were on voyages of discovery. The sloop, Martínez summed up in his diary after Kendrick had departed, was "in pursuit of the fur trade, which is the principal object of all the people who come to this coast." Kendrick, in fact, must have openly admitted as much, for the Spanish commandant entrusted 137 sea-otter skins to him, to be sold in Canton when Kendrick disposed of his own furs. The money, Martínez directed, was to be turned over to the Spanish ambassador at Boston to the credit of the Crown.

Even then, however, Kendrick appears to have been thinking not of a return to Massachusetts but of another season on the Northwest Coast. He "had not completely carried out his commission," Martínez wrote of Kendrick, "and asked me if he might operate on this coast next year after a trip to the Sandwich Islands and Canton." The commandant agreed, with the provision that Kendrick always carry an official Spanish passport. Presumably it was to be issued by Martínez himself. Kendrick said he expected to do so.

Before *Washington* sailed from Nootka on the way to China, doubtless with the usual exchanges of salutes, Martínez added a second proviso: Kendrick should buy in Macao on the Spaniard's account and bring back with him "two ornaments for the Mass, and seven pairs of boots for the officers of the San Carlos and of my own ship. However," Martínez added realistically, "I believe that none of this will be done."

Now aboard *Washington* in Macao after a stop in the Sandwich Islands, which seems to have passed with no sign of hostility from the natives, Kendrick sent a letter to Gray in Canton. He was, he said, "entirely destitute of every necessary or Cash to purchase unless I dispose of my Furrs which I wish to avoid till you can inform me what the Current Price is.... Therefore request your assistance," Kendrick wrote, "together with the owners instructions how to proceed."

Gray answered promptly, sending Barrell's instructions in all their confusion and followed his first letter with two more. All were clearly intended to discourage Kendrick from bringing his furs to Canton. "We are very sorry to inform," the first advised, "that our business is attended with the greatest trouble and difficulty. Mr. Randall, to whom we consign'd the Ship, (Mr. Shaw being absent) positively declines transacting the business of your sloop ... it is by no means advisable for you to attempt coming here." Nor could he or one of his officers go to Macao, Gray explained, with the excuse that to do so might involve the ship in difficulties with the Cantonese officials. Kendrick would be advised as quickly as possible, Gray assured him, of *Columbia*'s sailing date. The ship could safely stop at Macao on its homeward passage from Canton and the two captains could meet. "The price of skins is from fifty to seventy doll[a]rs provided you smuggle which in this port is impossible, without great danger." Gray's advice a few days later is even more positive:

> The report at Canton is that you are coming up. Believe me Dear Sir you will have immeasurable difficulties to struggle against at this late period of the Seson. Not only that but you will not receive one third of the Value for your Skins and once they have you here they will oblige you to give the Skins at their own price.... If it is not too late by all means remain below. You will find Merchants in abundance to take your Cargo of[f] your hands and supply you with whatever articles you are in want of. This Dear Sir is the opinion of Captain Douglas and everyone that wishes you well.

In view of Douglas's dark suspicions that Kendrick had a hand in Martínez's seizure of his *Iphigenia*, the last sentence has a hollow ring.

In his reply, Kendrick sounds more like his old self. He is undecided whether he should sell *Washington* in Macao, as Barrell suggests, return in the ship to Boston with a cargo of tea, or go back to the Northwest Coast. In stark contrast to Gray's insistence in his letter to Barrell that his furs were few and of indifferent quality, Kendrick proudly proclaims that the opposite is true of his own cargo of skins. He has aboard, he tells Gray, "320 Whole ones, 60 Garments, and 150 pieces both large and small. As to the quality we judge it equal to any that has been brought from the Coast." Back in the habit of giving orders, Kendrick demanded an accounting of *Columbia*'s return cargo of tea, and asked whether "Cordage, and sail Cloth, is to be procured at Canton"—he had not given up his old dream of converting the sloop to a brigantine—and inquired of the price of trade goods suitable for the Northwest Coast.

He had moved from the exposed roadstead off Macao, he concluded, "to Dirty Butter Bay where we lay Securely moored—and very lonesome." This was Lark's Bay, a secluded anchorage on Wong Kum Island, a few miles southwest of Macao. Lying beyond the reach of the Chinese authorities, it had long served as a convenient haven for ships carrying opium from India, and for any other vessel whose captain was contemplating a less-than-legal approach to the markets of Canton. Now the fur traders from the Northwest Coast, particularly the Americans, would make it a favorite rendezvous. The advantages Lark's Bay offered in freedom from the prying eyes of Chinese and Portuguese customs officers were sometimes offset by the appeal the rich cargoes lying there had for the ladrones, the Chinese pirates who infested these coastal waters.

Randall, meanwhile, had succeeded in selling *Columbia*'s furs, though for far less than even he had anticipated. The Chinese merchants had toyed with him unmercifully. "At last," Randall recorded unhappily, the hong merchant "Pinqua offered to settle with me for the whole price of the skins provided I took four thousand dollars less than the price agreed upon before, observing that he would not furnish me with a passport for the ship Columbia to depart, and that I might remain in Canton 'till the next season for ought he cared. . . . I therefore from necessity was constrained to accept Pinqua['s] proposition." The furs brought a total of $21,400. Commissions, customs duties, and the expense of getting the ship back in condition ate up nearly half of this, leaving only $11,241.51 for the purchase of a return cargo. This was less than a quarter of the amount Barrell and his partners had invested in the voyage. *Columbia* would carry back to Boston no fine porcelains or bright Chinese silks—only a partial cargo of not very fancy tea. This would be Bohea, an ordinary black tea from Fukien, some three hundred miles north of Canton.

Shaw and Randall had "engaged" 600 chests of tea for *Columbia*'s homeward voyage, but the ship's scanty funds were sufficient to pay for only 221. Many of the rest, to Joseph Barrell's annoyance, would be sent home as freight by the two brokers on their own account, to not one but two of Barrell's Boston rivals. First-mate Joseph Ingraham freighted for his acquaintance, the young Boston seafarer Thomas Handasyd Perkins, seventeen and one half chests of Bohea. Ingraham had met Perkins, then supercargo of the American ship *Astrea*, in Canton. The friendship would ripen when Ingraham returned to Boston, and he became captain of Perkins's brigantine *Hope* on a venture to the Northwest Coast in competition with *Columbia*'s second voyage. The balance of *Columbia*'s cargo, put aboard by Shaw and Randall, consisted of 341 chests of tea—more than the ship would carry home for her own owners!—consigned to Boston merchant Samuel Parkman. The freight charges on this latter, as Thomas Randall had so selflessly declared, would help keep *Columbia*'s homeward cargo from being a total disaster financially.

The bill of lading of this latter shipment deserves to be recorded:

Shipped by the Grace of God, in good order and condition, by Shaw and Randall, in and upon the good ship called the Columbia, whereof is master under God for this present Voyage Robert Gray, and now riding at anchor at Whampoa, and by God's Grace bound for Boston in America, to say, 220 chests Bohea Tea, 170 Half chests, 144 quarter chests d[itt]o to be delivered unto Samuel Parkman Esquire, or his assigns, and so God send the good ship to her desired Port in Safety— Amen

By 6 February, the date of Kendrick's last letter from Macao, Robert Gray had settled *Columbia*'s accounts with Shaw and Randall. Expenses ranged from six shillings for a new teapot to forty-nine pounds ten for fifteen barrels of salt pork. Helped by the presence of *North-West America*'s returning crewmen, *Columbia*'s people had evidently by this time eaten the last of the 150 live hogs purchased in Hawaii. Four pounds ten went for a new cabin table and six chairs. There were ten pieces of silk for new flags, perhaps the only silk the voyagers would bring back to Boston, and an advance of £111 to Captain Kendrick, "agreeably to Captn. K's order on the Agent of Ship Columbia."

For his part, Randall sent home with *Columbia* a letter to Joseph Barrell apologizing for the lack of profits the voyage would show:

Had this vessel been by the Owners regularly consigned to us, we should have advised Capt. Gray to have smuggled his Skins below, and when he came up to Canton reported he had nothing but money— however ... necessity obliged him to come up with his Skins and to value upon us, being destitute of money—we are Sorry to find that we have not been able to obtain more for the Cargo of the Columbia, which probably might have been done had we hazarded the risque of Smuggling the Skins at Whampoa.... We have often repented our accepting this consignment on the part of Capt. Gray and Mr. Howe as the Ship being without funds in ready money—involved us in heavy advances in Cash at a time when the State of trade here did not well admit of it.

One of *Columbia*'s final expenses was recorded as three pounds for "Cumshaw's for Grand Chop." Such cumshaws—sometimes small bribes, sometimes not so small—greased the way for nearly every transaction in old Canton. The grand chop was a huge and handsome document. It was always the same, printed in black and red from a carved woodblock

framed by a border of dragons and flying phoenixes. Spaces had been left
for insertion of the vessel's name and a listing of the number of crew
members, her "great guns," shot, swords, and muskets, and the quantity
of "fire-physic"—gunpowder—aboard. Handed out by the Hoppo, the
grand chop certified that all duties and taxes had been paid and that the
vessel was free to leave China:

> Chung, filling the office of Hoppo by Imperial edict, issues this in
> obedience to the Emperor's will. When Western Ocean ships have
> been measured, paid their duties, and departed, should bad winds and
> water drive them to the shores of another part of the Empire, if it is
> found that they possess this sealed discharge, they must be allowed to
> continue their voyage without delay or opposition. Which is on
> record.
>
> Now the foreign merchant ship Columbia, having loaded with
> goods, goes to the Flowery Flag Country, there to manage her busi-
> ness. . . . As she is now departing, this is given as a clearance into the
> hands of the said merchant to grasp and hold fast, so that, should he
> meet with any other customs house, he must not be detained. Military
> stations to which it may be shown must also allow the vessel to pass
> without delay, and not persuade her to remain and trade so they may
> benefit by levying charges and duties. Should they act otherwise, it
> will give rise to trouble and difficulties.
>
> According to old regulations, the guns, ammunition, and other
> weapons she carries for her defense are listed. An unnecessary number
> is not allowed, nor has she dared take on board contraband articles.
> Should it be discovered that these rules were broken, this permission
> to sail would assuredly not have been granted.
>
> Respectfully examine this and depart.

When the Hoppo had affixed his seal to the grand chop, *Columbia* was
free to start the return trip to Boston. A pilot had already been hired and,
on 12 February, just under three months since she arrived in China, the
ship caught a fair tide and headed out into the river. As she got under
way, Wyqua, the comprador through whom all of *Columbia*'s provisions
had been procured, descended to his sampan. "These compradores,"
wrote one early visitor sarcastically, "are respectable; they open an account, supply the vessel with fresh provisions, never cheat when they
have the slightest fear of detection, and take the pigs ashore occasionally,
squeeze the young ones breathless, and then bring them on board to

show that they died natural deaths." Now in appreciation of all the profits he had extracted from *Columbia*'s visit to Canton, Wyqua lighted a great mass of firecrackers hung out over the water on a long bamboo pole. The deafening crackle was intended to "awaken the gods to the vessel's departure and give her good wind and water." Firing a farewell salute in response, *Columbia* began her careful descent of the shallow, winding river to the Bogue Forts.

Gray, and New York-bound Thomas Randall only a couple of days after him, barely escaped Canton ahead of the Chinese New Year celebration. Their ships would have been held up by the Chinese over the long holiday, "during which time the public offices are shut, and no business transacted for near three weeks." Canton's merchants, observed an American visitor, "betake themselves to one of the flower boats, not always with the most virtuous female society, and leave the city for a fortnight. They go far up the stream, fire shooting crackers, feed on delicacies, overrun with good humor, and get very drunk before bedtime . . ."

In no mood to tarry, Gray put in at Macao only long enough to receive his clearance from the Portuguese customs house, but despite his promise he made no effort to stop at Dirty Butter Bay, only ten or twelve miles beyond, where Kendrick waited aboard *Lady Washington*. It is difficult to believe other than that Robert Gray saw a God-sent opportunity to race home ahead of Kendrick, and grabbed it. This was no time to look for complications; Kendrick could take care of himself. "We left Captn. Kendrick in a harbour below Macao," Gray and supercargo Howe would tell Barrell, "but a gale of wind prevented our seeing him. By what we could collect he intends returning on the coast."

Columbia now spread her sails before the dying northeast monsoon, moving down the South China Sea with her long, graceful homeward-bound pennant streaming from the masthead. This would be a nerve-wracking passage. It always was in those days. Fleets of Malay pirates cruised there in their swift praus, ready to pounce on any ship unlucky enough to become becalmed or to ground on one of the fanged reefs that lay between Borneo and Cochin China. *Columbia* would have to pass through Gaspar Strait or the Strait of Banka. One was as poor a bargain as the other. Then she would slip into the Java Sea, with probably a stop for provisions at Anjer. This was the place, wrote novelist Joseph Hergesheimer in his novel *Java Head*, where "the land breeze, fragrant with clove buds and cinnamon, came off to the ship like a vaporous dusk; and in the blazing sunlight of morning, the Anjer sampans swarmed out with a shrill chatter of brilliant birds, monkeys and naked brown humanity, piled high with dark green oranges and limes and mangosteen."

Sunda Strait, with Sumatra to starboard and Java to port, lay just ahead, with its treacherous currents and uncharted rocks that rose abruptly from the sea floor, and its gaunt mid-channel islands known to Western mariners as "The Button," "Thwart-the-Way," and "the Cap." Beyond these lay grim Krakatoa, its volcanic cone thrusting upward from the greasy waves. To Gray and his fellow captains, Krakatoa was merely a brick lying in the garden path, something one had to go around. Nearly a century would pass before that terrible day in 1883 when the craggy little island exploded, launching waves that swept thirty-six thousand people to their deaths and flinging aloft a girdle of volcanic dust that encircled the earth.

Finally they passed big, crab-claw-shaped Panaitan, or Princes, Island. "Thank God we are clear of Sunda Straits," reads the journal of one Boston shipmaster. " 'Tis surprising to see the joy depicted on every one's countenance at getting clear of these horrid straits." Then, as the dark, stony bulk of Java Head slipped below the horizon behind her, Columbia could enjoy a respite from South Asia's reef-fanged waters. Worn sails bellied gently to the northeast monsoon as the helmsman swung the ship due south to begin the long haul across the Indian Ocean. Homesick sailors would have watched happily as the vessel settled into a steady stride and a fine roll of white water curled from her bluff bow. This would be the "flying-fish weather" the chanteymen sang of, the easy passage through soft tropical seas that every deepwater mariner longs for. "I'm a flying-fish sailor, just in from Canton. Oh way-oh! Blow the man down."

With luck, theirs could now be an uninterrupted reach south and then west before the southeast trade winds, clear across this vast, wet wilderness to Africa, with rarely the need to hand a sail until they fetched Madagascar. There they could pick up the great Agulhas Current that would help shove Columbia south and westward around the stormy Cape of Good Hope and out into the Atlantic for the final run home. The ship probably stopped for wood and water at Simonstown by the Cape, or at Mauritius, the "Isle of France." She was at St. Helena by 16 June. Less than two months later, on 9 August 1790, Columbia passed Castle Island outside Boston Harbor and became the first vessel to have carried the new Stars and Stripes around the world. She had sailed twice the circumference of the earth—nearly fifty thousand miles—in the two years, eleven months, and nine days she had been away from Boston.

Profit or no, the Massachusetts capital was ecstatic. "On the Columbia's arriving opposite the Castle," Boston's *Columbian Centinel* reported, "she saluted the flag of the United States with 13 guns; which was immediately returned therefrom—and on coming to her moorings in the harbour fired a federal salute-which a great concourse of citizens assembled on the several wharfs, returned with three huzzas, and a hearty welcome."

For Boston's eighteen thousand or so residents, Gray and his crew were possessed of the same "right stuff" as later heroes Admiral Dewey, Lindbergh, and the Apollo astronauts. Before the day had ended, excited Bostonians had thronged the city's narrow streets to watch Gray marching at the head of the ship's company to the State House, to be received by Governor John Hancock. With the captain and first-mate Joseph Ingraham were the Sandwich Islands boys each had brought back to Boston. Attoo, marching alongside Captain Gray, was resplendent in his feather cloak "of golden suns set in flaming scarlet, that came halfway down his brown legs," wrote historian Samuel Eliot Morison. "Crested with a gorgeous feather helmet shaped like a Greek warrior's, this young Hawaiian moved up State Street like a living flame." Once the adulation died down, though, both Attoo and Opie would tire of the wonders of Boston and return as quickly as they could to the Pacific.

The day closed on an equally festive but much more patrician note. Crusty, gout-bedeviled Hancock entertained Gray, his officers, and *Columbia*'s owners in his great dining room where sixty could be seated at a time. As the ailing governor had himself pushed about the room in a wheelchair, Gray described his adventures—how he had struggled around Cape Horn despite the perils of icebergs, fierce storms, and darkness, and how he had endured Indian attack and the iniquities of the rascally Chinese. He might even have hinted to this all-male audience of the uninhibited pleasures of the Sandwich Isles, where no American ship had called before.

Sober assessments for the Bostonians as well as for the young Hawaiians took the place of that initial jubilation in the days that followed. As if *Columbia*'s "trifling cargo," as Barrell contemptuously called it, was not skimpy enough already, the ship had arrived at Boston to find that the federal government was now "organized under the new Constitution of 1789," which had led to heavy customs duties, particularly on tea. Also, some of the cargo had been damaged by saltwater during the voyage. Sold at auction, it brought only $304, a fraction of what it had cost in Canton. The balance would have sold well—tea was as essential as bread to an eighteenth-century Bostonian—but that would still be precious little return for Barrell and company's $49,000.

Some years later, Barrell indicated that he had received a letter of explanation from Kendrick for the voyage's poor showing when *Columbia* returned to Boston. Kendrick could hardly have been so casual as not to offer his employer some reason for the change of command between *Columbia* and *Washington* and for the financial failure of the whole endeavor. But his explanation, to whatever effect, would have counted for little at that moment. Someone had to be given the blame. Gray, and Haswell, if anyone asked him, would have lost no opportunity to fill Barrell's ears with the failings and follies of their absent commander. And to be sure, Kendrick had earned a great deal of what was being said about him.

Precocious young John Quincy Adams, then just twenty, was in Boston that eventful Monday. He wrote to his mother, Abigail, (John Adams Senior was then serving in London as the first United States Ambassador to Great Britain) that the

> principal topic of conversation this week has been the arrival of the Columbia from an expedition which has carried her around the world. The adventurers after having their expectations raised to the highest pitch, were utterly disappointed, and instead of the immense profits upon which they had calculated, will scarcely have their outsets refunded to them. This failure has given universal astonishment and is wholly attributed to the Captain, whose reputation now remains suspended between the qualifications of egregious knavery and of unpardonable stupidity.

General Henry Jackson commented in another letter that "the concerned in that enterprise have *sunk 50 per cent* of their capital. This is a heavy disappointment for them, as they had calculated every owner to make an independent fortune."

Young John Hoskins, Kendrick's friend in Joseph Barrell's counting house, probably summed up the situation to that date as fairly as anyone:

> Captain Kendrick's conduct was much blamed by the officers of the Columbia, who say he had it in contemplation to cheat the Owners

out of what property he has in his hands; and would have done out of all had they not rescued it.—that he never had cruiz'd the coast; and appear'd not to have the owner's interest at heart but only to gratify his own pleasures.

This much must be acknowledged: that Captain Kendrick had two good vessels on the coast. (and if his enemies may be believed,) had it in his power to make both for himself and the Owners a very handsome fortune; but he let those golden opportunities pass . . . but no Knavery has at present open'd. To be sure, the man was by no means calculated for the charge of such an expedition: but a better man might have done worse.

One thing, however, had been accomplished handsomely. Whatever the balance sheet said, and whoever got the blame, *Columbia*'s brave venture had launched the nation on a course that would not end until Yankee seafarers dominated the entire Pacific and the United States spanned its continent from one ocean to the other.

CHAPTER FOURTEEN

"Departed This Life Our Dear Freind Nancy the Goat"

★

"Mr. Barrell, I am informed, is not discouraged," John Quincy Adams wrote to his mother in London, "but intends to make the experiment once more, and if he should not meet with anybody disposed to second him, they say he will undertake it at his single risk and expense."

Boston talked of little else that summer save *Columbia's* voyage and the peccadillos of the absent Captain Kendrick. Young John Hoskins, clerking in Joseph Barrell's counting house, must have overheard many an hour of postmortem discussion among Gray, his officers, and their employers. They would have met in Barrell's office, which was decorated now with the souvenirs Gray had brought back from New Albion: "a hat, cloak, and mantle of the natives, several pieces of cloth manufactured there from the bark of trees, and other natural and artificial curiosities of that part of America."

Alongside these dun-colored relics flamed the vivid reds and golds of the great feathered helmet and sweeping cloak the young Sandwich Islander Attoo had worn on his triumphant march up State Street only a few weeks before. Both of these pieces had been built up a thumbnail-size piece at a time, with feathers torn from tiny birds that had darted like flames through the dim rain forests of the islands.

Attoo would leave this startling garb behind when he returned to his island home on *Columbia*'s second round-the-world voyage. Joseph Barrell, ever the patriot—and not averse, one guesses, to currying a little favor in high places—would later send the two curios with his compliments to George Washington in Philadelphia. He had already sent the general one of the silver medals struck to honor the first voyage. The hero of the Revolution, now his nation's first president, passed the cape and helmet on to his friend the artist Charles Willson Peale for preservation in Peale's museum of natural history. Sadly, the cloak has long since crumbled away, but that regal headpiece survives. A little timeworn now but still bright enough to evoke the drama of that long-ago march up State Street, it survives to this day in the collection of Harvard University's Peabody Museum of Archaeology and Ethnology.

But now the bows and arrows and that glorious cloak and helmet gazed down on a different scene. Even in the cool gloom of Barrell's counting house, where the Boston merchant and his partners huddled with Robert Gray and *Columbia*'s officers, those incandescent feathers would have cast a subtle spell. Along with their condemnation of Kendrick's behavior, Hoskins wrote, Gray and his people "gave such flattering accounts of the coasts; together with such noble prospects as were to be deriv'd from the quantity of skins, which with a little exertion are to be procur'd: at the same time promising from their abilities to produce a golden harvest; that the Owners notwithstanding the failure of the former voyage were again induced to fit the ship . . ."

Most of the investors were swayed by Gray's rhetoric. The New Yorker John Marsden Pintard, who had plunged into stock speculation and would become a bankrupt within two years, dropped out. So did John Derby of Salem. The rest, however, stayed on. The enterprise now rested entirely in Boston hands, with a total investment of $25,016, about half that of the first voyage. But that would be enough, since they already had their ship. Samuel Brown increased his stake in the venture by adding one more of the fourteen shares to the two he originally held. Joseph Barrell boosted his investment from four to five shares. Crowell Hatch and the Bulfinch family continued their two shares each, though now the latter appeared in the name of Dr. Thomas instead of that of his son Charles. The remaining two shares brought three entirely new names into the partnership. The only surviving document listing them, along with the four original owners who held onto their shares for the second voyage, reads simply "R. Gray, Davenport and McLean, 2/14ths." Gray's partners, if such they were, were apparently the "victualling merchants" Rufus Davenport and John McLean, who maintained a store dealing in West-India goods on Boston's Orange Street.

In the light of accusations that would later be made of shady dealings and illicit sales of furs at Canton by not one but three people—Hoskins, Kendrick, and John Howel, the first two of whom knew Gray long and intimately—one may be excused for wondering where the captain secured even a fraction of the $3,574 necessary to buy into the ownership of *Columbia's* second voyage. Gray's salary of three pounds twelve a month during the first voyage, less advances, had netted him barely more than one hundred pounds, about four hundred dollars, when *Columbia* reached Boston again.

There would have been little Barrell could do, however, other than give command of this new enterprise to Gray. He had brought *Columbia* safely if not profitably home, and he knew the problems of trading in China and on the Northwest Coast. *Columbia's* first mate, Joseph Ingraham, who might have been a candidate, had been snapped up by rival Boston merchant Thomas Handasyd Perkins to command the little seventy-ton brigantine *Hope* out to the Northwest Coast. She would sail a full two weeks ahead of *Columbia.* Losing Ingraham so angered Barrell that he issued a mean-spirited order that no letters were to be carried from Boston aboard *Columbia* to anyone on the *Hope.* Robert Haswell was probably adjudged not yet mature enough for the responsibility of commanding *Columbia*—he was then only twenty-one—though he later became captain of a sloop Gray built on the Northwest Coast and acquitted himself well. For now, though, it was Gray or no one.

Barrell was obviously nervous. Perhaps he had seen that inventory of sea-otter furs sent ashore by Gray at Canton: 1,215 skins plus one taken ashore under a seaman's jacket for Mr. Ingraham. That document is preserved to this day among Barrell's records of the first voyage, along with the inventory taken before *Columbia* left the Northwest Coast and Gray's letter from Canton to Joseph Barrell. Both of the latter declare *Columbia's* cargo as only seven hundred skins.

The truth of the matter would have pained Barrell even more deeply. In a letter written to Secretary of the Treasury Alexander Hamilton,

Thomas Randall in 1791, after his return to New York from China, wrote a detailed account of his handling of the sale of *Columbia*'s furs to the Chinese. The ship arrived in Canton, Randall informed Hamilton, not with 700, nor even with 1,215 skins, but "with about fifteen hundred sea Otter skins of various sizes and quality . . ." Randall, after many difficulties with the Chinese, sold *Columbia*'s cargo to the hong merchant Pinqua for $21,400. This, one surmises, could only have been the "official" cargo of 700 skins, which thus brought thirty dollars each, a believable figure, though far below the fifty to seventy dollars quoted by Gray to Kendrick as the going price at Canton only a few weeks earlier. It would make little sense to suggest that, even in that depressed time, the entire 1,500 skins could have fetched only $21,400—an average of only about fifteen dollars each. What happened to the other seven or eight hundred skins, and who pocketed the proceeds, can only be guessed at.

Barrell's principal salve for his growing unease was to replace Richard Howe, who had been *Columbia*'s supercargo the first time around, with his young and trusted clerk John Hoskins. Before the Revolution Hoskins's father, William, had been the senior member of one of Boston's most respected and prosperous shipowning and importing firms. During the war the elder Hoskins had carried out assignments for the Continental Congress with great credit to himself. William Hoskins died in 1786, when John was eighteen. Barrell took the son of his old friend into his own home and later into his business.

Now, looking for a way to allay his misgivings, Barrell put the twenty-one-year-old Hoskins in charge of all of the voyage's commercial endeavors. The choice proved to be a wise one, though it was no favor where young Hoskins was concerned. Considering him to be Barrell's "narker," a spy and a challenge to his integrity, Gray lost no opportunity to embarrass Hoskins and to make it as difficult as possible for him to keep the accounts Barrell expected. The attitude of Gray and his officers, Hoskins angrily reported in a letter to his employer from the Northwest Coast, was "Damn Jo. Barrell he does not know how to keep books or anything else, except his damn mean ways, of setting his damn clerks to overlook people . . ." In the long run, Barrell must have come to regret not his appointment of Hoskins but his handling of the younger man's assignment. He had given his young supercargo an awesome responsibility to be carried out in the company of men older and far more experienced than he. But he had failed to couple the responsibility with the authority

Hoskins would need to carry it out. This would seriously limit Hoskins's usefulness and become an impediment to the good business procedures Barrell demanded.

There might also have been a hint of concern in the Boston merchant's mind about Shaw and Randall and their handling of the ship's business at Canton. Randall had been forced to accept an absurdly low price from the Chinese for *Columbia*'s furs—enough to buy only a partial cargo of tea for the return trip to Boston. And if this were not enough, Barrell must have fumed at the idea that the cargo space thus made available had been taken up by tea consigned to his chief rivals in Boston, to their profit as well as Thomas Randall's, but precious little to his.

The cure for all this, Barrell decided, was to apply a touch of poetic justice. Randall himself had written that the skins would have brought more had they been sold in Macao rather than in Canton. Barrell would have Gray do just that. Instead of staying with Randall, Barrell decided to name John McIntyre, a longtime resident of Macao, as the broker who would handle *Columbia*'s second cargo. McIntyre's reputation, in fact, was not exactly unblemished. Ingraham had had dealings with him while *Columbia* had been tied up in Canton the first time around—of what kind one can only guess—and later would have sad experiences with him on his voyage in the *Hope*.

Barrell and his partners were determined to get *Columbia* out of Boston promptly, and that no time would be wasted on her way to the Northwest Coast. The ship had returned to the city on 9 August 1790. By 15 September she had been caulked and resheathed with copper and was ready for sea. For this voyage, unlike the first, we have a complete record of the work that was done on *Columbia* and the stores aboard—a fascinating look at the complexity of handling a sailing ship in eighteenth-century America.

John Derby, though no longer a shareholder, sold Joseph Barrell the extra guns he felt were necessary—probably taken from one of his father's no-longer-active privateers. A pair of four-pounders, two three-pounders, and four swivels cost the partners twenty-two pounds sixteen shillings. They paid D. Hathorne, great uncle of Nathaniel Hawthorne, eight shillings to freight them down from Salem.

For the rest, as they had for *Columbia*'s first voyage, nearly every merchant in Boston, it seems, had a hand in sending her off the second time. There would be no doctor aboard, so John Joy provided a medicine chest for something over ten pounds. Enoch James provided four whale irons and a shark hook and chain. Ten of Boston's ship chandlers had to be called upon to round up forty-four iron-bound water casks. Seventy-two pounds of Joseph Barrell's expensive Bohea tea would leave Boston, along with thirteen and a half tons of ship's bread, three-quarters of a ton of gunpowder, 135 barrels of salt beef, and five hundred pounds of cheese. Lewis Hayt was called on for twenty barrels of flour and three kegs of spruce essence, the latter of which, when mixed with water, molasses, and yeast, would make the unpalatable spruce beer that many ships of those days relied on—usually, with little or no success—to prevent scurvy among the crew.

With the status of *Lady Washington* in doubt—Barrell would hardly have depended on having her back—the partners took a leaf from the British fur trader John Meares. At their order, shipwright Thomas Thacker put aboard *Columbia* the frames and some of the planking for a sloop, to be built as *North-West America* had been, on the coast. Her name, Barrell instructed, would be *Nootka*. Boston chandler Shippie Townsend furnished blocks for the new sloop's rigging, and Benjamin Cushing the masts and yards.

The trade-goods fiasco of the previous voyage would not be repeated. *Columbia* had returned to Boston probably half the oddments the merchants had hoped would entice furs from the Indians. All of the Jews' harps came back, all of the butcher's knives, most of the egg slicers, and nearly all of the 461 looking glasses. The Indians had scorned pepper boxes and dippers, pewter porringers and combs. Despite its dismal record, much of this trading truck would go back for a second try. But this time, however, there would also be copper, 267 sheets of it, supplied by John Pintard and Herman Brimmer. Brimmer also put aboard blue and green duffle, a coarse woolen cloth, and a quantity of scarlet coating. Solomon Cotton forged for *Columbia*'s owners 4,261 half-pound "chissels." There would be no scruples this time, either, about trading guns to the Indians or to the Sandwich Islanders, if that was what they insisted on for furs or hogs. In addition to whatever arms remained aboard *Columbia* from the previous voyage, 125 old muskets, 100 of them purchased from the government for twelve shillings apiece, were put in working order and sent aboard. In all, the partners invested more than six thousand dollars in those trade goods that experience had taught Gray and Haswell the Indians would accept.

Amateur artist George Davidson appeared on the crew roster of *Columbia*'s second voyage simply as "painter." Probably he was exactly that—the *ship's* painter. Nevertheless, in his spare time he created one of the finest visual records in existence of an early American voyage, a gallery of naive but informative renderings that were handed down in the family of Robert Gray. Several appear in this book. Davidson seems later to have risen to become a captain himself, commanding at least one vessel in the China trade. He was lost when his ship, *Rover*, disappeared at sea in 1801.

(*Self-portrait, The Concord Antiquarian Museum, Concord, Massachusetts*)

Columbia was completely loaded by 25 September, and was ready for sea. In addition to Captain Gray and Robert Haswell, who was now the ship's first officer, four of *Columbia*'s complement were veterans of the first voyage. Only one of these, seaman Andrew Newell, had started out from Boston. Gray's cabin boy, Attoo, would return aboard *Columbia* to his native Hawaii, and seaman Joseph Barnes had signed on in Canton. The fourth, of course, was Nancy the goat, who had spent the past six weeks contentedly browsing some grassy backlot in Boston.

The rest of the crew embraced the usual specialties of a vessel setting out for a years-long voyage: John Ames and Benjamin Popkins, armorers; Bartlet Pease, cooper; Thomas Nichols, the captain's tailor; Obadiah Weston, sailmaker; and Thomas Truman, the ship's cook. Samuel Yendell (who had helped build the U.S.S. *Constitution*), and Nathan Dewley, the carpenter and carpenter's mate, would be responsible, in addition to making repairs at sea, for construction of the new sloop after *Columbia* reached the Northwest Coast. By a happy circumstance the ship's twenty-two-year-old painter, George Davidson, also fancied himself an artist. His naive but information-packed paintings of "Columbia Attacked by Indians," and "The Launching of the Sloop Adventure," as Gray renamed the *Nootka*, are among the few on-the-scene renderings of Northwest Coast fur-trading days in existence. In all, thirty-one men, including the captain, and one boy, Samuel Homer, who was probably not more than eleven or twelve at the time, made up the ship's complement.

The day before *Columbia* was to sail, Joseph Barrell handed Robert Gray a sheaf of paper embodying his detailed instructions for the voyage. One can imagine him as he wrote it, his serious, patrician face clouded by doubts about the whole affair. Throughout the lengthy and repetitious document, Barrell's nervousness is apparent. Much of it must have infuriated Robert Gray. Paying him a weak compliment, Barrell told his captain that "we place such confidence in you as to give you command." When it came to Hoskins's role, though, Barrell in the next sentence clearly showed who he thought he could trust. "In all matters of traffic on the northwest coast of America, China, or elsewhere," he ordered, "you will consult with Mr. John Hoskins . . . in whose industry, integrity, and honor we place the utmost confidence; we therefore expect the most perfect harmony to subsist between you, your officers, and him." If Gray were to send the sloop to China at any time, Barrell instructed, "we would have Mr. Hoskins go with her, and he will apply to such persons as will assist him in disposing of the furs to the best advantage ..." Nor did Gray escape without a lecture:

> We hope it is needless to remind you that you are now accountable for the conduct of the present voyage. You have seen and heard the pointed manner in which every one condemns the conduct of the last; if you have a proper spirit for this enterprise, or any regard for your own honor and rising reputation, or have respect to the sea letters with which the President of the United States has honored and indulged you, we trust you will doubly exert yourself to prevent such reflections in the future.

After such a vote of no confidence, Gray's distaste for Hoskins's presence aboard comes as no surprise.

Barrell touched every base. "We expect you do not stop until you reach the Falkland Islands; nor then a moment longer than is absolutely necessary." And about illicit private trade: "You will constantly bear in mind the absolute prohibition against every sort of traffic, or receiving any presents on this voyage; for, be assured, the owners will treat every breach of the contract in this particular with the utmost severity." Barrell also thought it important "to enjoin system, good order, prudence, and economy, which, with a tender treatment of the men under your command, will show you to be a father to your crew ..."

Barrell was still not through. A final inducement to honest and good business practices was thrown in. "For your encouragement, and that of your officers," he wrote, "we engage to allow you five percent.; to the first mate, one and one-half per cent.; to the third mate, one half per cent. upon the sales of the cargo in Boston." Now, like a spanked schoolboy torn between resolve and rebellion, Robert Gray was turned loose with a final admonition. "if the wind is fair on the morrow, we desire and expect you will embrace it and proceed on the voyage."

Despite Barrell's heartfelt desire and expectation, a leak in the stern and then contrary winds delayed *Columbia*'s departure until 1 October 1790, three years to the day since she had cleared Boston on her first voyage. The crossing to the Cape Verde Islands was uneventful. Sixteen-year-old fifth mate John Boit thought *Columbia* "sails dull, but is a fine sea boat," but Gray still managed to clip ten days from Kendrick's time in getting there. And true to his instructions, in the longitude of São Tiago, Gray swung his course southward toward Cape Horn. "It had been Captain Gray's intention of stopping at this last mentioned island," John

Hoskins wrote in his new journal, "but not being in any real want of any thing; and loath to loose the advantage of so fine a breeze; he could not be induced to waste the time."

There were now, in addition to the "official" ship's log, of which only the first volume has been preserved in its entirety, at least three journals recording the day-to-day events of *Columbia*'s second circumnavigation. Only one, kept by 16-year-old John Boit, the ship's fifth mate, covers the whole voyage. Sadly, it is the least informative. John Hoskins's literate and remarkably detailed journal, for an unknown reason, ends in mid-sentence on 29 March 1792, when the voyage still had more than a year to go. First mate Robert Haswell, whose earlier fragmentary journal provides our only account of *Columbia*'s first voyage, apparently kept a complete record of the second. Only the second volume, which begins on 14 August 1791, nearly a year after the ship left Boston, remains in existence.

Once again, little occurred to mark the passage to the Falklands. Hoskins talks of the pleasant custom, when vessels were sailing in the same direction, of exchanging visits at sea. On 11 November, *Columbia* sighted the whale ship *Aurora* of Bristol, also bound for Cape Horn. Captain Parker Butler came on board that afternoon. "He having lost his jib boom," Hoskins noted, "we supplied him with a spare topgallant mast to make a new one." The visits continued over several days as the two ships made their way south. On the fourteenth, Hoskins "was acompanied by Mr. Haswell on board the Aurora, w[h]ere we spent the day, the next Captain Butler honored us with a visit."

There were the usual squalls—one carried away *Columbia*'s fore and main topgallant masts, forcing her to heave to for three days so repairs could be made. Near Cabo Blanco, Gray fell into his old habit of "pursevearing in with the Land," and let the ship be driven so far inshore that she was nearly lost. In short, these were the hazards that square-rig sailors expected to encounter—and to survive.

As they neared the Falklands, *Columbia*'s seamen countered boredom by trolling for albatross, blissfully unaware of the ill luck it was supposed to bring. Trailing baited fishhooks behind the ship, they caught sixteen of these great sea wanderers one day and twelve the next. The largest measured twelve feet ten inches from wingtip to wingtip. The birds provided a welcome change to men who had lived for months on salted meat. "Though this bird is considered as coarse unsavory food; by those whose living has been more delicate," Hoskins confided to his journal, "yet by us, to whom fresh meat is a luxury, it was deem'd a noble acquisition, and eat both by ourselves and the people"—he was distinguishing here between the ship's officers and the sailors—"with great avidity . . . it eats exceedingly well, no ways fishy or unpallatable."

Lest some reader smile knowingly at young Hoskins's enthusiasm for so inelegant a meal as albatross, it might be worthwhile to ask just how bad the food aboard an eighteenth-century square-rigger really was. "Bread," actually hard, unsalted biscuit, had been put aboard by the ton —three and a half tons, to be exact. By the time *Columbia* had been at sea for a few months it would have become mostly stomach-turning gray shards and dead weevils. The water by now would have been so foul and slimy that it could be choked down only with the addition of a tot of rum. And there was good reason to call the daily boiled meat "salt horse." The victuallers who furnished ships' stores in those days were considered unprincipled thieves who would throw anything they could get away with into a cask and call it beef. A hoof or a horseshoe at the bottom of a barrel was welcome evidence that the seamen hadn't just eaten something even worse.

Whatever butter Barrell and company had put aboard back there in Boston would long ago have vanished or would have turned inedibly rancid by now and be fit only to slather on some of the ship's creaking gear in lieu of a better lubricant. So the sailors would fall glumly back on "slush" to help them choke down their meals. This was the scum of ugly yellowish fat that rose to the surface of the cook's "steeping tub" when salt meat was boiling. Following Captain James Cook's perceptive custom, most captains forbade their crews this delicacy, for they believed that it contributed to the ravages of scurvy. But the men would still wheedle it away from the cook or even promise him a few shillings at the end of the voyage for a steady supply.

And the cook himself? Chances are he totally lacked skills and so was utterly useless anywhere else on board. Or he had only one leg or one arm, or was too far gone in the head to follow an order on deck. But the cook's responsibilities were depressingly few. A *Sailor's Companion*, printed in London in 1740, listed them thus for the Royal Navy:

    1. He is to take upon him the Care of the Meat in the Steeping-tub.

    2. In stormy Weather, he is to preserve it from being lost.

    3. He is to boil the Provisions, and deliver them out to the men.

And that was all the cook had to do or to know. Little wonder that

Ashore in the Falkland Islands on his second voyage, Robert Gray supervises the filling of water casks before turning *Columbia* westward for another rounding of stormy Cape Horn. Behind Gray, Nancy the goat rests in the shade of a tent. In a fortnight here, crewmen careened and caulked the ship, while hunting parties added several hundred ducks and geese and a number of wild hogs to the galley stores. Though it was January, the Antarctic summer, squalls ceaselessly harried the Bostonians. The wind, noted one journal of the voyage, "sometimes blew so strong that we drag'd with 5 anchors a head." (*George Davidson, Oregon Historical Society, OrHi 983/1147*)

sailors jigged desperately for any bird, fishy tasting or not, that could be yanked in at the end of a line, and any fish they could haul flapping onto the deck.

Columbia's sailing time to the Falkland Islands, which they reached on 22 January 1791, once again bettered Kendrick's leisurely pace, this time by three and a half weeks. The ship remained for eleven days. One of George Davidson's splendid paintings shows a tent erected ashore, with Captain Gray, chart in hand, giving orders to a seaman. Behind the captain, looking soulfully up at him, rests a goat (it can only be Nancy!) while all around others of the crew busily repair and fill the ship's water casks. During *Columbia*'s stay at the Falklands, the officers shot half a dozen of the islands' wild hogs and "upwards of 1000 ducks. . . . The fowl was quite tame when we first arrived," Boit observed, "but they soon was taught the doctrine of self-preservation." The ship received an overhaul, and quantities of wild celery were collected.

With some trepidation, Gray turned *Columbia*'s bow toward Cape Horn. Hoskins gave expression to this concern: "Never did a deeper laden vessel, ever, attempt to double this formidable Cape." But where Cape Horn had shown its fury to the ship on her first passage, it now donned a benign countenance. A relieved and delighted Hoskins recorded that the ship "had the winds and weather much better than could be expected, and almost equal to what we could have wished." In three weeks *Columbia* had put several hundred miles of the Pacific under her keel and was at fifty-two degrees south.

The one casualty of the voyage occurred on 23 April. "Between the hours of 3 and 4 PM," Boit wrote in what was for him an unusually long entry while at sea,

> Departed this life our dear freind Nancy the Goat having been the Captains companion on a former voyage around the Globe but her spirited disposition for adventure led her to undertake a 2d voyage of Circumnavigation; but the various changes of Climate, and sudden transition from the Polar Colds to the tropical heats of the Torrid Zone, prov'd too much for a constitution naturally delicate, At 5 PM Committed her body to the deep. She was lamented by those who got a share of her Milk!!

Hoskins, writing a briefer but more realistic obituary, simply noted that "having some rice up to air," Nancy "got at it, eat so much that it swel'd in her belly, and caused her death; this was the more greivious as it

Slammed into her beam ends before an approaching downpour, stout *Columbia* heels before an approaching gale. This could be a moment of grave danger for any but the best-handled ship. In addition to the usual stones and gravel carried only for their weight, *Columbia* on her second voyage took aboard 43 barrels of tar and pitch, 2,000 bricks, 12,000 pounds of bar iron, and dozens of casks of fresh water. All of this heavy cargo would have been stowed amidships in the lowest hold. As long as it remained in place, the weight would counter the force of wind and hold the ship upright. But should this ballast shift, the vessel could become completely unmanageable, take on water, and sink. Artist George Davidson, who created this lively sketch, was himself later lost when his ship disappeared without a trace—probably the victim of just such a mishap.
(*Oregon Historical Society*, OrHi 984/1147)

depriv'd us of the greatest delicasy we had in the ship, her milk, which made our tea so much more palatable."

Once beyond the Roaring Forties and into calmer seas, Gray turned his attention to preparing the ship for whatever the Northwest Coast might have in store. The incident at Murderers' Harbor on the first voyage in which Gray's servant Marcus Lopius had been killed had left the captain in no mood to trust the Indians. Cannon were mounted—six four-pounders on the quarterdeck and four six-pounders on the fo'c'sle —and ten swivels were installed on the rails. The armorers and gunners readied the ship's small arms and prepared ammunition.

By late April, as she neared the equator, *Columbia* was nearly six months away from Boston and any significant amount of green foods. "Four seamen laid by, with the Scurvey," Boit noted. "Their Mouths and Legs are very bad." Mid-May found three more affected. "Their Gums is quite numb, (the worst of Complaints!!)." When *Columbia* reached Clay-oquot Sound, forty miles south of Nootka, on 5 June 1791, the first concern was to get the ailing seamen ashore.

> Landed the sick immediately on our arivall [Boit wrote], and pitch'd a tent for their reception, and although there was ten of them in the last stage of the Scurvy, still they soon recover'd, upon smelling the turf, and eating Greens of various kinds. . . . We buried sevrall of our sick, up to the Hips in the earth, and let them remain for hours in that situation. Found this method of great service.

Boit had several times grumbled during the Atlantic passage about the lack of attention paid to sanitation aboard *Columbia*. Now Hoskins took up the refrain, blaming Gray for the toll taken by scurvy. "This must in a great measure be attributed to our scanty supply of antiscorbutics," he wrote, "to an improper use of what we had; and to the small attention paid by the commander to the preservation of the health of his people." To which he might have added that the food provided to ordinary seamen of those days was much coarser than that enjoyed by land-lubbers and officers. Scurvy was more of a hazard of the common sailor's life than it was of the privileged few who commanded from the quarterdeck and ate at the captain's table.

★

CHAPTER FIFTEEN

Gray's Hostage-Taking
Casts an Ominous Shadow

★

Gray had been determined, at whatever the cost, to beat Kendrick's sailing time to the Northwest Coast, and he did—by nearly four months. Hoskins, of course, faulted Gray for not having stopped at some of "those islands so happily scattered," which offered ample supplies of fresh greens of various sorts. But, scurvy or not, the determined Gray reached the Northwest Coast in early June and had the best of a season ahead of him before winter would put a damper on trading.

From the Indians, Gray learned that only one ship lay at Nootka Sound. This would have been the *Concepción* of the new Spanish commandant, Lieutenant Don Francisco Eliza. After Kendrick's and Gray's old friend Martínez had been recalled by the viceroy of New Spain and the Spanish fort dismantled, a new viceroy had reversed his predecessor's order and reestablished Spain's presence at Nootka. Though the Americans had been treated with the utmost courtesy by the Spaniards on the first voyage, Gray decided to play it safe. If Martínez could seize English ships with impunity, Eliza might now have orders to do the same with American ships. Clayoquot Sound was as happily situated a harbor as

Nootka, the captain decided, and just as convenient to fur-trading areas up and down the coast.

Much had happened between Spain and Great Britain since July of 1789, when *Columbia* and *Washington* had left the Northwest Coast on their way to China, though even now—two years later—Gray would have been only dimly aware of the political volcano that had erupted over the status of Nootka Sound. John Meares had taken to London an exaggerated account of Martínez's confiscation of *Princess Royal*, *North-West America*, and *Argonaut*, and had demanded indemnity of more than half a million dollars from the government of Carlos IV. Britain's Parliament had in turn seized upon Spain's takeover of the land on which Meares had built his little outpost at Friendly Cove as a challenge to British rights in the Pacific. Nationalistic pride overrode reason as the two powers trumpeted the importance of perhaps half an acre of the North American wilderness. Britain's cabinet conferred with their allies, Prussia and Holland. The United States was approached to see what its attitude would be toward the mother country it had so recently been at war with. Parliament voted the funds for a conflict.

Dithering between bombast and apology, Spain finally decided in favor of arbitration. The "Nootka Convention," signed in October of 1790 restored to Britain the land and buildings at Nootka that the Spaniards were charged with usurping—the "building" being the one whose walls Captain Douglas had carried away on *Iphigenia* after giving the roof to Kendrick to burn for firewood—and awarding Meares $210,000 for the loss of his vessels and the skins he might have acquired. Within a year Nootka would become neutral ground, held by neither nation but open to the citizens of both. What the convention established, in fact, was that the same was true of that erstwhile Spanish lake, the Pacific Ocean.

At first, Gray's decision to stay clear of Nootka Sound and its political ramifications seemed no loss. Clayoquot itself appeared to offer encouraging possibilities for trade. When Gray first anchored there and allowed the Nootkans to throng *Columbia*'s deck, Chief Wickananish and six or eight members of his family had clambered aboard. All were "cloathed with two to four sea otter skins each; this was a most pleasing sight and the best introduction [*Columbia*] could have had." But as time passed the Indians seemed indifferent to the ship's trade goods, which they expected to receive as presents. Aching to get his hands on a cargo of furs—he'd show those doubters back in Boston!—Gray must have cursed inwardly as he watched Wickananish and his obedient braves scornfully carry away their precious sea-otter cloaks. Knowing how badly these men from Boston wanted their furs, the Indians not only refused to sell but took delight in showing how little they valued them. More than one greedy trader had been chagrined to see a splendid cloak flung carelessly across a boiling food pot, its edges tantalizingly near the flames, where the steam would drive out the lice so the owner could kill them by crushing them between his front teeth.

Thinking ahead to the winter he and his men would spend in Clayoquot, Gray brought up from the hold a peck of potatoes taken aboard ship at Boston, together with a quantity of onions and some vegetable seeds. One of the chief's brothers was induced to plant them. Gray sent an officer and several seamen ashore in the longboat to show the Indians how they should be put in the ground. Wickananish's elder brother, Tootiscosettle, appeared to be delighted with the honor the Americans were doing him. Gray was greeted the next morning, however, by a deputation of tribesmen who, having dug up both the potatoes and the onions, now brought them back to the ship and offered them for sale. "This seems sufficiently to shew the idle disposition of these people," Hoskins moralized, "and [their] present ignorance of civilization."

A few furs began to trickle in, but Gray had made up his mind to move on. The rigging had to be put in order after *Columbia*'s long voyage, the hull needed attention, and wood and water had to be taken aboard. In the midst of all this activity, the captain's cabin boy, Attoo, deserted from *Columbia*, apparently having convinced himself that life among the Indians would be preferable to that aboard the ship. With the high-handed approach that every fur trader adopted at times, Gray decided to get the boy back by making a hostage of the first chief who came along. This proved to be Tootiscosettle, who was cajoled into coming aboard with his servant. He denied all knowledge of Attoo's whereabouts until Gray threatened to carry him to sea on *Columbia*. The Indian took this as a threat to kill him and immediately sent his servant to the village with orders to bring Attoo. The canoe was "soon seen returning, with several others; hollowing as they came," and bringing the deserter. Making an example of Attoo, Gray had him flogged and demanded that the chief witness the punishment. This incident would have a disagreeable aftermath the following winter.

In mid-June, Gray took *Columbia* out of Clayoquot's snug harbor, on the way picking up six more skins from a canoeload of Indians. In all, he had acquired 112 pelts thus far, plus an assortment of pieces and tails. The natives had parted with them for sheet copper and clothing; iron chisels, Hoskins noted, "they would scarcely take as a gift." Despite their lack of appeal the first time around, Columbia had brought back to the Northwest Coast many of the unexpended trade goods of the previous voyage —knives, buttons, fishhooks, and the like—but these would procure little other than fish and vegetables.

Gray kept Columbia busy up and down the Northwest Coast that summer, making a mockery of Kendrick's reluctance to take the larger vessel into British Columbia's rocky, tide-swept coves and inlets. In late June Columbia had moved to the southern end of Vancouver Island and lay off the village of Nitinat, at the mouth of the Strait of Juan de Fuca. When "Cassacan the Chief and his Lady" brought their canoe out to the ship, Hoskins recorded a sad and all-too-typical story. "Cassacan we found troubled with the venereal to a great degree," he wrote. A trading vessel had come to Nitinat some time before, the chief explained, to whom Cassacan had sold a slave girl for several sheets of copper. When the vessel left, the girl was put ashore. From the girl Cassacan acquired the disease and afterwards transmitted it to his wife. "Thus this most baneful disorder will e'er long prove fatal to this pair, and possibly spread throughout the village." Poor Cassacan also showed the effects of smallpox, another gift of the traders. "Oh, miserable inhabitants," Hoskins wrote, "where is your native happiness? Is it not gone? Never, never more to return."

Working his way north, Gray on 23 July sighted the Hope, commanded by Columbia's one-time first mate Joseph Ingraham. The crew of that little brigantine had had an eventful voyage from Boston, discovering a group of islands in the Marquesas as they sailed northward from Cape Horn. The women there, Ingraham told the jealous officers of Columbia, were "much handsomer than the natives of the Sandwich Islands." Hope had then stopped for supplies at the Hawaiian Islands. There Ingraham bade farewell to Opie, the lad who had gone with him on Columbia to Boston, and from Boston home again on Hope to Hawaii. Now meeting Columbia on the Northwest Coast, Ingraham "received . . . letters from my friends in Boston, which although dated but ten days after our departure were yet great satisfaction." They had been carried by Robert Haswell in defiance of Joseph Barrell's ill-conceived order that Columbia's crew carry no letters to their friends on Hope.

In the closemouthed manner of every fur trader, Ingraham refrained from discussing his great trading discovery of the season. Seeing collars of wrought copper on some of the Indians, he had set his armorer to forging copies in iron, for which the natives eagerly gave two and three sea-otter skins. While Gray nervously jumped from one location to another, Ingraham stayed in one place for weeks at a time, letting the furs come to him and gathering them in three at a time for one of his strange necklaces. The technique would net him an enviably rich cargo in the two months —actually, forty-nine days of trading by his own count—that he spent on the coast that summer.

Gray early in August took his vessel to what is now the lower tip of southeastern Alaska and anchored in a sound he named Port Tempest. Second mate Joshua Caswell asked permission to fish in a nearby cove. Arming himself with only a musket and taking two seamen—Joseph Barnes, one of the two who had signed on in China, and John Folger— Caswell set off about nine o'clock in the jolly boat. Near midday a fresh breeze came up. Eager to be underway, Gray fired a gun as a signal for the party to return. Impatient after half an hour had elapsed, Gray fired another gun and hoisted a flag, meanwhile weighing anchor and hoisting sail. Alarmed now that the little party had run into trouble, Gray sent third mate Owen Smith and an armed crew to search for Caswell and the two sailors. The pinnace returned with its flag at half mast, towing the seemingly empty jolly boat.

"With this melancholy token," wrote John Hoskins, "they approached the ship and when they came alongside I saw my worthy friend Mr. Caswell laying dead in the bottom of the boat stripped perfectly naked and stabbed in upwards of twenty places. This was a sight too shocken ever to be effaced from my memory." Smith had found Caswell's body in the boat where he had fallen. Barnes lay dead on the beach, stripped by the Indians of all but his trousers. Folger had disappeared. Fearing an ambush, Smith took the jolly boat in tow and returned to the ship.

Next morning, as *Columbia*'s gunner fired a cannon at one-minute intervals, Caswell was buried ashore "with all the solemnity we was capable of. The place was gloomy," wrote the impressionable Boit, "and nothing was to be heard but the bustling of an aged oak whose lofty branches hung wavering o'er the grave, together with the meandering brook, the Cries of the Eagle, and the weeping of his freinds [adding]

Robert Haswell's journal of the second voyage begins just three days before the scene depicted here, when *Columbia* (left) met the brigantine *Hancock*, commanded by Samuel Crowell, in Masset Sound, Queen Charlotte Islands. The Queen Charlottes had been sighted and named in 1787 by a British trader. Unaware of that, Gray too "discovered" the islands two years later on his first voyage, and patriotically gave them the first president's name. Crowell bestowed the name Hancock's River, honoring the governor of Massachusetts, on Masset Sound. Going aboard *Hancock*, Gray and Haswell expressed keen disappointment that Crowell had brought no letters from Boston, though he had left there two months later than *Columbia*.

(*Massachusetts Historical Society*)

solemnity to the scene. So ends." *Columbia* made her way sadly from what Gray and his company would know henceforth as Massacre Cove.

Gray took *Columbia* south again toward Clayoquot Sound, where he planned to spend the winter building the sloop whose frame the ship had brought out from Boston. At midnight on 15 August, only a few miles from the site of Caswell's murder, the captain saw a sail on the horizon and shortly recognized the *Hancock*, Captain Samuel Crowell. Gray and Hoskins went aboard the brigantine that morning, eager for letters and news of home. She had left Boston only a month later than *Columbia*, so there was little news worth repeating and no letters.

After a stormy passage around Cape Horn, *Hancock* had stopped at Hawaii for fresh meat and vegetables. The islands were becoming a less and less comfortable stop for fur traders. Crowell had bought forty sea-otter skins from the natives, loot from the *Fair American*, a small Nor'west-man that had been seized the year before by the islanders and all of her crew murdered. Crowell himself had been threatened by Kaiana, Gray's old friend of Nootka days, who boasted that he had *Hancock* in his power but had told his people that they should not attack the vessel until the next day. Crowell prudently left Hawaii that evening.

Crowell had arrived on the Northwest Coast a month before his meeting with *Columbia* and had set up operations in a harbor only a few miles from Massacre Cove. Like *Columbia*, the *Hancock* had brought out from Boston the frame of a small sloop-rigged vessel, which the crewmen had completed in a few weeks. When Crowell's men finished the hull, the local Indians had appeared en masse and attempted to keep them from launching her. In the battle that ensued, four of the Indians were killed and a number wounded.

Hoskins found in the meeting with Crowell and his fellow Bostonians a lifting of the spirit after the depressing events at Massacre Cove. Boit, on the other hand, saw Crowell's affray at the boat launching as the seed of Caswell's and the two *Columbia* seamen's deaths. "Capt. Crowell had, upon some trifling offence, fir'd upon these Indians by which a number of them fell (such wanton cruelty throws him upon a levell with the savage), and perhaps this same fray was the means of our losing our worthy 2nd Officer as the places are not 20 leagues distant and mayhap they reck'd their Vengenace upon us, thinking us all of one tribe. If it was so, bad luck to Crowell. Amen."

After sailing in company with the *Hancock* for nearly a week, and trading for whatever skins appeared, Gray learned that it was Crowell's intention to finish out the season with a final cruise to the south of Clayoquot Sound before sailing for China. Such was the competition among Boston's Nor'westmen that Gray immediately decided to get to the southern trading grounds ahead of Crowell if he could manage it. When the two Boston vessels parted, *Hancock* had five to six hundred sea-otter skins aboard. *Columbia* had about the same number.

Late in August, *Hope* and *Columbia* crossed paths once more. Ingraham generously sent his ship's boat with an officer to tell Gray he was sailing shortly for China. Knowing that Gray would winter on the Northwest Coast and ignoring Joseph Barrell's order that *Columbia* carry no letters for him, he generously offered to take letters to Canton and forward them on other ships from there to America. Among the packet of letters sent to Boston that day from *Columbia* was one from Robert Gray to Joseph Barrell in which Gray pointedly noted that it would arrive courtesy of Captain Ingraham.

John Hoskins added a postscript, "please to inform my mama that I am well"—a commentary on the amazing youthfulness of some of the men who made those first long, adventurous voyages to the Northwest Coast.

CHAPTER SIXTEEN

The First American
to Reach Japan

★

Let us leave *Columbia* now as she hurries south to Clayoquot Sound, Captain Gray intent on scooping up as many furs as he can find before his rival Crowell can get his hands on them. Our last sight of Captain John Kendrick, remember, was eighteen months earlier, when we left him fuming impatiently aboard *Lady Washington* at Dirty Butter Bay, "very lonely" and awaiting a visit from Robert Gray as Gray started *Columbia* on her long westward passage from Canton. But Gray, in no mood to stop for anything, is determined to be the first one home to Boston. He pauses at Macao just long enough to pick up the ship's port clearance papers and then scurries past Dirty Butter Bay as fast as the wind will push him. Kendrick, he thinks, can take care of himself. "A gale of wind prevented our seeing him," he will explain to Joseph Barrell, at the same time tendering *Columbia*'s chief owner a proper accounting of Kendrick's multitudinous shortcomings.

Kendrick's future is clouded. After *Columbia* left the Northwest Coast in July, he continued trading aboard *Washington*, moving northward in August and September to the Queen Charlotte Islands, which then still

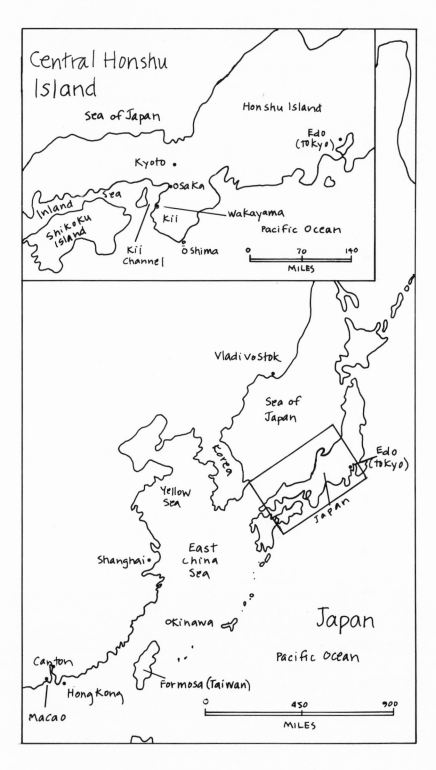

offered abundant furs for only modest outlays of trading goods. Now, at anchor in Chinese waters, after crossing the Pacific in *Columbia's* track (making his little sloop the second American vessel ever to put in at the idyllic Sandwich Islands) *Washington's* captain pondered his next move. He had a seaworthy boat, though not his own, and a cargo of other people's sea-otter pelts. His letters carry more than a hint of the possible courses he considered: Sell the vessel and her furs and return to Boston with a profit for the owners and a refurbished reputation for himself. Or sell his furs, rerig the vessel as a brigantine, and go back for another season on the golden Northwest Coast. In the end, weakness must have combined with optimism to dictate his choice. A fresh dream burned in his mind. He would go back across the Pacific and then return next year to China with the finest cargo of furs ever brought to Canton.

One wonders why he was not drawn back to Massachusetts by the wife and children waiting for him there in that "costly gambrel roof house" in Wareham. In the forgetfulness of this new life of his, nearly three years had slipped away since he had last seen Huldah and her brood. Little Huldah, the only girl, would be nearing nine. But he seems to have put them out of his mind. Next year, after another golden harvest of otter furs, would be time enough to start for Boston and home.

The old fur-trader's fantasy would not materialize that easily. Stricken with "a violent fever, which caused his life for a time to be despaired of," Kendrick lay for weeks aboard *Washington* at Dirty Butter Bay. Once recovered, he took a house ashore in Macao to be able better to arrange the sale of his furs and the refitting of the sloop.

After so many months either at sea or camping ashore in the wilderness of the Northwest Coast, the easy-going Kendrick would have dropped gratefully into the relaxed life of this strange European settlement somehow magically transported to the China coast. "Macao is one of the most romantic cities that imagination can picture," wrote an early visitor from Baltimore to this beguiling Portuguese colony. "There is nothing Chinese in its appearance. It resembles Naples. The same beautiful bay studded with green islands, the same gently curving beach, the same rising hills on either side, and the houses and buildings towering up the slope that stretched from the pier . . ." The Chinese town back of the city, though, he recorded with a shudder, was "a hole of filth and wretchedness."

The European residents of Macao, the same observer noted, "are of old decayed families, as proud as Lucifer, the men lazy and the women mischievous, and they doze away the days, and only appear as the night approaches. . . . In the evening they saunter along the beach, and the women, in the garb of old Portugal, turn a dark eye on the stranger." One can envision the problem-beset and sea-worn Kendrick in the Baltimorean's final estimate of this gently rotting enclave of Asian and European weaknesses. "A man sick of the world," the American wrote, "worn out and disgusted with himself and everyone else, would find Macao a home more suited to his pallid tastes and jaded spirit than any other spot I could name."

Macao in those early days of the American presence in Asia must have been an extraordinary place, a little enclave of Mediterranean Europe dropped fortuitously on old Canton's doorstep. The Portuguese had been there since 1557, long enough for them to establish the first senate in Asia and to build the three monasteries, the thirteen churches, and the convent that served the little colony's four thousand Christian residents. In addition to these, there was a military garrison of Eurasians and Africans and a Chinese population that outnumbered the Portuguese by perhaps two to one.

This mixture, rich enough already, was spiced each winter by the arrival from Canton of the staffs of the various East India companies, plus the few Americans there since 1786. These little groups of foreign devils could remain in their factories at Canton only during the trading season, and each year they gratefully took the last ship of their country downriver to their airy seaside villas and their Chinese mistresses in Macao. Added to this polyglot assortment were the crews and captains of the "country ships" from India, Burma, and Malaya, with their Hindu, Arab, and Javanese seamen, plus an occasional Filipino or Dyak tribesman from Borneo. The British and American vessels brought their Anglo-Saxons, who thought as little of jumping ship in this pleasant Asian port as they did of deserting in the sunny Sandwich Islands. Macao, long before Hawaii, had become a maritime clearinghouse where a crew could be patched together from the flotsam of the entire Pacific.

The little Portuguese colony even welcomed an occasional Hawaiian. The young chief Kaiana, who had come to the Northwest Coast with William Douglas, had before that sailed from Oahu to Macao with John Meares. The huge Polynesian—"nearly six feet four inches high, and remarkably stout"—must have added a striking note even to the amazing mix of a Macao street when he wandered out to buy oranges in his flaming bird-feather cloak and hat, carrying a spear so the Chinese he met would realize that he was "a person of grandeur and distinction." Understandably, the Chinese who encountered the gigantic Hawaiian felt more terror than admiration and dubbed Kaiana "the Great Stranger."

Moving from the spartan life aboard ship to a house ashore in cosmopolitan Macao was as customary for a captain wintering over in the sunny Portuguese colony as it was for those spending the summer in Canton, where they rented private quarters near the hongs while the ships' officers and crews remained with their vessels in the anchorage downriver at Whampoa. Kendrick would have looked forward to a time of socializing in the ebb and flow of Macao's crossroads community while he took his time selling his cargo of furs and planning the conversion of *Lady Washington* to a brigantine.

The captain, however, had failed to take into account the repercussions of his "alliance" with the Spaniard Martínez back in Nootka Sound. Now he ran afoul of Portuguese officialdom at every turn. Initially he had been refused permission to bring *Lady Washington* into the Typa, Macao's inner harbor. When he managed to overcome this galling restriction and moved ashore, his house was broken into, provisions were denied him, and he was arrested on the streets by Portuguese soldiers and ordered to leave Macao immediately on pain of imprisonment.

One need not look far to discover the cause of all this. Kendrick had openly allied himself with the Spanish commandant at Nootka Sound. While British vessels flying the Portuguese flag were seized and shipped off to Mexico as prizes and their crews imprisoned or sent back to China on Kendrick's *Columbia*, Kendrick himself enjoyed the freedom not only of Nootka Sound but of the entire Northwest Coast. John Meares, who commanded the British-Portuguese squadron, made no secret of his belief that Kendrick had actively conspired with the Spanish commandant in the seizures. Meares had come back to Macao on his way to England, and William Douglas, captain of *Iphigenia*, the first vessel Martínez had seized, was in Macao now. Despite his personal friendship with Kendrick, Douglas would have been as bitter as Meares. And there was João Carvalho, part owner of the enterprise and secret partner of the Portuguese governor of Macao. It was he who had prevailed upon his friend the governor to issue Portuguese papers to the three British ships. Bankrupt now and being dunned for his debts in connection with the seized vessels, Carvalho would have had no love for the American captain now so conveniently cast up on his doorstep.

Kendrick would have been picked clean before he escaped from Macao's clutches had a new governor not arrived to take the place of Carvalho's crony. In the end Kendrick managed to sell only part of his cargo, leaving two hundred skins still in Lady Washington's hold. But what he did sell brought a good price—an average of $48 each—which confirmed Samuel Shaw's judgment that Columbia's sea otters would have brought more had Gray too sold them in Macao and proceeded to Canton for a homeward-bound cargo with cash in hand.

Kendrick did even better with the 137 skins entrusted to him by Martínez. Most of them had been gifts to the Spanish commandant and would have been of the finest quality. They brought in $8,000—an average of $58 each. Solvent again—never mind whose money it was—Kendrick could finally turn in earnest to his old dream of transforming Lady Washington from a sloop, with its one vulnerable mast and great, unwieldy mainsail, to a brigantine with its two shorter masts and sail area broken up into smaller, more manageable units. But fourteen months slipped away in the process, as did the $18,000 Kendrick received for the skins he had sold from Washington's cargo as well as the money Martínez's furs had brought. An entire season on the Northwest Coast had also been lost. In desperation he borrowed another $3,000 to stay afloat until he could get back to the Northwest Coast.

Exactly who owned Lady Washington at this point no one really knows. Kendrick admitted in a letter to Joseph Barrell that he had sold her, "but I assure [you]," he told the little vessel's faraway owner, "it was nothing but a sham sale merely to help me through my difficulties and troubles." Be that as it may, the money he borrowed would not have been forthcoming from either the Chinese merchants or his fellow traders without some sort of security, and a share in Lady Washington was all he could have offered. But somehow Kendrick kept command in his own hands. Whatever the technicalities of ownership, he remained the little sloop's (or brigantine's, by now) master, and his dreams continued to set her course.

There was talk in the air even then of trade with Japan, both among the foreign captains wintering in Macao and the shipowners back in Boston. Joseph Barrell, in fact, in his orders for Columbia's second voyage, would suggest to Gray "your trying what can be done on the coast of

Japan . . . where, if you find safety in anchoring, and can dispose of your furs to advantage, we would advise you by all means to do it." This, of course, was more than half a century before Commodore Matthew Perry would open the ports of Japan to American ships. Only the Dutch had trading access there now, and their privileges were far more limited than were those of the foreigners at Canton.

Kendrick would have heard the talk too, and he still had two hundred prime skins stashed away on *Washington*. Perhaps Japan would be the key to overcoming this never-ending streak of bad luck. It was a beguiling dream, and Kendrick must have seized on it as he had on so many other will-o'-the-wisps.

Kendrick's erstwhile critic and competitor of Nootka days, the Scottish captain William Douglas, late of *Iphigenia Nubiana*, was now master of his own vessel, *Grace*. He had probably picked up the sloop at a bargain price because of the vessel's lack of proper papers, and now he flew— quite illegally—the American flag. He had either been convinced by the likeable Kendrick that he had not allied himself with Martínez against Douglas's interests or Douglas had simply agreed to forgive and forget. The American mariner Amasa Delano, in his *Voyages and Travels*, records that he served aboard *Grace* early in 1791, when Douglas took his sloop from Macao to nearby Lark's Bay to help his old friend Kendrick get *Washington* ready for another season on the Northwest Coast. Part of that help may have been a loan of $2,320, which still remained unpaid at the time of Kendrick's death. Interest by then had more than doubled the debt, to $5,000.

The two were ready for sea by the last of March and sailed for Japan together. Douglas, presumably, also had unsold sea-otter skins aboard. According to one of the few references to Kendrick during this period, he carried a crew of thirty-six, including two Chinese and two of the Pacific's wandering Hawaiians who had seen the wonders of China and now wanted to return to their island home.

With another golden dream to ride—the fantasy of opening Japan to Western trade and of making a fortune for himself in the bargain— Kendrick pretended to be seeking refuge from a storm and boldly took *Lady Washington* to the tip of the Kii Peninsula, the southernmost point of Honshu. There, on 6 May 1791, he anchored off the village of Kashinozaki, at the eastern end of an island called Ō Shima. Whether Douglas went in with him or lay offshore in *Grace* waiting is unknown.

Thanks to painstaking research in Japanese archives by a Japanese-speaking scholar, Howard F. Van Zandt, a surprising amount is now known about this fleeting but historically important first contact between Japan and the United States. Kendrick's ship, Van Zandt tells us, was quickly ringed by local vessels, and their passengers treated to odd Western foods and alcoholic drinks. Crew members from *Washington* explored the island in search of water and firewood and filled their casks from a spring beside a Shinto shrine.

The next day a typhoon forced the Americans to seek shelter in the harbor of Kashinoura, some distance to the northeast. There Kendrick's crewmen astonished the Japanese, who knew only clumsy matchlock firearms, by shooting ducks in flight with their flintlocks, bringing down two birds out of three, and using a dog to retrieve them. A physician named Date Koshikazu was summoned, suggesting that there might have been a medical problem aboard. A minor fracas developed when a farmer named Haruemon tried to prevent one of the Americans from chopping down a tree. The crewman fired a gun, and Haruemon fled.

Kendrick seems not to have been entirely comfortable among the Japanese, for he ordered his ship's guns to be fired periodically during the night. And indeed trouble might have ensued had he stayed long enough, for the local authorities wasted no time in sending a delegation of samurai to the prefecture's administrative center at Wakayama to seek instructions. Those orders would inevitably have been unfavorable to the Yankees. The people of Wakayama were conservative and violently xenophobic. They prided themselves on their aloofness even more than did the inhabitants of the rest of Japan. Luckily, the typhoon that had driven the Americans to shelter in Kashinoura had also raised the seas too much for the samurai to travel by boat. Forced to go overland, they did not return from Wakayama until 19 May 1791, two days after Kendrick had realized the hopelessness of his quest and left for Hawaii in the face of a stiff gale.

Even had he been able to stay, it seems a safe bet that the American captain's bluff, outgoing manner would not have impressed the reserved and tradition-bound Japanese. But that he did enter Japan and remain for a fortnight there exists no doubt. A curious note, written by one of the Chinese seamen aboard *Washington*, still survives in the Wakayama archives. Another version, in Dutch, has disappeared.

This ship [the note in Chinese characters reads] belongs to the Red Hairs from a land called America. Its cargo includes copper, iron, and fifty guns. In going from Flower Country to Skin Grass Country we do not pass your land, but we have drifted here under the stress of wind and wave. We shall not stay here more than three or five days. We shall remain as long as the wind continues to be adverse, and shall leave as soon as it becomes favorable. There are about one hundred persons aboard this ship. The cargo truly consists of copper and iron, and of naught else. The captain's name is Kendrick.

For all his courage in making the attempt, Kendrick must have been ill at ease about the whole venture, as one can guess from his boastful claim that his little vessel carried a crew of one hundred. Apparently learning that the Japanese looked with horror on the idea of anyone dressing in the skins of dead animals, he carefully avoided mention in his note of the furs he had brought. John Hoskins, who recorded Kendrick's account of his visit to Japan when *Washington* reached Clayoquot Sound that summer, wrote that the American had been "received by the natives with the greatest hospitality. Here Captain Kendrick displayed the American flag, which is probably the first ever seen in that quarter." Of the sea-otter skins *Washington* carried, Hoskins comments that "the Japanese knew not the use of them." But however ill-conceived the venture, Kendrick's attempt marks the first visit by an American ship to Japan.

Hoskins also noted that, a few days' sail from Wakayama, Kendrick and Douglas discovered a group of islands "to which on account of the natives bringing water off to sell was given the name of Water Islands." These were perhaps the Bonins. Kendrick commented to Hoskins that the people of the islands could not communicate in spoken Japanese or Chinese but could do so in writing.

From the "Water Islands," *Washington* and *Grace* made their separate ways to the Northwest Coast, both probably stopping in Hawaii for "refreshment." Finishing his second crossing of the Pacific, Kendrick took *Washington* into Houston Stewart Channel—he would still have called it Barrell's Sound—in the Queen Charlotte Islands. On 13 June, about three months after he had left Macao, he anchored off the village of the Haida chief Coyah, with whom he had traded two years before. This time, the Indians' welcome would take an unexpected turn.

★

CHAPTER SEVENTEEN

"Forgotten" Insult
Leads to a
Rude Surprise

★

Lady Washington's tragic encounter at Murderers' Harbor, in which Marcus Lopius was slain, and the ambush Columbia suffered at Massacre Cove were not the first violent encounters Northwest fur traders had with the Indians, nor would they be the last. The very first trader on the coast, in fact, had to fight to save his ship. This, as already mentioned, was the little brig Sea Otter, née Harmon, of Captain James Hanna, the Englishman who had sailed from China in the spring of 1785.

His sixty-ton vessel carried a crew of only twenty, and she must have seemed tiny to the Indians of Nootka Sound, who had previously seen only the great three-masted ships of Juan Pérez and Captain Cook. Maquinna and his tribesmen attempted to capture Hanna's vessel in broad daylight but were driven off with heavy losses. The Haidas of the Queen Charlotte Islands threatened Captain William Douglas's Iphigenia Nubiana in 1789, and in April 1791 the snow Gustavus III staved off an attack only by arming its crew in a show of strength that frightened away the Indians.

It is hardly surprising that Washington, as she cruised for furs in the spring of 1791, should run into similar—and nearly fatal—trouble. To understand the background of the attack, we must go back to the late summer or early fall of 1789. *Columbia*, under Gray, had left the Northwest Coast for China at the end of the previous July. Now Kendrick, on the move at last, took *Washington* through Houston Stewart Channel in the southern Queen Charlotte Islands. The western part of Kunghit Island, which lies south of the channel, was the territory of the Haida chief Coyah—"Raven"—a "little diminutive savage looking fellow as ever trod," noted John Hoskins in his journal. This was the same chief with whom *Washington* had done business, under Gray's command, earlier that same year. Iron "chizzles" were not in demand, Gray had discovered, but Coyah, trading for his people, eagerly accepted clothing in exchange for sea-otter skins. Now *Washington* was back, this time under Kendrick. And Coyah's eagerness for European clothing had not abated, nor had the Haidas' propensity for pilferage. Missing no opportunity to steal anything they could put their fingers on, Coyah and a cohort wound up by making off with Kendrick's clean linen from the line on which it was drying.

Kendrick in the past had always treated the Indians benevolently, perhaps more so than any other trader, and with this one exception and its bloody aftermath, he would continue to do so throughout his career on the Northwest Coast. But this time the Haidas had tried him too far. The captain's fiery temper went out of control. Seizing Coyah and Schulkinanse, another chief who was on *Washington*'s deck, Kendrick had a cannon dismounted from its carriage, which he used as improvised stocks. Thrusting a leg of each Indian into a depression that held one of the gun's trunnions, he locked the clamps in place and threatened to kill them both if the stolen articles were not returned. Coyah, who apparently maintained tight control over his tribesmen, managed to get them to return some of the pilfered goods. The rest Kendrick insisted the Indians pay for in sea-otter skins.

John Hoskins, supercargo of *Columbia* on her second voyage, penned a lengthy account of the whole affair. "Well knowing if he let those chiefs go," Hoskins wrote in his journal, "they would sell him no more skins, [Kendrick] therefore made them fetch him all their skins and paid them the same price he had done for those before purchased."

After the Coyah incident, in the fall of 1789, Kendrick sailed to China with his cargo of furs. Now he had arrived back on the Northwest Coast, where he went through Houston Stewart Channel again on 13 June 1791. The captain dropped anchor off Coyah's village, Ce-uda'o Inagai—"The

Village That Fishes Toward the South"—as if nothing had ever happened between the chief and himself. For the rest of the story, we have no fewer than six accounts: brief mentions in the journals of *Columbia*'s first mate Haswell and fifth mate John Boit; detailed versions recorded by Hoskins and Joseph Ingraham; a version in the journal of Kendrick's friend John Bartlett, who probably picked it up from Kendrick or one of his crewmen in Macao; and a doggerel ballad perhaps written by a member of *Washington*'s crew who took part in the affair. The latter was published as a broadside—sharing space with a sad little poem about a pair of Swiss orphans—by a part-time barber named Leonard Deming, whose place of business the sheet lists as "No. 62 Hanover Street, 2d door from Friend Street, Boston." The ballad had apparently long been a favorite aboard the fur-traders' vessels and in the homes of New England sailors, though Deming did not commit it to print until about 1834. Titled "Bold Northwestman," it makes no mention of Kendrick by name.

> Come all ye bold Northwestmen who plough the raging main,
> Come listen to my story, while I relate the same;
> 'Twas of the Lady Washington decoyed as she lay,
> At Queen Charlotte's Island, in North America.
>
> On the sixteenth day of June, boys, in the year Ninety-One,
> The natives in great numbers on board our ship did come,
> Then for to buy our fur of them our captain did begin,
> But mark what they attempted before long time had been.

Kendrick, says Ingraham, had allowed about fifty Indians aboard the vessel, including at least three chiefs. More than half of the crowd, adds another source, were the warlike Haida women. This was a dangerous departure from the traders' standing rule that all furs would be bargained for over the sides of the vessel. Perhaps a hundred more Indians had gathered alongside in their canoes. Bartlett, whose spelling was remarkable even in that day of outrageous orthography, adds an element ignored in all of the other journals; "The Captn wos in Lickqur," he claims, "And trusted More to the Natives then his own Peple."

The Indians, including Coyah, at first appeared to have forgotten the earlier incident and to be quite friendly. Kendrick, for his part, was loath to clear the deck of natives for fear they would take offense and leave with their furs. He had arrived late in the season and was anxious to quickly gather a cargo for China.

Abaft upon our quarter deck two arm chests did stand,
And in them there was left the keys by the gunner's careless hand;
When quickly they procuring of them did make a prize,
Thinking we had no other arms for to defend our lives.

Our captain spoke unto them and unto them did say,
If you'll return me back those keys I for the same will pay;
No sooner had he spoke these words than they drew forth
     their knives,
Saying the vessel's ours sir, and we will have your lives.

Bartlett again adds an element missing from the ballad, and from the other accounts. Kendrick's gunner, who had been overhauling the ship's weapons, "went On the qurter Deack and tould him that the Natives would take the Vessel from them and it wos Dangerous to Let So Many of them Come Onbord. The Captn Strock the Guner and Pushd him of[f] the qurter Deack So that he had Not time to take the Keyse Out of the Arms Chest." Here was Kendrick's temper, flaring again at the slightest challenge to his authority, as it had in the quarrels with Haswell and Woodruff.

This was the moment the Indians had apparently been waiting for. None of Kendrick's men was armed—another breach of common sense on this savage coast. Coyah seized the keys, then he and some of his warriors leaped onto the arms chests. More natives swarmed toward *Washington* from shore and began to climb aboard, making "a Tarible Norse whith thear war Songs."

Coyah taunted Kendrick, pointing to his legs. "Now put me into your gun carriage." Kendrick, still on deck, tried to pacify the crowd, meanwhile edging toward the companionway. All of this time an Indian held an improvised weapon—a marlinspike stolen from some previous trader and now fixed into a shaft—over Kendrick's head, ready to strike whenever Chief Coyah gave the order.

Our captain then perceiving the ship was in their power,
He spoke unto his people, likewise his officers;
Go down into the cabin and there some arms prepare,
See that they are well loaded, be sure and don't miss fire.

Then down into the cabin straightway we did repair,
And to our sad misfortune few guns could we find there;

We only found six pistols, a gun and two small swords,
And in short time we did agree "blow her up" was the word . . .

Bartlett tells this part of the story on a more realistic note: If the crewmen offered the least resistance, the Indians threatened, all would be killed. They began to drive the Americans down into the hold. Kendrick's friend Ingraham tells of the captain ordering his men to drop off the deck one by one into the hold and to prepare any weapons they could find. Accounts differ as to what they located—"two Pisstols One Musket and two Cutlashes," according to one, "4 musketts a blunderbuss and a pair of pistolls" in another. These, whatever the number, were probably the officers' personal arms.

In the meantime the exultant warriors were amusing themselves by tormenting the sailors who remained on deck by snatching away their hats and kerchiefs. Other Indians were gathering up the trade goods— chiefly sheet copper—that lay scattered about. Kendrick was still on deck grasping the only weapon he had been able to get his hands on—a bar of iron—while Indians surrounded him with daggers drawn.

At this point, Coyah made a tactical error. Probably assuming there were no weapons there, he leaped down the companionway into the hold. Kendrick reacted instantly by jumping down on top of Coyah. The chief's dagger grazed the captain's belly but did no other harm. Seeing a handful of armed crewmen around the captain, Coyah quickly scuttled back on deck. This was the diversion the Americans had been hoping for.

Then with what few firearms we had we rush'd on deck amain,
And by our being resolute, our quarter deck we gain'd;
Soon as we gain'd our arm chest such slaughter then made we,
That in less than ten minutes our ship of them was free.

Then we threw overboard the dead that on our deck there lay;
And found we had nobody hurt, to work we went straightway;
The number kill'd upon our deck that day was sixty good,
And full as many wounded as soon we understood.

As Coyah rushed back on deck, Kendrick had fired a musket from the companionway. Then, abandoning the last-ditch decision to blow up the vessel, he and his men charged after Coyah, shooting and shouting. Kendrick had snatched up a musket and two pistols. All this was too much for the Indians, who, after having held the vessel for nearly an hour, poured over the sides into their canoes. Only one Indian, "a proper amazon" who had urged the warriors on from a position in the rigging, seemed determined to brave it out. She continued to encourage them "with the greatest ardour until the last moment, though her arm had been previously cut of[f] with a [sword] and she was otherwise much wounded." She was the last one to leave the vessel. A crew member shot her as she attempted to swim away.

Though the Indians had fled with the keys to the arms chests, the chests had strangely remained closed but unlocked throughout the encounter. They were now opened, says Hoskins, "and a constant fire was kept up as long as they could reach the natives with the cannon or small arms after which they chased them in their armed boats making the most dreadful havock by killing all they came across."

The result of Coyah's attack was nearly as disastrous to the Indians as the exaggerated count in the ballad. Joseph Ingraham, cruising that area in *Hope* the summer after the encounter, learned that forty of the tribe had been killed. Coyah himself was wounded, as were two of his brothers and Schulkinanse, one of the other chiefs involved. Coyah's wife and two children were also among the dead.

> 'Twas early the next morning at the hour of break of day,
> We sail'd along abreast the town which we came to straightway;
> We call'd on hands to quarters and at the town did play,
> We made them to return what things they'd stolen that day . . .
>
> And now unto old China we're fastly rolling on,
> Where we shall drink good punch for which we've suffered long;
> And when the sixteenth day of June around does yearly come,
> We'll drink in commemoration what on that day was done.
>
> And now for to conclude, and make an end unto my song,
> Success to the commander of the Lady Washington!
> Success unto his voyages wherever he may go,
> And may death and destruction always attend his foe.

Summing up the encounter in his journal, Joseph Ingraham philosophized that "savages seldom forget insults or injuries. It is said of those [Indians] among us on the East side of the continent that they will never fail to revenge . . . an affront of any kind for years after the transaction has happen'd. Till oppertunity presents itself they are apparently on good terms with their adversary."

Ingraham ends his account on a moral tone: "it is sincerely to be hoped the termination of this affair will be of generall service to vessels trading as by convincing [the Indians] that they have little less than inevitable destruction to expect from attacking people who's Instruments of death are so far superior to their own it may render them peacable & content to enjoy what they possess by fair means only."

When *Columbia* on her second voyage reached the Queen Charlotte Islands in July of 1791, less than a month after Coyah's abortive attempt to capture *Washington*, Hoskins asked for the chief. He was no longer a chief, the Indians told him, but an "ahliko," or member of the Haida's lower class. They now had no head chief but many inferior chiefs. Coyah's fall from authority had happened, the Indians told Hoskins, when Kendrick "took Coyah, tied a rope around his neck, whipt him, painted his face, cut off his hair, took away from him a great many skins, and then turned him ashore." This, whether true or not, was obviously a reference to the events of 1789.

In fact, all of Coyah's people seemed to have undergone a dramatic change. "The tribe, when Captain Gray visited it in the Washington in the summer of 1789, was large and powerful; had many skins. but they are now dwindled to a few, as we did not see more than fifty different faces while here." This, Hoskins surmised, was due to Kendrick's having humiliated their chief two years before.

"They are covered with dirt and grease; most of them indeed had their faces painted black, and hair cut short," Hoskins recorded. "This, I have since been informed, is practiced in mourning for the loss of any of their Chiefs . . . or any other calamity."

The Haida women, Hoskins noted, were "always ready and willing to gratify the amorous inclinations of any who wish it, but Captain Gray very prudently forbid any of the ship's company having any connections with these women." Hoskins, however, was not above acting on the theory that it does no harm to look. He prevailed upon one of the mourners to have her face washed, whereupon he discovered "one of the most beautiful countenances my eyes have ever beheld; indeed she was a perfect beauty." Sad to say, she paddled away from the smitten Hoskins in her canoe to return shortly with her face as black as ever. Her friends, it seems, had laughed at her. "What a pity it is," Hoskins noted gloomily, "that these people delight so much in filth and nastiness."

The women of Coyah's village continued to fascinate the impressionable young Bostonian. "In trade, as well as in everything else," he marveled, these emancipated ladies "appear'd to govern the men; as no one dare to conclude a bargain without first asking his wife's consent; if he did, the moment he went into his canoe, he was sure to get a beating . . . and there is no mercy to be expected without the intercession of some kind female." Coyah and his fellow tribesmen, Hoskins concluded, for all their outward ferocity, were "entirely subject to a petticoat government, the women in all cases taking the lead."

Coyah himself turned up that evening. Coming aboard *Columbia*, he seemed to hold no grudge toward Kendrick. He exhibited a "blue coat and some nankin cloth" that he said Kendrick had given him. His "tarry was short," Hoskins wrote, "he appeared much frightened, being in a constant tremor the whole time." But he offered no hint of his disastrous attempt to capture *Washington*. Hoskins would not learn of that until August of 1791, when *Columbia* and *Washington* met in Clayoquot Sound.

The feisty Coyah did not remain an ahliko for long. In 1794, three vessels were actually captured by the Haidas of the Queen Charlotte Islands, and all but two men of their crews were murdered. Two of the three vessels fell to Coyah and his braves.

One, a still-unidentified British ship, had put into Houston Stewart Channel to replace storm-damaged masts. Seeing the vessel disabled, and with sickness among the crew, the Indians surrounded her and killed everyone aboard. John Boit, then captain of the sloop *Union*, recorded seeing in Coyah's possession "the riging of a large ship, whose shroud Hawser was above 9 inches." It was probably a trophy from that vessel.

In the same year, the Haidas under Coyah captured the brig of the American fur trader Simon Metcalfe, killing the captain and his entire crew with the exception of one man "who got up in the Main top and was taken alive." Later rescued by a Boston ship and carried to Hawaii, he told a story closely akin to Kendrick's. Metcalfe had cast aside his usual caution and, like Kendrick, had let a large number of Haidas come aboard. "The natives taken advantage of their superiority in numbers," wrote Boit, "clinch'd and stab'd, ev'ry man on board, except the one that sprung up the Shrouds. This horrid Massacre was executed in the space of a few minutes with no loss, on the side of the natives." The sole survivor suffered a brutal year-long enslavement before his rescue.

The third of these clashes must in a sense also be traced to Coyah. Cumshewa ("Juicy Grass"), a powerful chief on the same island, was inspired by Coyah's successes to attack a small schooner, the ninety-ton tender of the ship *Jefferson* of Boston. Again, all members of the company were murdered with the exception of one seaman who hid in a cask in the hold. Discovered while the Indians were looting the ship, he was enslaved by the Haidas—in fact, made a slave of their slaves—until his rescue about a year later. In an ironic twist of fate, Cumshewa's capture of the little vessel finally gave the Haidas the revenge they had sought for their humiliating defeat by Kendrick three years earlier. The captain's son, Solomon Kendrick, was killed along with the rest of the little vessel's officers.

CHAPTER EIGHTEEN

Land Purchases
Kindle
a Dream of Empire

★

Flushed with victory and rich with otter pelts, Kendrick turned *Lady Washington* southward from Coyah's village across the 150 miles or so of open sea that lay between the southern Queen Charlottes and the northern tip of Vancouver Island. Leisurely trading his way along the coast, he arrived at Nootka Sound on 12 July, nearly a month after the skirmish with the Haidas. Here on Vancouver Island Kendrick would be among the Nootka Indians, a tribe he knew and trusted—and who trusted him.

The territory of the Nootkans embraced some of the Canadian Northwest's most awesome scenery. Deep bays, where the Pacific surf crashes endlessly, lie between high, rocky headlands. Narrow fjords, folded between brooding spruce-clad hills, penetrated far inland. A scenic paradise even to the eighteenth-century's hard-bitten mariners, Nootka had, since Captain Cook's visit in 1778, been a magnet for fur traders, both British and American, and for Spanish dons intent on holding the traders off and extending Spain's dominion northward from California.

When Kendrick took *Washington* through the inlet into Nootka Sound, he was uncertain of the reception he might receive from the new

Spanish commandant but was determined to pick up whatever furs he could find there. Arming his men and loading both cannon and swivels, and with matches alight ready to open fire, he boldly approached the entrance, now guarded by Fort San Miguel. A voice boomed at him from a speaking trumpet, warning him not to enter. The captain pretended he had not understood and headed for his old anchorage at Marvinas Bay.

Partway there the wind died. A launch with an armed party from the fort reached *Lady Washington*'s side. Spanish courtesy alternated with nationalistic anger. The fort's gunners could have sunk Kendrick's vessel, he was told. But since they had not, he was given a warning against trading in the sound. Kendrick's response to the new commandant, Lieutenant Don Francisco Eliza, was properly deferential, as it had been with Martínez before him. He would stay only briefly. The Spaniards thereupon courteously towed the American vessel the rest of the way to Marvinas. Kendrick must have gratefully dropped anchor in this favorite retreat of his, where *Washington* could lie snug as a duck in a ditch. He would have been painfully aware that his little vessel was battered and desperately tired from so many Pacific crossings.

Kendrick promised to pay a call on the commandant, which he promptly forgot to do. But his agreeable reaction to the Spaniards' warning apparently won them over. A supply of the Iberian settlement's garden vegetables was sent to *Lady Washington* every day she remained in Nootka.

The only hint of dissension anywhere in the sound just then appears to have been on board *Washington*. Three of the brigantine's officers lodged a protest against their captain with the commandant and asked that they be allowed to stay at Nootka under Spanish protection. The cause of the difficulty was not recorded, but the Spaniards' response was. The request "was not considered." Kendrick's relationship with the Spanish authorities of "Northern California" had always been relaxed, and it continued to be so, even though Martínez was no longer in command (he had been shipped back to Spain when his wife complained that he had failed to support her and their child).

Despite his promise to move on, Kendrick tarried for nearly two weeks with another old friend, the Nootkan chief Maquinna. There was no question of Kendrick's popularity with the Indians of Vancouver Island. Joseph Ingraham commented on it during his voyage in the *Hope*. The natives, he wrote, "enquired particularly after Capn Kendrick saying they had plenty of skins for him and they would not sell them to any one else ... Indeed they all seem'd very fond of Capn Kendrick for he ever treated them with great kindness." A Spanish botanist, visiting Nootka in 1791, noted that Kendrick, alone among the traders, made a point of conforming to the Indians' customs, spoke their language, and even adopted their dress. He entertained the Nootkans with fireworks, and often gave them gifts.

As a relief from the cramped quarters aboard *Washington*, Kendrick would probably have relished a stay in one of the great Nootkan houses of red cedar. They were twenty feet or more wide and sometimes 150 feet long. The only permanent elements of these structures were four huge corner posts and a ridgepole made of a single great tree. Sailor John Jewitt measured one of the latter in Maquinna's house at Friendly Cove, "which I found to be one hundred feet long and eight feet four inches in diameter." The boards, great planks as much as five feet wide, were transported from one camp to another as the Indians moved from their winter village far inland, to another beside their principal salmon stream, to a third, where *Washington* now lay at anchor, convenient to summer fishing and whale hunting.

Inside these huge communal houses there were no rooms, but living areas were marked off by rows of baskets and elaborately painted and carved storage boxes, also of cedar. Away from the doorway, at the end screened from the incessant southwest winds, Chief Maquinna would have had his living quarters. Here, as everywhere else, kitchen scraps littered the floor, fish dried odorously, blubber on overhead racks dripped rancid whale oil, and a pall of cook fire smoke cast a bluish haze over the entire scene. This rich blend of smells was quite acceptable to the Indians—and, to Kendrick and his crew, probably would not have been much different from the flavor of a small ship below decks after a year or more at sea.

What bothered the Indians was the odor of cheese, which made them gag whenever they were offered it by the fur traders. Salt they also violently disliked. Ships' biscuit liberally sopped in molasses was a great treat, however, as were tea and coffee if heavily sweetened.

During the fine days of spring and summer the Indians caught huge quantities of herring that came to Nootka's sheltered coves to spawn. Eggs of sea birds were collected. Trolling lures of fresh herring were towed behind swift dugout canoes for spring salmon, and hair seal and sea lions were harpooned. And then there were the sea otters. When the wind dropped and the sea lay calm, Nootkan hunters would paddle out to the great beds of kelp that lay offshore. Here the female otters would leave their young while they dove for the big deep-water clams that were their favorite meal. The Indians found these sea-otter pups easy prey and used imitations of their cries, in turn, to lure the frantic mothers into killing range.

After *Washington's* long ocean voyage, all of this strange activity and the heady freedom of life ashore made it easy for Kendrick and his crew to put off their promised departure. Day after pleasant day slipped by. As he tarried and traded with Maquinna's people under the Spaniard's noses —while there he bought nearly eight hundred sea-otter skins—Kendrick launched a project that had been long in his mind. Instructions given him by Joseph Barrell and the expedition's other owners had directed that should "you make any fort or improvement of land upon the coast, be sure you purchase the soil of the natives, and it would not be amiss if you purchased some advantageous tract of land in the name of the owners."

Notice that there appear to be two separate ideas here. At least they can be read that way: that Kendrick purchase land, and almost as an afterthought, that he might also purchase a tract for the owners. That was certainly not the intent of Joseph Barrell and his associates. But then, Kendrick had never paid much attention to the fine print. And anyway, those instructions had long ago gone back to Boston with Gray aboard *Columbia*.

To Kendrick's visionary mind—he had once proposed shifting the direction of the Atlantic's prevailing westerly winds and, more than a century before it would become a serious possibility, creating a waterway across the narrow waist of Mexico to link the Atlantic and Pacific oceans —the idea of colonizing the remote Northwest Coast must have seemed a modest dream indeed. In exchange for ten muskets, a commodity naturally frowned upon by the Spanish authorities—though they seemed powerless to do much about it—Maquinna and five of his subchiefs affixed their marks to the following document:

> I, Macquinnah, of Nootka sound, on the north-west coast of America
> . . . do sell and grant unto John Kendrick . . . a certain harbor in said
> Nootka sound, called Chastacktoos, in which the brigantine Lady
> Washington lay at anchor on the twentieth day of July, 1791, with all

the land, rivers, creeks, harbors, islands, etc., within nine miles north, east, west and south . . . only the said John Kendrick does grant and allow the said Macquinnah to live and fish on the said territory as usual."

The deed made it clear that the eighty-one-square-mile tract belonged solely to "the said John Kendrick, his heirs, executors, and administrators, from henceforth and forever, as his property absolutely."

When Maquinna and his chiefs had each marked their X, nine of the *Washington's* crew added their names as witnesses. John Stoddard, the captain's clerk, had probably drawn up the deed. The others were second mate John Redman; the carpenter, Thomas Foster; sailmaker William Bowles; John Porter, carpenter's mate; gunner James Crawford; Robert Green, the cooper; and John Barber, the ship's blacksmith. Also signing was a mysterious Florence McCarthy, whose sex and occupation remain unknown to this day. The location of Kendrick's purchase, which he renamed Safe Retreat harbor in the deed, was in all likelihood his favorite retreat, Marvinas Bay, where he had anchored when he arrived back at Nootka.

Years later, a retired sailor named John Tremere of Boston, by then seventy-seven years old, recalled having entered Nootka Inlet aboard the ship *Jefferson* while Kendrick was making his deal with Maquinna. He told of seeing the chief climb up to the masthead of Kendrick's brigantine and point to distant parts of the territory. "The lands were taken possession of with much ceremony," another old seaman remembered, "the American flag hoisted, a bottle sunk in the ground, etc., and many Chiefs present at the ceremony." Kendrick had remembered well the pageantry when Martínez had taken possession of Nootka Sound in the name of the Spanish king.

At this point caution seems to have suggested itself to Kendrick. If he went boldly out of Nootka Sound the way he had entered, the Spaniards would be forcibly reminded of how little attention he had paid to their orders. More than that, he might be called to account for the $8,000 due Martínez for the sale in China of his sea-otter skins. Of course, that money had long ago disappeared into the pockets of Macao's and Canton's merchants. Kendrick decided to leave by way of the narrow channels behind Nootka Island. These were the waterways he and Robert Haswell had explored two years before, which the Indians had told him led all of the way around the island and back into the ocean again. Kendrick's son

John, Jr., had also made his way through them and probably thought at first he had found that Holy Grail of every Pacific navigator, the Northwest Passage that would lead him to the Atlantic. But the twisting waterway had only led him again into the Pacific.

This back route would be no picnic, Kendrick knew. Though only about thirty miles lay between "Safe Retreat Harbor," where he was now anchored, and Esperanza Inlet, where he could again slip into the open sea, the entire distance lay through narrow, fjord-like passages. Even little *Washington* would have no chance of maneuvering through under sail. If the winds were anything less than ideal, she might have to travel the whole way on an "ash breeze"—towed by oarsmen in the ship's boats. Racing tides would mean that even that could be done only when the tide ran fair.

By 2 August—and possibly before that—Kendrick had managed to reach the Pacific through this twisting maze. He anchored in Nuchatlitz Inlet, just south of Esperanza. Three days later, "in consideration of two muskets, a boat's sail, and a quantity of powder," the captain acquired from Tarrason, his two sons, and another chief "a certain harbor in said New Chatleck, called by the natives Hoot-see-ess, but now called Port Montgomery ... on the south side of the sound of Ahasset, and now called Massachusetts-sound, being a territorial distance of eighteen miles square."

Washington now moved across Esperanza Inlet, where Kendrick gave Norry-Youk and three other chiefs the usual muskets, sail, and powder, plus an American flag, for a square, again eighteen miles on a side, centering on the harbor of Chenerkintau, which the captain promptly renamed Kendrick's Harbor. Judge Frederic W. Howay, a lifelong student of early voyages to the Northwest Coast, tentatively identified Chenerkintau as the Indian village of Cheninkint, on beautiful Queen's Cove just inside Esperanza Inlet.

Presumably leaving *Washington* at anchor there, Kendrick now had himself rowed in the ship's boat back up Esperanza Inlet and through winding Hecate Channel to the northernmost tip of Tahsis Inlet, which lies, wrote John Jewitt, "between a range of lofty hills ... covered with the finest forest trees of the country." Kendrick and Haswell had camped overnight here on their shooting excursion two years before, and Kendrick had never forgotten those steep, wooded hills and deep dark waters. He must have been enchanted by this area, "abounding with the most romantic views, charmingly diversified, and fine streams of water falling in beautiful cascades from the mountains." He had hurried back only the day after he had completed his dealings at Esperanza. Here Kendrick obtained from Hannopy, a lesser chief who had also signed Maquinna's deed, and the chief of Tahsis, Caarshucornook, a tract "nine miles around said Tashees."

In all of this land speculation, Kendrick was following a path firmly established by his paternal grandfather. An immigrant from Lancashire who settled on Cape Cod about 1700, Edward Kenwrick the next year acquired a tract between Eastham and Harwich from the Wampanoag Indian John Sipson. The deed expressed "ye love" Sipson felt for "Mr. Edward Kindwrick, weaver," and acknowledged the payment of "valew-bel considerations." Kenwrick bought subsequent parcels of land from more than a dozen individuals, all of them Indians.

John Kendrick and his oarsmen now made their way back to *Lady Washington*, and the little brigantine headed south again past Nootka to drop anchor in Clayoquot Sound. When *Columbia*, on her second voyage, reached Clayoquot, about sixty miles south of Nootka, the Indians told Gray that Kendrick was already there and had been there some time. "Nothing can equal the pleasure I received," *Columbia*'s supercargo John Hoskins wrote, "on meeting my old friend or our mutual professions of happiness on the occasion, each being as eager to recount his various vicissitudes of fortune since parting as the other was to hear." They had not seen each other since October of 1787, when *Columbia* left Boston on her first voyage. Hoskins at that time was an eighteen-year-old clerk in Joseph Barrell's Boston counting house.

It was an odd but fortunate circumstance that a deep friendship had developed between young Hoskins and the then forty-seven-year-old captain. As soon as Kendrick came aboard *Columbia* in Clayoquot Sound, Hoskins began to fill pages of his journal with the best record we have of Kendrick's comings and goings between February 1790, when *Columbia* left Kendrick in Macao and sailed home to Boston, and *Columbia*'s and *Washington*'s reunion eighteen months later.

Kendrick must have delighted in regaling *Columbia*'s crew with the story of Coyah's treachery and his own success in regaining his vessel from the attackers. And well he might have, for he had displayed extraordinary courage and quick thinking throughout the affair. But he probably was even more enthusiastic about his purchases of the Indians' "landed estates," as Hoskins called them. Kendrick became fond of saying that he had bought his territories, while other nations stole theirs. Kendrick also liked to boast—perhaps when he was "in Lickqur," as John Bartlett phrased it—of having told the Spanish commandant at Nootka Sound that if the Spaniards became impertinent, he would raise the Indians and drive the Europeans from their settlements.

After having been entertained aboard *Columbia*, Kendrick reciprocated by inviting Captain Gray and Hoskins to breakfast. Going to Marvinas Bay in the ship's jolly boat, they were received "at a small Island which [Kendrick] had fortified and dignified with the appellation of Fort Washington in honour of our Illustrious President." Here was the last of Kendrick's land purchases, bought of Chief Wickananish, for "four muskets, a large sail, and a quantity of powder (they being articles which we at present stand in need of, and are of great value)." This statement seems to refute the claim, made by the Spaniards at Nootka, that Kendrick had at some point given Wickananish "more than two hundred guns, two barrels of powder, and a considerable portion of shot." It hardly seems possible that Kendrick would ever have had so many weapons aboard that he could hand them out in such wholesale portions.

During these days when *Columbia* and *Washington* were together again at Clayoquot, Kendrick must have agonized over the stories he surely knew had made their way back to Boston: his delays in reaching Cape Horn, which had cost both vessels the best of a season on the coast, his handling of *Washington* as if she were his own, his failure to make even a token accounting to the owners in Boston. Now with a cargo of a thousand sea-otter skins to show for his three months on the coast, he pondered his alternatives: Go on to China, sell his furs, and complete this voyage, at least, with credit to himself and a profit to Barrell and company, or turn the whole thing—ship, cargo, and all—back to Gray and Hoskins to carry on with as they thought best.

The captain—he was now fifty-two years old, an old man by the standards of the day—put the problem up to his young friend Hoskins, who as supercargo of *Columbia* was responsible for the ship's business dealings. If Hoskins would pay his crew's wages, Kendrick offered, plus the money he had borrowed in Macao in order to rerig his vessel and return to the coast, he would turn over to him both the vessel and the thousand skins. Kendrick would certainly have suggested that he carry on as *Washington*'s captain at least back to China.

Hoskins told Kendrick that his responsibility was only *Columbia* and her affairs. He had no authority to accept Kendrick's offer or to demand any payment of him, nor did he think anyone on the ship had.

So that was that. Hoskins's account contains no hint of whether his decision was a relief to the old trader or a disappointment. However it came down, Kendrick now had no choice but to continue his preparations for the trip alone back to Macao.

CHAPTER NINETEEN

Stirrings of Trouble
with the Indians

★

John Hoskins was by now complaining as bitterly about Gray's conduct of *Columbia*'s second voyage as Haswell had about Kendrick's handling of the first. The young supercargo grumbled at this point that *Columbia* was "subject to every inconvenience that can possibly attend a ship on an undiscovered coast save the knowledge derived from Captain Gray's former voyage, which is none. . . . But for Mr. Haswell, our chief mate, who was with Captain Gray . . . we should be totally ignorant of every part of the coast . . ."

In a letter to Barrell, Hoskins was more specific about Gray's shortcomings, both as a commander and as a loyal employee. Insisting that Gray had failed to exercise command of the ship, he charged that *Columbia* had "run many risks both in sailing along shore, and going into harbors, unknown, unsounded, and without a boat in the water." Certainly the incidence of groundings and near disasters on both *Washington* and *Columbia* while Gray was their captain had been and would continue to be alarmingly high.

As to business, Hoskins had a high regard for neither Gray nor

Haswell. One day, he reported to Barrell, "Captain Gray brought out several old fashion woolen coats and other articles, which I have heard him declare, if he could get an opportunity he would sell and convert the proceeds to his own use. . . . He has also said should the Ship go to Boston, he would not send any property of his own in her, he would send it to New York." In short, declared Hoskins, Gray was "a man, who has not the least principle of honour or honesty but appears to be divested of every virtue, and who is in grain if not openly a Knave and a Fool." Curiously, Hoskins's last comment was echoed almost word for word four years later by *Lady Washington*'s then captain, John Howel. "Except Mr. Hoskins," Howel wrote to Joseph Barrell after Kendrick's death, "I hardly ever saw a man in your N. W. employ, who was not either fool or Rogue, and your commanders united these characters."

As for Haswell, Hoskins told Barrell, he had been reported telling his fellow officers "that he would make 10,000 Dollars, he would then go to England that the Owners might go to hell and his wages and per Centage with them."

Some of this appears to have been known to Barrell by way of the first voyage. "If you will recollect," Hoskins wrote, "the Captain of our ship is a man of no principle." There is only one way that sentence can be read: that Barrell had learned of irregularities in Gray's conduct of the first voyage, a conclusion borne out by the language of the Boston merchant's orders to Gray for the second.

". . . I could wish there was some person in Canton," Hoskins continued, "who had your orders to take the Ship and Cargo out of the present hands. If there was I think it would be to your advantage." After the finish of the voyage, Hoskins concluded his indictment, "to you and their faces I will relate every circumstance." That Hoskins returned to Boston and became Joseph Barrell's personal agent in Europe and a successful merchant in partnership with one of Barrell's sons while Robert Gray looked elsewhere for employment suggests that Hoskins may have done exactly that.

As *Columbia* made her way south, Hoskins continued to snipe at Gray's every action. Why, he wanted to know, had Gray passed up the village of Tahtence, in the Queen Charlotte Islands? It was there that "Captain Gray on his former voyage procured more skins than at any other part of the coast nor did he get all for they broke him of trade [goods] and he was obliged to return to Nootka." In a few moments, Gray had purchased two hundred pelts there, and for only one chisel each. A British trader, two years before that, had acquired three hundred there at the same price in less than an hour. Now, with ample trade goods aboard, Gray sailed by without attempting to reach the village. Hoskins sarcastically explained that Gray did not know how to find it on his own "and was therefore loath to expose his ignorance after so much pretended vaunted knowledge."

On 29 August *Columbia* was back in Clayoquot Sound. Kendrick, who had been there a month already, waited with his tales of the encounter with Coyah's braves in the Queen Charlotte Islands and of his own land purchases at Clayoquot and in Nootka Sound. Despite the tension that might have been expected between Gray and Kendrick, *Columbia* and *Washington* and all on board the two vessels made up a warm and friendly community for the rest of that summer. Boit, to be sure, noted disapprovingly in his journal that Kendrick had still not remitted so much as a dollar to his owners in Boston. But Boit exaggerated when he described Kendrick as "under some mistrust that Capt. Gray was empower'd to seize the Brig, and kept himself always ready against attack."

Every other document makes clear the mutual confidence and fellowship that existed between the captains and officers of the two ships throughout this period. Haswell, for instance, notes that when *Columbia* and *Washington* met at Clayoquot, Gray greeted his fellow captain warmly, firing a gun and hoisting the ship's colors. When Kendrick came alongside *Columbia*, he was saluted with three cheers. Haswell, of course, could not let the meeting pass without some criticism. Comparing the fact that since the two vessels had parted in China eighteen months before, *Columbia* had sailed back to Boston, been completely refitted and resupplied, and then returned to the Northwest Coast by way of Cape Horn while *Washington*, so far as he knew, had merely sold her furs and come back across the Pacific, he concluded smugly that "our former commander is not a very urgent man of business."

Though a good many skins appeared to be available at Clayoquot, *Columbia* stayed there only briefly. Gray, navigator or no, was a determined trader, and he was not willing to let Crowell and the *Hancock* beat him to the last furs of the season. Whatever Clayoquot had to offer would still be around when he came back. After little more than a week at anchor, the ship bore away toward the Strait of Juan de Fuca and the southern end of Vancouver Island. This time Gray's foolhardy navigation came in for stinging criticism from all three of the chroniclers aboard.

On 11 September, offshore of Cape Flattery, surf-swept rocks suddenly appeared at dawn through the fog. The ship's boats barely managed to tow *Columbia* clear against a racing tide. "Our situation was truly alarming," said Boit in his journal, "but we had no business so near the land in thick weather. However Good Luck prevail'd." Haswell concludes his account of the occurrence by saying "we narrowly escaped our impending fate."

Next day Boit recorded another close call: "At 3 PM saw a rock about [a] stone's throw distant, and narrowly escaped being dash'd upon itt. Damn nonsense to keep beating about among rocks in foggy weather.... The Captain, at length, was frightned, and proceeded with the Ship to a good offing (this ought to have been done long before)." Hoskins, no longer alone in his condemnation of Gray's handling of the *Columbia*, probably summed up the encounters for all three: "There was not the least chance while this weather continued of the natives coming of[f] with skins. [The captain] therefore must be blamed by every body for sporting with the lives of so many people under his charge."

On 18 September 1791, with few new skins to show for so harrowing an adventure, *Columbia* again lay at anchor in Clayoquot Sound. Gray's first concern now was to select a location suitable for the building of the sloop, the frames for which had all of this time been waiting in the ship's hold. With the aid of Kendrick's boats as well as his own, *Columbia* was towed to a sheltered cove a few miles farther inland, where she was secured by cables to trees on either side. This snug anchorage, protected from every quarter, was christened Adventure Cove. The sloop to be built there would be named *Adventure* rather than *Nootka*, as Joseph Barrell had directed. Probably this was because another *Nootka*, John Meares's first ship, had already established a rather unsavory reputation on the Northwest Coast.

Ashore, a party was set to work laying the foundations for a house in which the ship's company could spend the winter. Hoskins, in his careful way, describes it minutely: thirty-six feet long and eighteen wide, with a lower story formed of logs held together by wooden pins. Seams were chinked with mortar the seamen made with clay and burned shells. Cedar boards "procured from the natives for a trifling consideration in iron" covered an upper story. Two ports for cannon and loopholes all around secured it against Indian attack.

A forge was set up for the blacksmith, and a brick fireplace was built to provide warmth and a cook fire. For this latter, Columbia's customs clearance when she left Boston listed two thousand bricks. In fact, Boston merchant Eliakim Morse, nominally an apothecary and grocer, had dipped into another line of trade long enough to stuff the ship's hold with 5,470 of them. To defend the little outpost, four cannon, forty muskets, a number of blunderbusses and pistols, and a quantity of ammunition were sent ashore from the ship. Finished on the last day of September and placed under the command of Robert Haswell, the establishment was dubbed Fort Defiance.

While Gray's stronghold was rising at Adventure Cove, Kendrick's own Fort Washington, farther up the sound, had been demolished and its guns put back aboard his brigantine. On 29 September Kendrick sailed out of Clayoquot Sound on his way back to China. Although he had proposed giving up Lady Washington and her cargo to John Hoskins (who, it will be remembered, turned the offer down), this may have been only a momentary gesture. The old mariner's head still buzzed with grandiose schemes that would recoup his fortunes—and perhaps even those of the ship's owners. Hoskins, ever Kendrick's friend, took "the most affectionate leave of him as he left the harbor." This would be their last meeting.

With Columbia laid up for the winter and the house ashore completed, the ship's company turned to the task of building the new sloop. The keel was laid and cedar logs were brought in the ship's boat to be sawed into planks. Two sawpits, a blacksmith's shop, and a boatbuilders' shed gave Adventure Cove, said Boit, "the appearance of a young ship yard." Clayoquot's Indians helped by supplying as many boards as the shipwrights could use. "They was all caeder, and appear'd to have been split with wedges from the Log."

Christmas at Adventure Cove, when "Wickananish with a number of other Chiefs . . . honored us with their company," must have been reminiscent of the first Thanksgiving at Plymouth with its Indian guests and bountiful foods. The Americans had decorated the house and fort, as well as the ship and the partially completed sloop, with "spruce boughs interspersed with the various flowers of the season," and the company was "allowed as many fowl such as geese, ducks, teals etca. as they could eat, also of grog and every other thing a double allowance."

The wives of the chiefs were also invited but shyly remained in their canoes, dining on "what we chose to send them from our festive board

Settling in for the winter of 1791-92, Gray picked a secluded cove in Vancouver Island's
Clayoquot Sound, safely away from the Spanish authorities at Nootka, where his
shipwrights could assemble the little sloop *Adventure* (center), the first United States
vessel built in the Pacific Northwest. Nearby, with her top mast lowered, *Columbia* lies at
anchor, while the crew lives ashore in a rough blockhouse armed with two of the ship's
cannon. Gray named his settlement Fort Defiance. In 1973 historian Samuel Eliot Morison
located the site on Meares's Island, and in 1977 amateur archaeologists confirmed the
identification with the discovery of the fort's chimney, built of bricks
brought from Boston aboard *Columbia*.
(*George Davidson, Oregon Historical Society*, OrHi 59298/1147)

which the Chiefs their husbands dictated." John Boit noted the Indians' surprise at seeing "20 Geese roasting at one immense fire ... At 12 Clock fir'd a federall Salute, and ended the day toasting our sweethearts and wifes." The ship's company, John Hoskins recorded approvingly, "returned to their duties not the least intoxicated with liquor."

For Gray's crew, accustomed to the rigors of New England winters, the mildness of the Northwest Coast came as a pleasant surprise. "The Weather was generally very fine," noted Boit, with his memories of harsh Massachusetts winters, "and very seldom had Snow, and never Ice thicker than a Spanish Dollar, but experienced frequent heavy rains. We pick'd Whurtle and Blue Berries, throughout the winter, which was very fine, and Whurtle Berry pudings was quite common with us. We kept the Crew continually supplied with Spruce beer, and their breakfast and supper was Tea boiled from the green Spruce boughs sweetned with Molasses. Perhaps this method kept the Scurvey off." Strange that they should not have realized that scurvy never occurred ashore, nor would it have at sea, so long as they could eat those fine blueberry puddings and the other bounty of that fertile shore.

Clayoquot's Indian residents continued to give every appearance of friendship. Groups of them, sometimes including Chief Wickananish, regularly visited Adventure Cove and marveled at the work going on. They still harbored a deep resentment, however, over Gray's having humiliated the chief's brother earlier the previous spring by taking him as a hostage when the Hawaiian cabin boy, Attoo, had attempted to desert.

This seems not to have been the only reason for Wickananish's animosity. Another instance of Gray's ruthless attitude toward the Indians was recorded by Captain Josiah Roberts of the Boston fur-trader *Jefferson*, on which Solomon Kendrick served as first officer. Gray, said Roberts, "having lent to Wickananish a great coat to wear on shore," grew angry when the garment was not returned as promptly as he expected. Gray once again took out his anger on one of the chief's brothers by seizing his sea-otter cutsark in payment "& presented a musquet to his breast with threats to shoot him unless he should produce more skins for the great coat." On the other side of that coin, Roberts added, Wickananish "seemed to have a marked confidence in Capt. Kendrick."

Gray's inability to get along with Wickananish contrasts starkly with the experiences of other traders. The chief, Captain Charles Bishop of the British fur-trader *Ruby* said, "is one of the most easy people to deal with I ever knew. He prides himself on having but one word in a barter. He throws the skins before you—these are the furs, I want such an article. If you object, they are taken back into the canoe and not offered again."

Though the Americans by and large maintained an easy relationship with their Indian friends, seemingly unbroken by these awkward incidents, an undercurrent of concern kept them from becoming careless. Suddenly awakened by a musket shot and a cry that the cove was full of Indians, Haswell one foggy October night rushed to the beach with an armed party. "But wonderful to tell, these mighty war equipped savages, turned out to be none other than some rocks, which the tide ebbing low, had left dry. . . . I did not chide the sentinel for a false alarm, for it were better to be alarmed when no danger is nigh than once to let it overtake us unprepared."

The next encounter proved a little more disconcerting. Captain Gray and John Boit, now third mate after the death of Mr. Caswell, took a crew in the jolly boat and went in search of geese. The boat dropped Gray at a place frequented by the birds and took Boit to the opposite side of the sound. Boit sent the boat off to still another location. Waiting quietly for the approach of game, Boit instead saw three canoes, each with four men armed with spears and the leader with a musket. A group of the Indians approached him and attempted to snatch his cartridge box, which fell to the ground. Boit, then barely past his seventeenth birthday, coolly put his foot on the box, leveled his gun at the chief, and told him he would be shot if the men continued to harass him.

After a tense face-off, during which the jolly boat returned, the Indians agreed to leave if Boit would tell them where Captain Gray was. Boit told them Gray was at the Indian village of Opitsat, Hoskins recorded in his account of the incident, "where he was not." The Indians "paddled away with the greatest precipitation." Boit picked up Gray from his shooting stand on the other side of the sound and the group returned to the ship.

That afternoon, reports Haswell, the same chief who had accosted Boit earlier in the day came to *Columbia* "and sold two geese with the greatest unconcern." Haswell judged the natives intended only to rob Gray and Boit. Hoskins took a different and, as it turned out, correct view. "It is very probable these were a parcel of fellows employed by Tootiscosettle [Chief Wickananish's brother] to get revenge for Captain Gray's taking him [hostage] some time since. . . . These people did not appear to have a wish to hurt anyone else and all their enquiries were for him." Boit, in his journal, modestly makes no mention of the incident.

The natives were at first puzzled as to how the Americans expected to move the sloop the seventy-five feet that lay between it and the water. Once it had been explained that ways would be built of logs between the finished boat and the cove, over which *Adventure* would slide, the visitors became particularly inquisitive as to the launching date. By February, with the sloop nearing completion and the trading season looming, plans were made to shift *Columbia* to a nearby bank where the ship could be careened and readied for sea. Hoskins objected to the plan, pointing out that by having ship and fort out of sight of each other, the Americans would effectively be divided into two companies and would thus be much less able to put up a strong defense in case of attack. Convenience and the seeming friendliness of the Indians overcame any qualms others among the Americans might have felt.

Hoskins's uneasiness was not helped by the sound of gunfire from the direction of one of the Indians' villages. A visiting chief explained next day that he had been teaching his people to shoot at a board on which he had drawn a figure the size of a man. They were going to war against another tribe and he wanted his villagers to know how to shoot in the darkness.

While plans proceeded both for the launching of the sloop and careening of *Columbia*, Wickananish and several lesser chiefs invited Hoskins to visit Opitsat. Everyone in the village appeared unusually busy. Wickananish superintended the making of canoes—to be used for whaling, he explained. In the houses men were fashioning spears and barbed arrows. Others were loading muskets and making shot. Shortly, the chief told Hoskins, his people were going to destroy a tribe not far away called Hichahats. The war was to start in two months.

In the house of Wickananish's father, Hoskins found a parade of Indians bringing arrows and spears for the old man's approval. He measured one against Hoskins's body, laughingly wondering if it would go through him. Wickananish made no secret of his interest in *Columbia*. Had the Americans finished graving the ship? If she still lay on the bank, would she be there all night? Hoskins gave him evasive answers, as he did to Tootiscosettle that afternoon when he found him hanging around Adventure Cove.

Coming atop the ominous tone of all he had seen and heard at

Opitsat that day, Hoskins was further disturbed to find the ship's company in a highly excited state when he returned. Owen Smith, *Columbia's* second mate since Caswell's death, had seen Attoo in deep conversation with one of the chiefs. He ordered the Hawaiian back to work but Attoo quickly contrived to start the conversation anew. Smith now spoke so harshly to Attoo that the boy sulked off to the blacksmith's shed. Attoo vented his anger to a shipmate, ingenuously asking if Smith thought he was plotting with the chief to attack the ship. This so aroused the man's suspicions that he forced Attoo to admit what he and the chief had really been discussing.

Attoo confessed that the Indians wanted him to wet the charges in *Columbia's* and the fort's guns and to remove the priming from all of the muskets and pistols. The Indians promised Attoo a sea-otter skin for each musket ball he would bring them. They had originally planned to come to the ship that night but now had decided to wait a day or two. They would approach through the underbrush and could easily jump onto *Columbia* where she lay on the bank, kill the sentry, and then murder everyone aboard. Attoo was to run to the Indians when the attack commenced. For his part in the plot, they promised to make the gullible youth a great chief.

Surprisingly, Attoo must have convinced Gray that he had refused to take part in the scheme and had voluntarily warned his shipmates of their danger. Had Gray believed otherwise he surely would have killed him.

There was only one thing to do: Finish graving *Columbia* that night and get her off the bank and into the water by morning. Once away from the beach and at anchor again in full view of the fort, they would be able to stand off an attack if it came. The entire company worked throughout that clear, starlit night. At high tide the ship was hauled farther onto the shore and the half of the bottom that had remained undone was scraped, burnt off, and retarred by the light of flaring torches. A "most dismal whoop" shortly after midnight indicated that the Indians had indeed decided to attack as they had originally planned. "The people who belonged to the Fort flew to their arms," Hoskins records, "and those who belonged to the ship was by no means behind them." But the Indians must have realized that their plot had been discovered. The attack never came. "We continued to hear the most dreadful shrieks or whoops till day began to dawn. I suppose those ... must have been the order for retreat."

By nine that morning the rising tide had floated the ship free. Eager to know what was going on, the Indians sent a canoe with three people into the cove, ostensibly to sell a few fish. Another canoe with three women came about midday, offering fish and vegetables for which they would accept only powder and shot. Gray angrily told them they would be given plenty of both when his ships came down to Opitsat—a promise he would keep to the letter.

Though they had worked all night, the ship's crew loaded all of the stores back aboard *Columbia* and got her off to her old mooring in the cove by sunset. Tools and other valuables were brought aboard, the guns at the fort were unloaded and taken from their carriages so they could not be used against the ship, and the unfinished sloop was secured as well as possible. That night the exhausted crew slept with their weapons, "but the natives did not think it prudent to disturb us."

CHAPTER TWENTY

More Trouble
—and a
Grim Revenge

★

Gray's anger with the Indians for their attempt to capture the ship surfaced often in the days that followed. When Tootiscosettle and the father of Wickananish showed up at the cove, clearly frightened, though they tried to act as if nothing untoward had happened, Gray seized the furs they had brought, told them they should seek their pay from their fellow tribesmen, and ordered them not to return on pain of death. Hoskins, with his eyes fixed firmly on business, expressed his regret at Gray's high-handed action, which "effectually shut up our source of trade. . . . We now have no longer a right to expect to be able to procure any more skins from this tribe, who as yet have done us no farther injury than alarm us [and] confine us to the cove and within reach of our vessels, out of which at present we have no bussiness."

Gray, on the other hand, wanted no more traffic with Chief Wickananish or any of his people. The Indians of the immediate area, through the eagerness of the traders for their sea-otter skins, had by now accumulated a stock of more than two hundred firearms and a large quantity of ammunition, and had learned how to use them. With a total force of

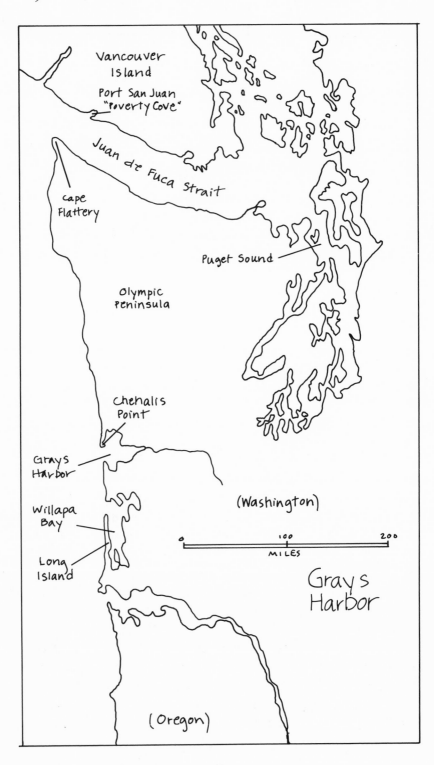

Vancouver Island

Port San Juan "Poverty Cove"

Juan de Fuca Strait

Cape Flattery

Puget Sound

Olympic Peninsula

Chehalis Point

Grays Harbor

Willapa Bay

Long Island

(Washington)

0   100   200
MILES

Grays Harbor

(Oregon)

around two thousand men gathered from their own and neighboring tribes, the Indians lacked only the resolution necessary to overwhelm this little group of strangers in their midst. Gray was both angry and realistic. It mattered not whether sea-otter skins were available here; he was determined to go elsewhere.

That meant completing the unfinished sloop as rapidly as possible, and at the same time getting *Columbia* ready for sea after her long winter lay-up. Haswell, in charge of all these shore operations, lost no time. First he sent four charges of cannister shot rocketing into the forest around the unfinished sloop to be sure no Indians lurked there. Then, under a strongly armed guard, the carpenters were ordered to finish and launch *Adventure* as quickly as possible so the entire group could move out of Clayoquot Sound. Within twenty-four hours the new vessel was ready to be run down the ways and into the cove.

Suddenly, with this proud symbol of accomplishment rising in their midst, the tension lifts and a spirit of celebration sweeps over the little company. Shipwrights worked in those days from first light to sunset, and these energetic Yankees have also spent a few nights frantically working by torchlight to finish *Adventure* and to ready *Columbia* for sea. Now they are desperately eager to put an end to this business of hammers and saws and get back to being sailors again. Here on this remote coast there has not even been that traditional benefit of shipyard life, the foreman's hearty call of "Grog O!" echoing off the dark cedars and firs in late morning and again as the sun begins to drop. *Columbia*'s supply of ardent spirits, sixteen months away from Boston now, is far too low to afford the quart of rum deemed a proper expenditure in a shipyard back home for every ton of vessel being built.

The launch, though, will be another matter. A flag flutters in the sea breeze now at *Adventure*'s stern, and others billow restlessly above *Columbia*, riding at anchor a few-score yards offshore. An agile seaman, with a bottle of precious rum in one hand, has ever so carefully slid and pushed himself out to the very tip of the new ship's stout bowsprit, to sit precariously there with bottle held aloft and legs clamped tightly around the spar while his mates knock out the wedges that keep the sloop from starting prematurely down the sloping ways.

As the last wedge clatters out and the little ship slowly moves stern-to toward the water, the man on the bowsprit raises the bottle to his own lips in a toast to this graceful new member of faraway Boston's merchant fleet. His Adam's apple bobbing, he rhythmically swallows gulp after gulp of the raw spirit, as much as he can hurry down without choking, amid shouts from the seamen below of "Ho, there. Save some for the ship!" Then, while at least a drop remains for this ceremonial birth rite, he calls out the name of the vessel—"I christen ye *Adventure!*"—and brings the bottle smashing down onto the tip of the bowsprit.

Alas, almost before the shards of glass have glistened for a sunlit instant and then hit the muddy ground, the ways have sunk into the muck and the sloop has ground to a halt barely her own length closer to the water.

Next day they try again. *Adventure* gains another thirty feet before the green wood of the ways buckles and once more halts her progress. Finally, on 23 February, with the aid of a hawser attached to a winch aboard *Columbia*, *Adventure* splashes into the cove, the first American-built vessel launched in the Pacific Northwest.

Now all was serious business again. The sloop was quickly made ready for sea. First-mate Robert Haswell, now Captain Haswell, went aboard as commander, taking with him *Columbia*'s fourth mate and a crew of ten. "She was one of the prettiest vesels I ever saw," John Boit wrote enthusiastically, "of about 45 Tons, with a handsome figurehead and false badges, and other ways touch'd off in high stile." *Adventure*'s hull and deck planking, sawed from the majestic cedars of the British Columbia coast, ran in continuous boards "not above nine inches wide" for the whole of her fifty-foot length.

Food and trade goods for a four-month cruise were put aboard *Adventure*. Gray, still seething with anger, insisted that the fort ashore be stripped of everything that might be of value to the Indians. On 26 March 1792, with the heady challenge of spring in the air, *Columbia* and her new tender left Adventure Cove and headed out of Clayoquot Sound for the open sea. But first, Robert Gray had a fateful appointment to keep.

The angry captain sent John Hoskins and a crew of seamen ashore when the ships came abreast of Wickananish's village, Opitsat. Hoskins found it had recently been deserted, apparently in great haste. Domestic utensils lay scattered about the houses and hidden in the brush behind them. Aware from Gray's explosive reaction of a few days before that their plot to seize the ship was fully known to the Americans, they probably had fled at the first sight of the ships. They might even have remembered Gray's threat the next time his ships passed Opitsat to give them the bullets and powder they continually asked for in exchange for their skins. Gray gave way to a cruel and vengeance-seeking streak in his nature when he followed through on that promise.

"I am sorry to be under necessity of remarking," John Boit penned in his journal for 27 March,

> that this day I was sent with three boats, all well man'd and arm'd, to destroy the Village of Opitsatah. It was a command I was no ways tenacious of, and am greiv'd to think Capt. Gray shou'd let his passions go so far. This Village was about half a mile in Diameter, and Contained upwards of 200 Houses, generally well built for Indians. Evr'y door that you enter'd was in resemblance to an human and Beasts head, the passage being through the mouth, besides which there was much more rude carved work about the dwellings some of which was by no means innelegant. This fine Village, the Work of Ages, was in a short time totally destroy'd.

Sadly, the wanton destruction of Opitsat, then probably the largest and arguably the grandest Native American settlement north of Mexico, was an omen of things to come. In his continued callous treatment of the Indians, no trader would have more to answer for than Robert Gray.

Now, agreeing to meet in Columbia's Cove, a sheltered harbor in Nasparti Inlet about one hundred miles above Clayoquot, Haswell headed *Adventure* northward toward the upper end of Vancouver Island in search of furs. Gray, on his own quest, would spend the next month moving slowly southward along the British Columbia and then the Washington and Oregon coasts, trading with the Indians who came out to the ship in their canoes.

The captain tried repeatedly to find a sheltered haven but without success. "Still beating about, in pursuit of anchorage," wrote the frustrated Boit on 22 April while *Columbia* lay off Willapa Harbor in the Washington coast. "Sent the boat in shore often, but cou'd find no safe harbour." But a trickle of trade continued. The natives, speaking a language new to the Americans, came alongside in their canoes to exchange sea-otter pelts and fish for whatever Gray would offer.

A century later at least one relic of that fleeting contact survived. Chief George A. Charley of Willapa, clad in an eagle-feather headdress and white-man's suspenders, posed for a portrait holding a hand-forged knife he inherited from his father, "Lighthouse" Charley Ma-Tote, who claimed it had been a gift from Captain Gray. The stubby double-edged blade was probably one of 528 "Cuttoe Knives" of various sizes—some with handles of "Buffelo"—that had been put aboard *Columbia* in 1790 by Boston merchants John Andrews and Mason & Wilson.

Finally, on 7 May, Boit recorded the sighting of "an inlett in the land, which had the appearance of an harbour." A boat was sent out to reconnoiter but found the entrance blocked by breaking waves.

> Capt. Gray was determin'd not to give itt up. Therefore ordering the boat a head to sound with nessescary signalls, the Ship stood in for the weather bar and we soon see from the Mast head a passage between the breakers.
>
> Vast many canoes came off, full of Indians. They appear'd to be a savage sett and was well arm'd, every man having his Quiver and Bow slung over his shoulder. Without doubt we are the first Civilized people that ever visited this port, and these poor fellows view'd us and the Ship with the greatest asstonishment.

The Indians, "stout made and very ugly," brought furs and fish, which the Americans purchased for "Blanketts"—squares of coarse cloth—and pieces of iron. "We was fearful to send a Boat [to shore] on discovery," Boit commented.

Gray also became convinced of the warlike character of the natives before the day was over. "This evening heard the hooting of Indians," Boit recorded. "All hands was immediately under arms. Sevrall canoes was seen passing near the Ship, but was dispersed by firing a few Musketts over their heads. At Midnight we heard them again and soon after as 'twas bright Moon light, we see the Canoes approaching the ship." Gray, for once holding his anger within bounds, continued to try to warn them off. "We fir'd sevrall cannon over them, but [they] still persisted to advance with the war Hoop. At length a large Canoe with at least 20 Men in her got within 1/2 pistol shot . . . and with a Nine pounder, loaded with langerege"—a deadly mixture of small shot and scrap iron—"and about 10 Musketts, loaded with Buck shot, we dash'd her all to pieces, and no doubt kill'd every soul in her. The rest soon made a retreat."

Boit and his fellow officers named the bay for *Columbia*'s captain, and it remains Grays Harbor to this day. The morning after the attack—if such it actually was—trade quickly regained its usual priority. Canoes full of Indians surrounded the ship, offering plentiful quantities of skins. These Indians were apparently from the upper reaches of the Chehalis River. They were permitted to come alongside to bargain, but the ship would have been protected against any hostile move by men in the rigging armed with pistols and blunderbusses. Other Indians, fellows apparently of "those unlucky savages who last Night fell by the Ball," pointed to the ship's cannon and tried to explain the noise they made. This, said Boit, "made us still more certain that they had no Knowledge of firearms previous to our Coming amongst them. I am sorry we was oblig'd to kill the poor Divells," he added, "but it cou'd not with safety be avoided."

Gray seems to have done his best to keep the Chehalis Indians of the harbor that bears his name in ignorance of firearms. Kaukauan, an aged chief of the village on Chehalis Point, at the mouth of Grays Harbor, told ethnologist George Gibbs many years later that he remembered Captain Gray. The American had traded his people a musket and some paper-wrapped cartridges, each of which held a charge of powder and a lead ball. Knowing the Indians had no understanding of firearms, Gray had removed the ball from each cartridge. The Indians supposed the gun was "intended merely to make a noise, and fired it off until their powder was gone," and then broke it up. As other traders came to Grays Harbor, Kaukauan learned how the first white man he ever saw had tricked him. The American, said the old Indian, had also given his people knives and axes. They received also a square of cloth for each dressed deerskin.

Stories preserved among the Indians of western Washington still convey some of the awe and fright the natives must have felt when a great white-sailed ship and its bearded strangers suddenly appeared on their shores. Gibbs recorded the memory of such a day in the life of Lakhkanam, an old man of the Puget Sound area. He had been that old, he said, pointing to a boy of about ten, when the first ship arrived. The Indians thought it was bringing their spirit Dokwebutl. They knew nothing of the white man, said Lakhkanam, and feared that a great sickness would follow the appearance of the ship.

"The old men and women went out and called Dokwebutl! Dokwebutl! The chiefs said to one another that they ought not to be afraid, and they accordingly washed, oiled, and painted their faces ... thinking to please Dokwebutl. They all went out in their canoes to the ship, when one man, a sailor, motioned to them not to come near till they had washed the paint from their faces. They went astern and did so, and then all were admitted to the ship."

The old man who told the story had been small then, and afraid, so he did not go aboard. A sailor got into his canoe and wanted to try to paddle it. The child cried until someone older than himself came down into the canoe and told him not to cry. The captain of the ship then made them all presents of buttons and knives.

Farther north, when the first ship arrived, the Indians thought it was bringing the spirit of the pestilence. Dancing on the shore, they waved their palms toward the newcomers to turn them away. When the traders landed, the Indians sent to them their old men, who had few years to live anyhow, expecting them to fall dead. When the traders began buying furs, the younger Indians got up their courage and traded skins for axes and pieces of iron. Firearms here, as at Grays Harbor, evoked the greatest fear. When one of the strangers shot a gun, an Indian said that the trader did so by striking it on the side. Another thought that he blew through it. A third said that a little bird sat on top and made it go off.

A single bullet was acquired by the people of this village. The belief arose among the Indians that if it were thrown at their enemies, all would be killed. Neighboring villagers were terrified at the idea and, until they all learned the truth about guns and ammunition, the bullet's possessors preserved that fear by keeping it always ready, carefully wrapped up in skins.

CHAPTER TWENTY-ONE

"We Directed Our Course Up This Noble River"

★

A rendezvous with immortality awaited *Columbia* as she plowed her way south from Grays Harbor. Others, of course—including *Columbia* herself —had already threaded this foggy, surf-lashed coast. The Spanish explorer Bruno de Hezeta in 1775 had even mapped what he could see there of a spacious harbor lying beyond the breakers and extending all the way to the horizon. His attempt to enter had been foiled by swift currents plus concerns about illness aboard his ship. Believing what he saw to be "the mouth of some great river," he named the broad body of water visible beyond the surf-swept bar Bahia de la Asunción de Nuestra Señora—Bay of the Assumption of Our Lady. Spanish cartographers eventually gave the name Rio de San Roque to the stream that presumably flowed into it.

The Englishman John Meares searched for Hezeta's great Bay of the Assumption but decided that he could now "with safety assert that no such river . . . exists, as laid down in the Spanish charts." So sure was he of this that he named the point north of the river Cape Disappointment. The mouth of the river itself became Deception Bay.

Captain George Vancouver, in his turn, made a similar mistake. Arriving at Deception Bay in April of 1792, he saw that "the sea had now changed from its natural, to river coloured water, the probable consequence of some streams falling into the bay.... Not considering this opening worthy of more attention, I continued our pursuit to the N. W. being desirous to embrace the advantages of the prevailing breeze...." Thus for a fair wind the English explorer cast aside a discovery that, had he made it for Great Britain, could have changed the entire history of the Pacific Northwest.

Vancouver, like his great predecessor Cook, was under orders to search for the fabled Northwest Passage that was believed to link the Atlantic and Pacific oceans somewhere across the top of the North American continent. John Meares, on his return to England, had spread the story that *Lady Washington* in 1789 had sailed into the Strait of Juan de Fuca and from there continued northward several hundred miles around the whole of Vancouver Island.

Two days after passing up the mouth of the soon-to-be-named Columbia River, Vancouver saw a sail, a "great novelty." Other than the *Chatham* of his own little flotilla, it had been eight months since he had sighted another ship.

> She soon hoisted American colours, and fired a gun to leeward.... She proved to be the ship Columbia, commanded by Mr. Robert Gray, belonging to Boston.... I desired he would bring to, and sent Mr. Puget and Mr. Menzies aboard.... On the return of the boat, we found our conjectures had not been ill-grounded, that this was the same gentleman who had commanded the sloop Washington at the time, we are informed, she had made a very singular journey behind Nootka.

The American captain expressed complete bewilderment at Meares's fabrication regarding the *Lady Washington*. "It is not possible to conceive any one to be more astonished than was Mr. Gray," wrote Vancouver. Gray had penetrated only some fifty miles into the strait in his search for sea-otter skins, he told the British captain, and finding none that far from the ocean, had moved to more likely areas. He had, however, he told Vancouver, only nine days before been "off the mouth of a river ... where the outlet, or reflux, was so strong as to prevent entering.... This," noted Vancouver, "was probably the opening passed by us on the 27th." Vancouver, for the second time, decided the river was not worth investigating and continued northward in his search for the nonexistent Northwest Passage. So it remained for Gray, after all these false starts—including his own—to move in decisively and make his discovery of the river and to give it a name that would be remembered.

The great event started off with no more excitement than had *Columbia*'s several dozen other approaches to land along this wave-lashed shore. "This day," John Boit recorded on 11 May 1792—though he erroneously dated his entry 12 May—"saw an appearance of a spacious harbor abrest the Ship, haul'd our wind for itt, observed two sand bars making off, with a passage between them to a fine river." Following the ship's boat over the bar, *Columbia*'s crew found that "the River extended to the NE as far as eye cou'd reach, and water fit to drink as far down as the Bars, at the entrance.

"We directed our course up this noble *river* in search of a village," continues John Boit's journal.

> The beach was lin'd with natives, who ran along shore following the
> Ship. Soon after, above 20 Canoes came off, and brought a good lot of
> Furs and Salmon, which last they sold two for a board Nail. The furs
> we likewise bought cheap, for Copper and Cloth. [The Indians]
> appear'd to view the Ship with the greatest astonishment and no
> doubt we was the first civilized people that they ever saw ...
>
> Capt. Grays named this river Columbia's, and the North entrance
> Cape Hancock, and the South Point Adams. This River, in my opinion,
> wou'd be a fine place for to sett up a Factory.

Young Boit's sound judgment was confirmed less than two decades later when the German immigrant John Jacob Astor established his trading post, Astoria, the first American settlement west of the Rocky Mountains, at the mouth of the Columbia River.

The ship tarried in the stream that would bear her name for nearly a fortnight while Gray traded with the Indians and put his vessel in order. The crew enjoyed the rare luxury of filling their freshwater casks from buckets dipped directly over the ship's side.

In the friendly Chinooks living along the river, Gray had at last encountered Indians who were as keen on trade as he was. They lived by bartering with other tribes up the river and along the shore for commodities as varied as berries, canoes, dried salmon, slaves, and, of course, furs and were traditionally the intermediaries for this whole area of the Pacific Northwest. During her stay, *Columbia*'s cargo grew by 150 sea-otter pelts, 300 beaver skins, and twice that number of other less-valuable furs.

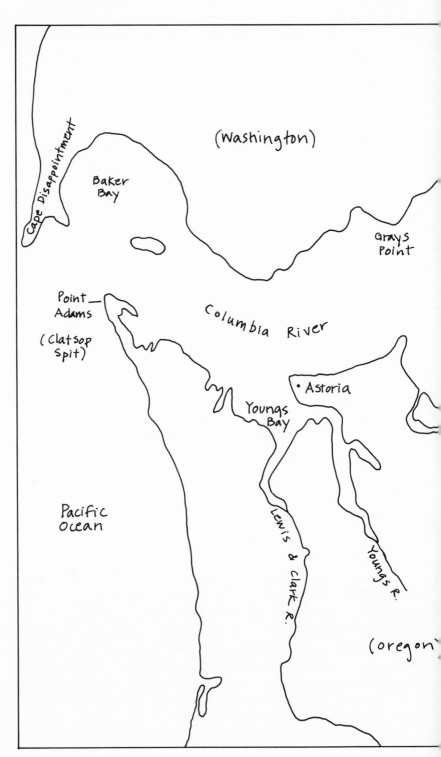

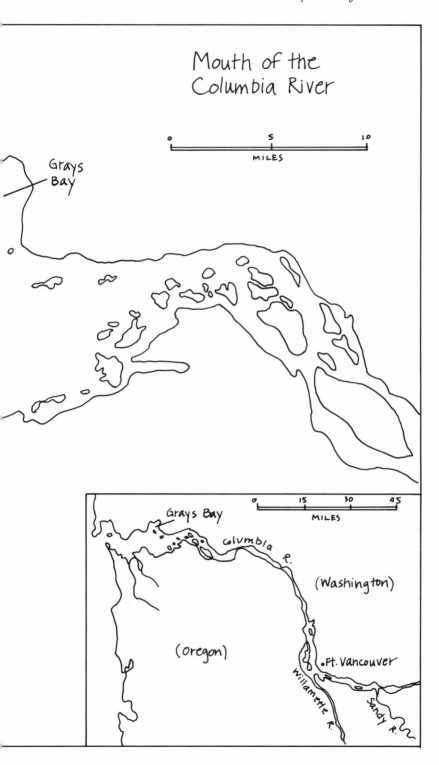

The Indians who brought the furs, Boit observed, were

> very numerous, and appear'd very civill (not even offering to steal). . . .
> The Men at Columbia's River are strait limb'd, fine looking fellows,
> and the women are very pretty. They are all in a state of Nature,
> except the females, who wear a leaf Apron (perhaps 'twas a fig leaf).
> But some of our gentlemen, that examined them pretty close, and
> near, both within and without reported that it was not a leaf but a
> nice wove mat in resemblance!! and so we go—thus, thus—and no
> Near[er]!—!

One of the Indians who must have come to marvel at the great ship
and its crew of strangers during that portentous visit in 1792 would have
been a twenty-seven-year-old Chinook brave named Comcomly, who
was later to play a leading role in much of the early history of the region.
Fortunately for that history, the friendly relations marking this first meeting between Americans and Indians there on the Columbia River established a degree of trust between the native peoples and the newcomers
that was rare elsewhere along this coast. Comcomly, by then a chief,
extended a helpful welcome to Lewis and Clark when the weary explorers reached the Columbia in 1805. He also offered a friendly hand to John
Jacob Astor when he established Astoria a few years later.

Thanks no doubt to his position within the tribe, the one-eyed Comcomly became the wealthiest man among the Chinooks. Fond of showing off his rank, Comcomly served as the nearest thing to royalty in what
was then the little frontier town of Vancouver, Washington, today an
across-the-river neighbor of Portland, Oregon, which lies on the south
shore of the Columbia. In those vanished days the chief would arrive for a
visit by ship with a retinue of as many as three hundred slaves. Before the
great man would consent to come ashore these unhappy serfs would be
compelled to lay down a carpet of beaver and otter pelts stretching
perhaps a hundred yards between the vessel and the nearest building.

But that was yet to come, and Comcomly now was just another
nameless Indian staring at Gray and his men as they made the first exploration of this great stream. "Took up the Anchor, and stood up River,"
Boit's journal for 15 May reads, "but soon found the water to be shoal. . . .
As we did not expect to procure Otter furs at any distance from the sea,
we contented ourselves in our previous situation which is a very pleasent
one. I landed abrest the ship with Capt. Gray to view the country and
take possession, leaving charge with the 2d Officer."

Interestingly, modern scholarship has shown that the words "and take possession" were added by a later hand and in a different ink. Probably the addition was made years later, when Robert Gray's and John Kendrick's heirs were importuning Congress for redress over their supposed losses in the matter of Kendrick's land purchases. Much of their case rested on the importance to the westward expansion of the United States of Gray's discoveries along the Oregon and Washington coasts.

From this three-word addition—"and take possession"—sprang a whole mythology. Congress was regaled with the details of an apocryphal ceremony. In 1852 the fantasy came to full flower. "Captain Gray sailed fourteen miles up [the Columbia] river," the legislators were solemnly assured (and that much *was* true), "and with the officers and marines of the ships, landed on its northerly bank, raised the American flag, and took possession of the country in the name of the United States." As if the addition of another ship and a contingent of marines was not enough, one of *Columbia*'s officers, long since departed, was quoted as having recalled that he had made it even more official by burying some Massachusetts pine-tree shillings beneath a tree on the river's bank.

In fact, however, nowhere is there a hint that Gray ever formally took possession of the Columbia River in any way, or that he ever looked on any of this territory as a future part of the nation. Both Boit's journal and the surviving fragment of *Columbia*'s official log for that period indicate that at least a week elapsed, while the ship lay at anchor in the newly discovered river, before Gray even thought to give it a name. Unlike Kendrick, with his impractical visions of American colonies at Nootka and Clayoquot, Gray seems to have been content to let the Spaniards and Britons argue over the status of the Northwest Coast while he focused only on gathering in its furs.

For all the drama of his discovery and the credit due him for going in where others had appraised the danger and then hurried away, Robert Gray was a very lucky man to have reached the mouth of the Columbia River at one of those rare times when the passage between the bars was visible through the surf. Hezeta had been foiled by the racing currents and crashing waves, as had Meares and Vancouver. Three years after Gray's successful entry into the river, Boit brought the little Boston sloop *Union* to the Northwest Coast and tried to find his way into the river again. He had, of course, been with Gray aboard *Columbia* on that historic day of its discovery, and he knew what to look for.

"It was impossible to tell the passage in," he wrote on 12 July 1795. Two days later he saw "the entrance of Columbia's River but we was too leeward of the bars with a strong breeze and current against us." The next day: "Sent in the yawl . . . to find a passage." None was visible in "an immense swell upon the bars, it breaking quite across from one shore to the other." On the following day Boit tried once more, but "could not fetch the river. Indeed, if I had, should have been afraid to venture over the bars as the sea was frightful." *Union's* young captain "kept beating off, and on . . . endeavouring to get into Columbia's River, but the attempt was vain . . . Came very near losing the sloop several times on the bars, but thank God we came off without damage." After some thirty approaches and well over a week spent in the attempt, Boit regretfully abandoned his determined campaign to enter the river. "Had I been fortunate enough to have accomplished it," he mourned, "many capital sea otter skins would have been procured."

"Mere description can give little idea of the terrors of the bar of the Columbia," wrote Charles Wilkes, then a lieutenant in the United States navy, in 1849. It was, he said, "one of the most fearful sights that can possibly meet the eye of the sailor." Understandably, Boit was not the last to be foiled by the fury of the Columbia River's bar. The U.S.S. *Ontario* gave up and sailed away in 1818, as did Wilkes's own U.S.S. *Vincennes* in 1841. Once inside, ships often spent weary weeks trying to get out again. Two, the U.S.S. *Peacock* in 1841 and the U.S.S. *Shark* in 1846, were wrecked in the attempt. In 1837 the *Nereid* and the *Lama* could cross the bar only after a wait of fifty days. Yet there were other times when tides, wind, and currents conspired to leave it almost as smooth as a lake.

Gray's luck seems to have held when he decided to leave the river. The brevity of Boit's journal entry for 20 May 1792—"This day left Columbia's River"—suggests that Gray on the way out was able to take his ship across the forbidding bar as uneventfully as he had sailed her in.

★

CHAPTER TWENTY-TWO

"In Blundering Along
. . . The Ship . . .
Struck a Rock"

★

Once clear of the Columbia River's mouth, Gray took his ship northward, past the Strait of Juan de Fuca and along the shore of Vancouver Island to an unidentified cove in what Gray called St. Patrick's Harbour. This was probably Esperanza Inlet, at the upper end of Nootka Island. At anchor there on 25 May 1792, the ship was quickly surrounded by canoes "full of Indians. They was all dress'd in War Armour, and completely arm'd with Bows, arows, and Spears, and had altogether quite a savage appearance." The suits of armor they wore were the same elkhide garments Haswell had noted on the first voyage. Made of several thicknesses of tanned leather, they covered the warriors from shoulders to ankles and would withstand not only arrows but spears. The Indians' heads also were sometimes protected by helmets of cedar bark, grass, and leather that would resist arrows.

The Indians appeared "much agitated," Boit observed. "I believe they was fearfull we shou'd rob their village, which was at no great distance." Even so, a brisk trade was initiated, and a number of otter furs changed hands. When a boat took some of the crew ashore for water, however, minor trouble developed between the traders and the Indians. "Indeed I was oblig'd to knock one of them down with my musket," says Boit. *Columbia* remained at anchor here for two more days, but Boit's journal jumps without comment from the 25th, when this first difficulty occurred, to the 28th, when *Columbia* moved southeast again to an anchorage in Columbia's Cove.

Boit's silence is troubling, for the incident that followed is the only one, so far as *Columbia* and *Lady Washington* are concerned, for which we have the Indians' side of the story. On 2 June—only a week later, and less than that from the two days on which Boit made no entries in his journal —a canoe arrived at Nootka Sound "with various natives asking help from the Commandant Don Juan de la Bodega against a ship which was in the Buena Esperanza Inlet," reads the account of the visit, written by a Spaniard traveling with the ships *Mexicana* and *Sutil*, which anchored in Friendly Cove in the spring of 1792.

The traders, charged the Indians, had attacked their village, killing seven men and wounding several others, and robbing them of the rest of their sea-otter skins. The Indians had brought a severely wounded man for the Spanish surgeon to heal. "As far as could be understood," reads the Spanish account of the visit, "the ship was the American frigate Columbia, Captain Gray, whom the Indians indicated by making signs that he was one-eyed, which we knew to be a characteristic of that captain." The Indians charged that the villagers had not wanted to sell their skins to the traders, who had used force to make them do so.

The Spanish surgeon extracted two bullets from the wounded man's thigh. Nootka's current commandant, Juan Francisco de la Bodega y Quadra, who was noted for his generosity toward anyone who turned up in the sound, offered to let him recuperate in the settlement's infirmary. Chief Maquinna tried to reassure the unfortunate Indian that he would be well treated by the Spaniards, but "the wounded man could not overcome his suspicions because of the recent memory of the evil handling he had received from [the traders] and had himself carried away."

Violent encounters with the Indians continued. In Columbia's Cove, about fifty miles above Nootka Sound, which had been named as the meeting place farther into the season for the ship and sloop, the natives exhibited a suspicious interest in the number of men aboard *Columbia*. Covering up the fact that the missing crewmen were actually hundreds of miles away aboard *Adventure*, Gray explained that they were asleep

An unhappy litany of clashes with the Indians dogged Gray on his second voyage as
he took *Columbia* into one remote anchorage after another in quest of furs. Here in
Queen Charlotte Sound, after an unprovoked attack two days earlier, twenty war canoes
converge on the ship, "with above 30 Men in each . . . Arm'd with spears and Arrows!
The captain humanely ordered a warning shop fired over the warrior's heads; only when
they persisted were two men killed, leading the flotilla to withdraw. On other
occasions, Gray's vindictiveness and sharp temper led to bloody encounters with
the Indians that might otherwise easily have been avoided.

(*George Davidson, Oregon Historical Society, OrHi 049264/1147*) below. The Indians, familiar with the ship's routines from previous visits, must have seen through the ruse, for that night a war canoe with about twenty-five men headed for the ship.

"We hail'd them, but they still persisted, and other Canoes was seen following, upon which Capt. Gray order'd us to fire, which we did so effectually as to kill or wound every soul in the canoe. She drifted alongside, but we push'd her Clear, and she drove to the North side of the Cove, under the Shade of the trees. 'Twas bright moonlight, and the woods echoed with the dying groans of these unfortunate Savages."

Gray continued trading his way northward, leaving behind at Columbia's Cove a sign that read "Ship Columbia arriv'd May 28th sail'd May 30th. Beware" as a warning if *Adventure* happened to reach the place of rendezvous ahead of them. In Queen Charlotte Sound, about eighty miles above Nootka, they again had trouble, this time when a couple of hundred Indians suddenly attacked a party that had been sent ashore to cut a tree for a new mizzen topmast. Boit, who was in command, managed to get his people together and reached *Columbia* under the covering fire of the ship's gunners.

Two days later and farther up the sound, hostile Indians suddenly appeared while members of another tribe were trading on the friendliest of terms. After again firing over their heads, the members of the crew shot two Indians, one for persisting in approaching the ship and the other for actually heaving his spear onto *Columbia*'s deck.

Columbia and *Adventure* met as scheduled as the two vessels approached their agreed place of rendezvous at Columbia's Cove. Haswell turned over to Gray the results of *Adventure*'s cruise through the Queen Charlotte Islands: 238 sea-otter skins, plus assorted fur garments, otter tails, and pieces. The crew aboard *Columbia*, according to Boit, had by this time collected nearly seven hundred sea otters, and the amazing number of fifteen thousand skins of less valuable land animals. Gray's sign warning of the possibility of attack had not been touched and the Indians of Columbia's Cove this time showed no sign of aggressive intentions.

Even more exciting for the moment than *Columbia*'s and *Adventure*'s combined tally of furs were the letters from home that Haswell unexpectedly handed to Captain Gray. Haswell had picked them up ten days earlier at Barrell's Inlet when *Adventure* had crossed the path of the ship *Margaret* of Boston, sailing under Captain James Magee. The packet, including a letter of instructions for Gray and Hoskins and "letters for the other gentlemen from their friends," had been dispatched from Boston in March of 1791—more than fourteen months before they finally reached the hands of *Columbia*'s commander and his crew.

It comes as no surprise that the originals of those wandering letters have never come to light. But *Columbia*'s careful owners, mindful of the uncertainty of sending messages to an unknown address on the shore of an all-but-unknown ocean, saw to it that any Boston vessel bound for the Northwest Coast carried duplicate letters addressed to Gray and Hoskins. One such, probably never delivered and hence carried back unopened to Boston months or even years later, still exists.

"This will be handed you by Mr. Thomas Francis, Super Cargo of the Ship President," the letter begins, and then reminds Gray and Hoskins of the suggestion in their original orders proposing their "trying what can be done on the coast of Japan and Pekin, if you find safety in anchoring and can dispose of your furs to advantage, we would advise you by all means to do it."

There had been much discussion back in Boston of the difficulties of doing business with the Japanese. There were tales abroad that the emperor's customs officials demanded that European merchants dramatically deny their Christianity as the price of being permitted entry to that forbidden land. But wishful thinking had apparently laid such fears to rest in Barrell's mind. "The chief intent of this letter," *Columbia*'s owners now declared, "is to add to the hint already given you respecting to your trying the Coast of Japan.... You will find there is no difficulty in the matter. The Idea of being obliged to trample upon the Cross and contemn the Christian Religion is without foundation."

The letter concludes with a bitter postscript:

> by the last advices from Canton Cap Kendrick was still at Macao,
> having spent above twelve months there, We have not recd a line
> from him since the Columbia left that place.
>
> We are Gentlemen
> Your friends & Owners
> Sam Brown
> Joseph Barrell Junr
> for Joseph Barrell Senr
> who is now on a journey to Philadelphia

After a week at anchor, during which time the Americans hauled *Adventure* ashore and graved the vessel's bottom, Gray and Haswell resumed their search for furs. Both this time started toward the northern trading grounds. After only a couple of days at sea, what looked like another example of Gray's daredevil navigation put an entirely new complexion on the whole enterprise. "I was surprised," Haswell recounted what he had seen from *Adventure*, "to find Capt. Gray standing in for the land in a place that looked to me very dangerous. . . . He had all sail on his ship, steering sails below and aloft. I had seen as I passed several sunken reefs of rocks, and as the Columbia passed not looking out properly, she struck."

Hoskins, aboard *Columbia*, was even more critical of Gray as he cataloged the times in which pure luck had kept the ship from disaster. "At last, however, fortune refus'd any longer to smile, and in blundering along (for I can call it by no better name) without any lookout kept, within three miles of a most inhospitable & rocky shore, the Ship going six knots with a crowd of sail, struck a rock about four feet under water. . . . Mr. Haswell says he in the Sloop saw the rock break & haul'd away from it."

Columbia was badly damaged, though how badly Gray at this point had no way of knowing. The ship, heretofore tight, now leaked "1000 smart strokes per hour." This meant that, with both pumps working continuously, she could still barely keep abreast of the water flooding into the hull.

This most dreaded of a seaman's duties kept eight men at a time—four at each pump—swinging heavy levers up and down until their arms felt as if they were being torn from the sockets, the pain so intense that no amount of determination could force them aloft for another stroke. But there could not be a moment's let-up in this grueling, fear-propelled exercise, for then the pumps would go dry. Precious time would be lost repriming the clumsy contrivances with bucketfuls of water hoisted laboriously onto deck at the end of a line. New men had to take the places of exhausted comrades without an instant's interruption of the steady once-every-four-seconds rhythm that at each upstroke coughed out a gallon or so of seawater to slosh past their feet and tumble overside into the Pacific where it belonged. Black, foul-smelling water that had lain in the bilges for months would have drawn a welcome shout. The water that gushed onto the deck now was as clear as the sea itself. The stuff was pouring into *Columbia*'s hull faster than her frantic crew could draw it out.

Adventure responded to a signal from the stricken ship and put aboard a number of men to help with the pumping. Gray and Haswell agreed to stay together and make their way south again to Columbia's Cove where they could haul the ship ashore and assess the damage. Despite firing a cannon periodically during the night so that Adventure could keep track of her position, Columbia lost contact with the sloop in a gale. "Our feelings was not the most agreeable," Boit noted unhappily.

Columbia's crew now had to rely on their own ingenuity. Taking one of the ship's sails, they folded it back on itself and stuffed the inside with oakum, bits of old rope, and any other padding they could lay hands on. Maneuvering it under the ship's hull, they pulled it up tight around the damaged section. The word for this is "fothering," and it is a technique that saved many a wooden ship in distress. Columbia's leak was not stopped, but when the padded sail was in place the flood of water had been reduced by half—enough that the men at the pumps could keep up with it. Within a week of the accident, the ship had limped back to Adventure Cove.

The damage was serious. The ship's keel had been split, and a portion of the stem had been torn away. Much of her copper sheathing had been ripped off, and three underwater planks on the port side were stove in. Columbia's carpenters could restore the planking, but the rest of the damage would require more assistance than could be found in a wilderness inlet. Gray would have to disregard Joseph Barrell's stern admonition that he keep Columbia away from any Spanish port in Northwest America. Only at Nootka Sound could he hope to put his ship back in condition for the long voyage home.

Square-riggers were never easy to handle, and the damage Columbia had suffered made her even more difficult. Contrary winds drove Gray past Nootka and he had to take refuge in Clayoquot Sound. He found Wickananish aboard the Boston ship Margaret, which had anchored there a few days earlier. The chief had at first refused to go on the ship's deck and finally did so only when a hostage from the ship's crew was left on shore during the visit. This was John Howel, the Margaret's English "historian," about whom we shall hear much in tracing the later movements of John Kendrick and Lady Washington.

Amazingly, Gray in his turn had the gall to invite the chief, whose village he had so recently ordered destroyed, to visit him aboard Columbia. More amazing still, the chief agreed, though "he did not appear happy. However," Boit adds with the cynicism typical of even the best of the fur

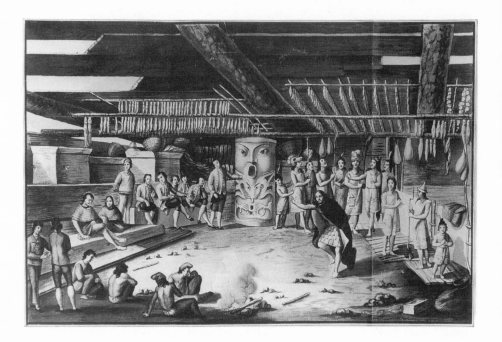

Clad in regal sea otter, Maquinna dances a welcome to European guests in his winter house at the head of Tahsis Inlet. The British explorer George Vancouver and Spain's Don Juan Bodega y Quadra visited the Nootkan chief in September of 1792 to reassure the tribesmen of their two nations' friendship. In a scene dominated by Maquinna's family totem, carved from the trunk of a huge red cedar, Spanish artist Atanasio Echeverria y Godoy portrayed the chief's four wives and several children behind him. European sailors crouch in the foreground. Overhead, smoked fish and whale blubber hang from drying racks.

The visit turned into a culinary contest, with the Indians offering a banquet of "Stews and Fricasees of Porpoise, Whale, Seal, and such delicious Meats." The Europeans countered with a table improvised from one of the great cedar planks that supported Maquinna's roof, on which the don's servants laid down a meal brought from Friendly Cove, twenty miles away, and served to the highest-ranking guests on silver plates. The rest of the Indians, reported one of the Britons, "entertained themselves at a Mess no less grateful to their palate." It consisted, he noted, "of a large *Tunny* & a Porpus cut up in small pieces entrails & all into a large Trough with a mixture of Water blood & fish oil, & the whole stewed by throwing heated Stones into it."
(Moziño, *Noticias de Nutka, translated by Iris H.W. Engstrand, University of Washington Press, 1991*)

traders, "twas the means of getting more skins than we otherways should have done."

When *Columbia* finally passed the Spanish fort guarding the approaches to Nootka Sound, the reception could not have been more cordial. The new Spanish commandant, Don Francisco de la Bodega y Quadra, had already sent boats to *Columbia's* aid where she lay wallowing helplessly at anchor outside the sound. Now at Friendly Cove the Americans were offered every assistance in getting their ship underway again. In a month, with the help of the courtly don's shipwrights and those of an English vessel anchored in the cove, the Americans put in a new stem and part of the cutwater, graved the ship, and had her afloat again.

Spanish hospitality had not changed with the departure of Martínez, but the primitive little settlement Gray remembered from *Columbia's* first voyage had been dramatically improved. "From being a wilderness," wrote one visitor, the cove, "was now become a garden producing every kind of vegetable. The village consists of sixteen houses.... They had several storehouses, blockhouses, and a hospital. Cattle, sheep, and hogs they had, and poultry in abundance."

The immaculately bewigged, finery-loving Bodega y Quadra, a man of generosity and warmth, took an honest delight both in showing off and in sharing the perquisites of his station in life. Among those Don Francisco had snuggled under his wing was Maquinna, who by now had become a habitual visitor at the Spanish settlement and aboard the ships of whatever Europeans or Americans happened to have cast their anchors in Friendly Cove. The great Nootkan chief would arrive imperially, trailed by his retainers and splendid in a cloak of sea-otter furs—and nothing else, to the embarrassment of an occasional newcomer unaccustomed to viewing nakedness. At other times Maquinna would appear in deer hides or an "exquisite cloak of weasel skins."

The Spanish commandant's gifts and concern for the appearances of the chief's sovereignty had so influenced Maquinna that he had by now come to live alongside Friendly Cove, where the ships of so many distant nations appeared for his kingly amusement and the favors of his trade. Maquinna ate every day, recorded a Spanish chronicler, from Bodega y Quadra's table, "not at it . . . yet very near, using a knife and fork like the most cultivated European, allowing his servants to wait on him, and delighting all with his festive behavior. He drank wine with pleasure," the Spaniard reported, "and in order that his mind not be fogged left others to determine the amount which he should drink of that which he called 'Spanish water.'" Maquinna had learned a few words of Spanish and regularly excused himself from the don's presence with a "Buenas noches, señor," and a courteous bow.

Extending his bountiful hospitality to the Americans who had limped into Nootka Sound aboard their crippled ship, Don Francisco insisted that Gray and Hoskins be his personal guests and gave them a separate storehouse in which they could safely keep the ship's gear while *Columbia* was being repaired. Climaxing the stay at Nootka was a grand entertainment to which all of the ships' officers—Spanish as well as British and American—were invited. Wide-eyed John Boit reported that

> fifty four persons sat down to Dinner, and the plates, which was solid silver, was shifted five times, which made 270 Plates. The Dishes, Knifes and forks, and indeed evry thing else, was of Silver and always replaced with spare ones. There could be no mistake in this as they never carried the dirty plates or Dishes from the Hall where we dined (as I thought, on purpose to let us see the quantity of plate used by Spaniards in South America).

Gray must have been relieved by his good fortune, and Boit was plainly overwhelmed. "May such fine fellows Never be in want of the like assistance shou'd they ever stand in need of itt from the hands of any American."

It was now late August and imperative that *Columbia* and *Adventure* wind up their affairs on the Northwest Coast. Gray hurried north in the newly repaired *Columbia* toward the Queen Charlotte Islands, where he and Haswell in the sloop had agreed to rendezvous. Once again, the two vessels met as they approached Port Montgomery, the appointed harbor.

A plan had lately been developing in Gray's mind: He wanted to sell *Adventure* to the Spanish. He had certainly mentioned *Adventure* while he was at Nootka overhauling *Columbia* and would have seen the Spanish commandant's look of interest. There would have been no reason to risk crew members by taking the little vessel back to Boston. To catch the Spaniards' eye again at Nootka, the sloop was graved and otherwise put in order before she left Port Montgomery.

When *Columbia* and *Adventure* moved south for their last visit to Nootka, Bodega y Quadra confirmed his interest in the sloop, which he wanted as a present for the viceroy of New Spain. "Haswell," Boit noted, "was not backward in displaying her to the best advantage." The bargain was easily sealed. Bodega y Quadra would buy the sloop if Haswell would bring her south as far as the small Spanish outpost at the Strait of Juan de Fuca, only a day or two from Nootka Sound. Gray and the don agreed on a price: seventy-two prime sea-otter skins, each worth fifty-five dollars at the hongs of Canton.

In a letter of explanation to Barrell, Gray and Hoskins dismissed *Adventure* as having sailed "very dull." This was a direct contradiction of Haswell's and Boit's enthusiastic opinion of the trim little sloop's performance. "I had the satisfaction to find her a very good seaboat," Haswell had noted shortly after launching, "and [she] outsailed the Columbia." But this disagreement was really beside the point. *Adventure* was absurdly small even for a crossing to Hawaii or Canton, much less a voyage all the way home to Boston. And Gray would have been desperately short-handed aboard *Columbia* without the help of Haswell and his men.

Columbia and *Adventure* sailed from Nootka Sound for the last time on 22 September 1792. In less than a week, Haswell delivered the sloop to "Don Arrow"—Bodega y Quadra's second in command, the Spanish Lieutenant Gonzalez López de Haro—and took his belongings and his crew aboard *Columbia*. After taking on wood and water at Poverty Cove, today's Port San Juan on Vancouver Island, Gray on 3 October turned the ship's bow toward Hawaii, China, and then home.

★

CHAPTER TWENTY THREE

Back to the Hongs
of Canton

★

Homesickness suddenly swept through *Columbia*'s crew as they saw the mountains of western America disappear behind them. Two years and two days had passed since the ship had sailed from Boston on her second voyage. Said John Boit, "Our freinds at Home and ev'ry endearing idea rush'd so full upon us and made us so happy, that 'twas impossible, for a while to get the ship in readiness for bad weather." But get it ready they did, helped by a full ration of grog.

Twenty-six days later, *Columbia* raised the island of Hawaii, visible dimly forty-five miles away. Hogs and fresh vegetables came aboard from canoes that met the ship before she reached an anchorage. The hogs cost from five to ten large spikes, and half a dozen fowls could be acquired for a chisel. Boit, with his usual eye for a pretty face, noted that the women in the canoes were "quite handsome," but that "not many of the Columbia's crew prov'd to be Josepths."

At Niihau, westernmost of the islands, Gray expected to say farewell to Attoo, the young Hawaiian who had now been around the world aboard *Columbia*. Boit records Attoo's reunion with his parents, who came

276

aboard the ship from their canoe. "The meeting was very affectionate, but still our Lad refused to go on shore and Capt. Gray did not think proper for to force him. However [we] made his freinds many presents." Boit then drops the subject. Haswell mentions only that the ship stopped at Niihau to pick up a supply of yams. Young Attoo, who had held all Boston in thrall when he strode up State Street beside Captain Gray in his cloak and helmet of red and gold feathers, simply disappears from history, either as a seaman somewhere in the Pacific or into the obscurity of his island home.

"Bore off and made sail for the Coast of China," reads Boit's journal, "and soon lost sight of these beautifull Isles, The Inhabitants of which appear'd to me to be the happiest people in the world. Indeed there was something so frank and chearfull that you cou'd not help feeling prepposses'd in their favor."

Gray and Hoskins had now to decide upon the wisdom of "trying what can be done on the coast of Japan and Pekin," as Barrell and the other owners had twice urged in their orders. The decision took little time to make and even less discussion. *Columbia*'s misadventures up and down the Northwest Coast had left a tired and wounded ship. Jury-rigged repairs might give way at any moment. She leaked dangerously, and rotting sails and chafed rigging would be unlikely to survive a serious storm. One can almost overhear Gray and Hoskins reach one of their few agreements of the voyage. The only course for sensible men, they concluded, is to forego any more adventuring on unknown shores. They would get on to Canton as quickly as possible—Gray, at least, knew what to expect from the Chinese merchants—and hope for the best.

On 7 December 1792, as *Columbia* passed Grand Lema Island, off the coast of China, she again picked up a pilot who agreed to guide her to the Typa anchorage at Macao, this time for only twenty-five dollars. That information forms the last entry in Robert Haswell's journal. Hoskins had abandoned his in mid-sentence eight months earlier. For the rest of *Columbia*'s voyage home, we have only the often brief journal entries of young John Boit. He tells us that another pilot took over at Macao, for forty dollars, and saw the ship to the Pagoda anchorage at Whampoa.

Gray would have been all business on this second trip, and of course he elected as a captain's prerogative to spend his days in the relative luxury of Canton. Boit, new to China and helping to look after the ship at Whampoa, was all eyes.

When we arriv'd [he wrote] there was upwards of a dozen fine Hogs
on deck, which we had reserv'd for the Passage home. The rasscles of
the Chinese found means to throw them some poisenous stuff, which
kill'd the whole of them. But we took notice as soon as they was
thrown overboard, they was eagerly seiz'd, and no doubt was feasted
upon by the poor of the River. Indeed nothing escaped their clutches.
The entrails of Poultry, or Dead rats serv'd equally alike to appease
these half starv'd wretches . . .

Boit's complaint about the sharp practices of the Chinese with whom
the foreigners came in contact was an old one. The compradors who
supply the ships with food, lamented a British captain, "use . . . every art
to make their hogs, geese, ducks &c. weigh heavy. They cram them with
stones, and give them salt and water to make them thirsty . . ." Another
foreign visitor to old Canton bought a cage full of bright-plumaged birds
only to have their bold hues wash off when they were inadvertently left
out in a shower. But there were compensations. "I always remark'd," Boit
concluded, "that [the Chinese] was very nice in their cookery, and Rice
was always part of ev'ry Mess."

Why Gray chose for a second time to ignore Joseph Barrell's instructions to sell the ship's cargo in Macao is unknown. He had ample opportunity on the Northwest Coast to talk with other fur traders. Probably they
had convinced him that Canton now offered the best market. Certainly
it was the safest. On the basis of the scanty documents surviving, it appears that this time Gray chose the better course when he took the ship
directly to the Whampoa anchorage.

This was not apparent at first. In two doleful letters to Barrell,
Hoskins and Gray warned that furs were "almost impossible to get rid of
for money." Even in goods, the best skins were bringing not more than
thirty dollars retail and only a fraction of that—six to twenty-five dollars
—wholesale.

The situation was not helped by the number of foreign vessels in port
that were eager to get rid of their cargoes—fifty-three of them when
Columbia arrived, including six other Americans. *Columbia*'s furs, Gray and
his supercargo concluded gloomily, were not expected to bring more
than forty thousand dollars. As if this were not bad enough, leaks continued to plague the ship. She would have to be overhauled at high cost
before she could head for sea again. If Barrell received his letters from
Gray and Hoskins before he saw *Columbia* herself, he must have groaned.

Before *Columbia* left Canton, Boit summed up the ship's affairs in a single entry spanning the period from 12 December 1792 to 2 February 1793. "We hauled the Ship a shore on Dutch Island beach and graved. This business cost 150$ (paid to the Propri[e]tors of the beach). The Whole expence accruing to the Columbia at Canton amounted to the enormous sum of 7000 Spanish $. The otter Furs where landed at Canton and d[e]l[ivere]d to the Hong Merchants for 90,000$, average 45 Dollars each. The Land furs sold quite low in proportion."

First-mate Haswell, responsible at this point for making daily entries in the ship's log, was more specific, noting that "979 Sea otter Skins and 116 Coatsacks" were sent ashore, and the next day another "768 Sea Otter skins and 116 inferior pieces." Both statements work out to about two thousand skins.

It becomes almost impossible to reconcile Gray's and Hoskins's pessimistic letters and Boit's account of *Columbia*'s transactions in Canton. There is no letter or ledger to explain what happened to change the ship's fortunes so dramatically for the better. Whatever the reason, *Columbia* would take home nearly $100,000 worth of China goods. That Boston-bound cargo, says Boit, consisted of tea and nankeen, plus small quantities of sugar and Chinese porcelain. It would occasion no huzzas in the countinghouses of Boston, but at least it was a better showing than the first time around.

Joseph Barrell had sternly enjoined *Columbia*'s fo'c'sle hands against any private trade with the Indians and encouraged them as well to inform on their officers if they saw anyone else doing so. All transactions were to be solely "for the benefit of the owners." Barrell relented, however, to the extent of allowing crew members to draw as much as three-month's pay for their personal expenditures in Canton and permitted them to send home to Boston free of freight charges any goods so purchased. How successful this was in keeping *Columbia*'s transactions in legal channels remains a question. The financial returns from the ship's two voyages, as will become evident, suggest that not much attention was paid on either one to Barrell's admonitions once the vessel was a continent and more away from Boston Harbor.

In any event, the crew this time would take home their share of nankeens and satins, umbrellas with whalebone ribs, fans, tortoiseshell combs, stone dogs, perhaps even a depiction on canvas or glass of *Columbia* by one of Canton's skilled port painters. There would also have been many small decorated chests of tea for wives at home, or wives-to-be. Gray himself, though still a bachelor, invested in a table service of blue-and-white "willow-ware" china. Most of it survives to this day.

By the time *Columbia* had her cargo and her grand chop aboard, and her officers and crew had stowed away their sea chests of souvenirs, only seven other ships, from Sweden and England, remained at Whampoa. On 8 February Gray dropped *Columbia*'s pilot at Macao and headed for the Cape of Good Hope. There was still the leak, uncorrected since she struck the rock on the Northwest Coast. But even that failed to dampen the spirits of *Columbia*'s homeward-bound crew. "Find the ship requires one Pump pretty steady," an unconcerned Boit wrote, "however as it has been a steady leak for some time, it is not looked on as a serious affair." They were well and hearty, and looking forward to meetings with "Sweethearts and Wives. How can we be otherways than happy when anticipating the joys that awaits us there."

Little occurred at first to mar that elation. *Columbia* threaded the South China Sea without incident and sailed cautiously through the narrow, reef-beset strait behind Banka Island, which presses tight against the Sumatran shore. Then dead south she plunged through the Java Sea, where spiderweb oil rigs today extort twentieth-century wealth from these once forbidding waters.

There was enough company to make *Columbia*'s passage a worrisome one. "Many proas about," reported John Boit. Once Gray was forced by the narrowness of the channel to pass disturbingly close to one, "a *Moorish* sloop, (*at anchor*). She was strongly man'd and arm'd. I believe she was a *pirate*," Boit noted with many nervous underlinings. But the "Moors"— actually Malays—would have seen that these New Englanders also stood by their guns, primed and ready, and forebore any notion of a challenge.

At North Island, deadly sea snakes, their tails flattened vertically like those of fishes, writhed lazily in seas turned a hard green-grey under a glowering sky. Here *Columbia* found company more to her liking: the sixty-four-gun ship-of-war *Lion*, Captain Gower, and the British East India Company's *Hindustan*. The little flotilla was headed in the opposite direction, carrying the person and considerable entourage of Lord George Macartney, King George III's hopeful emissary to the court of the Emperor of China. He too would experience the scorn and contempt that had already met so many of China's Western visitors. Within a few months this proud ambassador from the earth's most powerful nation would find himself being escorted up the Pei Ho toward Peking in a junk to which the Chinese had affixed a derisively worded pennant announcing to all who could read that here was "the English Ambassador bringing tribute to the Emperor of China."

But now aboard the *Lion* and *Hindustan* there was no hint of failure of the king's grand mission. Moods on both British ships matched those of homeward-bound *Columbia*, and a warm friendship prevailed between Americans and Britons who less than a decade before had concluded a bitter and deadly war. Gray readily accepted dispatches from Macartney, to be dropped off at lonely St. Helena in the Atlantic for forwarding to London. By evening the two British ships were on their way to Dutch-ruled Batavia, today's Djakarta.

Now, before *Columbia* could sail, there was water to be brought aboard and fresh meat and fruit to be bought of the Malays ashore. John Boit drew the detail. (One realizes how often this amazingly competent teenager was picked for the dangerous jobs over the heads of his older, more experienced shipmates!)

Despite the beauty of the situation here, where the tips of Sumatra and green Java almost meet, with clear streams splashing out of jungly growth into the sea, and the warm breezes yet "fragrant with clove buds and cinnamon," the realistic Boit was in no mood for poetics.

> I found above 200 Malays round the watring place. They was completly *arm'd*, with *Creases* (or *Daggers*), but was quite *freindly*. However I did not allow the *boats* to touch the beach and only let 6 men beside myself land, and swam the water casks off to the boats, *when fill'd*. This method I thought but prudent, as the *Malays* had *kill'd* one of the *Lions* crew, while washing cloaths at the brook.

"I cannot say," Boit admitted to his journal, "that I experienced the most agreeable sensations while on this duty."

Now with wood and water aplenty and the decks noisy with cooped fowl and heavy with the scent of tropical fruits, *Columbia* weighed anchor for the passage through dreaded Sunda Strait. Past the Button, Thwart-the-Way, and the Cap—craggy hazards Gray remembered from his first voyage home—*Columbia* stood to windward between big Princes Island and Krakatoa and then "came very near depositing the Ship upon the Qu Klip rocks, however good luck prevailed." Then Boit could happily note that "Princes Isle bore East and Java Head ESE 5 leagues. Wind from NW. Stood to the southward."

Now, almost as if she sensed that only open sea lay between her bowsprit and Boston, sea-weary *Columbia* seemed to strain ahead in the warm breezes. In less than a month the ship had driven southward across the Indian Ocean and was struggling against head winds off Africa's southern tip. "At length, thank God," wrote Boit, "the wind chang'd.... Bore off to the North[war]d and West[war]d ..." That meant that Agulhas, last of the stormy capes in *Columbia*'s path, now lay behind her.

At St. Helena, where Lord Macartney's optimistic dispatches were handed to Lieutenant Governor Robinson—"he appear'd to be an excellent man"—Boit learned of the Napoleonic Wars in Europe, and, as he put it, "that poor Louis was a head shorter." As usual, his eyes quickly strayed elsewhere. "The sight of an English Lady made my heart feel all in an uproar, and alas! the poor Sandwich Isle girls where entirely forgot. So it is, and we cannot help itt."

But a more immediate matter quickly displaced Boit's reverie. *Columbia* had been at sea now for nearly three months. Having passed up the settlements at Simon's Town and Table Bay by Africa's southern tip, she was desperately short of provisions. Gray had depended on finding them at St. Helena. Unhappily, the island had not long before suffered a drought that, wrote Boit, "carried off the greatest part of their stock and greatly distress'd the inhabitants." Water there was in plenty, and to Boit's amazement it was "convey'd to the Port by pipes under ground." There was even another wonder, a crane on the pier to give help in loading the filled casks. But where food was concerned, British ingenuity could offer almost nothing. And if Gray wanted the advantages of favoring winds and currents on his homeward leg, he would have to head straight across something like six thousand miles of empty ocean that lay between St. Helena and Boston's beckoning wharves. There was nothing to do but run for it.

Predictably, *Columbia*'s final sprint across the Atlantic was made on dramatically short rations. A month out of St. Helena, Gray and his crew were desperate. Luckily, they crossed the path of a coastal trader, an American brig bound for Grenada with a cargo of livestock. Boit's journal reveals the bluntness that sometimes prevailed in the days of sail. "Was oblidg'd to fire sevrall shot a head of him before he wou'd stop," he noted blandly. Gray induced the captain of the brig to sell "many Sheep and Hogs etc., with two tierces Bread. This was quite a seasonable supply, as we had been eating Maggotty bread for ... some time."

Three weeks later—and only a day out of Boston—food again became a problem. A fishing boat, itself short of meat, sold *Columbia* three
barrels of salt mackerel and a few hundred ship's biscuit, which were
doled out among the crew. But the men were too close to home now to
worry about a minor thing like hunger. The next afternoon, 25 July 1793,
Columbia

> pass'd Castle William, and gave a federall salute, which was re-
> turn'd. . . . At 7 anchor'd off the Long Wharfe in the Stream and
> saluted the town with 11 Guns which was return'd from the Wharfes
> with three welcome Huzzas.
>
>   'Tis impossible to express our feelings at again meeting with our
> freinds

Boit says as he ends his journal. But the young man's homecoming was not
spared a cloud. ". . . the loss of an affectionate and much lov'd Sister
during my absence was a great obstacle to the happiness I shou'd otherways have enjoy'd."

CHAPTER TWENTY FOUR

Final Reckonings

★

This time *Columbia's* homecoming would have been less of a festive event than her arrival from around the world three years before. The people of Boston had by now grown accustomed to the almost daily comings and goings of ships, China and otherwise, and to the sight of Sandwich Islanders on the city's narrow, cobbled streets. No one would have expressed much interest yet, either, in Robert Gray's discovery of a "noble river" somewhere on the Spanish coast of western America. What quickened the interest of Boston's merchants just then—especially after *Columbia's* dismal showing the first time around—was the mundane matter of dollars and cents.

The balance sheet made a little better reading than that of the first voyage, though not much. Joseph Barrell could write to his brother Colburn Barrell in London, "The Columbia has safely returned but by no means made the voyage we had reason to expect, nor near eno[ugh] to extricate me from the Demands of the Bank." And to his friend John Webb, Barrell in another letter dropped a clear hint as to his opinion of Robert Gray's conduct of the enterprise. "Through the vigilance of Mr.

Hoskins," he wrote, *Columbia* "has made a saving voyage of some profitt."

The fragmentary ledgers that survive indicate that *Columbia*'s second voyage appears to have returned roughly fifty thousand dollars—about twice the investment put forward by Barrell and the adventure's other backers. Of course, there was still a loss of several thousand dollars to recoup from the first voyage. The remainder was not exactly the return *Columbia*'s owners had envisioned when they launched the expedition. Nor would subsequent voyages to the Northwest Coast for other owners do as poorly. Within a very few years fur-trading ships dispatched from Boston would be returning profits of as much as 400 percent at the end of their three- and four-year voyages.

This leads to some interesting speculations about the conduct of both of *Columbia*'s voyages. Gray in 1789, by his own count, took seven hundred sea-otter skins to China. (Never mind for the moment the inventory that showed 1,215 skins being taken ashore at Canton, and Thomas Randall's statement to Alexander Hamilton that *Columbia* carried "about fifteen hundred sea Otter skins of various sizes and quality.") The furs purchased on that first voyage were almost all acquired by Gray in the *Lady Washington*. Kendrick in *Columbia* had collected few while he lay inert at Nootka Sound during the entire period, leaving virtually all the trading to Gray. He, in a little over four months of cruising with the sloop, bought most of those seven hundred skins at the rate of perhaps 150 a month. On the second voyage, with Gray cruising the coast in *Columbia* and Haswell taking command of *Adventure*, two thousand skins were acquired over a total time for the two vessels of fifteen and a half months. This works out to about 130 per month for each vessel.

Kendrick remained on the coast to trade for no more than two months—and probably a little less—after *Columbia* sailed for China the first time. When he reached Macao in December of 1789, he had by his own count 320 skins, 60 cutsarks, and 150 pieces. This would total 540 skins; we know that one cutsark was made up of three skins, and the traders considered that four "pieces" equalled one skin. This estimate is borne out by the price Kendrick received for the 340 of his skins he was able to sell, $18,000, which averages out at fifty-three dollars apiece— about as much as one would expect for Macao compared with the thirty dollars each that Gray took in for *Columbia*'s cargo of seven hundred when it had to be sold in Canton.

What does not tally is that Kendrick, never a man in a hurry, had gathered in his skins at nearly three hundred a month, roughly twice Gray's rate, and in an area that had presumably been swept clean by Gray's cruises earlier in the year. In a little more than three months he collected one thousand skins—again at the rate of about three hundred a month. There was also William Douglas in *Iphigenia*. After having been freed by Martínez, he picked up seven hundred skins during the one month he traded in the Queen Charlottes before returning to China.

All this might still be dismissed as happenstance were it not for Joseph Ingraham's harvest of skins aboard *Hope* during the summer of 1791. After two months and three days on the Northwest Coast at the same time and on the same trading grounds as Gray in *Columbia* and Haswell in *Adventure*, Ingraham crammed the hold of his brigantine with "cutsarks and skins equal to 1400 sea otters, over 300 sables, and some beaver, wolverines, etc." The otter skins came aboard *Hope* at the rate of seven hundred a month, more than four times Gray's acknowledged take on either of *Columbia*'s voyages.

The list could go on, but one more example makes the point: the Boston ship *Margaret*, commanded by Captain James Magee. Haswell, who met Magee while trading in *Adventure*, called *Margaret* "as fine a vessel as ever I saw of her size, and [she] appeared exceedingly well fitted for this voyage, and I believe there was no expense spared." Magee traded on the Northwest Coast from late May until mid-November of 1792, during which time he collected nearly 1,200 sea-otter skins. Leaving a crew at Nootka Sound with the materials needed for construction over the winter of a small schooner—an uncanny parallel with the details of *Columbia*'s second voyage—Captain Magee took the *Margaret* to Hawaii for "refreshment." Returning in early April of 1793, Magee found his schooner completed, and the two vessels traded through the spring and summer, amassing a total of 3,025 more sea-otter skins. Thus Magee acquired, in all, more than 4,000 pelts in almost exactly the length of time that *Columbia* and *Adventure* had taken to purchase their declared cargo of less than half as many—not to mention the fact that by 1793 Magee was facing the competition of at least ten other fur-trading vessels operating in the same area. *Margaret*'s two seasons on the coast are estimated to have yielded a profit of some sixty-four thousand dollars for her owners. In another uncanny parallel with *Columbia*'s voyage, Captain Magee himself was one of them.

It begins to look as if the inventories prepared for Joseph Barrell's eyes might have listed no more than half the sea-otter skins *Columbia* actually carried to Canton and sold there. The rest would have been smuggled ashore and the proceeds diverted to the pockets of whoever had stashed them away during the voyage. And lacking the firmly established authority Joseph Barrell had failed to include with John Hoskins's responsibility as supercargo, there would have been little he could have done to stop it. On each voyage, the bootleg furs, had they been sold for the benefit of the owners, would have made the difference between profit and loss.

There exists no reason to suspect that either Kendrick or Ingraham would have padded their counts to make them sound larger than they were. Kendrick had by this time certainly given up any serious idea of making a settlement with *Washington*'s owners. Trading now on his own account, there would have been no logic in stating anything but the actual number of skins he had aboard.

The same can be said of Joseph Ingraham, though for a different reason. Of the three traders—Gray, Kendrick, and Ingraham—he seems to have been the only one who attempted to live up to the trust his backers placed in him. Sadly, he arrived in Macao with his furs at a moment when the Chinese were at war with the Russians. Thinking the sea-otter trade was in some way benefitting their enemies, they had prohibited the importation of otter skins in March of 1791. The embargo would be lifted by the time *Columbia* reached Canton on her second voyage, but for Ingraham the ban was ruinous. A bond signed by him in China in the names of *Hope*'s owners suggests that the little brigantine ended her voyage more than forty thousand dollars in debt to the hong merchants.

What passed between Barrell, Gray, and, presumably, Hoskins, after *Columbia*'s final return to the Massachusetts capital can only be guessed at. Within a few months of his homecoming, the bachelor Gray—he was then thirty-eight—bought a lot and brick house on Back Street in Boston, presumably in anticipation of his wedding three weeks later to Martha Atkins, eldest daughter of one of the city's wealthiest merchants. She was sixteen years his junior. Their first son, Robert, born in 1794, received the middle name Don Quadra, after the courtly and generous Spanish commandant Don Juan Francisco de la Bodega y Quadra.

Gray continued in the merchant service, though not on vessels owned by Barrell or his associates, and voyaged both to England and to ports in the Carolinas. In 1793 he sailed from Salem for the east coast of

South America in command of a ship newly launched earlier that year. Alas, the "Good Brig Alert," as Gray referred to her in a pathetic letter of explanation to her owners, had not been coppered. Sixty-seven days out of Salem, he reported, slowed by a fouled bottom, she was overtaken by a French privateer and escorted as a prize of war to Montevideo. Thus, unwillingly, *Alert* became the first North American ship to sail into the Rio de la Plata. The Spaniards, to whom the French sold her, promptly sent her out again as a privateer under their own flag. Gray was released and made his way home to New England via Baltimore. A century would pass before the heirs of *Alert*'s original owners would receive compensation for the loss of their ship.

In 1799, Gray took command of the privateer *Lucy*, which carried twelve guns and a crew of twenty-five. Her commission, signed by President John Adams and dated 4 November of that year, authorizes the capture of "any armed French vessel which shall be found within the jurisdictional limits of the United States, or elsewhere on the high seas." Whether he avenged the loss of *Alert* is unknown. Lack of record to that effect suggests that he did not.

In the spring of 1800, Gray was in command of a ship sailing between Boston and ports on the Irish Sea. He was back again on the Rio de la Plata in 1801, by way of Rio de Janeiro, as master of the topsail schooner *James* and probably carried home a cargo of "Buenos Ayres Hydes," thus becoming a pioneer in the great trade of subsequent years in hides and lumber between Argentina, Uruguay, and New England ports. The following year, forty-four American vessels—eighteen of them from Massachusetts—brought mixed cargoes to the same South American ports and carried away hides. Gray may well have commanded one of them.

Beyond these bare facts and suppositions, Robert Gray's later years are almost as little remembered as his youth. In a petition to Congress of 17 January 1846, Gray's widow placed her husband's death, believed to have been from yellow fever, in the summer of 1806. He is thought by some to have been buried in Charleston, South Carolina. Others conjecture that he was buried at sea. He left, Mrs. Gray attested, "four daughters and very little property."

It is difficult to assess Robert Gray other than in the light of his having almost accidentally made his way into the mouth of the Columbia River on that historic day in May of 1792. That act of Gray's gave his country a gift worth more than all the sea-otter skins ever yielded by the North-

west Coast. The man himself emerges only dimly. His actions were duti-
fully recorded in the journals kept aboard *Lady Washington* and *Columbia*—
the repeated murderous fights with the Indians, the constant flirting
with disaster along the rocky, tide-swept, Northwest Coast, the way he
pushed his men and ships to cover more ground in less time than Kendrick—but none of his contemporaries seems to have commented on
the personality behind those events.

As well as he knew Gray, John Hoskins still could only project the
image of a cold and distant figure when he compared him with Kendrick.
"Captain Gray . . . cruiz'd the coast more; and appear'd to be more perse-
vering to obtain skins, yet his principles were no better, his abilities less,
and his knowledge of the coast, from his former voyage, circumscribed
within very narrow limits." Driven by ruthless ambition and few scruples,
Gray nonetheless harvested fewer skins—if we are to believe the accounts submitted to the vessels' owners—than almost any other captain
who worked the Northwest Coast in those first palmy days of the sea-
otter trade.

John Hoskins continued his association with the Barrell family for a
decade, carrying on a business at Codman's Wharf in Boston with one of
the sons of his long-time employer under the name of Barrell and
Hoskins. He later spent several years in Europe, acting as personal agent
for the elder Barrell as well as searching out investment possibilities for his
own firm. "His Business in France," wrote Joseph Barrell in one letter of
introduction, "is to form Commercial Connections . . . & if any promising
Speculations offers [to] engage them, for which purpose he will have the
command of a very handsome Sum of Money—you will find him a man
of honour and ability. . . ."

Hoskins returned to Boston for a time at Barrell's urging to take a
larger role in the business. About 1804, however, after the death of his
wife, he moved back to France, where his brother William lived, and
there married Catherine Girard, a sister of the Philadelphia philanthropist
and banker Stephen Girard. Hoskins died sometime in his fifties while on
a visit to the island of Mauritius, where his daughter Lydia made her
home.

After his return from China in 1793, *Columbia's* first-mate Robert
Haswell successively became master of the Boston-owned ships *Hannah*, in
which he voyaged to the East Indies, and the *John Jay*. At this point
Haswell, then only twenty-seven, seems to have had serious second

thoughts about the mariner's life. "My last voyage has been twenty-seven months long," he wrote to his sister Susanna Rowson in 1796, "and on the winding up of it I think it will not be an unprofitable one.... I think I shall tarry ashore this winter, and in the spring seek my fortune again. I hope in a few years to acquire enough to purchase a small farm, and then sit down in homely ease and enjoy the few years that may be left.

"For the sea my love has almost worn me out ... it has impaired my constitution beyond measure and has not been productive of the gain that should be expected from such hazardous enterprises."

But go to sea again he did. In 1799 he became a lieutenant in the United States Navy and served aboard the frigate *Boston*. During the troubles with France, Haswell earned a share of the prize money, $286.35, for *Boston's* capture on 12 October 1800 of the corvette *Le Berceau*. Under Haswell's command, the captured vessel was brought into Boston Harbor. After two years of service in the Navy, Haswell's familiarity with the fur trade earned him a master's berth on the ship *Louisa* of Boston for a voyage to the Northwest Coast and China. Leaving Boston in August of 1801, the *Louisa* was never heard from again.

The sea took a heavy toll of *Columbia's* veterans. Joseph Ingraham, first mate on the ship's first voyage and then captain of the brigantine *Hope*, also turned to the Navy after he came back to Massachusetts. Barred from further involvement in the Northwest fur trade because of the financial failure of *Hope's* voyage, he petitioned Secretary of the Navy Henry Knox in 1797 for a commission. After an agonizing wait, probably in desperate poverty, Ingraham became a lieutenant and was assigned aboard the brig *Pickering*. She cleared Newcastle, Delaware, on 20 August 1800. Like Robert Haswell's *Louisa*, she disappeared without a trace.

Columbia's young ship's painter and sometime artist George Davidson went to sea a year or so after his return to Boston, and seems to have risen quickly to positions of command. In 1799 he left the city as captain of the *Rover*, bound for the Northwest Coast. Two years later, the ship cleared Hawaii for Canton with two thousand sea-otter skins and, like *Louisa* and *Pickering*, was never heard from again. "We understand," reported Boston's *New England Palladium* of 9 October 1801, "that there is no doubt that the schooner Rover, Davidson, of this port, foundered on her passage from the Sandwich Islands to Canton."

Columbia herself survived only briefly. Though probably only six years old when she returned to Boston harbor that summer evening of 1793, she had led a hard life. Rot would have taken its toll, as would the improvised repairs on wilderness beaches and the wear and tear of one hundred thousand miles of struggle against the unforgiving sea. Sometime in the summer of 1801 her owners, whoever they were by then, gave up the struggle to keep her afloat. *Columbia*'s register in the National Archives, canceled on 15 October of that year, bears the terse epitaph "ript to pieces."

CHAPTER TWENTY-FIVE

Kendrick Tries
Once Again

★

Captain Robert Gray and *Columbia* have played out their roles now, but what about Gray's fellow captain John Kendrick and stout little *Washington*, with her ragtag crew?

When Kendrick took his ship out of Clayoquot Sound in September of 1791 on his way back to Hawaii and China, Robert Gray was laying *Columbia* up for the winter and starting his preparations for building the sloop *Adventure*. Gray and Kendrick's young friend John Hoskins had gone aboard *Lady Washington* at Adventure Cove to take leave of the old mariner for the last time. They would never see one another again.

Now, with his golden dreams of fortunes to be made, his deeds to Indian lands, and another cargo of sea-otter furs in *Washington*'s hold, Kendrick started across the Pacific for the third time. This would be the third time, too, that he would bring his ship to Hawaii. The possibilities of trade in those idyllic islands had always intrigued him. On his first visit he had seen sandalwood trees growing in the lush mountain forests of Kauai and the island of Hawaii. Chinese and Indian merchants would pay handsomely for even small quantities of this wonderfully aromatic wood.

On his crossing from the Northwest Coast to China two years before, Kendrick had left three of his crew behind in Hawaii with orders to gather a cargo of sandalwood against his return in the spring of 1790. The men were also to trade for pearls. The venture was ill-fated. Two of the men, probably left with little in the way of provisions or the wherewithal for trading, quickly tired of the project and got a passage back to Macao when Captain William Douglas's *Iphigenia* stopped in Hawaii on her way from the Northwest Coast. The other shortly thereafter was "improving his lifestyle" by making himself useful to one of the chiefs on Oahu.

The lure of pearls and sandalwood remained in Kendrick's mind. Now, just before starting back to Macao again after his stop for "refreshment" in Hawaii, he suddenly decided to try again. At Niihau he put three more men ashore, telling them he would pick them up after he had sold his furs in Canton, returned to New England, and then spent another season on the Northwest Coast. Kendrick's fantasy soared to ever greater heights. Gathering up the men and the "Sandars wood and Pearls," *Washington* would then continue on to the fur markets of Canton and thence, as Joseph Barrell had suggested so long ago, to India to dispose of the rest of the cargo.

Captain George Vancouver, stopping at Hawaii as he followed the track of Captain Cook in the Pacific, found all three of the men living on Oahu. An English seaman of about seventeen, John Roebottom, with a Welshman, John Williams, and an Irishman, James Coleman, were each to expect wages of eight dollars a month, he learned, while they awaited Kendrick's return in about twenty months from Boston and the Northwest Coast.

The realistic Vancouver was unimpressed. The sandalwood of Hawaii, he observed, "seemed but slightly to answer the description of the yellow sandalwood of India." As for the pearls, the "white were very indifferent, being small, irregular in shape, and possessing little beauty." The yellow, though, and those of a lead color, "were better formed, and, in point of appearance, of superior quality.

"Mr. Kendrick," Vancouver concluded, "must, undoubtedly, flatter himself with great emoluments from these branches of commerce, or he would not thus have retained three men in constant pay for such a considerable length of time, with a promise of further reward if they conducted themselves with fidelity towards his interest." This last proved to be a hollow hope. All three of the men quickly left their duties in favor of a less spartan existence as retainers of the Hawaiian chiefs.

Coleman, to the displeasure of the fastidious Vancouver, had "adopted the customs of the natives, particularly in dress, or rather in nakedness. . . . I asked him what he had done with his former clothes; to which he answered with a sneer, that they were hanging up in a house for the admiration of the natives; and seemed greatly to exult in having degenerated into the savage way of life."

Despite his disapproval, Vancouver saw to it that the three men were given a hundred young orange plants to be distributed about the island. One of the men also received from the British explorer a quantity of vegetable seeds "to amuse him in making a garden . . . and [to] instruct the natives in the method of rearing and using them."

Kendrick's whole venture, Vancouver commented, appeared "to have been the effect of a sudden thought." It was not until *Lady Washington* was weighing anchor, the men told the British captain, that Kendrick made his decision and put them ashore. "In consequence of such short notice, (they) had no means of equipping themselves, and were left almost destitute of apparel." Vancouver generously gave the Americans clothing, "to make them respectable in the eyes of the people with whom they were yet to remain for several months," along with tools and "some books, pens, ink, and paper, for their amusement."

Vancouver was wrong about the quality of Hawaiian sandalwood but correct when he surmised that Kendrick would reap no profit from this hastily conceived venture. It remained for Yankee shipmasters of two decades later to make Hawaiian sandalwood a profitable commodity on the Canton market. By 1827 the aromatic wood was paying for the Chinese tea that sea-otter skins had previously bought. Five thousand islanders labored in the forests, stripping them of ten thousand tons of sandalwood a year, to be sold to Yankee shipmasters at four dollars a picul (133⅓ pounds). Of this money the king received half. After another decade of this, during which time the Hawaiian royal family greedily exploited both their subjects and the islands' shrinking forests, Hawaii's fragrant sandalwood went the way of the Pacific's sea otters, and the trade died out.

Kendrick hastened on to Macao after dropping off his three seamen, arriving only two and a half months after leaving the Northwest Coast. The Chinese prohibition against the importation of sea-otter furs that had ruined Joseph Ingraham's chances of making a "saving voyage" were still in effect. Any furs that were disposed of would have to be smuggled, with all the attendant risks. It was not until March of 1792 that Kendrick could report to Joseph Barrell that he had sold his second cargo of more than a thousand sea-otter skins to the Chinese, this time for "twenty one thousand Spanish head dollars."

Kendrick's letter to Barrell, his first so far as anyone knows in more than two years, is a curious document. He has obviously given up his grandiose scheme for a return to Boston and then another voyage to the Northwest Coast, Hawaii, China, and on to India—if, in fact, this was ever more than a vagrant daydream. Instead, he brusquely informs *Lady Wash-ington*'s owners, "I am now fitting out the Brig for another voyage to the North West Coast, where it is my intention to winter, consequently shall not be in China again until the month of November, 1793."

In a rambling recounting of his financial misadventures, Kendrick mentions the various sums that have come into his hands—and for the most part, slipped out again: the eighteen thousand dollars his first cargo of skins brought, plus eight thousand for the sea-otter skins entrusted to him by Martínez; the money borrowed from Captain Douglas to help him through his troubles with the Portuguese authorities; and now the twenty-one thousand dollars for his second cargo of furs. Despite it all, the "Vessel is now so far in debt, that I really wish not to turn her on your hands." As an alternative, Kendrick proposes that he buy the vessel, allowing Barrell "fourteen thousand dollars with an interest of 12 per cent . . . until payment is made."

In case Barrell preferred to continue him in his employ "as Captain and Super Cargo . . . according to our first agreement when I left Boston," Kendrick continues grandly, "I shall consider the Columbia as consigned to me, and shall expect a commission on the sales, and purchases of her cargoes of this her second voyage to the North West Coast of America." He would, he told Barrell, also expect the customary perquisites of a commander, five hundred sea rupees per month as wages, and 5 percent commission as supercargo.

Not surprisingly, Kendrick adds his bit to the allegations made in connection with Gray's conduct of the first voyage. Shaw and Randall, Kendrick charges, sold *Columbia*'s cargo of furs for five thousand dollars more than was indicated on the account taken home to the owners in Boston. "There was too much smuggling, and the officers even encouraged the people to follow their examples. . . . When I was on the Coast the last voyage, the natives gave me information of their selling numbers of skins to the officers and people, which was sold at Canton.

"In my last Voyage," the captain added, "I purchased of the natives five tracts of land, and copies of the deeds which was signed shall be sent you the first opportunity." Kendrick failed to mention the important fact that only his own name appeared in them as owner. Nowhere would Barrell find reference to ownership by himself or his partners. "You may depend on my honor and integrity," Kendrick concluded. "Firm and steady to my first agreement, and . . . content to stay and prosecute the voyage or voyages to the end."

One can see in this strange letter Kendrick's regret at the lost opportunities and wasted years of his long and lonely odyssey. He could not seriously have thought Barrell would reinstate him as *Columbia*'s commander *and* supercargo, or that his halting explanation would brush aside the criticisms he knew had been leveled at his conduct of the venture. He must have known, too, that he was far too entangled in a web of his own spinning ever to see Boston again. Whatever his culpability, it was a bitter realization for an old man half a world away from all he had ever known.

There was only one possible course. He had put his finger on it in his letter to Barrell. Stay and prosecute the voyage or voyages to the end. But Kendrick would have been in no hurry. He rarely was. And he would have found it hard to tear himself away from the pleasantly raffish life of Macao, with its European amenities and Asian luxuries. He would again have taken a house ashore, where there was the constantly changing company of other captains from most of the world's ports. Eleven months slipped away while he slowly got *Lady Washington* ready for another Pacific crossing. With them must have gone whatever of the twenty-one thousand dollars had not been paid out to people Kendrick owed for advances on his previous voyages.

Holding to his plan of wintering on the Northwest Coast, Kendrick sailed from Macao in September of 1792. With *Lady Washington* on this voyage went a small tender. Since the brigantine was only about sixty feet long, the tender must have been absurdly small for a Pacific crossing. Only one reference to this boat has been found. John Bartlett refers to her in his journal as being "called the Venger." In the light of Bartlett's highly individual style of spelling, one can guess that the boat's name might actually have been *Avenger*.

Lady Washington and her miniature consort had barely made their way into the South China Sea when a typhoon overtook them. In his usual economical and understated way, John Boit, who arrived from Canton aboard *Columbia* after Kendrick had limped back to Macao, penned the only account we have of the disaster, a description that he received secondhand. Kendrick had been away from Macao only "four days when the Tuffoon overtook him. The brig laid on her Beam ends for some time before they cut away the Masts. She then righted, and the gale abating [Kendrick] steered for Macao."

The storm struck as *Washington* threaded her way through the fleet of fishing vessels that swarmed around the approaches of Canton. "The whole surface of the sea was cover'd with the Wrecks of Chinese Boats, and many of the poor fishermen was still hanging to pieces of the Boats. Capt. Kendrick pick'd up above thirty of the poor fellows, and was oblig'd to pass a great many that he cou'd not assist." Lacking masts, Kendrick somehow set up a jury rig and made his way back to Macao by the seventh day after the storm, almost certainly without the tender he had depended on to bring in more furs when he reached the Northwest Coast.

The old man's determination to make yet another voyage regardless of this stroke of ill fortune must have counted for something. By the end of October, Kendrick and James Bosma of the Dutch East India Company witnessed an agreement giving John Green, *Lady Washington*'s chief officer, and one David Wood a 9-percent interest in "the neat produce of the Skins, that may be brought in the aforesaid Lady Washington, on her return from the NW coast of America." What aid Wood and Green were able to offer Kendrick so that he could refit his ship after the typhoon, and how many others acquired an interest in the voyage, no one knows. But somehow, Kendrick would manage to patch up his vessel and start out again.

Lady Washington still lay at Dirty Butter Bay refitting when *Columbia* arrived at Macao homeward bound on her second voyage early in December of 1792. Gray spent the night ashore, where he learned of Kendrick's disastrous attempt to return to the Northwest Coast, but apparently neither he nor any of his officers visited Kendrick aboard the brigantine to get the details firsthand. The next morning *Columbia* started up the river to Canton.

The lands Kendrick had acquired from the Indians on Vancouver Island in 1791 were very much on the old fur trader's mind at this time.

Unlike Gray, Kendrick had a full awareness of the importance to the infant United States of the Northwest Coast. Whereas Gray seems to have had no thought of establishing an American claim to the territory around his "Columbia's River," Kendrick's lively imagination quickly seized on the possibilities that would open up if the United States established a settlement on the coast of Vancouver Island. There was Kendrick's age, as well. He was fifty-three now and may have felt an uneasiness in once again facing the perils of a Pacific crossing. It would be best to get his deeds on record.

Thomas Jefferson was now Secretary of State in President Washington's Cabinet. Although he was aware of Jefferson's position, Kendrick could scarcely have known of the Secretary's long and continuing involvement with the Northwest Coast—his friendship while Ambassador to France with that restless and frustrated genius John Ledyard, and their ill-fated attempts to establish an American fur trade at Nootka Sound—but almost as if he sensed that kinship of interests, Kendrick turned now to Jefferson with his own dream of American establishments on Vancouver Island. As we shall see, Jefferson was even then trying again to send an explorer—one André Michaux, a French botanist—across the continent via the "Oregon River," which he thought entered the Pacific somewhere in the vicinity of Nootka Sound.

Kendrick's letter to Jefferson still exists. Dated 1 March 1793, it was written at "Port Independence, on the Island of Hong Kong." This poses something of a mystery. The British would not establish their Crown Colony there until the 1840s. Before that, Hong Kong was a rocky, inhospitable island with few inhabitants save the Chinese coastal pirates who hung around the sea lanes leading to Canton. Kendrick may have taken refuge there when the Portuguese grew nervous about the many American trading vessels lurking on their doorstep at Dirty Butter Bay. "Port Independence" was probably just another of Kendrick's patriotic conceits, like giving the name Fort Washington a few years earlier to his little stronghold at Clayoquot Sound.

> I have the honor of enclosing to you [Kendrick's letter began] the
> copies of several deeds by which tracts of land . . . situated on islands
> on the north-west coast of America have been conveyed to me and
> my heirs forever by the resident chiefs of those districts. . . . I know
> not what measures are necessary to be taken to secure the property of
> these purchases to me, and the government thereof to the United

States; but it cannot be amiss to transmit them to you, to remain in
the office of the Department of State.

Once again, Kendrick makes it clear that he thinks of the lands as his own,
though they were bought with the property of his vessel's owners and in
direct contravention of their orders. Equally clear is the fact that Kendrick
foresaw the inevitable westward expansion of the thirteen American
states so recently freed from British rule.

The commercial possibilities of the Northwest Coast, Kendrick suggested
to Jefferson, "may perhaps render a settlement there worthy the
attention of some associated company under the protection of government.
Should this be the case, the possession of lands previously and so
fairly acquired, would much assist in carrying the plan into effect. Many
good purposes may be effected by the Union having possessions on that
coast, which I shall not presume, sir, to point out to you . . ." Nor did he
need to. Within a decade, Jefferson would dispatch Lewis and Clark on
their triumphant journey westward, an adventure that had certainly
been given impetus by Kendrick and Gray among others, and by John
Ledyard before them.

Kendrick's letter to Jefferson was probably written for him by John
Howel, who would play a major role in the later career of *Lady Washington.*
Certainly the poorly educated Kendrick could not have composed it
himself. Howel was an interesting figure. Captain George Vancouver,
who knew him well in Hawaii, wrote that "he appeared to possess a good
understanding, with the advantages of a university education, and had
once been a clergyman in England, but had now secluded himself from
European society." Born probably in 1753 and eventually ordained an
Episcopalian minister, Howel seems to have arrived in America about
1790 with second thoughts about the clerical life. Early in 1791 he purchased
Boston's twice-weekly *Herald of Freedom* and acted as its editor and
publisher until 19 July of that year, when he announced that "it now dies
and . . . on Friday like the Phoenix from her ashes will arise The Argus."

This reincarnation lasted only until October, when editor-publisher
Howel underwent another change of profession. On 24 October he sailed
for the Northwest Coast as "historian" aboard Captain James Magee's
ship *Margaret*, with the duty of writing a now-lost journal of the voyage.
In Macao, where he left the ship in January of 1793, the mercurial clergyman
switched again and signed on as clerk aboard *Lady Washington*, with
the avowed intention of sailing to the Sandwich Islands and settling

there. In fact, the affairs of the little vessel's captain were by then so disordered and the brig so far in debt to the merchants of Macao and Canton that Howel may already have been acting as a sort of supercargo on behalf of *Washington*'s creditors. As will appear later, Howel all along seems to have had his eye more on the here than the hereafter and, as he said, wanted badly to make himself "a large, and very rapid fortune." He may also have fallen under the spell of Kendrick's beguiling visions of wealth and glory to be found in the far reaches of the Pacific.

Clearing Macao with Howel aboard sometime in the spring of 1793, Kendrick missed receiving Joseph Barrell's reply to his long and involved letter of twelve months before. Barrell briefly acknowledged Kendrick's purchase of lands on the Northwest Coast but predictably had no ear for his errant captain's further involvement with *Columbia*'s affairs. Nor was he interested in Kendrick's optimistic thought of finding enough money to purchase *Lady Washington* and continue with her on his own.

"We acceded to go [as] farr as this," he recollected in a letter written to one of the venture's original shareholders, "if he would send us to any part of the Continent 400 Chests of Bohea Tea of the best quality, he paying the freight, but we running the Risque, we would discharge him." One guesses that the Boston merchant made the offer only in the forlorn hope that the improvident old trader would somehow strike so rich a bonanza that he might yet clear up his debts and send back to Boston a profit for his backers and a renewed reputation for himself. There was little else Barrell could do.

"I place no dependance on this," Kendrick's employer added realistically, "but am told he can procure the tea if he wishes it & Mr. Hoskins, who went on the second voyage of Columbia, is of the opinion that Kendrick will yet turn out an honest man . . ."

It was just as well that Kendrick had left Macao before Barrell's reply arrived. There was no chance that he could ever pay his debts and above that find the money he would need to send those four hundred chests of tea to Boston.

So, with rosy dreams still bright in his mind, Kendrick took the brigantine back to the Northwest Coast by way of Hawaii. Probably he steered first for Clayoquot Sound, where he seems to have established a remarkably sophisticated system of trade with Wickananish. This suggests that the bad blood between Clayoquot's chief and Robert Gray never extended to *Washington*'s captain. The chief, one of Vancouver's officers noted, "frequently receives in advance from the Masters of vessels (particularly Mr. Kendrick) the value of from 50 to 100 Skins to be paid in a certain time which hitherto he has commonly fulfill'd. When the Butterworth & Jenny were together in that part I have understood they could not purchase a skin as Wickananish was making up a quantity he owed and had likewise made a promise ... to keep all the skins for him that he collected." Thus Kendrick, in a brief summer season, could comb the Queen Charlottes and the Nootka area and then, without wasting time, gather up whatever Clayoquot offered as well.

Lady Washington was back at the Sandwich Islands with a partial cargo of furs about the first of December 1793. Howel, who seems to have stayed on as Kendrick's clerk up to this point, now moved ashore as he had planned. When Vancouver's *Discovery* anchored in Kealakekua Bay on 13 January 1794, the British captain found the *Washington* already there and invited Kendrick and Howel to dine with him aboard the ship. Archibald Menzies, *Discovery*'s botanist-surgeon, recorded in his diary that Kendrick, during the six weeks he had been in Hawaii, had continued to cast about for any new items of trade the islands might supply. One of them proved to be charcoal, some of which an islander had brought to Vancouver for sale. Kendrick, it seems, had lacked fuel for his forge and persuaded a seaman stranded ashore there to burn some for him. The Hawaiians adopted the technique and were now offering charcoal, along with their hogs and vegetables, to passing ships.

Another commodity, one that few save he would have recognized, caught Kendrick's eye. Vancouver recorded that the American captain had obtained from the natives at Waikiki a lump of "beeswax" that weighed some eighty pounds and had bought smaller quantities of the substance at other islands. This, of course, would have been ambergris, that strange, waxy substance sometimes expelled by the Pacific's deep-diving sperm whales. Foul-smelling when first cast up, it quickly develops a subtle, sweet, earthy odor prized by the world's perfume makers. Here was a rarity worth a prince's ransom to the scent merchants of India—worth its weight in silver, anyhow—if he could just get it there. Kendrick would have heard in Macao of that great mass of ambergris the French East India Company had got its hands on, 225 pounds of it, on which they had put a price of fifty-two thousand dollars. Kendrick's father had been a whaler, and he himself had made at least two whaling voyages. He would have recognized ambergris instantly.

There were few possibilities for commerce, however unlikely, that Kendrick overlooked. Even the island's famed feather cloaks had him dreaming of profits to be made, though where and to whom he proposed to sell them remains a mystery. But buy them he did. Archibald Menzies recorded that Kendrick purchased from one of the chiefs "a feather Cloak of nine feet deep & four & twenty feet wide in the spread at the bottom, the largest perhaps that was ever made at these Islands, for which he gave his two stern chasers mounted on their carriages." These were cannon used at a ship's stern, pointing aft, to be fired in case of pursuit by a hostile vessel. Kendrick's willingness to part with such a crucial element of *Lady Washington's* defenses suggests the magnificence and rarity of the cape, while the chief's agreement to make the trade shows how desperately eager the islanders were to acquire modern weapons from their visitors.

On a more mundane level, *Washington's* commander made good use on Kauai of a small sugar mill left there by another trader, "by the assistance of which Mr. Kendrick was enabled to make about 50 Gallons of good Molasses during his short stay." The market for this was clear. The Indians of the Northwest Coast loved the sticky syrup above almost anything else a foreign trader might bring them and would eagerly part with their furs for a bottleful.

CHAPTER TWENTY-SIX

"& Kill'd Capt. Kendrick As He Sat at His Table"

★

Ravenous after the privations of their long passages at sea, Kendrick's and Vancouver's crews gorged on the good foods of Hawaii: canoeloads of coconuts and ruddy yams, piles of plantains and golden bananas, sugar cane "of prodigious size," calabashes brimming with starchy pounded taro, and watermelons and fragrant muskmelons, both introduced to the islands only a decade earlier by Captain Cook.

Village firepits yielded a steady bounty of freshly roasted pork, fish, chicken, and dog—the latter, observed Thomas Manby, one of Vancouver's younger officers, the only animal food the women of the islands were permitted. Pork and, oddly, the region's plentiful bananas, were forbidden to them on pain of death.

The foreign seamen, with the eighteenth-century's lack of sentiment toward pets, happily downed banquets of dog meat as a special treat. "The hind leg of Bow-wow," Manby reported enthusiastically, "made an excellent breakfast; I picked the bone all but the Petty toes; them I made over to my next neighbor who was highly gratified with the delicious bit."

For the most part, a warm camaraderie prevailed between Americans and Britons of lesser ranks during that last pleasant winter in Hawaii. On at least one occasion, though, feelings were openly ruffled. Elegant feathered helmets, it seems, were presented by the Hawaiians to Captain Kendrick and one of Vancouver's officers. "We could not help remarking," wrote a fellow Briton acidly, "that the one given to Mr. Kendrick was much superior to that given to Mr. Puget. This, upon consideration, was only natural. These people only value the rank of their visitor, by the extent of their commerce with them."

For his part, Captain Vancouver was even more openly critical of Kendrick for "buying the chief part of his refreshments with Swivels, Muskets, and Gun Powder," which the humane Briton had himself steadfastly refused to put into the hands of the islanders. Nor did Vancouver look kindly upon what he called the "banditti of renegadoes that had quitted different trading vessels in consequence of difficulties with their . . . commanders." These included one Chinese, one Genoese, and one Portuguese. The rest "appeared to be subjects of Great Britain, as seemed also the major part of the crew of the brig Washington, although they called themselves Americans."

Vancouver warned the ruling chiefs against alliances with these foreigners, six or seven of whom had moved ashore and become their retainers. The Hawaiians, however, saw the seamen as "great acquisitions, from their knowledge of fire-arms."

Up to this point, Kendrick himself had apparently taken no overt hand in island affairs other than by his willingness to sell firearms to the chiefs. At least three one-time members of his crew, however, were in the service of the Hawaiian king Kamehameha. One of them, an Englishman named Boyd, who had been a mate on the Washington, "had put a plan into To Maiha Maiha's head of building a large Boat in the European style, which would . . . be of infinite advantage to him, in case of going off to War with the Leeward Islands, and had succeeded so far, that the keel and most of the timbers and Planks of the Boat were already cut out . . ." Unsure of his abilities as a shipwright, Boyd and the two ex-seamen who worked with him on the project appealed to Vancouver for the help of his carpenters and engineers in laying down the keel and setting up the frames. With this aid, Boyd and his friends "seemed to entertain no doubt of accomplishing the rest of their undertaking."

Vancouver seized on Kamehameha's eagerness for a vessel "after the

European fashion" as an opportunity to bring at least a part of the Hawaiian chain under the protection of Great Britain. Kamehameha agreed to
"cede" the island of Hawaii to "his Britannic Majesty, and acknowledged
his people to be subjects of Great Britain"—though the chief's idea of
cession was undoubtedly different from that Vancouver had in mind—
in return for help in completing his ship. Only thirty-six feet long, it
would be named, surely at Vancouver's suggestion, *Britannia.* The British
captain saw only laudable motives in Kamehameha's ambition that his
people learn to build boats for themselves. The chief, however, looked
on the possession of armed vessels as the one sure way to settle accounts
with his enemies and further his conquest of the neighboring islands.

Kamehameha's task was made easier by the volatile rivalries that
existed among the islands' ruling chiefs, and the increasing willingness of
the traders wintering there to take a hand in settling their affairs—for a
price, of course. Sometime during the winter of 1793-94, Inoino, chief of
the Waimea district of Oahu, attempted to usurp the leadership of the
ailing King Kahekeli and extend his sway over both Oahu and neighboring Kauai.

Kendrick, according to Vancouver, thereupon changed his role from
that of onlooker to active participant. Inoino, the captain reported, was
"assisted by Mr. Kendrick's people, and the rest of the European and
American renegadoes." Relying on the guns and muskets of the foreigners, Inoino was emboldened to declare his independence of Kahekeli.

When the King of Oahu learned of this, he sent a party, says Vancouver, to enquire democratically of Inoino if this change of rule was
"countenanced by the chiefs and people of the island." Assuming the
mission of Kahekeli's emissaries to be hostile, Inoino's faction, assisted by
Kendrick's crewmen, "with their muskets drove them with great slaughter from the island, and pursued them in their flight until they left few to
relate . . . the untimely fate of those who had fallen." What Kendrick had
been promised for his intercession in the affair is unknown. The old
trader was by now so deeply in debt that he would probably have
grasped at any faint hope of reward.

Vancouver was unusually harsh in his condemnation of the foreigners' role in the incident. "This melancholy event would not, most probably, have happened," he fumed, "had not these strangers advised and
assisted in the perpetration of this diabolical and unprovoked barbarity;
in extenuation of which they plead, that they were compelled to act this

savage part in order to preserve the good opinion of, and keep themselves in favor with, the chief."

Whatever the change, if any, Inoino may have effected in Kendrick's fortunes, the American left the islands in the spring of 1794 and took *Washington* back to Nootka Sound. Since the year before, the Spanish had been warning away all vessels other than those flying the Spanish and British flags. Kendrick, of course, casually continued to flout the rules, though he expressed some bitterness at being denied permission to take *Washington* up to his favorite anchorage at Marvinas Bay. But his little brigantine was contentedly riding at anchor in Friendly Cove on 31 August, when Vancouver, who had followed Kendrick eastward, arrived with *Discovery* and *Chatham* for the third time on the Northwest Coast.

The British captain was surprised to find five other vessels, in addition to Kendrick's, lying at Nootka—the British fur traders *Prince Lee Boo* and *Phoenix*, and three Spanish ships of war, the familiar *Princesa* and *San Carlos*, and the supply ship *Aranzazú*. The latter was now under the command of John "Juan" Kendrick. After having piloted the captured schooner *North-West America* to Mexico as a prize following his entry into Spanish service in 1789, the old fur trader's son had risen steadily. The two John Kendricks, father and son, would be together at Nootka until 11 September, when the young Captain Kendrick would take *Aranzazú* out of the sound on his way back to Monterey and San Blas. It would be the last time father and son would meet.

In this final encounter, John Kendrick and his father had expected to be witnesses to a historic moment. After having been the nearest thing to participants in the seizure of John Meares's vessels by Martínez, which had sparked the long-festering diplomatic struggle between Spain and Great Britain over Nootka Sound, they were now here as the quarrel was about to be resolved. Brigadier General José Manuel de Álava, Spain's new commissioner for Nootka, had arrived aboard *Princesa*. Captain George Vancouver would negotiate for his government in London. The two envoys only awaited word from their respective capitals.

As it turned out, the British and Spanish negotiators waited throughout the summer for word from their governments and finally left Nootka Sound with the issue still unresolved. It would not be until the following spring, with Juan Kendrick again present, that the Nootka controversy, which had threatened to plunge Europe into war, was finally put to rest.

Vancouver had noted, when he reached Nootka Sound that previous summer, that Kendrick's little sloop-turned-brigantine was again undergoing repairs. This probably had nothing to do with disasters at sea. Except for the typhoon that had dismasted the ship the year before, Kendrick had weathered whatever the sea had given him. He was cautious enough not to get himself in the fixes Robert Gray had seemed to court. *Lady Washington* was simply tired. She had been continuously in service now for at least seven years and considerably longer than that if she had been the privateer *Lady Washington* before Joseph Barrell acquired her for the fur trade. Like *Columbia*, she had been patched up and eked out with whatever materials and in whatever places could be found.

With his seemingly never-ending repairs to *Washington* again completed, Kendrick took the brigantine northward to Norfolk Sound, now Sitka Sound, Alaska. There, noted Captain Roberts of *Jefferson*, he obtained a large number of skins and "disposed of all his trade." With nothing left to barter for furs, Kendrick headed south again to Nootka Sound.

In his two seasons on the coast, he had done well. The palmiest days of the sea-otter trade, when almost unlimited numbers of skins could be obtained for two or three bits of iron apiece, were only a tantalizing memory now. Even so, *Washington*'s final cargo included more than a thousand pelts and 643 tails.

Now in October 1784, Nootka Sound was only a ghost of itself. *San Carlos* alone lay at Friendly Cove, where the Spanish garrison was settling down for the winter to await final settlement of the controversy. Juan Kendrick had taken *Aranzazú* south in September. Vancouver, with *Discovery* and *Chatham*, and Álava aboard *Princesa*, had sailed for California. John Kendrick took a final lingering look at the familiar tree-shrouded hills ringing Nootka Sound and headed back to Hawaii.

Lady Washington dropped anchor in Fairhaven, today's Honolulu Harbor, on 3 December 1794. Kendrick found two vessels already there. Both were familiar, the British fur traders *Jackal*, under Captain William Brown, and the *Prince Lee Boo*, under one Captain Gordon. These belonged to the so-called Butterworth squadron, which had been sent to the Pacific from England in 1792. Like Kendrick, Brown had since then shuttled his three vessels between the Northwest Coast and the fur markets of China, with occasional time out to sell guns to the various factions struggling for supremacy in the Hawaiian Islands. The *Butterworth* had now been sent home to England. Brown remained behind with the two smaller vessels.

The English captain had been one of the first, if not the first, European to discover the narrow channel that allowed ships to slip through a reef into the protected waters of Honolulu Harbor. Becoming a regular visitor and seeing the commercial possibilities of the place, which he named Fairhaven, Brown talked Kalanikupule, the chief of Oahu, into "ceding" the island to him in return for his help in defeating the forces of his half-brother Kaeokulani—Kaeo, as he was usually called. Cession of his island, of course, probably meant no more in the chief's mind than allowing Brown the use of the harbor whose entry the English captain claimed he had discovered.

In Brown's mind, however, ownership of the island—and four others along with it—was his without question. Kendrick, noted Archibald Menzies in his journal,

> show'd us a copy of a letter which Mr. Brown of the Butterworth left
> in Dec[embe]r last with James Coleman at Woahoo, importing that
> [Kalanikupule] had in the most formal manner ceded to him that
> island together with the four islands to windward, in consideration of
> some valuable presents he had made to the said Chief, & to render his
> claim more solemn & binding he had an instrument drawn up, which
> was signed by himself & four of his officers on the one hand & four of
> his principal Chiefs on the other, after which he appointed James
> Coleman as resident on the island of Woahoo in charge of his claim.

Brown had sold and traded guns indiscriminately to the island leaders. Now he and Kendrick, who by now had been at Fairhaven for more than a week, took a direct hand in Hawaiian affairs. Kaeo had invaded Oahu, and Kalanikupule's fortunes suddenly plunged. Probably to protect his own interests, Brown saw to it that the mate of *Jackal* and eight of his sailors joined Kalanikupule's forces. The guns of the Englishmen and almost certainly those of some of Kendrick's Americans proved decisive in what came to be called the Battle of Kalauao. Kaeo's forces fled into the hills overlooking Honolulu and finally sought shelter in a small ravine near the shore.

Kaeo might have escaped had his *ahuula*, his brilliant cloak of scarlet and yellow feathers, not given away his position. Brown's and Kendrick's gunners, in small armed boats lying inside the eastern arm of Pearl Harbor, fired on Kaeo as he fled, pinpointing him for Kalanikupule's soldiers. The Oahu chief's men came down on Kaeo from still higher ground and killed him along with his wives and warrior chiefs.

Some question lingers as to how active a role Kendrick played in the engagement. The two surviving references to his presence at Fairhaven that December are in direct contradiction. John Boit, calling at Hawaii in the sloop *Union* only a year after the battle, got his facts from the Englishman John Young, a deserter from the fur trader *Eleanora*, who had settled in the islands and had become confidant and adviser to Kamehameha. Boit's lengthy account, presented in his usual meticulously detailed way, says that victory "was gain'd by the King of Whawhooa, by the assistance of Capt. Kendrick." He makes no mention of Brown. Sheldon Dibble, in his *History of the Sandwich Islands*, just as flatly insists that "Captain Kendrick took no part in it."

Dibble's history was not published until nearly half a century after these events took place and must have relied in the main on other than eyewitness accounts. The question remains unanswered. Kendrick may well have had a vision of sharing in Brown's "ownership" of the island by also taking part in the action on the side of Kalanikupule. His definite involvement the winter before in Inoino's attempted coup on Oahu strengthens the likelihood that Boit's account is the correct one.

For the balance of the story, too, Boit's account, in its careful circumstantial detail, is by far the most believable. Kendrick's *Lady Washington* still lay anchored close to Captain Brown's *Jackal* and *Prince Lee Boo*. Immediately after the battle, Boit writes, Kendrick "inform'd Captain Brown that on the morrow he should cause the Flag of the United States to be hoisted, & fire a federal salute, which he beg'd might be answer'd by the two Englishmen." It seems unlikely that Kendrick would have initiated such a salute were he not celebrating his own victorious involvement in the affair. Brown, undoubtedly elated at his friend Kalanikupule's success, agreed and ordered the shot to be removed from three guns on each of his ships.

About ten the next morning, *Lady Washington* hoisted her colors and fired a salute, and *Jackal*'s gunner responded. "On coming to the 3'd gun it was discover'd not to be prim'd. So the Apron of the 4th Gun was taken of[f], which was fir'd, & being shoted with round & Grape Shot, it peirced the side of the Lady Washington & kill'd Capt. Kendrick as he sat at his table, & kill'd & wounded many upon deck."

The body of the fifty-five-year-old Kendrick, with those of his crewmen who had been killed, was taken ashore that afternoon and buried in a secluded grove of coconut palms back of Honolulu's muddy, coral-girt beach. Kendrick's clerk, the one-time clergyman John Howel, would have read the Prayer Book burial service. The puzzled islanders took the ceremony, the first they had seen, to be "an act of sorcery to procure the death of Captain Brown." That night they opened Kendrick's grave and stole what was to them a not inconsiderable prize, the dead man's winding-sheet.

Thus, on 12 December 1794 passed Captain John Kendrick, dead ironically as the result of one of the little patriotic gestures he so delighted in. Perhaps it came as he might have hoped. For all his failings and failures, one cannot quite wish the burly old captain the mediocrity of settling into the quiet obscurity of some house ashore. There were still too many dreams to chase, too many seas to follow. Had William Brown's gunner not carelessly gone on to his fourth cannon when he found the third unprimed, some other mishap would have carried the improvident old trader off as he stubbornly continued to make his way back and forth across the lonely Pacific.

In reading through the many contemporary references to him, one finds that despite his all-too-obvious failings, Kendrick seems to have evoked a warm response in nearly everyone who came in contact with him. The Spaniards Don Esteban José Martínez and José Mariano Moziño, the Englishman George Vancouver and the Scot William Douglas, the Americans John Hoskins and Joseph Ingraham, the Indian chiefs Maquinna and Wickananish each in his way testified to this.

It may have been Kendrick's personal appeal, more than anything else, that led Joseph Barrell to appoint him to the command of *Columbia* and *Lady Washington* in the first place. Even John Howel, who was second only to Haswell in the scope of his criticism—it was he who condemned both Gray and Kendrick as fools and knaves—succumbed in the end.

". . . with all his fooleries," Howel wrote to Barrell after the captain's death, "he was a wonderful man, and worthy to be remembered beyond the gliding Hours of the present. He was ruined by his appointment to the Columbia. Empires and fortunes broke on his sight. The paltry two-penny objects of his expedition were swallowed up in the magnitude of his Gulliverian Views. North East America was on the Lilliputian, but he designed N. W. America to be on the Brobdingnagian scale. Had you known him as well as I did, you would have sent some Glumdalclitch or other as nurse with him."

The American voyager Amasa Delano, whose life and adventures at

sea equalled Kendrick's both in length and variety, was as aware as anyone of Kendrick's faults when he eulogized him in his *Voyages and Travels*,
published in 1817:

> Captain Kendrick was the first American that burst forth in the world
> and traversed those distant regions which were before but little
> known to the inhabitants of this part of the globe. He taught many of
> his countrymen the way to wealth, and the method of navigating
> distant seas with ease and safety. . . . As a seaman and a navigator, he
> had but few equals. He was very benevolent, and possessed a heart
> filled with as tender feelings as any man I ever was acquainted with. . . .
> I wish to impress it strongly on the minds of every American, not to
> let his rare merits be forgotten, and to cast a veil over his faults, they
> being but few compared with his amiable qualities.

CHAPTER TWENTY-SEVEN

Phantom Land Purchases
Raise False Hopes

★

Within a week of Kendrick's death, *Lady Washington* sailed for Canton under the command of John Howel. That the ship's clerk so quickly took control of the vessel suggests one of two things: that all of her officers were among those killed when Captain Brown's grapeshot smashed into the brigantine's cabin, or that Howel had in some manner acquired a part ownership in the *Washington*. Both may have been true. The latter, in the light of Howel's subsequent actions, seems particularly likely.

After having been dismasted in the South China Sea the year before, Kendrick would have been desperate for funds to put his ship right again. Howel may even have been a sort of supercargo, looking out for the interests of others in Macao or Canton who owned shares in the ship. There is, in fact, one contemporary reference to Howel that supports this belief. Charles Bishop, captain of the *Ruby*, wrote in his journal that after Kendrick's death *Lady Washington* "belonged to several other proprietors." Howel, he said, was only a part owner and "ship's husband."

Whatever his reasons, Howel followed the right instincts in getting the little brigantine and what was left of her crew out of Fairhaven

Harbor as quickly as possible. Before the end of December, Kalanikupule had turned against his one-time British allies and conceived a plan to seize their ships. Offering Captains Brown and Gordon a large number of hogs in payment for their services in defeating Kaeo, the islanders lured the crews of *Jackal* and *Prince Lee Boo* ashore, ostensibly to kill and salt down the animals. Brown and Gordon remained alone aboard their ships. In a surprise attack, with no losses to themselves, the Hawaiians boarded the ships and murdered both captains. The crewmen, including the first mates of both vessels, were rounded up and marched off to the village of Honolulu, where they found the body of Captain Brown stripped and tied by the hands and feet to a pole.

Unaware of the fate he had perhaps escaped by his fortuitous departure from Honolulu Harbor, Howel brought *Lady Washington* into Macao early in February 1795. He would not learn of his good fortune until *Jackal* and *Prince Lee Boo* arrived in China a few weeks later. After having been forced with their crews to refit and arm the two ships so that Kalanikupule could use them in an invasion of Kamehameha's home island, Oahu, the two first mates had launched a desperate gamble, a night attack to recover their vessels.

The plan succeeded. After the natives had been driven from the ships, *Jackal* and *Prince Lee Boo* stopped at the island of Hawaii, where they traded Kamehameha the guns and ammunition left on board by the Oahu warriors for the supplies they needed to take them to Canton. By April of 1795 Kamehameha had invaded Oahu. On 1 May the battle of Nuuanu, in which Kamehameha defeated Kalanikupule and his chiefs with their own weapons, had made him monarch of all the islands except Kauai.

Once across the Pacific with *Lady Washington*, Howel seems quickly to have established himself in Canton and Macao as an agent for American ships bringing cargoes to China. John Boit, then captain of the sloop *Union*, wrote in December of 1795 that "Mess'r John Howell & Co, Compradore," had supplied ships' stores to both his and another Boston vessel, the *John Jay*. Howel's and *Lady Washington*'s subsequent careers are known chiefly from three letters the Englishman wrote to Joseph Barrell. In the first, dated at Canton in May of 1795, Howel informed the Boston merchant that he had sold the ship's cargo of sea-otter furs for $16,756, more than $11,000 less than the accumulated total of Kendrick's debts. The brigantine *Washington* had been sold for $1,300.

"I bought her," Howel wrote, "and am going to the N. W. Coast on my own account, connected with some Chinese merchants. I expect to be back next December, and shall then write to you very fully respecting every thing; wind up all the accounts; and transmit you the papers, which I believe, will be the only remittance you ever have had, or ever will have, from the Washington."

Instead of going to the Northwest Coast himself, Howel wound up sending *Washington* there under the command of another captain. William Broughton recorded seeing the brigantine at Nootka Sound in March of 1796. Howel meanwhile continued as agent for American ships at Canton. Captain Bishop consigned the cargo of the *Ruby* to a "gentleman of respectability here named Howel, who it seems does a good deal of business in this way."

The following year Howel was apparently the only "American" among Canton's little colony of foreign residents, and *Lady Washington*, "the property of Mr. Howell," is recorded in the East India Company's archives as having brought to Macao from Java a cargo of spices worth thirty thousand dollars. This trading venture, in association with an official of the Dutch East India Company, may have been what Howel referred to when he told Joseph Barrell in a second letter that, "as you well know I am a poor man, though I have a fair prospect of making a large, and very rapid fortune."

In that same letter from Macao, written a year and a half after the first, Howel was still promising Barrell an accounting of Kendrick's affairs and transmission of his papers. Howel, and presumably *Lady Washington*, were in Manila in May of 1798, when his last letter to Barrell was dispatched. Once again, the promises are effusive. "As I am in daily expectation of my papers, and among them your deeds of the lands on the N. W. Coast, you shall certainly have them transmitted—But do not think, my good Sir, they are worth 2d per 1000 acres."

Barrell's answer to Kendrick's letter telling him of the land purchases from the Indians of the Northwest Coast, addressed to Macao, never reached Kendrick, who had then left on his last trip to Hawaii and the Northwest Coast. In it, Barrell displayed the true merchant's instinct: buy cheap and sell dear. "The copies of the deeds of the lands you have purchased are not yet at hand," he told *Washington*'s captain. "I hope to receive them by next conveyance from you. At present they appear to be of little value, but in some future time they may be worth possessing."

Barrell had clearly been excited, however, by exaggerated stories about the quality and extent of the lands purchased by Kendrick, and saw in them a way of recouping his losses from this whole sorry adventure. His letters to Howel had been, more than anything else, efforts to get his hands on the deeds. Howel, for his part, took a more realistic view. "I have had an opportunity of seeing most parts of Capt. Kendrick's purchases on the No. Wt. Coast of America; and cannot flatter you with any hopes of profit from them even to your great, great grand children. They cost but little, it is true; and when the Millennium shall arrive, and all the nations of the earth shall be at peace, your Posterity may, perhaps, settle them."

Barrell, unaware that the deeds for which he was so desperately eager had been made out not in the names of himself and the expedition's other backers but in that of Kendrick alone, allowed his imagination full rein. Queries were dispatched to India as well as to Canton in an effort to turn up the missing documents. Each month they remained beyond his grasp, Barrell's rosy vision of the lands increased in extent and grandeur. Even before he had received the second and third of Howel's letters, Barrell had informed his brother Colburn Barrell in London that he and his partners had for sale a tract of land on the Northwest Coast embracing four degrees of latitude. Somehow, Kendrick's five separate pieces of land, the largest of them thirty-six miles on a side, had now grown in Barrell's mind to a square two hundred forty miles on a side—in the neighborhood of six million acres! "Better land and better climate," Barrell boasted, "than Kentucky."

A circular letter issued in 1795 by the London firm of Barrell and Servantes of 24 Threadneedle Street, offered the lands to investors and immigrants who might have the inclination "for settling a Commonwealth on their own Code of Laws, on a spot of the Globe no where surpassed in delightful and healthy Climate and fertile Soil;—claimed by no civilized Nation and purchased under a sacred treaty of Peace and Commerce ... of the friendly Natives." Directed "To the Inhabitants of Europe," and issued in English, German, Swedish, and French, it dealt only in the most glittering generalities and neglected altogether to mention where these marvelous lands were located.

The whole thing, of course, was a total failure. Any interest on the part of a potential investor or settler would have vanished when he learned where this earthly paradise was located.

In the long run, Barrell's enthusiasm vanished too. "If . . . any enquiry is seriously made," he wrote to Barrell and Servantes, "see what they offer for my share, as I should be fond of selling at a low rate." And to John M. Pintard, one of the venture's original shareholders, who also thought he owned a seventh part of Kendrick's northwest domain, Barrell opined of the land's location that "if it is not in the Moon, 'tis but a little this side." Barrell was by now deeply involved in the rush to buy land almost anywhere that a settler could reach overland and owned large parcels in Ohio and Georgia, but his bright dreams of a fortune to be made by settling the Northwest Coast had disappeared with the sobering influences of time. "If the rage for land speculation continues," he went on, ". . . I shall take the first offer, even if the pay is in wine." Not even that was forthcoming.

Joseph Barrell died as he had lived, swathed in comfort and respectability. *Columbia*'s losses had been only minor annoyances in an otherwise smiling career. Putting much of his business in the hands of John Hoskins and one of his own sons, he spent his last years lavishly furnishing the mansion in Charlestown that Charles Bulfinch had designed for him, with its "oval parlor projecting on the garden side," like that of the president's house in Washington. When Barrell died in 1804, one of the Boston papers (there were already half a dozen in that fiercely literate city) honored him with phrases like "unshaken patriot" and as a man "bold and noble in his designs."

To satisfy the nineteenth-century public's morbid preoccupation with the last moments of its betters, the writer also noted that Joseph Barrell had "often expressed his desire that his departure out of life might be sudden; in this . . . he was gratified. In half an hour from the commencement of his last illness, previous to which he had been in perfect health, he was a corpse."

When enthusiasm for Kendrick's lands disappeared, so too for many years did all interest in Kendrick's and Gray's explorations on the Northwest Coast. Kendrick, of course, never returned to Boston to tell about his. If Gray, who did return, attached any importance at all to that momentous day in May of 1792 when he took his ship across the Columbia River's wave-lashed bar, not so much as a suggestion to that effect survives. In his practical, dollars-and-cents mind, one supposes, it was just another river, not so very different from the others he had been the first American to enter. Grays Harbor, after all, which his crew had named for him, would likely have bulked larger in his affections. So his "Columbia's river" (he had not even bothered to name it until a week after its discovery) was just one more of a long string of anchorages *Columbia* had put her nose into—and was not half so profitable as some.

Whatever the reason—Gray's lack of interest, or Boston's—the discovery of the Columbia River remained for more than a decade one of the best-kept secrets of North American geography. The first public announcement was not made until 1798, six years after the fact, with the publication in London of Captain George Vancouver's *Voyage of Discovery,* which gave Gray credit only for having found the river's mouth.

More detail than that, still with no real credit to Gray, was gained by one of Vancouver's officers, Lieutenant William R. Broughton, who returned to the Columbia River in His Majesty's ship *Providence* and explored the river almost to the place where it tumbled from the Cascades to begin its last headlong rush to the sea. But the results of Broughton's explorations would not appear in print, again in London, until 1804; by that time Lewis and Clark were already well on their way across the continent.

In short, as far as Boston of the 1790s was concerned—the federal government, too, for that matter—Robert Gray might just as well not have entered the Columbia River. Eventually his discovery would take the majestic waterway out of the hazy uncertainty that had so long cloaked it. But that would not happen for a few years yet. It was still not on the map.

CHAPTER TWENTY-EIGHT

Lewis and Clark
Reach the Columbia River

★

The news Robert Gray brought back to Boston, if Joseph Barrell and his merchant rivals were aware of it at all, had stirred not a quiver of interest in the handsome mansions and noisy countinghouses of the Massachusetts capital. Never mind such trivial details of that distant shore. The only question in Boston heads just then was how to wring more money out of it. And more than a decade would pass before the existence of the Columbia River would penetrate the Atlantic seaboard as far south as the banks of the Potomac.

There in the young nation's swampy capital, Thomas Jefferson, whom we last met as he tried unsuccessfully to arrange for John Ledyard's "chimerical" journey across Russia and then afoot over the North American continent from Nootka Sound to Virginia, was now President Jefferson. He had brought his love of good company and good conversation to the parlors and dining rooms of the yet unfinished White House. Fortunately for the nation's future, that keen and penetrating mind of his also retained its compelling curiosity about the great wilderness that lay on the other side of the Mississippi River.

If anything, his interest had grown with the years. John Kendrick, we will remember, had in 1793 sent Jefferson, who was then secretary of state in George Washington's cabinet, the deeds to those lands of his on the Northwest Coast. The old captain, ever the patriotic visionary, had viewed his purchases from the Indians as potential sites for American settlements along the rim of the Pacific. That idea would have fanned the flame that never ceased to glow in Jefferson's mind—the dream of an overland exploration of the westernmost reaches of North America.

The Virginian had never lost an opportunity to learn more about the farther reaches of his continent. Somehow, for instance, he had got his hands on the original of Joseph Ingraham's fine and richly factual journal of his 1790-92 voyage to the Northwest Coast in the brigantine *Hope.* While he was secretary of state—spurred on perhaps by John Kendrick's optimistic dream of United States colonies on the western shore of North America—Jefferson had, in fact, already made another brave attempt to launch an expedition, one that would span the continent from east to west rather than the other way around, as he had originally proposed to Ledyard. This time he was encouraging the botanist André Michaux, who had been for some years in North America seeking plant species that he might introduce to his native France.

This had been a project that appealed to the horticulturist in Jefferson. So when Michaux applied to the American Philosophical Society in Philadelphia (of which Jefferson was a member) for support of an exploration into the Louisiana Purchase, the secretary gave the project his immediate backing, including a contribution of $12.50 toward the fund the society was raising. Alexander Hamilton gave an equal amount; George Washington bettered them both by adding $25 to the expedition's finances. This was in 1793, while Robert Gray was still on his way home with another skimpy cargo and (if he thought to mention it) the news of his great discovery.

Michaux's proposal, as Ledyard's had been, was quickly transformed by Jefferson. The Frenchman, he directed on behalf of the society, should "explore the country along the Missouri, and thence westwardly ... to find the shortest and most convenient route of communication between the United States and the Pacific Ocean.... It would seem by the latest maps," Jefferson went on, "as if a river called Oregon interlocked with the Missouri for a considerable distance, and entered the Pacific Ocean not far southward of Nootka Sound." Note well that reference to the

Oregon River, though Jefferson admitted at the time "that these maps are not to be trusted so far as to be of . . . any positive instruction to you." Despite Robert Gray's entrance into the Columbia in 1792, Jefferson, like the rest of his countrymen, would remain in virtual ignorance of the river's existence, thinking instead of the will-o'-the-wisp "Oregon," until Lewis and Clark gave real meaning to the Columbia River by reaching it overland a dozen years later.

Jefferson's orders to Michaux throw an amusing light on the state of our knowledge of the American West in 1793. Were there living mammoths grazing there, Jefferson charged Michaux to learn, to match the one whose fossilized remains he had exhumed some years earlier in Virginia? He was eager to learn "whether the Lama or Paca of Peru, is found in those parts of this continent . . ." Jefferson would also have Michaux record all he could of the "names, numbers, and dwellings of the inhabitants . . . their history, connection with each other, languages, manners, state of society, and of the arts and commerce among them"—a hint that he, like so many others of his time, would not have been altogether surprised by the discovery of some highly advanced Indian culture somewhere out there in the unknown west.

To protect such startling discoveries as Michaux might make, Jefferson suggested that "noting them on the skin might be best for such as may be most important, and that further details may be committed to the bark of the paper-birch, a substance which may not excite suspicions among the Indians, and [is] little liable to injury from wet or other common accidents."

Alas for Jefferson's and the Philosophical Society's grand plans and grander hopes, Michaux's expedition, like Ledyard's before it, failed early. The Frenchman was foolish enough to become embroiled in European politics at the moment Secretary of State Jefferson was trying to steer his fledgling nation through a thicket of Franco-Spanish rivalries in the Louisiana Purchase, the very area Michaux would have had to traverse first. The whole effort, Jefferson ruefully noted later, "proved abortive."

The Virginian's inauguration as president in 1801 put a new face on the whole enterprise. Now he had the authority to *make* things work. By mid-point of his first term, Jefferson had in a secret message successfully asked Congress for $2,500 to mount a third expedition. He chose as its leader a fellow Virginian, Meriwether Lewis, his private secretary. Lewis in turn chose as his co-leader the red-haired Virginian William Clark, a

boyhood friend and younger brother of the Revolutionary War frontiers-
man-soldier George Rogers Clark. Now for the third time Jefferson
penned instructions he hoped would finally carry Americans across the
continent. "The object of your mission is simple," he told Lewis and
Clark, "the direct water communication from sea to sea formed by the
bed of the Missouri, and perhaps the Oregon." The Columbia? He still
seemed barely to have heard of it, though others had tried to tell him it
was there. "The river you wish to discover," the French naturalist Bernard
Lacépède, for instance, had written to Jefferson in 1803, "could well be
the Columbia which Monsieur Gray, your fellow citizen, discovered in,"
he noted incorrectly, "1788 or 1789."

The expedition, forty-five strong including William Clark's slave
York, plus Lewis's huge dog, a Newfoundland named Seaman (not Scam-
mon or Scannon as so many have misread Clark's original journals), left St.
Louis on 14 May 1804, and by the following summer had forced its way
against the river's roaring currents to the headwaters of the Missouri.
They found no Oregon River "interlocked" with it, nor was there any
Oregon River there at all. Switching from their now-useless boats to
horses bought from the Indians, the expedition—joined by French-Ca-
nadian trapper Toussaint Charbonneau and his eighteen-year-old Shosho-
ne wife, Sacajawea—struggled across the Rockies afoot, relegating their
horses to duty as pack animals.

After false starts along rivers that might have led them toward the
Pacific but did not and then still more mountains to cross, Lewis and Clark
reached the Clearwater, followed it to the Snake, and then reached not
the mythical Oregon but the very real Columbia. The river's racing currents carried them perilously but swiftly to the Pacific shore. "Ocian in
view! O! the joy!" Clark penned ecstatically in his notebook. Later he
would cut into the trunk of a tall yellow pine the words "William Clark
December 3rd 1805. By Land from the U. States in 1804 and 1805."

There was no doubt where they were, that this was the same river
entered, often at such peril to themselves and their ships, by Robert Gray
and the maritime fur traders who had followed him for a decade after.
Though Jefferson had been only hazily aware of the Columbia and had
confused it with the fanciful Oregon as recently as in his orders to Lewis
and Clark, the two leaders themselves had known very well what they
were looking for. They had made themselves thoroughly familiar with
Vancouver's description of the Columbia (as far as it went) and may even

have gained some information on its upper course by word of mouth from Broughton's still unpublished account. Somehow—one can only guess how, but their journals prove that they did—these gifted men recognized the Columbia from the very moment they reached its confluence with the Snake, more than three hundred miles east of where it flows over that raging bar into the Pacific.

If there *had* been any doubt, the Chinooks at the river's mouth would soon have dispelled it. "The Indians inform us," Meriwether Lewis recorded in one of his elkhide-bound journals, that the traders who had preceded him to the mouth of the Columbia "speak the same language with ourselves and give us proof of their varacity by repeating many words of English, as musquit, powder, shot, nife, file, damned rascal, sun of a bitch, &c."

Clark recorded the names of some of the traders and their vessels, including one the Indians spoke of as the "Skooner Washilton," whose captain, they said, was a favorite of theirs. *Lady Washington,* so far as anyone knows, traded for skins under Kendrick's command no nearer the Columbia River than the Strait of Juan de Fuca. The "Washilton" must have been a garbled tribal memory. The Chinooks, great traders that they were, had probably heard from their northern neighbors years before of Kendrick's little brigantine and the generous way her amiable captain paid for furs.

The electrifying news of Jefferson's Louisiana Purchase in 1803, which at a stroke roughly doubled the area of the United States, had already turned American minds forcefully at last to the trans-Mississippi wilderness. Now Lewis and Clark's crossing of that vast, unknown expanse made it certain that every American would quickly become aware also of Robert Gray's Columbia River and the lands that lay around it. Jefferson was ecstatic. "I received, my dear sir, with unspeakable joy, your letter of Sep. 23," he congratulated Meriwether Lewis, "announcing the return of yourself, Capt. Clarke & your party in good health to St. Louis . . . the length of time without hearing from you had begun to be felt awfully."

In that simple, heartfelt letter lay the triumphant end of a long, desperately hard campaign. Cook the explorer, Jefferson and Ledyard, Barrell and Gray, Kendrick with his vagrant dream of colonizing the remote Northwest, even the clumsy Michaux, and now Lewis and Clark each had played out their roles in this heady drama. Together, and at last, they had changed the consciousness of an entire nation. Where Americans had until then thought of themselves as inhabitants of a narrow ribbon of colonies striped along the Atlantic shore, now they perceived themselves not as clinging to that narrow beachhead looking east toward Europe but as gazing westward from the threshold of a vast and empty continent awaiting the bark of the plainsman's rifle, the bite of the plow, the crunch of the iron-tired wheel.

The Northwest Coast and its Columbia River could at last beckon waves of overland settlers as they earlier had summoned the first little shiploads of American mariners who braved the voyage to the Northwest Coast around perilous Cape Horn. By 1813 the drift toward United States ownership of the Columbia and the lands around it had become an inexorable march. Thomas Jefferson, like every other thoughtful American, now knew very well where the river was, and what it was.

Away from the cares of the presidency now, in the study of his beloved Monticello, Jefferson answered a letter from the German immigrant John Jacob Astor.

> . . . I learn with great pleasure the progress you have made towards an
> establishment on Columbia river. I view it as the germ of a great, free
> and independent empire on that side of our continent, and that
> liberty and self-government spreading from that as well as this side,
> will ensure their complete establishment over the whole . . .

The Revolutionary War was yet too soon over for Jefferson to have lost his bitterness toward the British. He saw clearly, too, the pitfalls ahead. "It would be an afflicting thing indeed," he warned, "should the English be able to break up the settlement. Their bigotry to the bastard liberty of their own country, and habitual hostility to every degree of freedom in any other, will induce the attempt; they would not lose the sale of a bale of furs for the freedom of the whole world."

Induce the attempt the British did, of course. Astor's letter to Jefferson had barely left the fur merchant's fortified trading post, Astoria, at the mouth of the Columbia River, when a ragged group of British traders hammered at its gates and demanded the fort's surrender. Britain and America, it seemed, were again in open conflict in what would come to be called the War of 1812. The order was quickly given teeth by the guns of His Majesty's man-of-war *Raccoon.* Astor, ever a merchant, genially hauled down the Stars and Stripes and sold out his establishment, lock, stock, and good will, to Britain's rival North West Company.

Even this proved only a minor bump on the road toward eventual

United States ownership of the Columbia's lush and dramatic valley and the region around it. In 1816—twenty-three years after *Columbia*'s return from her second voyage—President James Madison initiated a search for records of her explorations that might be of value in bolstering United States claims to the Oregon Country. The existence of Boit's, Haswell's, and Hoskins's journals was at that time probably unknown. A search turned up the official logbooks of *Columbia*'s second circumnavigation in the possession of a brother of Gray's widow. Charles Bulfinch, one of only two of the original owners of *Columbia* then still living, made an excerpt —shorn of some of Gray's bloody encounters with the Indians, which might not have gone down too well with the legislators for whom the excerpt was intended—covering the two-week period during which the great river was first explored by other than its own natives, and the original logs were returned to their owner.

Until 1819 Spain, Russia, Great Britain, and the United States testily proclaimed their "inalienable" right to overlapping slices of the Pacific Northwest. The Spaniards, with their hands full elsewhere, became the first to back down. In a treaty ceding Florida to the United States, Spain also reluctantly transferred to the Americans her long-standing claims to lands north of "Upper California." Five years later the Russians bowed out, so far as the Oregon Country was concerned, by recognizing latitude fifty-four forty, which today marks the southernmost tip of Alaska, as the lower boundary of their North American sphere of interest.

By 1837, with a permanent American settlement in the Willamette Valley, there was no question that "Old Oregon," which included not only the present-day state but Washington and Idaho, whatever might be its precise boundaries, would in some fashion become a part of the United States. A new search was initiated for material on *Columbia*'s great discovery.

Charles Bulfinch, now an old man of seventy-four, and his son Thomas, were by then the only survivors of the bold New Englanders who had twice sent Robert Gray and the *Columbia* around the world. At his father's request, Thomas undertook once again to find the official logs of the second voyage. A niece of Mrs. Gray was found to be in possession of the captain's papers. "She very readily handed to him one log-book of the Columbia, containing minutes of her voyage from Boston to the straits of John de fuca in 1791," Charles Bulfinch wrote in a deposition, "but stated that another log-book, which contained the proceedings at Columbia river in 1792, had been used as waste paper, and was entirely destroyed."

Happily, Bulfinch saw to it this time that the surviving volume was not used to light cooking fires in a nineteenth-century Boston kitchen. He presented it to the Department of State, from whose archives it was eventually transferred to the manuscript collection of the Library of Congress.

Matters came to a boil in 1845 when James K. Polk swept into the White House on a battle cry of "Fifty-four forty or fight!" Predictably, the British were unwilling to let the Yankees link hands with Russian Alaska, thus shouldering them away from any door at all onto the Pacific Ocean, but they might have dismissed the whole thing as election hysteria had Polk not seemingly made it official in his inaugural address. "Our title to the country of Oregon," he thundered, "is clear and unquestionable." The British people, stung by this Yankee effrontery, declared their readiness for war. Letting these one-time colonies get away with this, trumpeted the *London Colonial Magazine*, would simply "pave the way for fresh insults." But in truth the Parliament, behind a facade of proper indignation, yearned for peace after so many years of war with her rebellious colonies. And so, it seems, did the outwardly belligerent Americans.

All it took was time. In July of 1845 James Buchanan, Polk's secretary of state, quietly (and secretly) forwarded an offer of compromise at the forty-ninth parallel to Richard Pakenham, Great Britain's minister in Washington. Fearful that the proposal might be accepted, the ambassador took it upon himself to turn it down. Cannily, Polk withdrew the offer and waited for the British to make a move. He was sure they would.

Nearly a year ticked by before the British came forward, on 6 June 1846, with their own offer of compromise at the same forty-ninth parallel that the Americans had so often suggested. In almost unseemly haste, President Polk sent the proposal to the Senate only four days after he had received it. Within two more days that body had given its stamp of approval, thirty-eight to twelve. On 15 June Polk signed the Treaty of Washington by which Britain held its title to the lands between Alaska and the Strait of Juan de Fuca, and the United States finally acquired clear title to the whole of Old Oregon. Now the dreams of John Ledyard and Thomas Jefferson, of John Kendrick and Lewis and Clark, could become a sharp-edged reality. The gates to manifest destiny had opened wide,

While the march toward statehood for Washington, Oregon, and Idaho gathered momentum, the heirs of Joseph Barrell, joining those of

Kendrick, petitioned Congress in 1838 and again in 1840 either to confirm their title to the lands Kendrick had purchased on Vancouver Island—the site of all five parcels—or to make some grant to them of equal value. The whole thing should finally have been put to rest by the Treaty of Washington, in which British sovereignty over Vancouver Island was recognized by the United States.

In 1852 and 1853, however, the widow of Robert Gray joined with the other heirs in once again bombarding Congress for some form of compensation. By this time imaginations had soared. Kendrick's five real-enough land purchases lay on Vancouver Island, of course, and the Treaty of Washington had once and for all put them firmly in Canada's jurisdiction. But wishful thinking does wonders. Kendrick *must* have extended his purchases to what was now United States territory and thus into the realm of the honorable senators—this despite the fact that the old mariner, as far as anyone knows, never so much as set eyes on what are present-day Washington or Oregon. But never mind the facts. Somehow these eager supplicants now added—on what mysterious evidence no one knows—a mythical sixth parcel, thought variously to be either in the vicinity of the Columbia River or extending south from the Strait of Juan de Fuca to Grays Harbor and the Chehalis River. This, wherever it was, they claimed in a flurry of accompanying documents, encompassed four degrees of latitude . . . extended eight days' journey on each side . . . and embraced upwards of sixty thousand square miles! Thus their unchained fantasies came to picture Kendrick's purchases as spanning not only the whole of 675-mile-long Vancouver Island—now, alas, beyond the purview of the United States Congress—but the whole of Washington State and probably much of Oregon.

The committee to whom the petition was referred recommended that five sections of land be given for each of these interests, and in a separate application, ten sections were to be given to the widow of Robert Gray. If such bills were actually introduced, they failed of passage. Mrs. Gray died in 1857.

In 1866, and again in 1882, Kendrick's heirs advanced their claims, now on their own, but still relying on the grossly exaggerated notions of the captain's land purchases that had buttressed the attempts of 1838 and 1842. Claims were even made that it had been Kendrick and not Gray who had discovered the Columbia River! By now there was common agreement among the captain's heirs that their ancestor had been done out of credit for the acquisition of, if not actual title to, most of the United States Northwest.

"On the discoveries and purchases of our ancestor rested the chief claim of this nation to that part of our territory now included in the State of Oregon and the Territories of Washington and Idaho," the organizers of the attempt trumpeted in their appeal for financial support. Predictably, these last feeble efforts also came to nothing. Thus vanished one more of John Kendrick's grandiose dreams.

Nothing remains now of the story of America's first great adventure into the Pacific except to follow *Lady Washington* to her end. Ebenezer Dorr, who had sailed with Joseph Ingraham as supercargo of the brigantine *Hope,* and who returned to Macao on another voyage in 1796, reported that at some subsequent time *Lady Washington,* probably not then under John Howel's command, "had been cast away in the Straits of Malacca," the reef-fanged passage between the Malay Peninsula and Sumatra. She would have been on her way to Calcutta, almost as if she were finally carrying out her longtime captain's old fantasy of a trading voyage from Canton to India.

CHAPTER TWENTY-NINE

Boom Times for the Fur Buyers

★

Twice was enough. After one "sinking" voyage and a second that still fell short of their golden vision, Joseph Barrell and most of his partners left the Northwest fur trade for good. But the track that *Columbia* and *Lady Washington* had pioneered, around Cape Horn to Nootka Sound and then across the Pacific to China, would still be busy with Yankee ships, bringing unheard-of wealth to other Boston merchants.

At the peak of the fur trade, American vessels would carry five million dollars worth of goods a year to Canton—much of it in the form of furs and sandalwood—and bring home cargoes of tea, textiles, and porcelain worth twice that in Boston. The best of the voyages would return profits of as much as $160,000 on an original investment of no more than $40,000 in ship, outfit, and cargo. This, remember, in a day when a chicken cost fifteen cents and ninety-two cents would buy a pair of "blue duffill Trowsers."

This would be slow in coming, however. There would be other modestly profitable voyages while Boston's shipmasters learned the tricks of the China trade and developed the ingenuity to meet the changing tastes of the Northwest Coast Indians. There was another complication. When Captain James King brought the value of sea-otter skins to the attention of American and British merchants—Washington Irving remarked of that discovery that "it was as if a new gold coast" had been discovered—a prime pelt sold for as much as $120 at Canton. By the early 1790s, fifty ships—only fifteen of them American, the rest British—had combed the Northwest Coast and disposed of their furs to the Chinese. Each of these vessels brought to the Canton hongs as many as two to three thousand skins.

The result was obvious. From that initial peak in 1779 of $120 for a prime skin, the price dropped to a quarter of that. It would take a clever captain to find the skins, to have aboard the right trade goods to buy them from the Indians, then to pay the six or seven thousand dollars in port expenses at Canton and still take home a profitable cargo. Yet many of them did.

One of the most ingenious, Captain Josiah Roberts, arrived on the Northwest Coast in May of 1793 aboard the 152-ton *Jefferson*—about midway in size between *Lady Washington* and *Columbia*. Owned by J. and T. Lamb of Boston, *Jefferson* had spent the previous winter in the Marquesas, where a small schooner, the *Resolution*, had been built to serve as a tender to the larger vessel. Solomon Kendrick, as we already know, was *Resolution*'s second officer.

Starting to trade at Barkley Sound, on the southern coast of Vancouver Island, Roberts found that pelts were plentiful, but few were for sale. The Indians informed him that they were saving them for Wickananish. Roberts would learn, of course, that the Clayoquot Sound chief was in turn putting them aside for his friend Captain John Kendrick, who was meanwhile busily trading at Nootka Sound and elsewhere in the *Lady Washington.*

At Nootka, *Jefferson* and *Resolution* found *Washington* there ahead of them, leading to that joyous and unexpected reunion between Kendrick and his son. There were also two other American fur traders in the sound, plus a British brig. Competition would be heavy, all right.

With no prospect of worthwhile trade at Nootka, Roberts moved his two ships north toward the Queen Charlotte Islands. At Coyah's harbor there were, as usual, large quantities of skins available, but the Indians now insisted on a new medium of trade, dressed elk hides, called "clamons" by the traders, with which they made their arrow-proof armor.

Elsewhere, sea-otter skins that had not long before been traded for a single chisel now cost an overcoat, a jacket and trousers, or ten pounds of thick sheet copper. *Jefferson*'s trade goods would not last long at that rate. But Roberts was adaptable. When an Indian took a fancy to the captain's sea trunk, he was given it for a prime skin.

At Bucareli Bay, Alaska, little other than tanned elk hides and thick copper were acceptable. Roberts had neither. He dispatched *Resolution* to the Columbia River to trade for a quantity of hides. *Jefferson* stayed on alone at Bucareli Bay for nearly a month but acquired only two dozen sea-otter skins. Each cost a musket and two pounds of powder or six and a quarter square yards of cloth and a couple of the blacksmith's iron collars. When Joseph Ingraham had created the first of these ornaments and the style was new, he had bought as many as five skins for a single collar.

Dejectedly sailing back to Barkley Sound, *Jefferson* encountered *Resolution*. In a surprisingly fast passage, the schooner had been to the Columbia River, where she had traded all the copper and cloth on board for sixty-three prime sea-otter skins and twenty-seven elk hides. *Resolution* was sent south once more before both vessels would be laid up for the winter. This time, as happened more often than not, roaring surf kept the schooner from crossing the bar at the Columbia River's mouth.

Resolution would try again in the spring, carrying among other trade goods several hundred crudely forged iron swords created by *Jefferson*'s blacksmith. This departure would be Captain Roberts's last sight of the little schooner and her crew, including second-mate Solomon Kendrick. As already mentioned, she later that season moved north to the Queen Charlotte Islands. Anchoring to trade near the village of the Haida chief Cumshewa, she was suddenly surrounded by Indians, and every man aboard save one was murdered.

Trading at Barkley Sound during the winter, Roberts was forced to give a musket each for tanned elk hides. This could not go on for long, even though the hides would purchase three prime skins in the Queen Charlottes the following summer. Then Roberts remembered the Indian who wanted his sea trunk and saw to it that the chiefs had a look at everything that *Jefferson* carried. One of them bought the cabin carpet for five elk hides.

As his elk hides disappeared the following summer, Roberts once again fell back on the ship's fixtures. The curtains of the cabin's stern windows brought in two skins. The ship's tailor began transforming old sails into women's garments. These were snapped up as fast as he could fashion them. A Japanese flag was good for a skin. The cabin mirror and the officer's sea chests went to the Indians, as did ten rockets and most of the ship's crockery. Twenty-nine more sea trunks, actually simple boxes made by the ship's carpenter, brought in still more skins.

By mid-August of 1794, when *Jefferson* was ready to sail for China, her cargo consisted of 1,475 sea-otter skins, plus 13,000 seal skins obtained at Ambrose Island on the way from Cape Horn to the Marquesas, plus an assortment of otter tails and miscellaneous land furs. Josiah Roberts's ingenuity had turned what could have been a sinking voyage—for which he would have had every excuse—into one that must have returned at least some profit to his merchant-owners back in Boston.

Another of the brightest chapters in those still early years of the American fur trade was written by young John Boit, *Columbia's* fifth mate on her second voyage. He had celebrated his sixteenth birthday just two weeks after the ship cleared Boston and was not yet nineteen when she returned in July of 1793.

Crowell Hatch, one of Joseph Barrell's partners in both of *Columbia's* voyages, was John Boit's brother-in-law. The young fifth mate had handled himself so well on *Columbia*—one would not soon forget his cool competence in some of those encounters with the Indians—that he shortly became first mate on the brig *Eliza* on a voyage to Dublin. Again he did well and apparently had no trouble convincing his brother-in-law and another shipowner, Caleb Gardner, that he could handle the responsibilities of a fur-trading voyage to the Northwest Coast. He had his eye on *Union*, a sloop essentially identical with *Lady Washington*, though a trifle larger—ninety-eight tons to *Washington's* ninety. Owned jointly by Hatch and Gardner, *Union* would have been just about seventy feet long on deck.

Boit took command of *Union* at Newport, Rhode Island, in July of 1794, just a year after he had arrived home on *Columbia*. Provisions for three years were put aboard the little sloop, plus the trading goods Boit would need on the Northwest Coast: sheet copper, bar iron, blue cloth, and blankets, plus an assortment of trinkets "suitable for traffick with the NW Indians," he wrote in his log, "for firs propper for the Canton markett." Remembering *Columbia's* constant troubles with the Indians, Boit would take no chances. *Union* carried an adequate crew, twenty-two in all, and mounted ten carriage guns and eight swivels on the rails.

Wherever he had gone on *Columbia*'s circumnavigation—the Northwest Coast, Hawaii, even during the ship's brief homeward-bound stop at St. Helena—Boit had kept an eye open for the local beauties. By the end of August, when *Union* slipped her lines and headed past Block Island into the Atlantic, the handsome young captain had been in the Rhode Island capital some six weeks—ample time to turn the heads of some of the city's daughters. His log reflects his mixture of excitement for the adventure ahead and sadness for the friends he was leaving behind. "Got all in readiness for Sea," Boit wrote. "Adieu to the pretty girls of Newport."

After an easy passage around Cape Horn, Boit reached Columbia's Cove, on the coast of Vancouver Island, on 16 May 1795, eight and a half months since he had left Newport. Though the young captain criticized the sloop as a "dull sailer," he made the passage in only a month longer than it had taken Gray in his determined effort to better Kendrick's performance.

Boit was surprised to find himself warmly welcomed by the Indians. "It is three Years Since I was in this Sound before, with Capt. Gray in the Ship Columbia, but the Natives knew me instantly & though we where oblig'd to kill Some of there Unfortunate Countrymen at that time, Yet they seemed to forget that, & are as chearfull as I ever saw them." Trading began immediately, and Boit soon learned that furs had doubled in price since his earlier visit. Most were acquired for some of the sloop's cargo of blue cloth. "Chizz'l[es] they wont take as presents," Boit observed, and copper was not much better.

In less than four months on the coast, *Union* ranged as far south as the Columbia River where, as we have already seen, Boit spent a harrowing week trying unsuccessfully to get across the breaker-lashed bar at its mouth. Nootka Sound he found deserted by both the Spanish and British. Chief Maquinna's village had been moved back to its old site at Friendly Cove. No trace remained of the busy European settlement save a few vegetables, "Green peas & Beans, Cabbges etc," which the Indians gleaned from the neglected Spanish gardens.

Boit's superb seamanship and the caution born of his earlier experiences on the Northwest Coast resulted in a season almost devoid of incident. Only once was the smooth rhythm of the captain's log entries —"purchased many valuable furs," "a fine lot of Skins," "a Capitall lot of prime furs"—punctuated by anything like the troubles that had marred Gray's operations in *Columbia*. Moving north to the Queen Charlotte

Islands, Boit brought *Union* to the same place Kendrick had anchored *Lady Washington* when Coyah and his Haida warriors had so nearly captured her.

Boit knew Coyah as "Skoich-Eye," and from his previous voyage on *Columbia* was familiar with the chief's evil reputation. The young Bostonian suspected trouble, keeping his boarding nets up and allowing only the various chiefs aboard to trade. On *Union*'s third day there, "above 40 canoes came into the cove full of Indians (at least 30 men each) . . . Eight chiefs were on board at this time who began to be very saucy & the war canoes kept pressing alongside & the indians getting upon the nettings."

Coyah seized *Union*'s second mate as the Indians alongside began shouting hideously and trying to board the ship. "However," Boit relates calmly, "we paid them for their temerity & killed their first chief Skoich-eye in the 2nd mate's arms while they was struggling together. I dispatched him with a bayonet. The rest of the chief[s] on deck was knock'd down and wounded & we kill'd from the nettings & in the canoes alongside above 40 more when they retreated, at which time I could have kill'd 100 more with grape shot but I let humanity prevail & ceas'd firing."

Next morning canoeloads of fearful Indians, waving green boughs as signs of peace, arrived with quantities of furs to ransom their surviving chiefs, who had been kept "strongly iron'd" on the ship during the night. "Order'd the irons off them & got the poor devils up and not with standing the treatment I paid full price for the skins. Believe I got every piece of fur they had in the village."

Union returned to Columbia's Cove at the end of August, and Boit spent the next fortnight buying whatever remaining furs the Indians had and preparing for the passage to China. After a month at sea he sighted the island of Hawaii. "The females," Boit observed as canoes crewed by island women brought supplies off to the ship, "were quite *amorous.*" Hogs were at first offered for a few nails or an iron hoop. The word arrived next day that Chief Kamehameha had decreed that the animals would henceforth be sold only for guns and ammunition. Boit notes that he "thought it proper to refuse." On reflection, however, he changed his mind and the next day acquired nine large hogs for a single musket.

Six weeks out from Hawaii, the little sloop, joining seven larger American vessels, was riding at anchor below Canton. To Boit's dismay the value of sea-otter skins had fallen disastrously since his visit in *Columbia* three years before.

However, as fortune is fickle it's no use to repine at our ill luck. . . .
Sold the cargo tolerable well so as to make a saving voyage for the
owners. Invested the returns in nankeins & pelts which enabled me to
take some freight to the Isle de France which helped the voyage very
much. A number of my people having took the small pox at Canton
was obliged to leave them behind as 'tis death for any commander to
take the small pox to Mauritius knowlingly.

At Mauritius—"the Isle de France"—Boit completed his cargo with
a quantity of pepper and coffee "& took Mr. Bowen, a crazy man, as
passenger." The poor man came aboard *Union* in chains. After the sloop
was at sea, *Union's* humane captain observed that he seemed far less
dangerous than his shackles suggested and had them removed to make
his passage more comfortable. "I find Mr. Bowin to be quite rationall,"
the captain noted a few days later. His thoughtfulness seems not to have
been misplaced. The journal includes no further reference to problems
with Mr. Bowen.

Except for severe gales as he rounded the Cape of Good Hope, during
which a wave smashed away *Union's* starboard bulwarks and swept a
chicken coop from her deck, Boit made a smooth passage of it from
Mauritius almost back to Boston. On the city's very doorstep, only two
days out, Boit saw

a sail stand'g towards us. Shortly after she fired ten muskets & two 18
pound shot at us, one of which went through the foresail. They then
hail'd me & order'd all our sails to be taken in. Their boat boarded &
took me on board with my papers. She proved to be the English
Frigate Reason. John Berriford Captain from Halifax. Finding they
could not make a prize of the sloop, suffer'd us to pass after treating
me in a rough, ungentleman like manner. Bad luck to him!

At noon on 8 July 1796, John Boit brought *Union* to anchor in Boston
Harbor and saluted the town. There were the customary three welcoming huzzas from the wharves. That was all. "Having sail'd round the globe
to the westward, have lost one complete day, it being Saturday at Boston
and only Friday with us." Boit was accepted home without fuss, though
his voyage was, as he noted, the first time around the world by a sloop.
The *Columbian Centinel*, under arrivals, gave his accomplishment one line of
very small type. "Sloop *Union*, Boit, Canton," was all it said.

What made John Boit's quiet homecoming so special, however, was
that this seasoned mariner, back now from his second voyage around the

Writing a remarkable chapter in the annals of the Northwest fur trade, young John Boit
served as fifth mate aboard *Columbia* on her second voyage. After rising to first mate for
an Atlantic crossing on the ship *Eliza*, he took command of the sloop *Union* for a trading
venture to the Northwest Coast and China. Despite the customary hazards—Cape Horn,
the threat of scurvy, an Indian attack, and the perils of doing business with the
Chinese—Boit could celebrate the completion of a successful voyage with this joyful
drawing in his log. The Boston shipping list for 13 July 1796 reported his safe arrival in just
four words: "Sloop Union, Boit, Canton." Typically, in an age accustomed to youthful
seamen, no one thought to note that this seasoned mariner, after two voyages around
the world, the second in command of the ship, was still only twenty-one years old.
(*Massachusetts Historical Society*)

world—this time as captain of his ship—was still only twenty-one years old!

After only a month ashore, Boit set out once more, this time for Mauritius, as master of a leaky ex-British store ship named *George.* "God send," he wrote of the rotten old tub, "that I may never sail in the likes of her again." Not long after his return, he married Eleanor Jones, one of those "pretty girls of Newport."

CHAPTER THIRTY

The End of
the Sea-Otter Trade

★

By the turn of the century American vessels, the majority of them sailing out of Boston, dominated the Northwest Coast fur trade. In the period from 1795 to 1804, fifty-nine voyages are recorded, of which only nine were made under the British flag.

These were the years when the first traders on the coast could scoop up several hundred pelts in a few days, and a careful trader could take one or two thousand skins to Canton for a summer's work. In 1799 alone, seven American ships took to China some eleven thousand skins, which brought an average of twenty-five dollars each—a total of more than a quarter million dollars. In the following year the American trade jumped to eighteen thousand skins, fifteen thousand of them collected by Boston ships and the rest by vessels from other New England ports.

Among the New Englanders who put his stamp on this period of the maritime fur trade was William Sturgis, another of those precocious Boston shipmasters in the mold of John Boit. Starting his career as a countinghouse clerk at fourteen, he went to sea in 1798 as a sixteen-year-old foremast hand on the ship *Eliza*, owned by his wealthy relative Thomas Handasyd Perkins. Young Sturgis did so well on that Northwest Coast voyage that he was made mate of J. and T. Lamb's *Caroline*, on which he sailed for the Northwest Coast and China in 1800. The captain, dying of tuberculosis, left the ship at Hawaii in 1802 and Sturgis, then only nineteen, took over command of the vessel. He sailed to Canton, disposed of *Caroline's* furs, and brought her safely and profitably home to Boston.

It was on that voyage that Sturgis observed the use of ermine skins as a form of currency among the Indians of the Alaska coast. Scarce there and highly valued by the Indians, the ermine was a common animal in Europe. Sturgis brought home a sample from China and arranged to buy five thousand in Leipzig the following year. On his next voyage to the coast as captain of the *Caroline*, his ermine skins were an even bigger hit than Joseph Ingraham's iron collars had been. Sturgis acquired in one morning 560 prime sea-otter skins, at that time worth fifty dollars each at Canton, for five ermine skins each. All of his ermine were traded out at the same rate, bringing him a thousand sea otters. All told, Sturgis collected 2,500 skins that season as he ranged the Northwest Coast from the Columbia River to southeast Alaska. The voyage brought its backers a net profit of more than seventy-three thousand dollars.

Samuel Eliot Morison paints an affectionate portrait of Sturgis, who became one of Boston's wealthiest merchants and for nearly three decades was a member of the Massachusetts legislature. "When he occupied a Boston seat in the Great and General Court," wrote Morison, "one of the professional orators of that body got off a long Greek quotation. Captain Bill couched his reply in one of the Indian dialects of the Northwest Coast, which, he explained, was much more to the point, and probably as well understood by his colleagues, as that of the honorable and learned gentleman."

Fashion among the Indians was fickle. The ermine skins that Sturgis brought to the coast in 1804 quickly lost their value as other traders tried the same trick. Within two years they were practically valueless in the eyes of the natives. Another trader established a short-lived fashion, also akin to Ingraham's iron collars, by bringing to the Northwest Coast thousands upon thousands of ordinary steel thimbles. The Indians purchased them with sea-otter skins and then strung them like so many tiny bells from the fringes of their ceremonial garments.

In this period, however, another commodity, even more damaging to the welfare of the Indians than the muskets and gunpowder the

Perhaps chastened by his failure in 1785 to capture James Hanna's little *Harmon*,
which had fired on his men in response to the theft of a chisel, the Nootkan chief
Maquinna for nearly two decades steadfastly refrained from violence toward the stream
of visitors to Vancouver Island. But the provocations of the fur traders were many.
An insulting tirade from Captain James Salter of the ship *Boston*, shown here surrounded
by canoeloads of warriors, proved too much for the proud chief to swallow. Maquinna
returned with his men the next day and, feigning forgiveness, suddenly turned on
the Americans and slaughtered all but two. One of those spared was John Jewitt, the
ship's armorer, who spent two years as Maquinna's captive, fashioning new
weapons for the tribe and repairing old ones.
(*Oregon Historical Society*, OrHi 086321)

earlier traders had introduced, had already become a regular item of barter in the sea-otter trade. When the ship *Boston*, under Captain John Salter, anchored in Nootka Sound in the summer of 1803, she was ready to offer Chief Maquinna and his people not only guns from her stock of two thousand muskets and fowling pieces, but all the rum they could pay for —in sea-otter skins, of course. *Boston* carried twenty puncheons, about two thousand gallons, stowed in her hold. She also carried an assortment of other liquors for those with fancier tastes.

Chief Maquinna and his people got both the rum and the guns but not exactly as Captain Salter and his backers had planned. A bitter argument occurred aboard *Boston* over a double-barreled gun Salter had given Maquinna on his arrival at Nootka. The chief had almost immediately broken the gun and now brought it back to see if it could be repaired. Salter angrily accused him of carelessness with the present and compounded the insult by declaring that Maquinna was mean and difficult to trade with and had the appearance not of a chief but of a low-born and insolent rascal. Salter threatened Maquinna with a musket and ordered him ashore.

For a chief who for more than a quarter of a century had associated as an equal with such cultivated and worldly visitors as the British explorer George Vancouver and the courtly Spaniards Martínez, Eliza, Bodega y Quadra, and Álava, plus a succession of trading-ship captains and their officers without once losing his dignity or letting his temper take control, this was too much. Pretending to have shrugged off the affront, Maquinna in a display of renewed friendship contrived to get enough of his people on *Boston*'s deck that they were able suddenly to overpower the crew and seize the ship.

In a show of savagery that indicated how deeply Maquinna felt his honor had been compromised, Salter and all but two of his twenty-six men were killed with their own knives, their heads cut off, and their bodies thrown overboard. The survivors, armorer John Jewitt and John Thompson, the ship's sailmaker, endured a brutal captivity as slaves of the tribe until their rescue two years later.

Boston's story was not typical, of course. Despite the rising cost of furs on the Northwest Coast, the ever-present danger of Indian attack, and the lowered prices at Canton, these were the peak years of the sea-otter trade. In 1805 alone, American ships carried to China 17,445 skins. These were years, too, in which the King George men had been almost entirely squeezed out of the competition by the Boston men. In the decade from 1805 to 1814, only three of the forty-five fur traders on the coast flew the Union Jack.

Though not the biggest years in total number of furs taken, the seasons of 1808 and 1809 saw the most successful voyage ever made to the Northwest Coast. After having sailed as mate and assistant supercargo on the ship *Pearl*, twenty-six-year-old Virginia-born John Suter was promoted to captain and supercargo for the vessel's second voyage. Suter spent two seasons on the coast gathering sea-otter skins, taking to China an all-time record for a single voyage of six thousand pelts. He then completed his cargo at Hawaii by taking on a large quantity of sandalwood. The combination brought in enough to pay the always high expenses at Canton plus $156,743.21 for *Pearl*'s return lading of China goods. Suter's own accounting of the sale of his cargo at auction, one of the few such to have survived, tells a great deal about the goods Boston men brought back to the city's wharves and warehouses.

Sales of Ship Pearl's Cargo At Boston, 1810

50 blue and white dining sets, 172 pieces each		$ 2 290.00
480 tea sets, 49 pieces each		2 704.80
30 boxes enameled cups and sauces, 50 dozen each		1 360.00
100 boxes Superior Souchong tea		795.87
100 chests Souchong		3 834.66
235 " Hyson		13 290.65
160 " Hyson Skin		5 577.40
400 " other teas		13 668.48
200 chests Cassia of 2208 "matts" each		8 585.52
170 000 pieces 'Nankins'		118 850.00
14 000 " (280 bales) blue do		24 195.00
5 000 " (50 ") yellow do		6 800.00
2 000 " (50 ") white do		6 580.00
24 bottles oil of cassia		466.65
92 cases silks (black 'sinchaws,' black 'sattins,' white and blue striped do. dark brown plains, bottle green and black striped 'sattins,' for Gentlemens ware'		56 344.61
And sundries, bring the total to		261 343.18

Expenses of sale, including auctioneer's commission,

Wharfage, truckage, "advertising in Centinel and Gazette, 5.50," "advertising and crying of sales, 30.31," "liquors, 5.88"	2 129.06
Captain Suter's 'primage,' 5% on balance	12 960.70
Balance to owners	246 253.42
On this were paid customs duties, within 12 months	39 602.95
Net profit on voyage	206 650.47

There still remained the costs of the ship, her cargo of trading goods, and such items as the crew's pay, to be deducted from the voyage's "net profit." But that would have added up only to about $40,000. With $160,000 left after all expenses had been paid, *Pearl*'s owners would chalk up a return to themselves of nearly 400 percent on their original investment, and on his "primage" of 5 percent John Suter had put by on this voyage alone a tidy fortune of nearly $13,000. After seven voyages around the world, he left the sea a wealthy man and settled into a quiet life ashore in Boston.

Sadly, wrote Samuel Eliot Morison, little survives of this quintessential Nor'westman "but bare facts and one anecdote. He was more deeply religious than most New England-born sea captains, and read the Bible aloud daily on shipboard. One young scamp of a supercargo amused himself by putting back the bookmark at the conclusion of every day's reading, until the Captain remarked mildly that he seemed to be having headwinds through the Book of Daniel!"

From the peak catch of John Suter's triumphant voyage, with its six thousand sea-otter skins, the trade began its inevitable decline. It seems incredible that the animals survived as long as they did in the face of the murderous pressures put on them by the demands of Chinese fashion and international greed. In fact, a decade before Suter's great voyage, their numbers had already been drastically reduced, but the total catch stayed high because of the willingness of Yankee traders to pay higher and higher prices and the increasing intensity with which the remaining populations were hunted down.

Up to this point the Spanish coast of both Californias had been largely off limits to the American fur traders. As the animals disappeared from the Northwest Coast, however, the plentiful sea otters to be found in the kelp beds farther south became increasingly attractive. The fact that the

Americans could not openly harvest the animals or trade for them ashore in Spanish territory led to a remarkable partnership between the Russians, who were also feeling the pinch of diminishing catches on the coasts of Alaska and Kamchatka, and the Boston men.

The Russians, in their ruthless pursuit of furs, had long exploited the Aleuts of Alaska. These skilled hunters had become virtual slaves of the fur seekers, who forced them to take their swift *baidarkas*, as the Russians called the Aleuts' kayaks, to sea in quest of otters. Children were taken hostage—two from each family—to ensure their fathers' willingness to cooperate. Hunters who failed to fill their quotas were beaten or killed. But even such brutality eventually failed. The sea otter was becoming scarce all across the northern Pacific rim. And so, for a decade beginning in 1803, the Russians entered into an unusual arrangement with Yankee ship captains, which opened up to both groups the still populous sea-otter colonies of the California coast.

Prime mover in this late-blooming chapter in the trade was an adventurous son of the Boston Irish named Joseph O'Cain, who first reached California in 1795 aboard an English ship. Asking to be left ashore at Santa Barbara, he twice journeyed as far north as Kodiak Island, trading much-needed supplies to the Russians for sea-otter skins. After hurrying home to Boston in 1799 to be married, O'Cain was back in California in 1804, this time in command of his own ship, also named *O'Cain*. Coasting northward to New Archangel, today's Sitka, Alaska, he arranged with Aleksandr Baranov, the Russian factor there, for the assignment of some 150 Aleuts and their baidarkas, whose catch was to be shared equally— between himself and the Russians, that is.

By this time, New England vessels operating in Spanish waters were accustomed to carrying a "*Carta de Amistad*," a bogus passport alleging to have been issued by some such dignitary as "*Don Juan Stoughton, Consul de S. M. C. para lost Estados Unidos de New Hampshire, Massachusetts.*" A Yankee ship captain hungry for furs could piously claim to have been driven into His Catholic Majesty's coastal waters "*par mal Tiempo o otro acontecimiento imprevisto,*" which, this dubious document assured the officials of remote Spanish outposts, was quite permissible. So ill luck or unexpected peril, wrote Samuel Eliot Morison in his classic *Maritime History of Massachusetts*, was pretty sure to overtake a wandering fur trader whenever "the land breeze smelt sea-otterish."

And sea-otterish it did smell when O'Cain returned to California with his Aleut hunters. "Putting out from the ship in their skin canoes, like Gloucester fishermen in dories," says Morison, the Aleuts gathered "eleven hundred sea-otter pelts for Captain O'Cain. Kills were made under the very walls of the Presidio." By now, at least in theory, the Aleuts were being paid for their services, though the Russian and American shares of O'Cain's profits, some $80,000 each, suggest that there could have been little left for the hunters themselves. On a subsequent cruise, the indomitable O'Cain "chartered his ship Eclipse of Boston to the Russian-American Company, traded their furs at Canton, visited Nagasaki" (this forty-six years before Commodore Matthew Calbraith Perry established an American presence in Japan), ". . . lost the vessel in the Aleutian Islands, built another out of the wreck, and returned to trade once more."

Well over a thousand Aleuts were still operating off the coast of northern California in 1811. Ten cooperative ventures, teaming American ships and the Russians' captive Aleut hunters, took place prior to 1812, when the Russians managed to establish their own fur-trading settlement on the California coast. Together the ten voyages yielded some twenty-five thousand skins.

As it became increasingly difficult for a ship to gather a profitable cargo of otter skins on the Northwest Coast, more and more desperate measures were tried by the traders. Typical of this later period of the sea-otter trade was the voyage of the 281-ton brig New Hazard. Technically not a Boston vessel, though she sailed from there, she was owned by a group of Salem merchants, among them John Derby, one of the shareholders in Columbia's first voyage. The one surviving account of New Hazard's voyage, which began in October 1810, was written by Stephen Reynolds, one of the vessel's foremast hands. Thus it offers that great rarity among journals of the fur trade, a glimpse into the life of an ordinary deckhand.

That life, the journal reveals, was a far cry from the romantic image that exists today. Less than a month out, Reynolds records, first-mate John Iverson "threatened to break my head." A few weeks later Iverson struck seaman Ephraim Sampson with a handspike. The sorry record continues through the journal: "Sampson got the cat." "Iverson gave Sampson a severe flogging." Seaman Perez Bumpus was flogged by Captain David Nye, Jr., for not reeving a topgallant sail line properly. "Sampson got a flogging by the captain, after which he jawed us, called us thieves, country boogars, infernal scoundrels . . ."

In another entry, Reynolds notes that the captain "flogged cook for not getting victuals enough. Ends a beautiful day." The journal records twenty-eight rope's endings and floggings. Only eight of the brig's nineteen seamen escaped punishment. Not surprisingly, nine of the foremast hands had managed to change their berths to other vessels by the time *New Hazard* made her way back to New England.

The ship carried a cargo typical of the times. The day when beads and crudely fashioned "chisels" would coax furs from an Indian had long vanished. *New Hazard* stocked muskets and gunpowder, the molasses and sugar the Indians loved, clothing, India cottons, tobacco, rice, matches, paints—a variety quite adequate to serve as a seagoing general store. The dishonest practices of *New Hazard*'s traders would have matched those of the meanest of small-town shopkeepers. "Mixed sugar with bran," Reynolds records one day, "to sell to Indians." Other commodities were regularly adulterated whenever the traders could get away with it. A favorite trick was adding a quantity of charcoal to the gunpowder they sold. Small wonder that by now the Indians mistrusted nearly every Boston man they dealt with.

Captain Nye found otter skins increasingly difficult to acquire, in spite of the varied cargo on board the *New Hazard*. He looked about for some other commodity that would bring in more skins and was probably not the first Nor'westman to see it in human flesh. Most of the Indians of the Northwest Coast kept slaves, unfortunate wretches seized in their constant warring with neighboring tribes. Some villages had an abundance of them, others few.

On 17 June 1811, Reynolds records that the captain "bought two slaves in the morning." Three days later they were sold: "one slave five skins, one, three." Not long after, Nye sold "a little girl slave for five skins." In July four more slaves were bought. One was sold for eight skins. Two of them escaped three weeks later, and the fourth was disposed of late in August, price undisclosed.

For all the brutality aboard and the difficulty of prying skins from the Indians, *New Hazard* made a saving voyage. Much of her cargo from the Northwest Coast would have been land furs on which the traders increasingly relied as the sea otters disappeared. The brig also spent a week in Hawaii taking aboard a cargo of sandalwood. She also would pick up extra income by freighting still more sandalwood and a quantity of sealskins from Hawaii to China for the ship *Albatross*. The New Bedford *Mercury* for Friday, 24 December 1813, recorded the arrival of "Brig *New Hazard*, Nye, of Salem, 8 months from Canton, with a cargo of teas, silks, etc., valued at 300,000 dollars." After 1813 there would be few Northwest Coast voyages as successful as this one.

Though sea-otter skins would continue to trickle onto the market for many years thereafter, the great three-cornered fur trade—from Boston to the Northwest Coast with trade goods, then to China with furs, and back again to Boston with tea and, increasingly, "China goods"—was effectively dead by 1817. Not only were there no longer enough otters to make the voyages profitable, but American tastes and American imports were changing. Instead of the familiar Canton willowware that had for so long graced the tables of well-to-do Bostonians, Staffordshire, Royal Worcester, and French porcelains became the style. European textiles imitating the Chinese nankeens were as durable and cheaper. And Boston was prosperous enough now that her ships could carry plentiful British manufactures instead of hard-won sea-otter skins to Canton to exchange for their tea and their teacups.

The end of the American sea-otter trade closed what was probably the most adventurous chapter—Yankee whaling alone excepted—in the lengthy chronicle of our country's maritime commerce.

EPILOGUE

The Sea Otter Itself

★

They copulate in the human manner. Altogether, in life it is a beautiful and pleasing animal, cunning and amusing in its habits, and at the same time ingratiating and amorous. Seen when they are running, the gloss of their hair surpasses the blackest velvet.... The male caresses the female by stroking her, using the fore feet as hands, and places himself over her; she, however, often pushes him away from her for fun and in simulated coyness, as it were, and plays with her offspring like the fondest mother. Their love for their young is so intense that for them they expose themselves to the most manifest danger of death. When [their young are] taken away from them, they cry bitterly like a small child.... When struck, [the sea otter] prepares itself for death by turning on its side, draws up the hind feet, and covers the eyes with the fore feet. When dead it lies like a dead person, with the front feet crossed over the breast.

From naturalist Georg Wilhelm Steller's journal of
Vitus Bering's voyage to the northernmost Pacific, 1741.

347

The end of the classic China trade brought no respite to the hard-pressed sea otter. For too many decades more animals had been harvested than their natural increase could replace. As fewer and fewer reached the market, the values of prime skins soared, putting an irresistible price on the heads of the rare surviving animals. By 1846, said fur-trader William Sturgis, "the whole amount collected annually ... does not exceed 200, and those of very ordinary quality." The values of these had risen by then to $150—more than the Chinese had paid for those first skins brought to Canton in 1779 by Captain Cook's men.

By 1903 the sea otter teetered at the edge of extinction. So far as anyone knew, the California otters were gone, as were those of the coasts of Alaska and British Columbia. In Washington and Oregon there had not been many to begin with. But the appetite of the wealthy for these lustrous furs had if anything been stimulated by their scarcity. The occasional prime skin offered on the London fur market sold for more than $1,100. One, in 1910, brought $1,703.33!

Through all of this, scarcely anyone thought about the sea otter itself. The animal was simply a piece of currency, a way to translate a small amount of money, by way of the Indians of the Northwest Coast and the hong merchants of Canton, into a larger amount of money. Among all the writers of ships' logs and journals of fur-trading voyages, only a few mention seeing the animals in their natural habitat. The Boston merchants, thousands of miles away in their comfortable countinghouses, probably never saw so much as the skin of one.

Help for the sea otter came almost too late and then as if by accident. In 1911, Great Britain, Japan, Russia, and the United States joined to prohibit the killing of fur seals, which likewise had been slaughtered with wanton disregard for their future. Sea otters were also covered by the ban, though their inclusion seemed almost academic.

So far as anyone knew, there were no sea otters left to protect. One animal, the last seen there, was killed in California in 1913. A survey of the Aleutian Islands, made in 1925 when that Alaskan chain was declared a wildlife refuge, seemed to confirm the biologists' gloomy picture for the animals' northern range. Not an otter was observed.

Small seed populations, however, had managed to hang on in isolated, rarely visited areas. In 1931 a female sea otter with a pup was seen in a kelp bed off Amchitka, in the Aleutians. By the 1940s, small herds of the animals had become a familiar and heartwarming sight to the airmen stationed during World War II on that bleak and isolated island.

Five or six years after the first sea otter was sighted at Amchitka, a couple saw some strange diving animals in the Pacific south of Monterey, California. They had stumbled on what state game wardens had known about for some time but had kept quiet to guard against the possibility of losing them to poachers. Several hundred sea otters survived, it turned out, along the rugged and beautiful Big Sur coast. The state declared a stretch of one hundred miles of shoreline south of Monterey an otter refuge and banned firearms between the coastal highway and the sea.

Curiously, it was not until the 1950s, when the otter populations had already begun to recover and biologists initiated studies of the animals, that people learned what a fascinating creature the world had so nearly lost. Unique among sea mammals, *Enhydra lutris* is the single marine member of the order Carnivora. Related to the familiar weasel, mink, and skunk—and of course to the land otter—it differs from all other marine mammals in having no layer of body fat to insulate it from the numbing cold of northern seas. That function falls to the little bubbles of air trapped in the billion or so silky hairs of its pelt. Thus the animals are particularly susceptible to marine pollution. Even a small amount of oil can destroy the fur's ability to retain those tiny air pockets. When that happens, cold water reaches the animal's skin and it dies of exposure as quickly as a human would in near-Arctic waters.

The otters spend their entire lives in the water—except in the roughest of storm-lashed seas—eating, mating, and delivering and raising their young. Even asleep, they remain at sea, snoozing comfortably on their backs with forelegs folded and a strand of kelp drawn over their chests to keep them from drifting ashore. To feed, the powerful otters use their large, webbed hind feet to drive their air-laden bodies as deep as 180 feet to the sea urchins, clams, mussels, and crabs on which they feed. Staying under as long as four minutes, though the average dive is about a third of that, an otter will return with as many as two dozen sea urchins and clams tucked into the pouch of loose skin that extends across its chest and under each foreleg.

Back on the surface, the animal adopts its relaxed back position again, lays out the meal on its chest, and leisurely opens the seafood as its fancy dictates. California sea otters, unlike their northern cousins, habitually bring a rock to the surface along with the catch. Balancing it on the middle of their chest, these tool-using animals pound open abalones and rock oysters on their improvised anvils. Northern sea otters, accustomed to feeding on mollusks they can crush with their powerful jaws, apparently do not use rocks, but quickly pick up that behavior in captivity. All sea otters are ravenous eaters, requiring a fifth or more of their body weight in food each day. This can be as much as twenty pounds for a large, full-grown male.

The animals multiply slowly, having a single pup at intervals of two to three years. Birth, like everything else in the life story of these unusual animals, takes place at sea where the kelp strands lie in a matted tangle on the water's surface. This becomes the baby's nursery, where it remains quietly while the female forages for food. The young stay with the mother throughout their first year, sleeping contentedly on her chest. Nicknamed "clowns of the kelp beds," females and their offspring will play together for hours at a time.

More than fifty years have elapsed since the rediscovery of sea otters in the 1940s. Thriving in their protected waters, California's sea otters now number roughly 1,500. To the north, from Alaska east to Kamchatka and the Kurile Islands of the Soviet Union, the little populations of northern sea otters discovered before World War II have swelled to some fifty thousand animals. Even the horrifying Exxon oil spill of March 1989, though it claimed at least one thousand sea otters in Prince William Sound, failed to halt Enhydra lutris's triumphant return from the brink of extinction. Though confined now to about a quarter of their original six-thousand-mile habitat along the northern arc of the Pacific rim, these grizzled "old men of the sea" face what appears to be a secure future. To the long, often tragic history of the sea otter's struggle to survive human greed we can now add that all-too-rare element of such tales, a happy ending.

Even the very waters plowed two centuries ago by Columbia and Lady Washington—waters once stripped bare by successive waves of fur seekers —now see a glimmer of hope for the continued presence of the once-plentiful sea otter. But the prospects at first were touch and go. An effort in 1972 to reintroduce sea otters to the coast of Washington came to naught. Similar attempts were made in the late 1960s along the coast of Vancouver Island, where no otters had been observed for thirty years, and they also failed. But renewed efforts there in 1970 and 1972 appear to have succeeded. Small but apparently stable populations took root along Vancouver's rugged northwest shore. Most heartening of all, a handful of sea otters—fifteen were counted in 1977—again live at Nootka Sound itself, where they can once more frolic at dusk off the shingled beach at Friendly Cove.

Seeing these living reminders of a long-vanished age, one's imagination changes the reflections of the cove's tall spruces and cedars cast back by the dark tide into quivering images of *Columbia* and *Lady Washington* floating again on these history-laden waters. Other shadows spring to life. Robert Gray paces beside the dimly visible shore and seems to whisper to burly John Kendrick. Britain's George Vancouver is there, and Spain's courtly Don Esteban José Martínez. Regal Chief Maquinna stands in glistening fur robe and dusting of eagle down. Handsome, scheming John Meares and his Chinese shipwrights gather beside Joseph Ingraham, Robert Haswell, youthful John Boit. Behind them crowd others, Indians and ships' crewmen—some remembered by name, most long forgotten— who made possible these stirring events of two centuries ago. All stand in ghostly rank on the shadowed shore, as if waiting to resume their varied roles.

The spell is broken by a flash from the stumpy lighthouse that guides today's British Columbian fishermen into Nootka Sound. The whispering wraiths of yesterday become once again only the wind-rippled reflections of cedars and spruces ringing this quiet harbor. Of the whole ghostly company, only the sea otters remain.

Sources

★

Abeel, David. *Journal of a Residence in China . . . from 1830 to 1833.* London, 1835.

Adams, John Quincy. *Writings.* New York, 1913.

Akrigg, G.P.V., and Helen B. Akrigg. *British Columbia Chronicle, 1778-1846.* Victoria, B.C., 1975.

Alexander, W.D., "Early Visitors to the Hawaiian Islands." *Thrum's Hawaiian Annual* (1890): 37-43.

Allen, Gardner Weld. *Massachusetts Privateers of the Revolution,* Massachusetts Historical Society Collections, Vol. 77. Boston, 1927.

Anson, George. *A Voyage Round the World in the Years* MDCCXL, I, II, III, IV. Compiled by Richard Walters, M.A., London, 1748.

Asiatic Pilot, Vol. 4. *Shores of the China Sea From Singapore Strait to and Including Hong Kong.* 1915. Washington, D.C.: Government Printing Office.

Augur, Helen. *Passage to Glory—John Ledyard's America.* New York, 1946.

Baker, William A. *Sloops and Shallops.* Barre, Mass., 1966.

Bancroft, Hubert Howe. *History of California.* San Francisco, 1886.

——. *History of the Northwest Coast.* 2 vols. San Francisco, 1884.

——. *History of Oregon.* 2 vols. San Francisco, 1886.

——. *History of the Pacific States of North America.* 2 vols. San Francisco, 1884.

Barbeau, Charles Marius. *Pathfinders in the North Pacific.* Caldwell, Idaho, 1958.

Barrell, Joseph. Manuscript journals and ledgers. Baker Library, Graduate School of Business Administration, Harvard University, Cambridge.

———. Manuscript letterbook, March 9, 1791-February 1, 1797. Massachusetts Historical Society manuscript collection. Boston.

Barrow, John. "Journal of an Embassy from the King of Great Britain to the Emperor of China." In *Some Account of the Public Life of the Earl of Macartney.* 2 vols. London, 1807.

Barry, J. Nelson. "Who Discovered the Columbia River?" *Oregon Historical Quarterly* 39 (1938): 152-61.

[Bartlett, John.] "A Narrative of Events in the Life of John Bartlett of Boston, Mass., in the Yrs. 1790-1793 During Voyages to Canton and the NW Coast of No. America." In Snow, Captain Elliot, intro., *The Sea, the Ship, and the Sailor, Salem.* 1925. Original manuscript in Peabody Museum, Salem.

Beaglehole, J.C. *The Life of Captain James Cook.* London, 1974.

Beeching, Jack. *The Chinese Opium Wars.* London, 1975.

Beinecke Rare Book and Manuscript Library of the Yale University Library, New Haven, Connecticut: manuscript collection.

Bell, Edward. "Log of the *Chatham.*" *Honolulu Mercury*, Honolulu, September 1929-January 1930.

Bernier, Olivier. *Lafayette: Hero of Two Worlds.* New York, 1983.

Bishop, Charles. *The Journals and Letters of Captain Charles Bishop on the North-west Coast of America . . . 1794-1799.* Edited by Michael Roe. Cambridge, 1967.

Bloxam, Andrew. *Diary of Andrew Bloxam.* Bernice P. Bishop Museum Special Publication 10. Honolulu, 1925.

Boit, John. "John Boit's Log of the Second Voyage of the *Columbia.*" In Howay, *Voyages*, 363-431. Also in *Massachusetts Historical Society Proceedings* 53: 218-75, and *Oregon Historical Quarterly* 22 (December 1921): 265-349.

———. *Log of the* Union. Portland, Oregon, 1981.

Boit, Robert Apthorp. *Chronicles of the Boit Family.* Boston, 1915.

The Boston Directory, Containing a List of the Merchants, Mechanics, Traders, and others, of the Town of Boston. Boston, 1789.

Boston Directory, Containing the Names of the Inhabitants, Their Occupations, Places of Business, and Dwelling Houses. Boston, 1796.

Bradley, Harold Whitman. *The American Frontier in Hawaii: The Pioneers, 1789-1843.* Gloucester, Mass., 1968.

Broughton, William Robert. *A Voyage of Discovery to the North Pacific Ocean . . . performed in His Majesty's Sloop Providence, and her tender, in the years 1795-1796, 1797, 1798.* London, 1804.

Buell, Robert Kingery, and Charlotte Northcote Skladal. *Sea Otters and the China Trade.* New York, 1968.

Bulfinch, Ellen Susan. *The Life and Letters of Charles Bulfinch, Architect, With Other Family Papers.* New York, n.d.

Bulfinch, Thomas. *Oregon and Eldorado, or Romance of the Rivers.* Boston, 1886.

Bushnell, David Ives. *Drawings by John Webber.* Washington, D.C., 1928.

Cape Verde Islands, Editions Delroisse. Paris, 1975.

[Cardero, José]. A Spanish Voyage to Vancouver and the North-West Coast of North America, Being the Narrative of the Voyage Made in the Year 1792 by the Schooners Sutil and Mexicana to explore the Strait of Juan de Fuca. Translated from the Spanish with an introduction by Cecil Jane. London, 1930. (Actually written by José A. Espinosa y Tello.)

Carse, Robert. The Seafarers, A History of Maritime America, 1620-1820. New York, 1964.

Cartwright, Bruce. "The First Discovery of Honolulu Harbor," Hawaiian Historical Society Annual Report (1922): 10-28.

Caruthers, J. Wade. American Pacific Ocean Trade: Its Impact on Foreign Policy and Continental Expansion, 1784-1860. New York, 1973.

Cary, Thomas G. Memoir of Thomas Handasyd Perkins: Containing Extracts from his Diaries and Letters. Boston, 1856.

Chickering, William H. Within the Sound of These Waves. New York, 1941.

The China Trade: Romance and Reality, Catalogue of an Exhibition in Collaboration with the China Trade Museum (at the De Cordova Museum). Lincoln, Mass., 1979.

Chinese Repository, Canton.

Christman, Margaret C.S. Adventurous Pursuits—Americans and the China Trade, 1784-1844. Washington, D.C., 1984.

Clark, Arthur H. The History of Yachting, 1600-1815. New York and London, 1904.

Clark, Malcolm, Jr. Eden Seekers: The Settlement of Oregon, 1818-1862. Boston, 1981.

Clark, William Bell, ed. "Journal of the Ship Empress of China." The American Neptune 10 (1950): 83-107, 220-29, 288-99; 11 (1951): 59-71, 134-44.

Cleveland, H.W.S. Voyages of a Merchant Navigator. New York, 1886.

Collis, Maurice. Foreign Mud: The Opium Imbroglio at Canton in the 1830s and the Anglo-Chinese War. New York, 1942.

Colnett, James. James Colnett's Journal Aboard the Argonaut from April 26, 1789 to November 3, 1791. Edited by Frederic W. Howay. Toronto, 1940. (Also contains portions of Estéban José Martínez's diary.)

Columbian Centinel, Boston.

Columbia, Official Log of the. Vol. 1, kept by first-mate Robert Haswell from 28 September 1790 to 3 October 1791, and by second-mate Owen Smith from 4 October 1791 to 20 February 1792. In Manuscript Division, Library of Congress. Also excerpt from the official log, Vol. 2, describing Gray's entry into the Columbia River, in Howay, Voyages, 435-38. Also published in Greenhow, History of Oregon and California; Oregon Historical Quarterly 22 (December 1921): 352-56; and Senate Document 470. (Another fragment from this same volume of the log, kept by Haswell and covering the homeward-bound passage from the Northwest Coast to St. Helena, appears to have survived only in a copy made in 1896, now preserved in the rare book collection of the Multnomah County Library, Portland, Oregon.)

Continental Congress, Journals of: Report on Sea-Letters to Columbia and Lady Washington. New York, 24 September 1787.

Cook, James. *Journals of James Cook*. Edited by J.C. Beaglehole. 3 vols. London, 1955-74.

—— and James King. *A Voyage to the Pacific Ocean . . . in 1776, 1777, 1778, 1779, and 1780*. 3 vols. London, 1784.

Cook, Warren L. *Flood Tide of Empire—Spain and the Pacific Northwest, 1543-1819*. New York and London, 1973.

Coughlin, Sister Magdalen, C.S.J. "The Entrance of Massachusetts Merchants into the Pacific." *Southern California Quarterly* 48 (1966).

Cowley, J. *Sailors Companion and Merchantman's Convoy*. London, 1740.

Crossman, Carl L. *A Catalogue of Chinese Export Paintings, Furniture, Silver, and Other Objects* (at the Peabody Museum). Salem, Mass., 1970.

——. *The China Trade*. Princeton, 1972.

Cutler, Carl C. *Greyhounds of the Sea: The Story of the American Clipper Ship*. New York, 1930.

——. *Queens of the Western Ocean, The Story of America's Mail and Passenger Sailing Lines*. Annapolis, 1961.

Cutter, Donald C. "Early Spanish Artists on the Northwest Coast." *Pacific Northwest Quarterly* 54 (1963): 150-57.

Davis, Felix G. *Captain Robert Gray, Tiverton's Illustrious Son*. Fall River, Mass., 1945.

Daws, Gavan. *Shoal of Time, A History of the Hawaiian Islands*. New York, 1968.

Delano, Amasa. *Narrative of Voyages and Travels*. Boston, 1817.

De Voto, Bernard, ed. *The Journals of Lewis and Clark*. New York, 1953.

Dibble, Sheldon. *History of the Sandwich Islands*. Lahainaluna, Hawaii, 1843.

Dixon, George. *A Voyage Round the World, but more particularly to the North-west Coast of America: Performed in 1785, 1786, 1787, and 1788, in the King George and Queen Charlotte, Captains Portlock and Dixon*. London, 1789.

Dmytryshyn, Basil, E.A.P. Crownhart-Vaughan, and Thomas Vaughan. *Russian Penetration of the North Pacific Ocean*. Vol. 2, *To Siberia and Russian America; Three Centuries of Eastward Expansion*. Portland, Oregon, 1988.

Dockstader, Frederick J. *Great North American Indians*. New York, 1977.

Downing, C. Toogood. *The Fan-qui in China in 1836-37*. 3 vols. London, 1838.

Drucker, Philip. *Cultures of the North Pacific Coast*. San Francisco, 1965.

——. *The Northern and Central Nootkan Tribes*, Washington, D.C., 1951.

——. *Indians of the Northwest Coast*, New York, 1955.

Dulles, Foster Rhea. *The Old China Trade*, Boston, 1930. Reprint. New York, 1970.

——. *Yankees and Samurai—America's Role in the Emergence of Modern Japan: 1791-1900*. New York, 1965.

Eames, James Bromley. *The English in China*. London and New York, 1974.

Eitel, Ernest John. *Europe in China—the History of Hong Kong From the Beginning to the Year 1862*. London and Hong Kong, 1895.

Ellis, William. *An Authentic Narrative of a Voyage Performed by Captain Cook*. 2 vols. London, 1782.

Espinosa y Tello, José A. See Cardero, José.

Essex Institute, Salem, Mass.: manuscript collection.

Fairbank, John K. *Chinese-American Interactions: A Historical Summary*. New Brunswick, New Jersey, 1974.

Fairburn, William A. *Merchant Sail*. 6 vols. Center Lovell, Maine, 1945-55.

Falconer, William. *A Universal Dictionary of the Marine*. London, 1769.

Felch, Alpheus, "Explorations of the North-west Coast of the United States. Report on the Claims of the Heirs of Captains Kendrick and Gray." *Historical Magazine* (September 1870): 155-75.

Fisher, Edna M. "Prices of Sea Otter Pelts." *California Fish and Game* 27, no. 4 (October 1941): 15-31.

Fleurieu, Charles Pierre Claret de. *A Voyage Round the World, 1790-1792*. Performed by Etienne Marchand, 2 vols. London, 1801.

Forbes, Robert B. *Remarks on China and the China Trade*. Boston, 1844.

Fry, Jack. "Fort Defiance." *The Beaver* (Summer 1967): 18-21 (excavations at Adventure Cove).

Gibbs, George. "Tribes of Western Washington and Northwestern Oregon." In *Tribes of the Extreme Northwest*, edited by W.H. Dall, 157-361. Washington, D.C., 1877.

Gibson, James R. "Bostonians and Muscovites on the Northwest Coast, 1788-1841." In *The Western Shore*, edited by Thomas Vaughan, 81-119. Portland, Oregon, 1976.

Golder, Frank Alfred. *Bering's Voyages*. 2 vols. New York, 1925.

Gough, Barry M. *Distant Dominion: Britain and the Northwest Coast of North America, 1579-1809*. Vancouver and London, 1980.

Greenbie, Sydney, and Marjorie Barstow Greenbie. *Gold of Ophir: The China Trade in the Making of America*. New York, 1937.

Greenhow, Robert. *The History of Oregon and California & Other Territories on the North-West Coast of North America*. Boston, 1844.

Gunther, Erna. *Indian Life on the Northwest Coast of America as Seen by the Early Explorers and Fur Traders during the Last Decades of the Eighteenth Century*. Chicago and London, 1972.

Hamilton, Alexander. *The Papers of Alexander Hamilton*. Vol. 9. Edited by Harold C. Syrett. New York and London, 1965.

Haswell, Robert. *Robert Haswell's Log of the First Voyage of the* Columbia. In Howay, *Voyages*, 4-107.

———. *Robert Haswell's Log of the Second Voyage of the* Columbia. In Howay, *Voyages*, 293-359.

Hawkesworth, John. *An Account of the Voyages Undertaken by the Order of His Present Majesty for Making Discoveries in the Southern Hemisphere*. 2 vols. London, 1773.

Henderson, Daniel. *Yankee Ships in China Seas*. New York, 1946.

Henry, John Frazier. *Early Maritime Artists of the Pacific Northwest Coast, 1741-1841*. Seattle, 1984.

Herrick, Lucinda Joy. "Revisiting the *Rediviva*." Master's Thesis. Portland State University, 1989.

Hergesheimer, Joseph. *Java Head*. New York, 1918.

Hewes, Edwin B. "Thomas Handasyd Perkins, Supercargo of the *Astrea* of Salem." *Essex Institute Historical Collections* 71 (July 1935): 203-15.

Hill, Hamilton Andrews. "The Trade, Commerce, and Navigation of Boston, 1780-1880." In *The Memorial History of Boston*, Vol. 4, edited by Justin Winsor, 195-234. Boston, 1881.

Hoskins, John. *John Hoskins' Narrative of the Second Voyage of the* Columbia. In Howay, *Voyages*, 161-289.

Howay, Frederic W. "Ballad of the Bold Northwestman: An Incident in the Life of Captain John Kendrick." *Washington Historical Quarterly* 20 (1929): 114-23.

———. "A Ballad of the Northwest Fur Trade." *New England Quarterly* 1 (January 1928): 71-79.

———. "Captains Gray and Kendrick; the Barrell Letters." *Washington Historical Quarterly* (October 1921): 243-71.

———. *The Dixon-Meares Controversy*, New York, 1969.

———. "An Early Colonization Scheme in British Columbia." *British Columbia Historical Quarterly* 3 (January 1939): 51-63.

———. "Early Relations of Hawaii with the Pacific Northwest." In *The Hawaiian Islands*, edited by A.P. Taylor and R.S. Kuykendall, 11-38. Honolulu, 1930.

———. "Indian Attacks Upon Maritime Traders of the North-west Coast, 1785-1805." *Canadian Historical Review* (1925): 287-309.

———. "John Kendrick and His Sons," *Oregon Historical Quarterly* 23 (December 1922): 277-302.

———. "Letters Relating to the Second Voyage of the *Columbia*." *Oregon Historical Quarterly* 24 (June 1923): 132-52.

———. A *List of Trading Vessels in the Maritime Fur Trade, 1785-1825*. Edited by Richard A. Pierce. Kingston, Ontario, 1973.

———. "An Outline Sketch of the Maritime Fur Trade." *Report of the Annual Meeting*, 5-14. Canadian Historical Association, 1932.

———. "The Ship *Margaret*: Her History and Her Historian." *Hawaiian Historical Society 38th Annual Report for the Year 1929*, 34-40. Honolulu.

———. "A Short Account of Robert Haswell." *Washington Historical Quarterly* 24 (1929): 83-90.

———. "Some Additional Notes Upon Captain Colnett and the *Princess Royal*." *Oregon Historical Quarterly* 26 (March 1925): 12-22.

———. "Some Remarks Upon the New Vancouver Journal." *Washington Historical Quarterly* 6 (April 1915): 83-89.

———. "The Spanish Settlement at Nootka." *Washington Historical Quarterly* 8 (July 1917): 163-71.

———. *Voyages of the* Columbia *to the Northwest Coast, 1787-1790 and 1790-1793*. Boston, 1941. Reprint. Portland, Oregon, 1990.

———. "Voyages of Kendrick and Gray in 1787-90." *Oregon Historical Quarterly* 30 (June 1929): 89-94.

———. "A Yankee Trader on the Northwest Coast, 1791-1795." *Washington Historical*

Quarterly 21 (1930): 83-94.

———and Albert Matthews. "Some Notes Upon Captain Robert Gray." *Washington Historical Quarterly* 21 (1930): 8-12.

Hunter, William C. *The "Fan Kwae" at Canton Before Treaty Days, 1825-1844.* London, 1882. Reprint. Shanghai, 1938.

———. *Bits of Old China.* London, 1885. Shanghai, 1911.

Ingraham, Joseph. *Journal of the Brigantine Hope on a Voyage to the Northwest Coast of North America, 1790-92.* Barre, Mass., 1971. (Original manuscript in the Library of Congress.)

Jackson, Donald, ed. *Letters of the Lewis and Clark Expedition, with Related Documents, 1783-1854.* 2d ed., with additional documents and notes. 2 vols. Chicago, 1978.

———. "Call Him Good Old Dog, but Don't Call Him Scannon." *We Proceeded On* 11 (August 1985).

Jarves, James Jackson. *History of the Hawaiian Islands.* Honolulu, 1872.

Jefferson, Thomas. *The Papers of Thomas Jefferson.* Edited by Julian P. Boyd. 18 vols. Princeton, 1950-72.

———. *The Writings of Thomas Jefferson.* Edited by Andrew A. Lipscomb and Andrew E. Bergh. 20 vols. Washington, D.C., 1903.

[Jewitt, John.] *A Narrative of the Adventures and Sufferings of John R. Jewitt, Only Survivor of the Crew of the Ship Boston, During a Captivity of Nearly Three Years Among the Savages of Nootka Sound.* Middletown, Connecticut: 1815.

Johansen, Dorothy O., ed. *Voyage of the Columbia Around the World with John Boit, 1790-1793.* Portland, Oregon, 1960.

——— and Charles Gates. *Empire of the Columbia, A History of the Pacific Northwest.* New York, 1957.

Johnson, William Weber. *The Story of the Sea Otters.* New York, 1973.

Kelley, Hall J. *On Oregon—A Collection of Five of His Published Works.* Edited by Fred W. Powell. New York, 1972.

Kenyon, Karl D. "The Return of the Sea Otters." *National Geographic Magazine.* October 1971: 520-39.

Kimball, Marie. *Jefferson: The Scene of Europe.* New York, 1950.

Kuykendall, Ralph S. *The Hawaiian Kingdom, 1778-1854.* Honolulu, 1938.

———. "James Colnett and the *Princess Royal.*" *Oregon Historical Quarterly* 25 (March 1924): 36-52.

———. "A Northwest Trader at the Hawaiian Islands." *Oregon Historical Quarterly* 24 (1923): 112-31.

Labaree, Benjamin W. *A Supplement (1971-1986) to Robert G. Albion's Naval and Maritime History, An Annotated Bibliography.* Mystic, Conn., 1988.

Latourette, Kenneth Scott. "The History of Early Relations Between the United States and China, 1784-1844." In *Transactions of the Connecticut Academy of Arts and Sciences* 22: 1-209. New Haven, 1917.

Lavender, David S. *Land of the Giants: The Drive to the Pacific Northwest, 1750-1950.* New York, 1958.

———. *The Way to the Western Sea; Lewis and Clark Across the Continent.* New York, 1988.

Lee, Jean Gordon. *Philadelphians and the China Trade, 1784-1844.* Philadelphia, 1984.

Ledyard, John. *John Ledyard's Journal of Captain Cook's Last Voyage.* James K. Munford, ed. Corvallis, Oregon, 1963.

Leitch, Barbara A. *Concise Dictionary of Indian Tribes of North America.* Algonac, Michigan, 1979.

Lower, Arthur J. *Ocean of Destiny: A Concise History of the North Pacific, 1500-1978.* Vancouver, 1978.

McClellan, Edwin North. "John Kendrick, American." *Paradise of the Pacific* 39, no. 10 (1926): 17-19.

McCracken, Harold. *Hunters of the Stormy Sea.* New York, 1957.

Makato, Horiuchi, ed. *Nan-ki Tokugawa Shi.* Vol. 2. Wakayama, 1930-33.

———. *Tsuko Ikiran.* Vol. 8. Tokyo, 1912-13.

Malham, John. *The Naval Gazeteer, or Seaman's Complete Guide.* 2 vols. London, 1801.

Malone, Dumas. *Jefferson and the Ordeal of Liberty.* Boston, 1962.

Manby, Thomas. "Journal of Vancouver's Voyage to the Pacific Ocean (1791-1793)." *Honolulu Mercury* (June-August 1929).

Manning, William Ray. "The Nootka Sound Controversy." *Annual Report of the American Historical Association,* 179-478. 1904.

"The Manuscript of Rev. S. Greathead." *The Friend* 29 (June 1862): 42-43.

Martínez, Estéban José. *Journal: see* James Colnett.

Massachusetts Centinel, Boston.

American Portraits, 1620-1825, Found in Massachusetts. 2 vols. Boston, 1939.

Massachusetts Historical Society, Boston: manuscript collection.

Massachusetts Historical Society, Proceedings. Vol. 1. 1791-1835.

Mayer, Brantz. "China and the Chinese." *Southern Quarterly Review* 23 (July 1847): 1-51.

McKelvie, Bruce Alastair. *Maquinna the Magnificent.* Vancouver, 1946.

Meany, Edmond S. "The Widow of Captain Robert Gray." *Washington Historical Quarterly* 20 (1921): 192-95.

Meares, John. *Authentic Copy of the Memorial . . . By Lieutenant John Meares, of the Royal Navy; Dated 30th April, 1790 . . . Containing Every Particular Respecting the Capture of the Vessels in Nootka Sound.* London, 1790.

———. *Voyages Made in the Years 1788 and 1789 from China to the N.W. Coast of America.* 2 vols. London, 1791.

Menzies, Archibald. *Hawaii Nei 128 Years Ago.* Honolulu, 1920.

Millar, John F. *Early American Ships.* Williamsburg, Va., 1986.

Morison, Samuel Eliot. "Boston Traders in the Hawaiian Islands, 1789-1823." *Washington Historical Quarterly* 12 (1921): 166-201. Also in *Massachusetts Historical Society Proceedings* 54 (October 1920): 9-47. And in Morison, *By Land and By Sea—Essays and Addresses,* 66-98. New York, 1966.

———. *John Paul Jones: A Sailor's Biography.* New York, 1959.

———. *Maritime History of Massachusetts, 1783-1860.* Boston and New York, 1921.

———. "The *Columbia's* Winter Quarters of 1791-92 Located." *Oregon Historical Quarterly* 39 (March 1938): 3-7.

Morse, Gideon Nye. *Tea: and the Tea Trade.* New York, 1850.

Morse, Hosea Ballou. *The Chronicles of the East India Company Trading to China, 1635-1834.* 5 vols. London, 1926-29.

———. "Currency in China." *Journal of the North-China branch of the Royal Asiatic Society.* Vol. 38. Shanghai, 1906.

———. *The Trade and Administration of China.* New York, 1908 (reissued 1967).

Mortimer, Lieut. George. *Observations and Remarks on a Voyage to . . . the North West Coast of America, Tinian, and from thence to Canton, in the Brig Mercury, Commanded by John Henry Cox, Esq.* London, 1791.

Moziño [Suarez de Figueroa], José Mariano. *Noticias de Nutka. An Account of Nootka Sound in 1792.* Translated by Iris Higbie Wilson. Toronto and Montreal, 1970.

Munford, James. *John Ledyard, An American Marco Polo.* Portland, Oregon, 1939.

Murray-Oliver, Anthony. *Captain Cook's Hawaii as Seen by His Artists.* Wellington, New Zealand, 1975.

New England Genealogical and Historical Register, Boston.

Newcombe, C.F., ed. *Menzies' Journal of Vancouver's Voyage, April to October, 1792.* Victoria, B.C., 1923.

Norman-Wilcox, Gregor. "American Ships in the China Trade." *Bulletin of the Los Angeles County Museum* 7 (Winter 1955). Catalogue of an exhibition, 4 February-20 March 1955.

Niles National Register. Vol. 53 (25 November 1837), 196.

Ogden, Adele. *The California Sea Otter Trade, 1784-1848.* Berkeley, 1941.

———. "New England Traders in Spanish and Mexican California." In *Greater America, Essays in Honor of Herbert Eugene Bolton,* 395-413. Berkeley and Los Angeles, 1945.

Orange, James, ed. *The Chater Collection: Pictures Relating to China, Hong Kong, Macao, 1655-1860, with Historical and Descriptive Letterpress.* London, 1924.

Oregon Historical Society, Portland: manuscript collections.

Paine, Josiah. *Edward Kenwrick, the Ancestor of the Kenwricks or Kendricks, and His Descendants,* Library of Cape Cod History and Genealogy, No. 35. Yarmouthport, Mass., 1915.

Parkinson, C. Northcote. *Trade in the Eastern Seas, 1793-1813.* New York, 1966.

Peabody, Robert E. *The Derbys of Salem.* Salem, 1908.

———. *Logs of the Grand Turks.* Boston and New York, 1926.

———. *Merchant Venturers of Old Salem.* Boston and New York, 1912.

Peterson, Merrill D. *Thomas Jefferson and the New Nation.* New York, 1970.

Pethick, Derek. *First Approaches to the Northwest Coast.* Vancouver, B.C., 1976.

———. *The Nootka Connection.* Seattle and Vancouver, 1980.

Ping, Chia Kuo. "Canton and Salem: The Impact of Chinese Culture Upon New England Life During the Post-Revolutionary Era." *New England Quarterly* 3 (1930): 420-42.

Pipes, Nellie B. "Later Affairs of Kendrick: the Barrell Letters." *Oregon Historical Quarterly* 30 (1929): 95-105.

Porter, Edward G. "The Ship Columbia and the Discovery of the Oregon River." *New England Magazine* 6 (June 1892): 476-81.

Portlock, Nathaniel. A *Voyage Round the World; But More Particularly to the North-West Coast of America, Performed in 1785, 1786, 1787, and 1788, in the* King George *and* Queen Charlotte. *Captains Portlock and Dixon.* London, 1789.

Quincy, Josiah. *Journal of Major Samuel Shaw, With a Life of the Author.* Boston, 1847.

Rasmussen, Louise. "Artists With Explorations on the Northwest Coast." *Oregon Historical Quarterly* 42 (December 1941): 311-16.

Restarick, H.B. "The First Clergyman Resident in Hawaii." *Hawaiian Historical Society 32d Annual Report,* 54-61. 1923.

Reynolds, Stephen, *The Voyage of the* New Hazard *to the Northwest Coast, Hawaii, and China, 1810-1813.* Edited by F.W. Howay. Fairfield, Washington, 1970.

Rickard, T.A., "The Sea Otter in History." *British Columbia Historical Quarterly* 11 (1947): 15-31.

[Rickman, John.] *An Authoritative Narrative of a Voyage to the Pacific Ocean Performed by Captain Cook, and Captain Clerke, in His Britannic Majesty's Ships the* Resolution, *and* Discovery, *in the Years 1776, 1777, 1778, 1779, and 1780.* Philadelphia, 1783.

Rigdon, Paul. *Captain Robert Gray's Charts Discovered After Almost Two Centuries.* Spokane, Washington, 1975.

Robinson, John, and George Francis Dow. *The Sailing Ships of New England,* 3 vols. Salem, Massachusetts, 1922-28.

Ruby, Robert H., and John A. Brown. *The Chinook Indians—Traders of the Lower Columbia River.* Norman, Oklahoma, 1976.

Sakamaki, Shunzo. *Japan and the United States, 1790-1853.* Tokyo, 1940. (Reprinted from *Transactions of the Asiatic Society of Japan,* 2d series, Vol. 8).

Seed, Alice, comp. *Sea Otter in Eastern Pacific Waters,* Seattle, 1972.

Sellers, Charles Coleman. *Mr. Peale's Museum.* New York, 1980.

Smith, Barbara Sweetland, and Redmond J. Barnett, eds. *Russian America: The Forgotten Frontier.* Tacoma, Washington, 1990.

Smith, Francis E. *Achievements and Experiences of Capt. Robert Gray.* Tacoma, Washington, 1923.

Smith, Philip Chadwick Foster. *The* Empress of China. Philadelphia, 1984.

Snyder, James Wilbert, Jr. "A Bibliography for the Early American China Trade." *Americana* (April 1940): 297-345.

Sparks, Jared. *The Life of John Ledyard, the American Traveler.* Cambridge, Mass., 1828.

Sperlin, Otis B. "Earliest Celebration of Independence Day in the Northwest." *Pacific Northwest Quarterly* 35 (1944): 215-22.

Stackpole, Edouard A. *The Sea Hunters: The New England Whalemen During Two Centuries, 1635-1835.* New York, 1953.

Starbuck, Alexander. *History of the American Whale Fishery.* 2 vols. Waltham, Mass., 1878.

Stokes, J.F.G. "Honolulu and Some New Speculative Phases of Hawaiian History." In *Hawaiian Historical Society Report* 42: 40-102.

Strange, James. *Journal and Narrative of the Commercial Expedition From Bombay to the North West Coast of America.* Madras, 1928.

Strathern, Gloria M., comp. *Navigations, Traffiques, and Discoveries, 1774-1848: A Guide* to *Publications Relating to the Area Now British Columbia*, Victoria, B.C., 1970.

Sturgis, William. *The Journal of William Sturgis*. Edited by S.W. Jackman. Victoria, B.C., 1978.

——. "The Northwest Fur Trade." *Hunt's Merchant's Magazine* 14 (June 1846): 532-38; *see also*, Howay, F.W., ed. "William Sturgis: the Northwest Fur Trade." *British Columbia Historical Quarterly* 8 (January 1944): 11-25.

Swanton, John R. *Contributions to the Ethnology of the Haida*. Leiden and New York, 1905. Reprint New York, 1975.

Thrum, Thomas G., comp., "The Sandalwood Trade of Early Hawaii." In *Thrum's Hawaiian Annual*, 43-74. Honolulu, 1905.

Torre Revello, José. *Los Artistas Pintores de la Expedicion Malaspina*. Buenos Aires, 1944.

Tiffany, Osmond, Jr. *The Canton Chinese*. Boston and Cambridge, 1849.

Treaty of Washington, Papers Relating to: Vol. 5. Berlin Arbitration. Washington, D.C., 1872.

U.S. Congress. House. *Lands in Oregon*. Report prepared by Charles Bulfinch, et al. 26th Cong., 1st sess., 1840. H. Doc. 43.

U.S. Congress. House. *Memorial of Martha Gray*. 29th Cong., 1st sess., 1846. H. Rept. 172.

U.S. Congress. House. *Widow of Robert Gray*. 29th Cong., 1st sess., 1846. H. Rept. 456.

U.S. Congress. House. *Widow of Robert Gray*. 30th Cong., 1st sess., 1848. H. Rept. 502.

U.S. Congress. Senate. *Memorial of Geo. Barrell and S.V.S. Wilder*. 32d Cong., 1st sess., August 11, 1852.

U.S. Congress. Senate. *To Authorize the President to Occupy the Oregon Territory*. 25th Cong., 2d sess., Serial 318, June 6, 1838.

Vancouver, George. "A New Vancouver Journal." *Washington Historical Quarterly* (April 1914): 129-37; (July 1914): 215-24; (October 1914): 301-8; (January 1915), 50-68.

——. *A Voyage of Discovery to the North Pacific Ocean and Round the World*. 6 vols. London, 1801.

——. *A Voyage of Discovery, etc.,* 5 vols. London, 1798.

[—— and Richard Hakluyt.] *A Voyage of Discovery to the North Pacific Ocean and Round the World, 1791-1795*. Edited by W. Kaye Lamb. 4 vols. London, 1984.

Van Doren, Carl. *Benjamin Franklin*. New York, 1938.

Van Zandt, Howard F., *Pioneer American Merchants in Japan*, Tokyo, 2d. ed., 1981.

Vaughan, Thomas. *Soft Gold: The Fur Trade and Cultural Exchange on the Northwest Coast of America*. 2d. ed. Portland, Oregon, 1990.

——, E.A.P. Crownhart-Vaughan, and Mercedes Palau de Iglesias. *Voyages of Enlightenment: Malaspina on the Northwest Coast, 1791/1792*. Portland, Oregon, 1977.

——, ed. *The Western Shore, Oregon Country Essays Honoring the American Revolution*. Portland, Oregon, 1976.

Villiers, Alan. *Captain James Cook*. New York, 1967.

——. *The Way of a Ship*. New York, 1953.

Wagner, Henry R. *The Cartography of the Northwest Coast of America To the Year 1800*. 2 vols. Berkeley, California, 1975.

——, ed. and trans. "Journal of Tomas de Suria of his Voyage with Malaspina to the Northwest Coast of America in 1791." *Pacific Historical Review* 5 (1936): 243-76.

———, ed. *Spanish Explorations in the Strait of Juan de Fuca.* Santa Ana, California, 1933.

Walker, Alexander. *An Account of a Voyage to the North West Coast of America in 1785 & 1786.* Edited by Robin Fisher and J.M. Bumsted. Seattle, 1982.

Walter, Richard. *A Voyage Round the World.* New York, 1974.

Walworth, Arthur. *Black Ships Off Japan— The Story of Commodore Perry's Expedition.* New York, 1946.

Washington, George. *Diaries of George Washington.* 4 vols. New York, 1925.

———. *Writings of George Washington.* 39 vols. Washington, D.C., 1931-44.

Wathen, James. *Journal of a Voyage in 1811 and 1812, to Madras and China ... in the* H.C.S. Hope, *Captain James Pendergrass.* London, 1814.

Watrous, Stephen D., ed. *John Ledyard's Journey Through Russia and Siberia, 1787-1788.* Madison, Wisconsin, 1966.

Weeden, William B. *Early Oriental Commerce in Providence.* Cambridge, Massachusetts, 1908.

Whitehill, Walter Muir, ed. "Remarks on the Canton Trade and the Manner of Transacting Business." *Essex Institute Historical Collections* 73, no. 4 (October 1937).

Wildes, Harry Emerson. *Aliens in the East, a New History of Japan's Foreign Intercourse.* Philadelphia, 1937.

Wilke, Joyce A. *Effect of the Maritime Fur Trade on Northwest Coast Indian Society.* Ph.D. diss. Columbia University, n.d.

Wilkes, Lt. Charles. *Narrative of the United States Exploring Expedition During the Years 1831, 1839, 1840, 1842.* 5 vols. Philadelphia, 1849.

Williams, Glyndwr. *The British Search for the Northwest Passage in the Eighteenth Century.* London, 1962.

Winther, Oscar Osburn. *The Great Northwest: A History.* Westport, Conn., 1981.

Wright, E.W., ed. *Lewis and Dryden's Marine History of the Pacific Northwest.* Portland, 1895. WPCo

★

Index

★

364

★

North Pacific Studies Series

★

Log of the Union: *John Boit's Remarkable Voyage to the Northwest Coast and Around the World, 1794–1796.*
Edited by Edmund Hayes, foreword by Thomas Vaughan.
1981

Civil and Savage Encounters: The Worldly Travel Letters of an Imperial Russian Navy Officer, 1860–61.
By Pavel N. Golovin. Translated and annotated by Basil Dmytryshyn and E.A.P. Crownhart-Vaughan, introduction by Thomas Vaughan.
1983

For Honor and Country: The Diary of Bruno de Hezeta.
Translated and edited by Herbert K. Beals, foreword by Thomas Vaughan.
1985

The Wreck of the Sv. Nikolai: Two Narratives of the First Russian Expedition to the Oregon Country, 1808–1810.
Edited with introduction and notes by Kenneth N. Owens. Translated by Alton S. Donnelly.
1985

To Siberia and Russian America: Three Centuries of Russian Eastward Expansion, 1558–1867. A Documentary Record.
Edited and translated by Basil Dmytryshyn, E.A.P. Crownhart-Vaughan, and Thomas Vaughan.
> VOLUME ONE: *Russia's Conquest of Siberia, 1558–1700.*
> 1985
> VOLUME TWO: *Russian Penetration of the North Pacific Ocean, 1700–1797.*
> 1988
> VOLUME THREE: *The Russian American Colonies, 1798–1867.*
> 1989

Juan Pérez on the Northwest Coast: Six Documents of His Expedition in 1774.
Translation and annotation by Herbert K. Beals, foreword by Donald Cutter.
1990

Voyages of the Columbia *to the Northwest Coast 1787–1790 and 1790–1793.*
Edited and annotated by Frederic W. Howay, foreword by Bruce Taylor Hamilton.
Second edition, revised
1990

Soft Gold: The Fur Trade and Cultural Exchange on the Northwest Coast of America.
Historical introduction and annotation by Thomas Vaughan, ethnographic
annotation by Bill Holm.
Second edition, revised
1990

Bering's Search for the Strait: The First Kamchatka Expedition, 1725–1730 [*V Poiskakh Proliva:
Pervaia Kamchatskaia Ekspeditsiia, 1725–1730*].
By Evegnii Grigorevich Kushnarev. Edited and translated by E.A.P. Crownhart-
Vaughan.
1990

The Last Temperate Coast: Maritime Exploration of Northwest America, 1542–1794. [map and
broadside]
Research, exploration routes, and text by Herbert K. Beals.
1990

Ranald MacDonald: The Narrative of His Life, 1824–1894.
Edited and annotated by William S. Lewis and Naojiro Murakami.
Second edition, revised
1990

The Shogun's Reluctant Ambassadors: Japanese Sea Drifters in the North Pacific.
By Katherine Plummer.
1991

Hail, Columbia: Robert Gray, John Kendrick and the Pacific Fur Trade.
By John Scofield.
1993

COLOPHON

John Scofield's fine work, *Hail, Columbia*, has been brought into print by a full complement of publishing and printing professionals. The editing of the book was done by Kim Carlson, and the design of the interior layout the product of the mind of the late George T. Resch. Susan Applegate supervised the early scheduling and production. Bruce Taylor Hamilton completed the latter and with Karen Bassett designed the cover. Jean Brownell took on the task of indexing *Hail, Columbia*. Others involved in this book's long voyage from its manuscript to its bound form were:

Cover illustration:	Dennis Cunningham
	Portland
Original maps:	Christine Rains
	Portland
Typesetting:	Irish Setter
	Portland
Printing *&* binding:	Edwards Brothers
	Ann Arbor, Michigan

The book was typeset in Cartier, printed on sixty-pound Glatfelter, and bound in a twelve-point stock.

Hail, Columbia is the eighteenth volume in the Oregon Historical Society Press's North Pacific Studies Series, a distinguished set of publications begun in 1972.

The Author

★

John Scofield, a descendant of Captain John Kendrick, has had a lifelong interest in maritime history. A journalist who has traveled extensively around the world on assignment, Mr. Scofield retired from *National Geographic* magazine in 1978 and now lives in Florida.